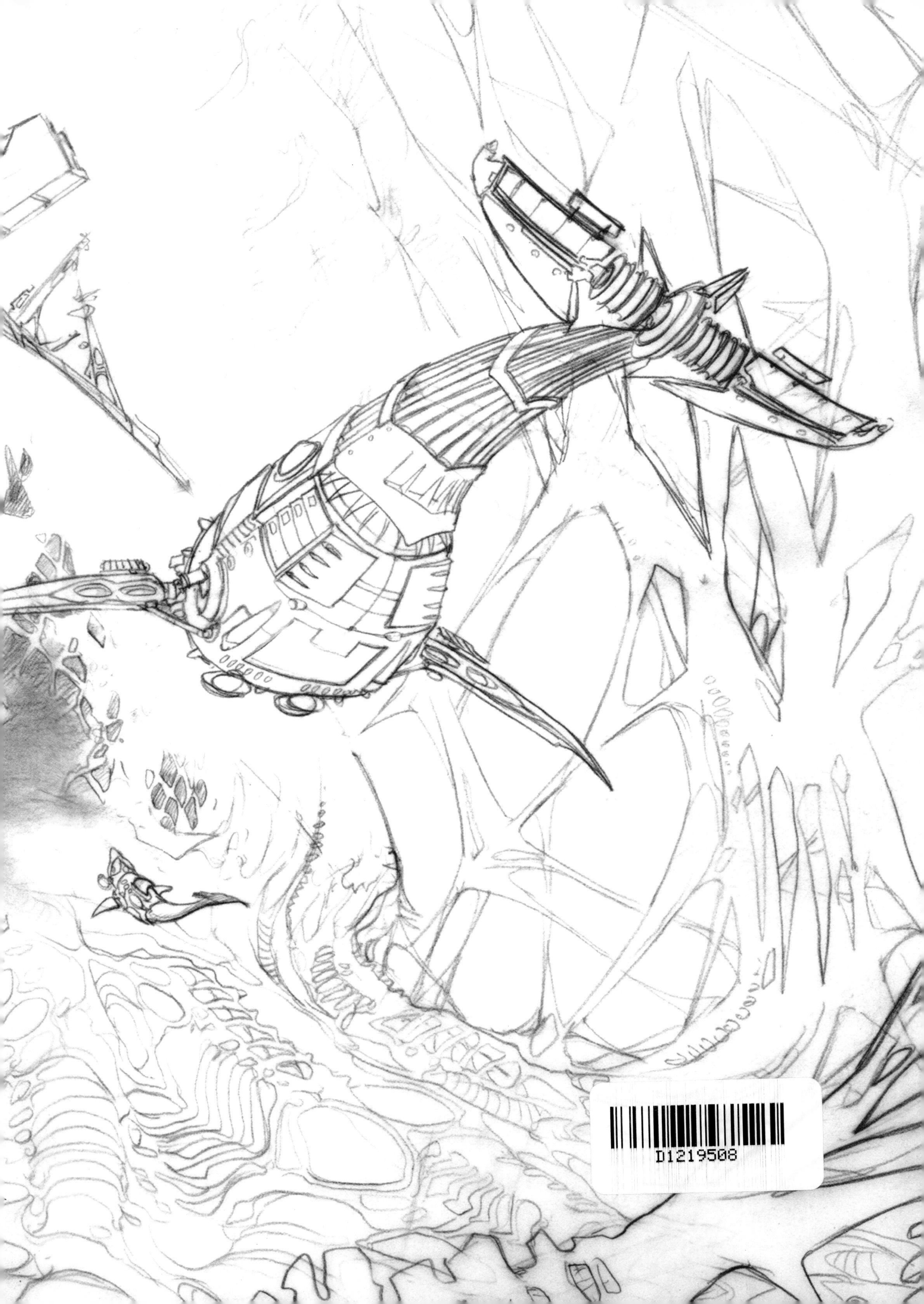

SHOCK™

AFTERSHOCK™

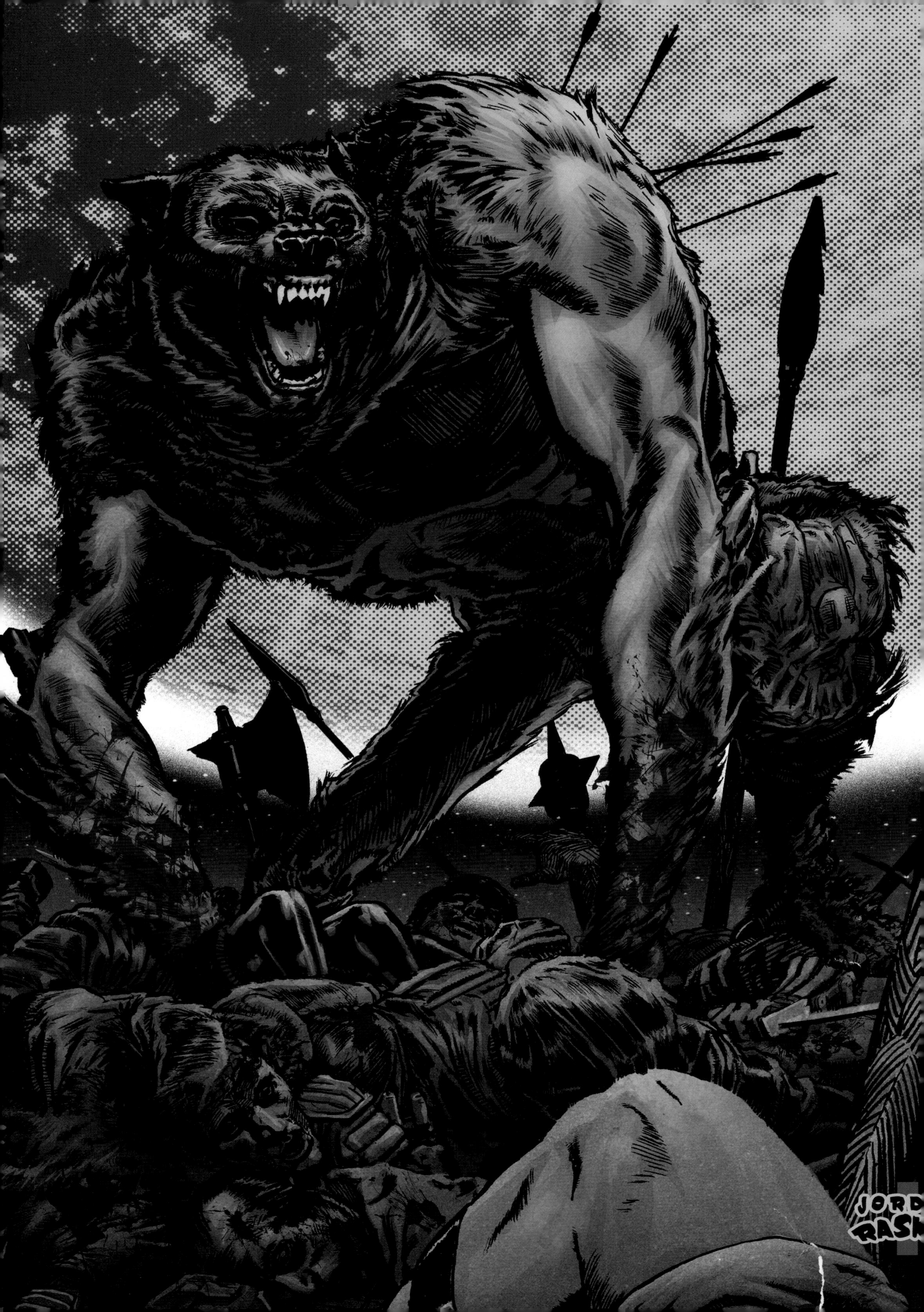

W E L C O M E

Welcome to SHOCK.

Anthologies are in my blood. I can't help myself. I always hear that anthologies don't sell. Who cares? I love them. The creators love them (look at this creative line-up and tell me that they don't!). I assume you do as well, since you're reading this introduction. Thank you for that.

For those of you who are familiar with AfterShock Comics, you already know that as a company we like to push the envelope in terms of story and art. From our initial launch in December of 2015, we have continued to publish what we think are cutting-edge, yet sophisticated stories by the comic book industry's most respected creative talent, alongside the fresh new voices of tomorrow. It's a fresh, yet experienced eclectic mix of talent. Much like the series that we choose to publish.

"We have the comics that you're looking for." That's a motto we've been using at AfterShock recently. We use it because it's true. This anthology is no exception. Like our regular monthly series, this anthology defies the common perception of what an anthology should be. It's not genre-based and it has no theme, but it does have something for everyone. I've never been one to read, watch, or view one particular type of book, show, or film, so why should I only focus on one thing?

If any of you are familiar with me or my career in comics, you'll know that my first real success in the comic industry was with a similar type of anthology. That anthology was the multiple Eisner and Harvey Award nominated series *Negative Burn*, whose first issue was published way back in 1993. *Negative Burn* helped to introduce the world to such amazing talent as John Cassaday (this volume's cover artist), Paul Pope, Brian Michael Bendis, David Mack, Terry Moore, Andrew Robinson, Paul Jenkins, Mike Wieringo, and, of course, myself. In addition, I was lucky enough to bring in established talent such as Alan Moore, Brian Bolland, Moebius, Warren Ellis, Neil Gaiman (you'll see his name in this volume as well), among others. I also liked the notion of publishing the top established talent and sprinkling in the most promising new talent. That's a trend that continues to today, and continues in this volume.

Negative Burn was the jumpstart to my career. AfterShock Comics is the culmination of that journey. SHOCK is both a return to my distant beginnings and a start to the exciting journey still in front of me. Consider this a "thank you" to the fans who have been with me from the start and a friendly "hello" to those just now joining the adventure.

Now prepare for a treat.

Joe Pruett
Atlanta, Georgia
April 2018

CONTENTS

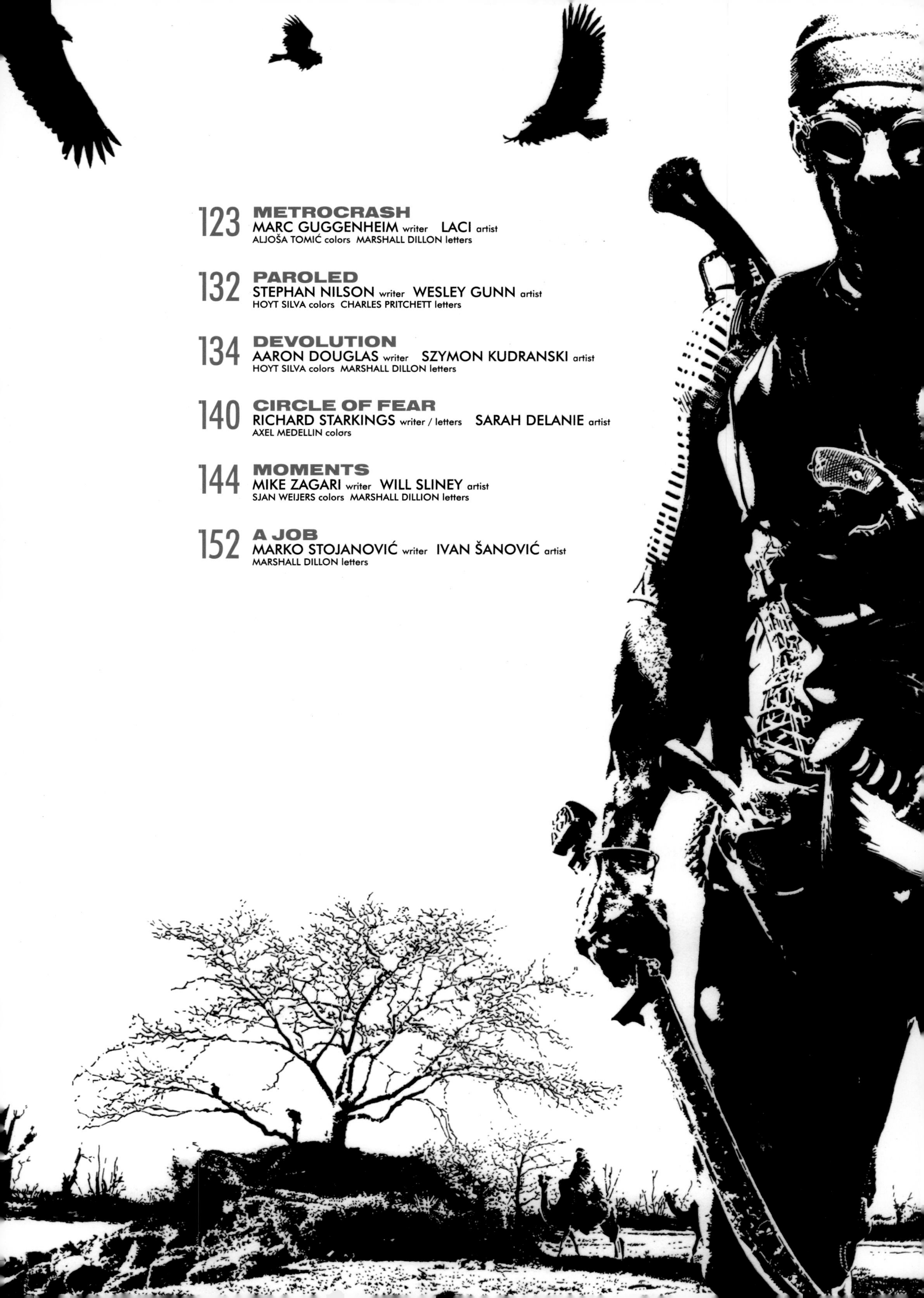

FRONT COVER ART REGULAR EDITION
JOHN CASSADAY artist   LAURA MARTIN colors

BACK COVER ART
MICHAEL GAYDOS

CONTENTS PAGE ART
TIM BRADSTREET

FRONTISPIECE ART
JORDAN RASKIN

VARIANT COVER ART
DAVE DORMAN
FRANCESCO FRANCAVILLA
BRIAN STELFREEZE

LOGO DESIGN
JOHN J. HILL

PRODUCTION
MARSHALL DILLON
STEPHAN NILSON
CHARLES PRITCHETT
JOE PRUETT

EDITOR
JOE PRUETT

FIRST EDITION
April 2018. 10 9 8 7 6 5 4 3 2 1

ISBN
978-1-93500-265-9 REGULAR EDITION
978-1-93500-259-8 SIGNED / LIMITED EDITION

Follow us on social media
𝕏 ⦿ f

AFTERSHOCK COMICS
MIKE MARTS - Editor-in-Chief   •   JOE PRUETT - Publisher/CCO   •   LEE KRAMER - President
JAWAD QURESHI - SVP, Investor Relations   •   JON KRAMER - Chief Executive Officer   •   MIKE ZAGARI - SVP, Brand
JAY BEHLING - CFO   •   STEPHAN NILSON - Publishing Operations Manager   •   LISA Y. WU - Retailer/Fan Relations Manager
ASHLEY WYATT - Publishing Assistant

AfterShock Trade Dress and Interior Design by JOHN J. HILL   •   AfterShock Logo Design by COMICRAFT   •   Proofreading by DOCTOR Z.
Publicity: contact AARON MARION (aaron@publichausagency.com) & RYAN CROY (ryan@publichausagency.com) at PUBLICHAUS
Special Thanks to: SVEN LARSEN, CHRIS LA TORRE, TEDDY LEO, LISA MOODY, KIM PAGNOTTA

WITCH WORK

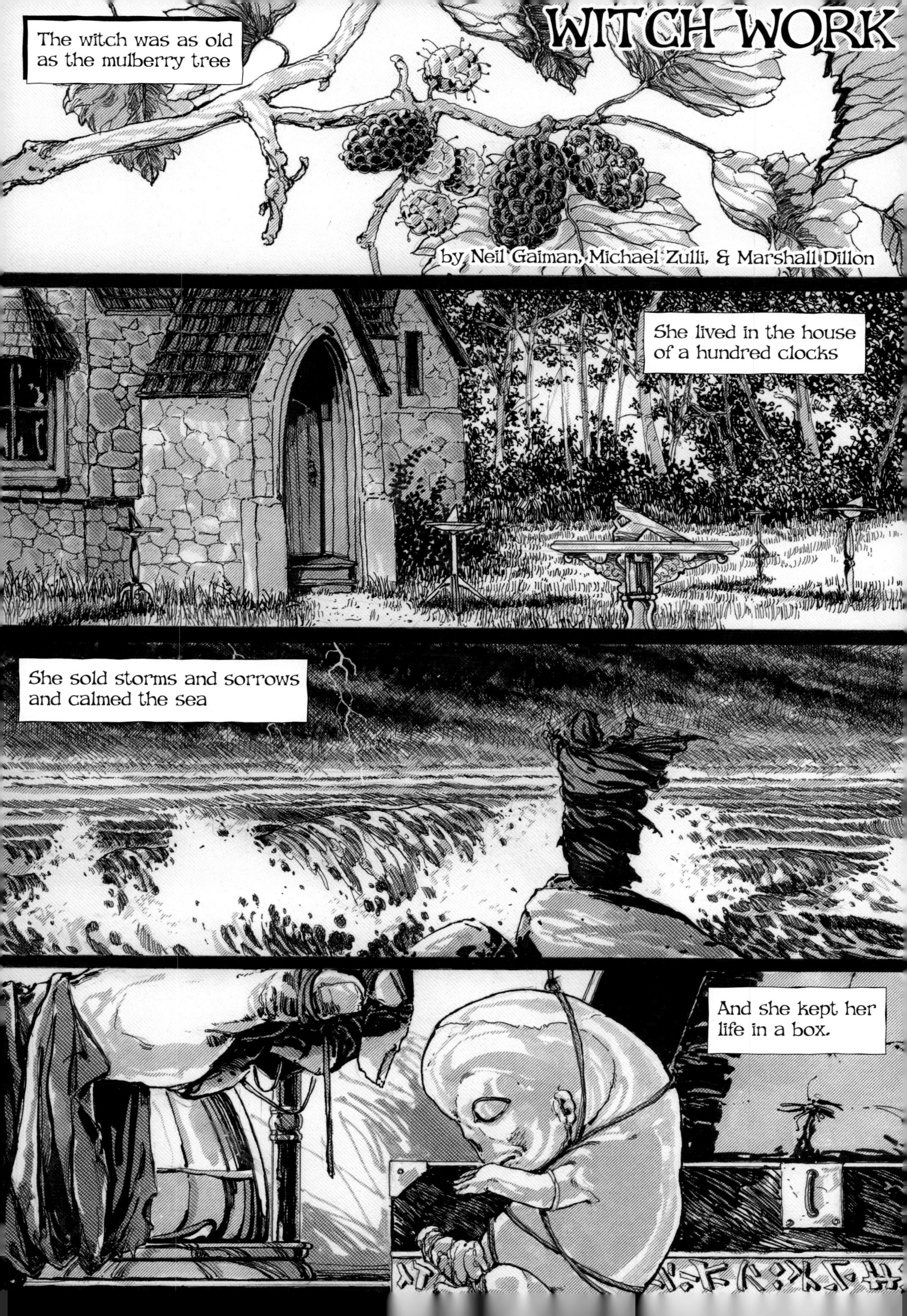

The witch was as old as the mulberry tree
by Neil Gaiman, Michael Zulli, & Marshall Dillon
She lived in the house of a hundred clocks
She sold storms and sorrows and calmed the sea
And she kept her life in a box.

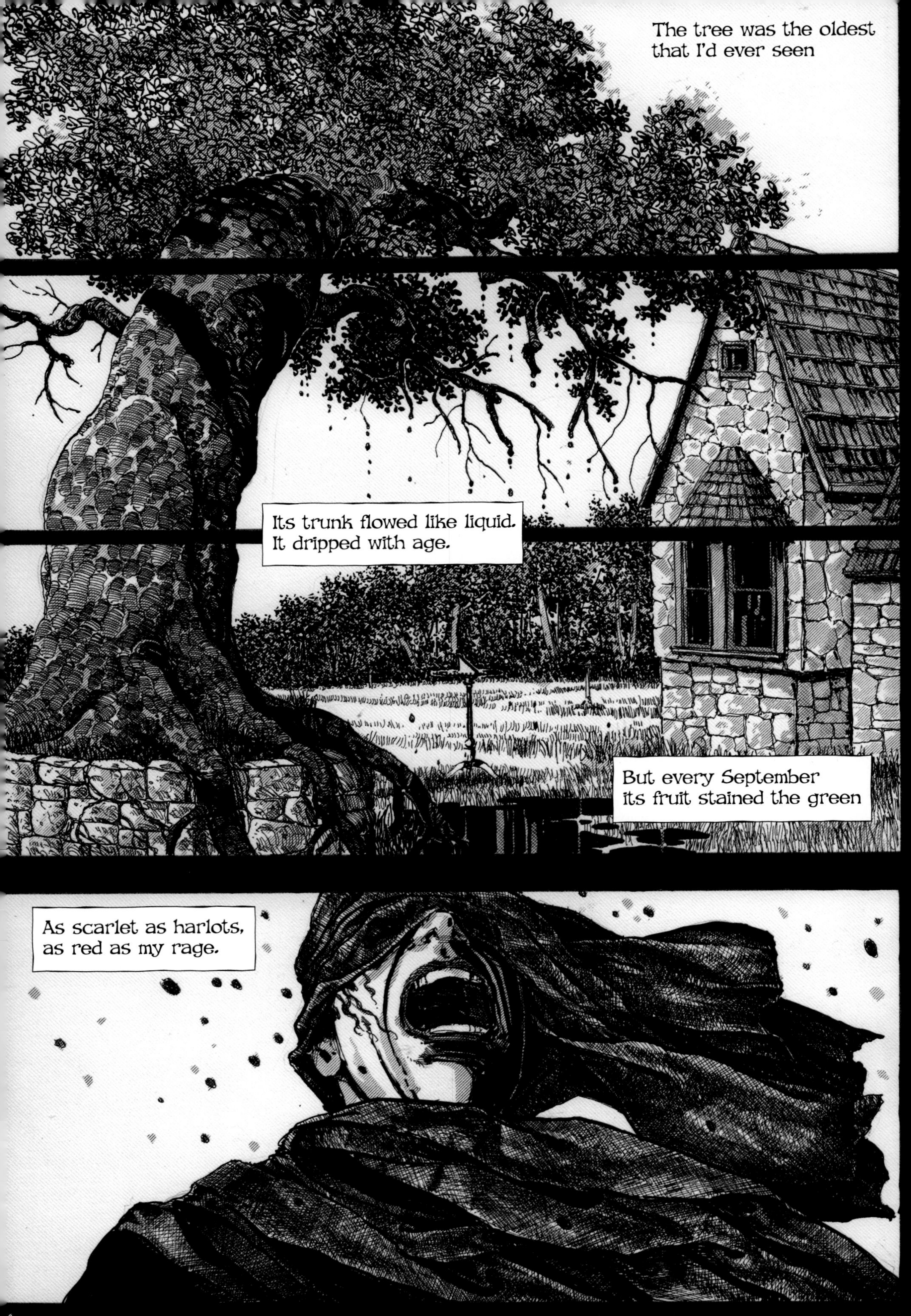
The tree was the oldest that I'd ever seen
Its trunk flowed like liquid. It dripped with age.
But every September its fruit stained the green
As scarlet as harlots, as red as my rage.

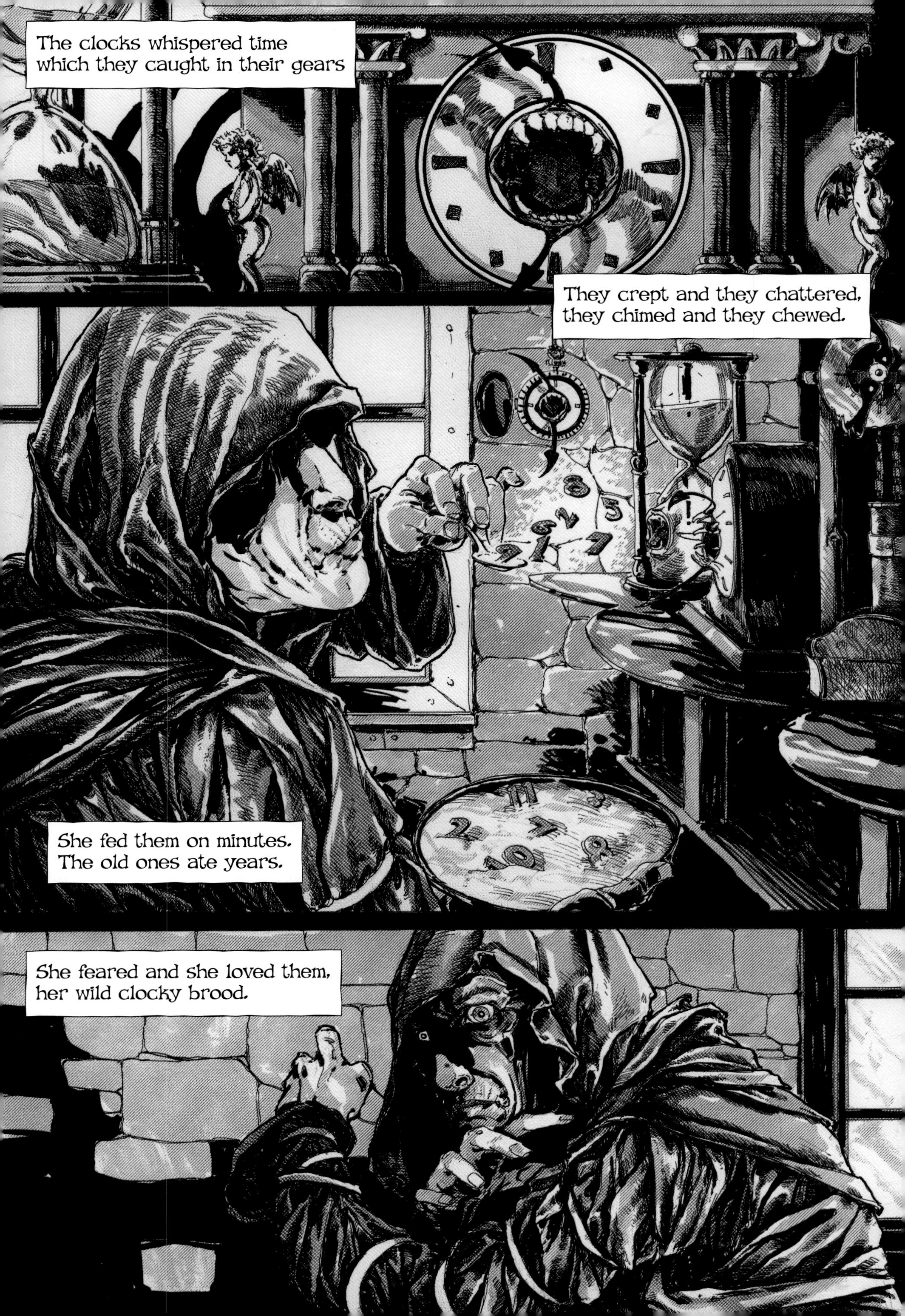
The clocks whispered time which they caught in their gears
They crept and they chattered, they chimed and they chewed.
She fed them on minutes. The old ones ate years.
She feared and she loved them, her wild clocky brood.

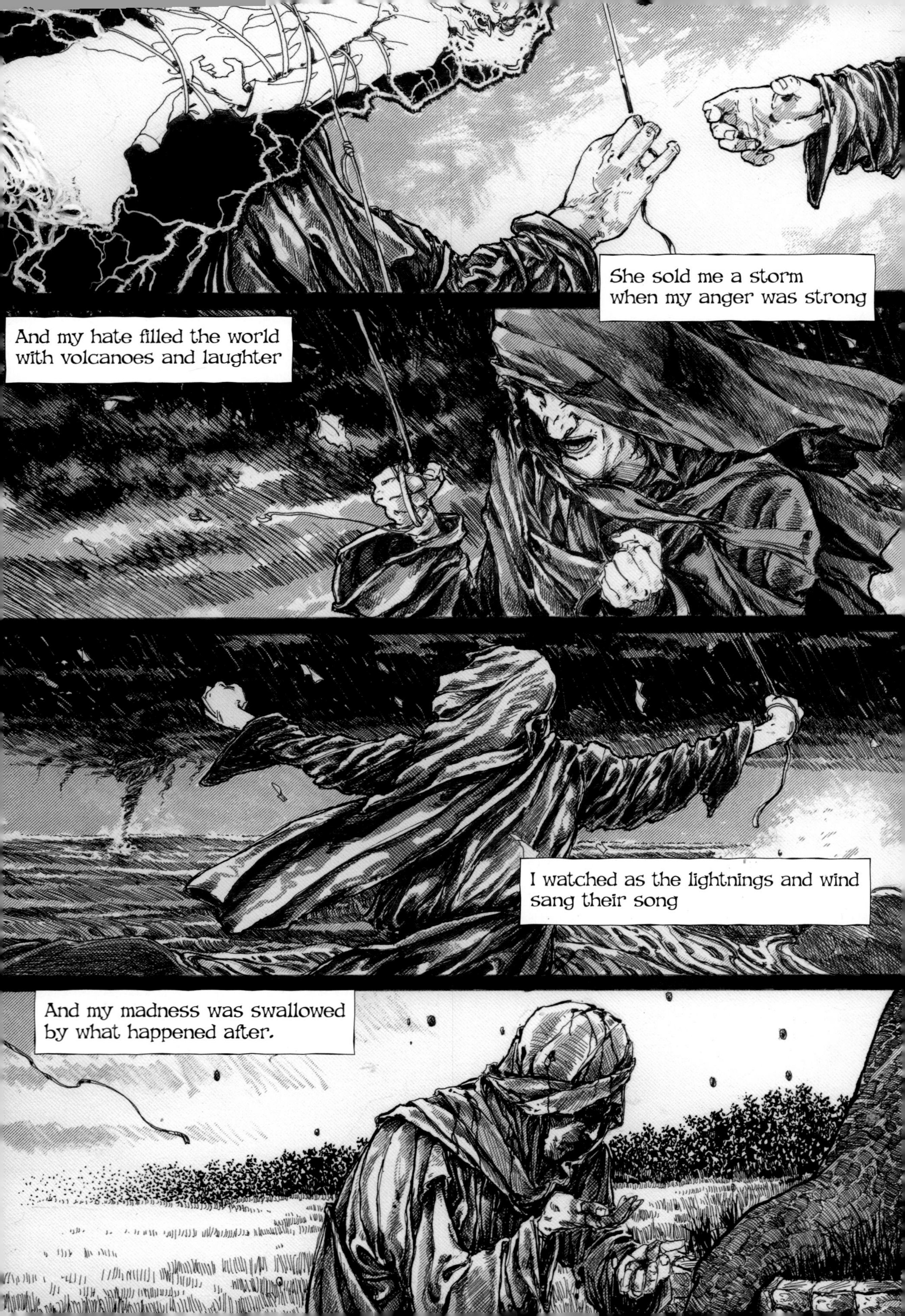
She sold me a storm
when my anger was strong
And my hate filled the world
with volcanoes and laughter
I watched as the lightnings and wind
sang their song
And my madness was swallowed
by what happened after.

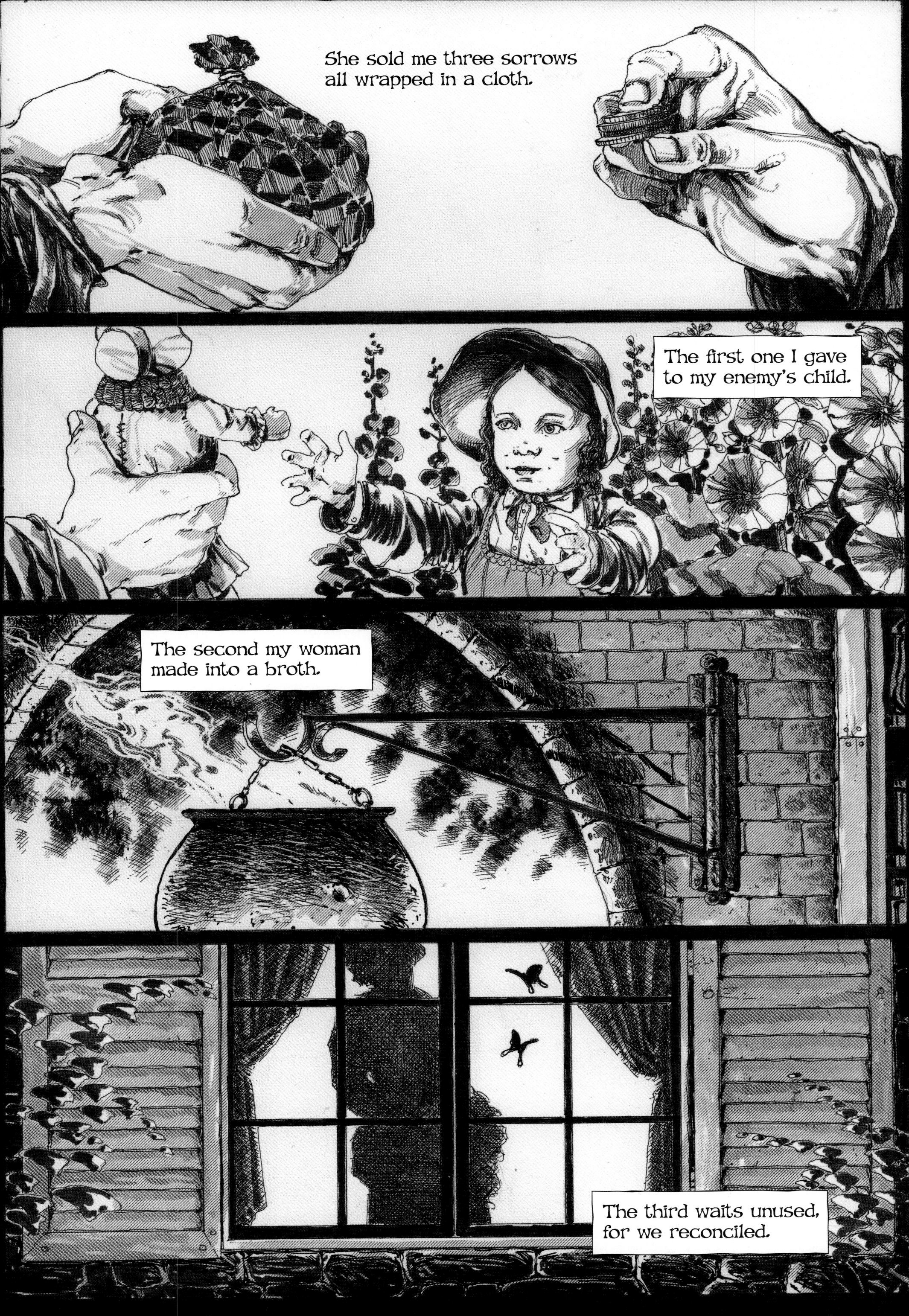
She sold me three sorrows all wrapped in a cloth.
The first one I gave to my enemy's child.
The second my woman made into a broth.
The third waits unused, for we reconciled.

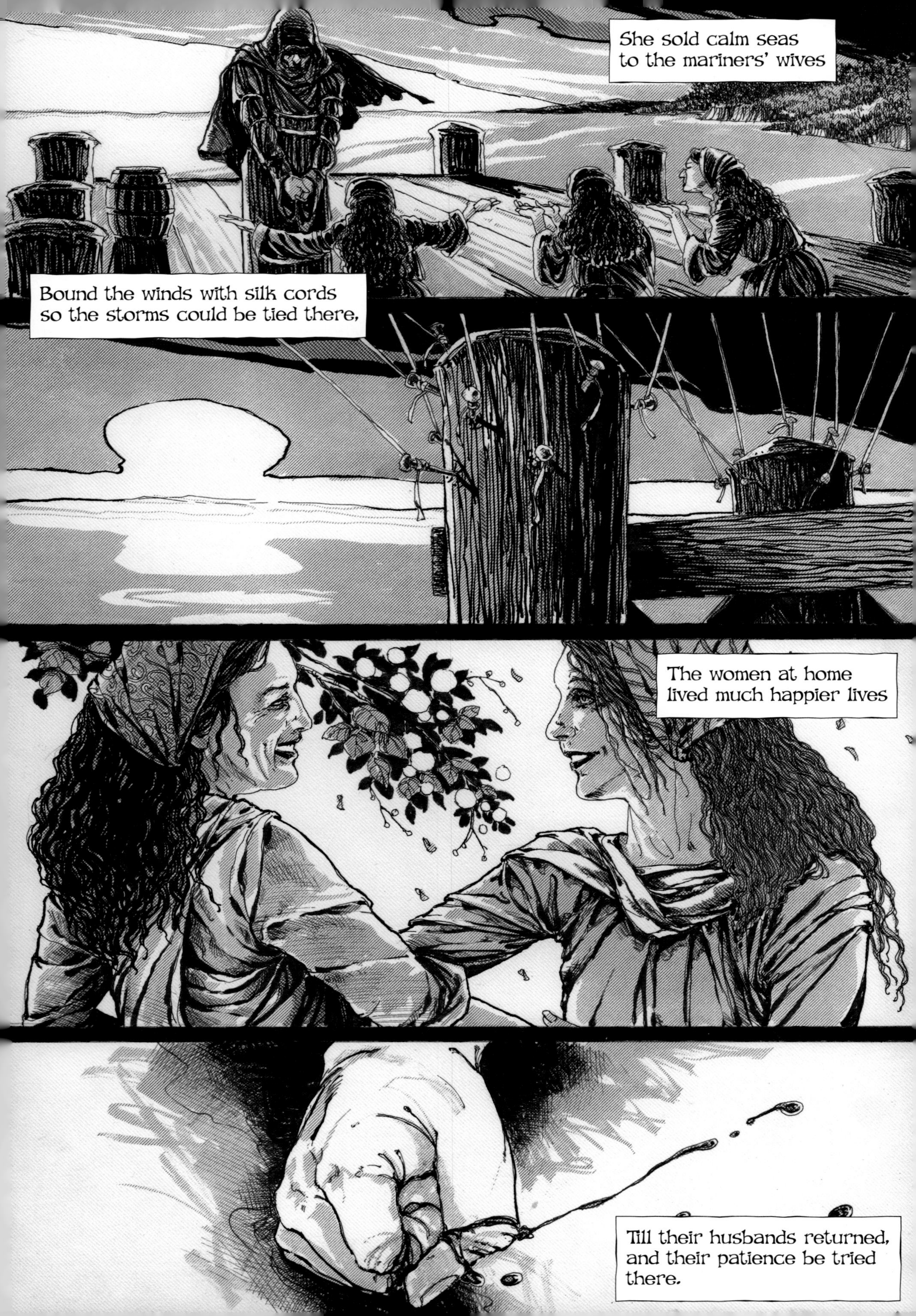
She sold calm seas to the mariners' wives
Bound the winds with silk cords so the storms could be tied there,
The women at home lived much happier lives
Till their husbands returned, and their patience be tried there.

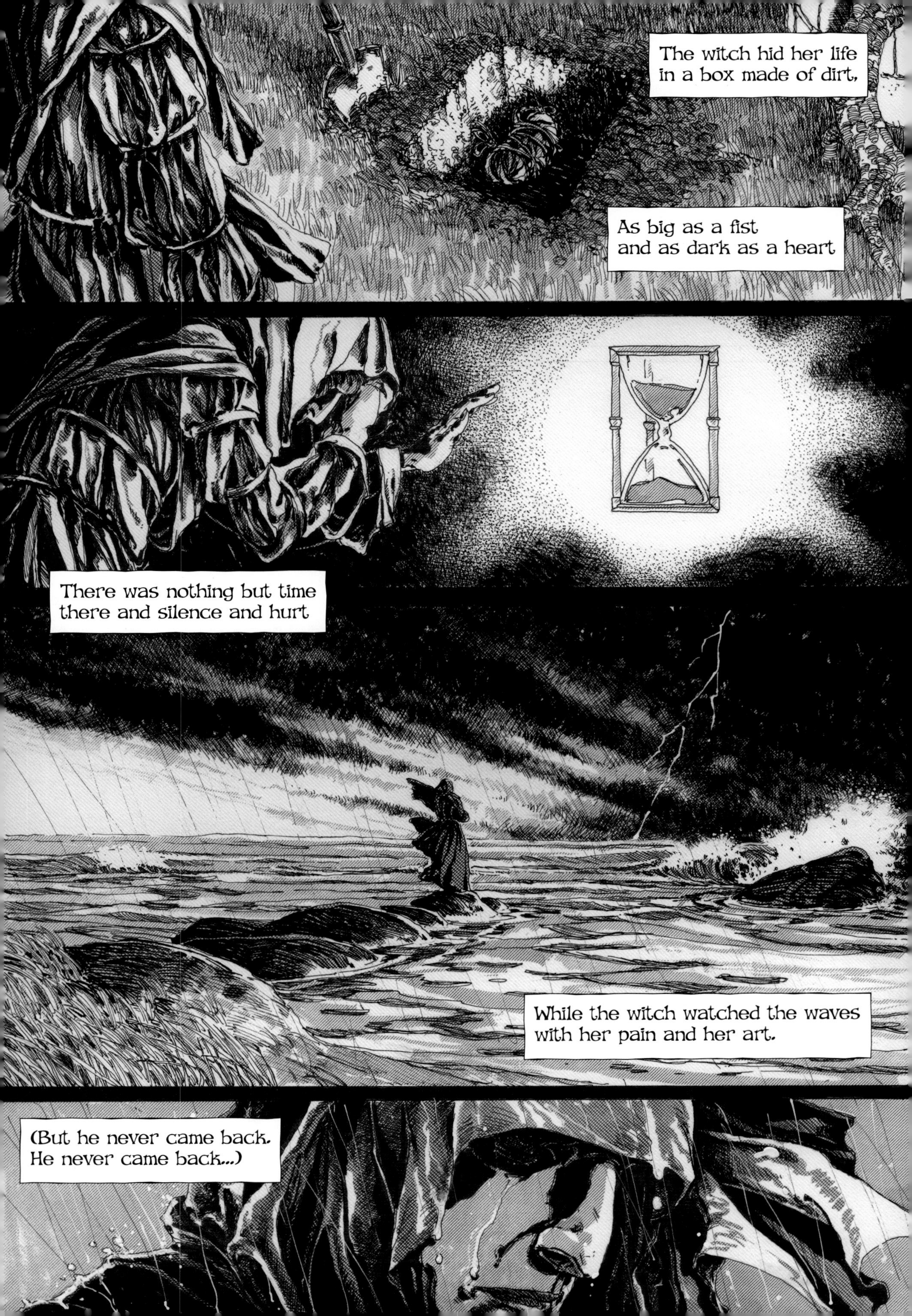
The witch hid her life in a box made of dirt,
As big as a fist and as dark as a heart
There was nothing but time there and silence and hurt
While the witch watched the waves with her pain and her art.
(But he never came back. He never came back...)

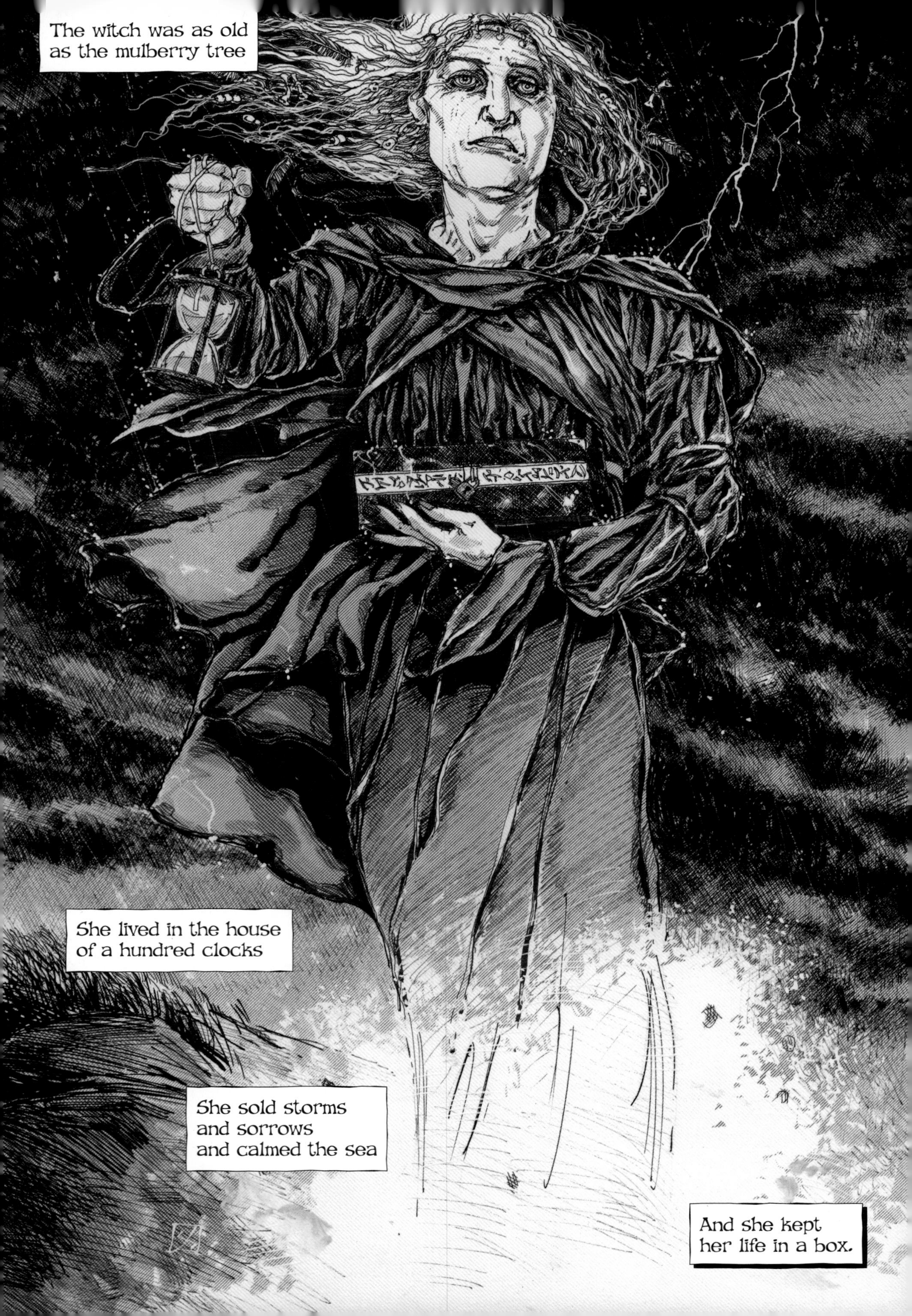
The witch was as old as the mulberry tree
She lived in the house of a hundred clocks
She sold storms and sorrows and calmed the sea
And she kept her life in a box.

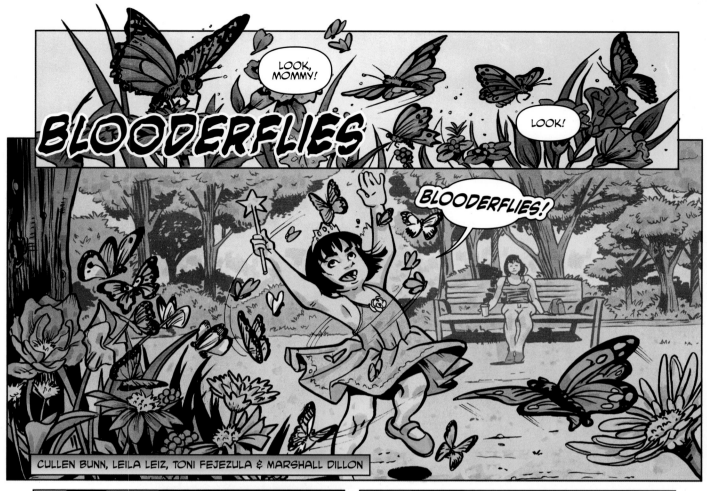

BLOODERFLIES

LOOK, MOMMY!

LOOK!

BLOODERFLIES!

CULLEN BUNN, LEILA LEIZ, TONI FEJEZULA & MARSHALL DILLON

BUTTER-FLIES, MAISY.

I THINK YOU MEAN BUTTER-FLIES.

THAT'S WHAT I SAID, SILLY!

HAHAHAHA!

BLOODER-FLIES!

BLOODER-FLIES!

WHATEVER YOU SAY, SWEETIE.

HAHAHAHA!

THEY TICKLE!

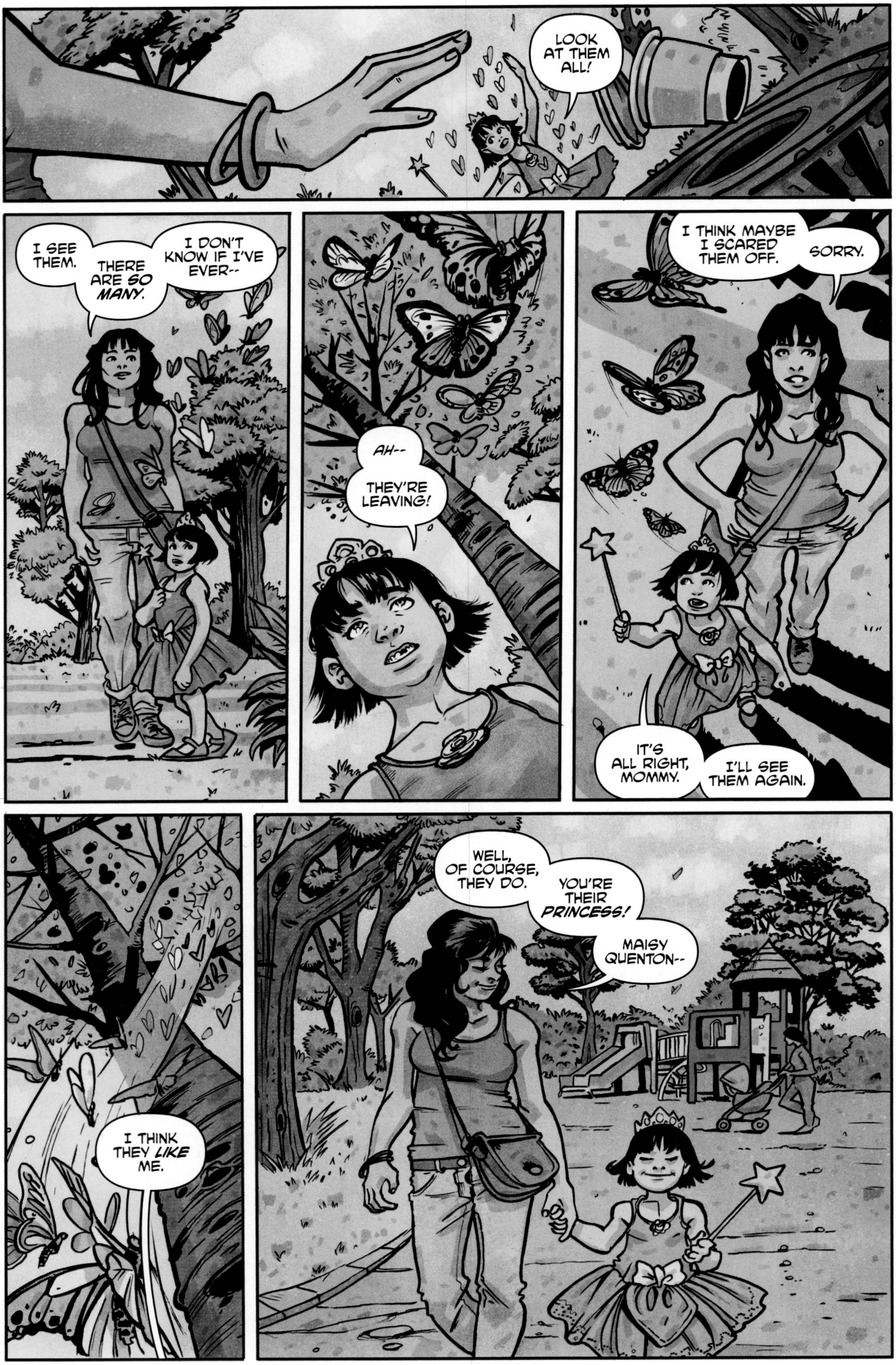
LOOK AT THEM ALL!
I SEE THEM.
THERE ARE SO MANY.
I DON'T KNOW IF I'VE EVER--
AH--
THEY'RE LEAVING!
I THINK MAYBE I SCARED THEM OFF.
SORRY.
IT'S ALL RIGHT, MOMMY.
I'LL SEE THEM AGAIN.
I THINK THEY LIKE ME.
WELL, OF COURSE, THEY DO.
YOU'RE THEIR PRINCESS!
MAISY QUENTON--

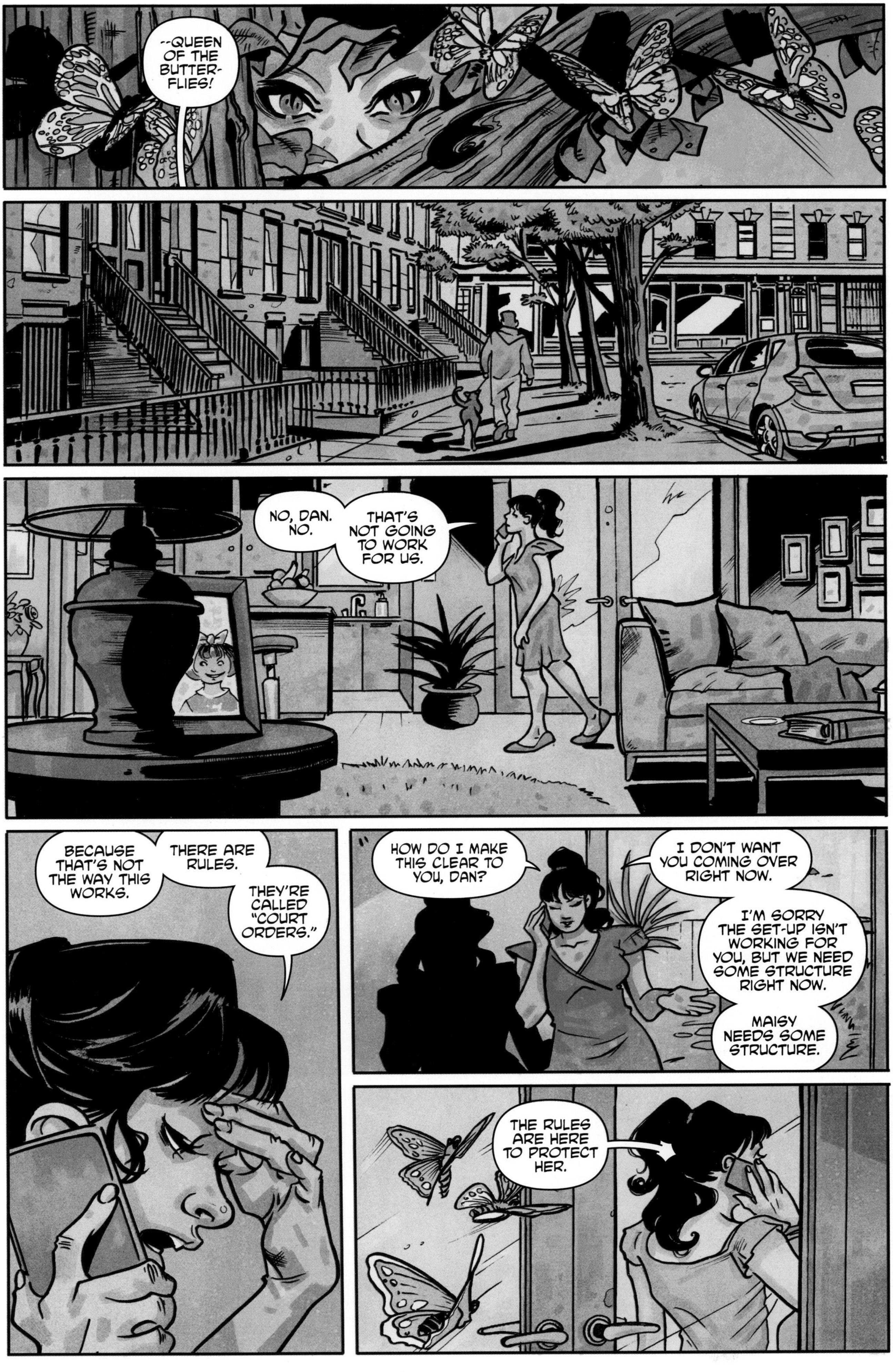
--QUEEN OF THE BUTTER-FLIES!
NO, DAN. NO.
THAT'S NOT GOING TO WORK FOR US.
BECAUSE THAT'S NOT THE WAY THIS WORKS.
THERE ARE RULES.
THEY'RE CALLED "COURT ORDERS."
HOW DO I MAKE THIS CLEAR TO YOU, DAN?
I DON'T WANT YOU COMING OVER RIGHT NOW.
I'M SORRY THE SET-UP ISN'T WORKING FOR YOU, BUT WE NEED SOME STRUCTURE RIGHT NOW.
MAISY NEEDS SOME STRUCTURE.
THE RULES ARE HERE TO PROTECT HER.

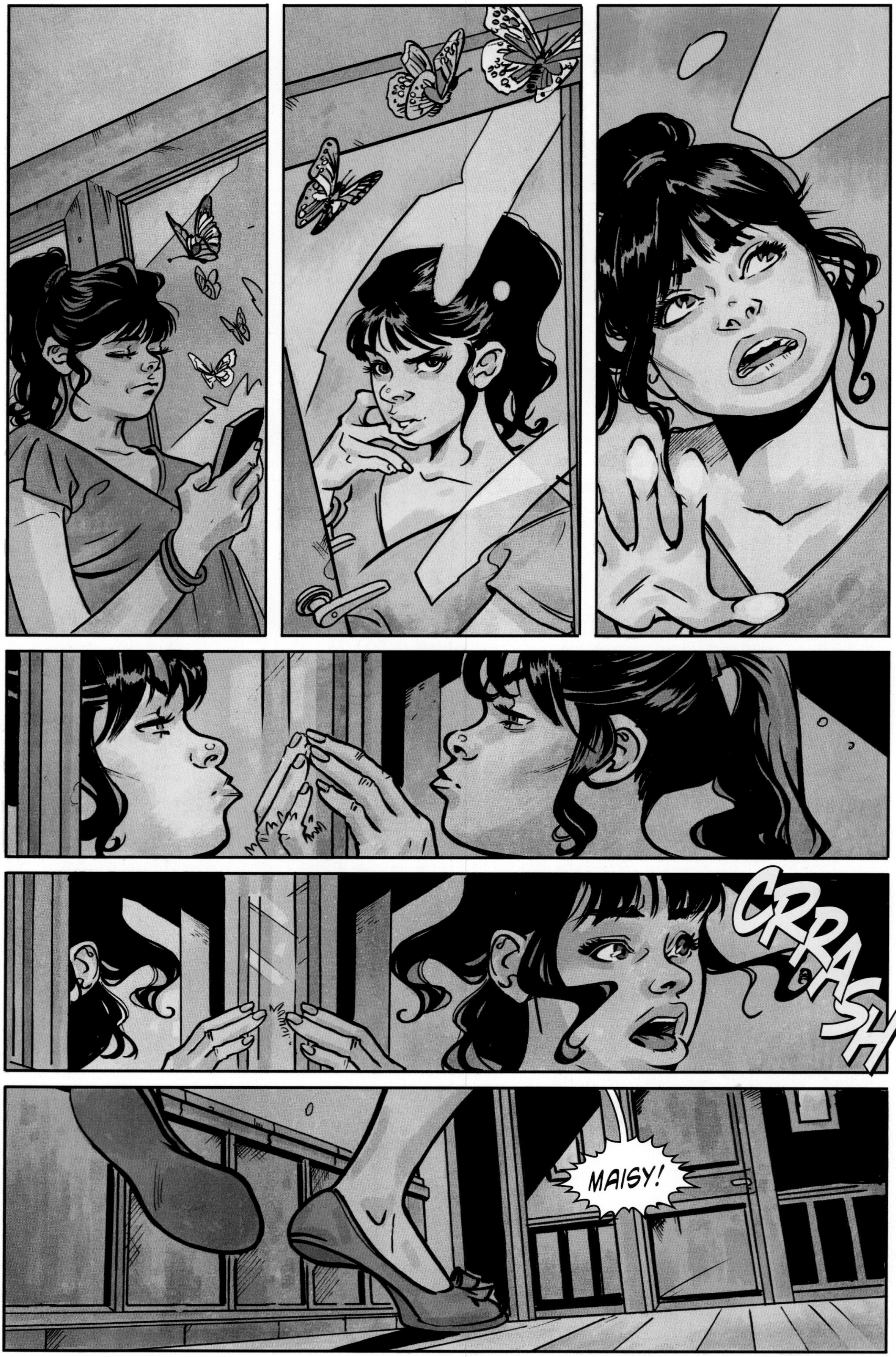
CRRASH
MAISY!

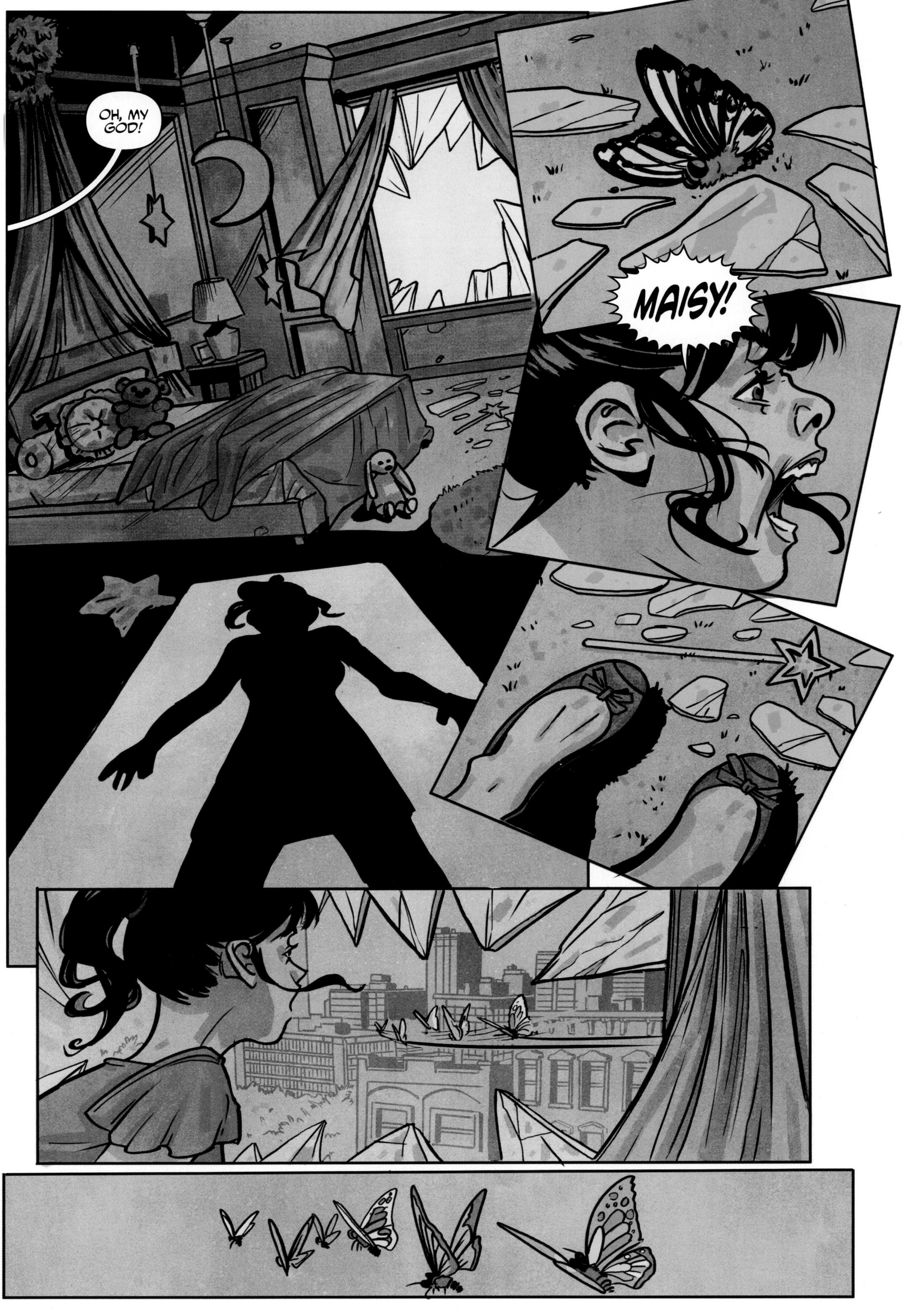
OH, MY GOD!
MAISY!

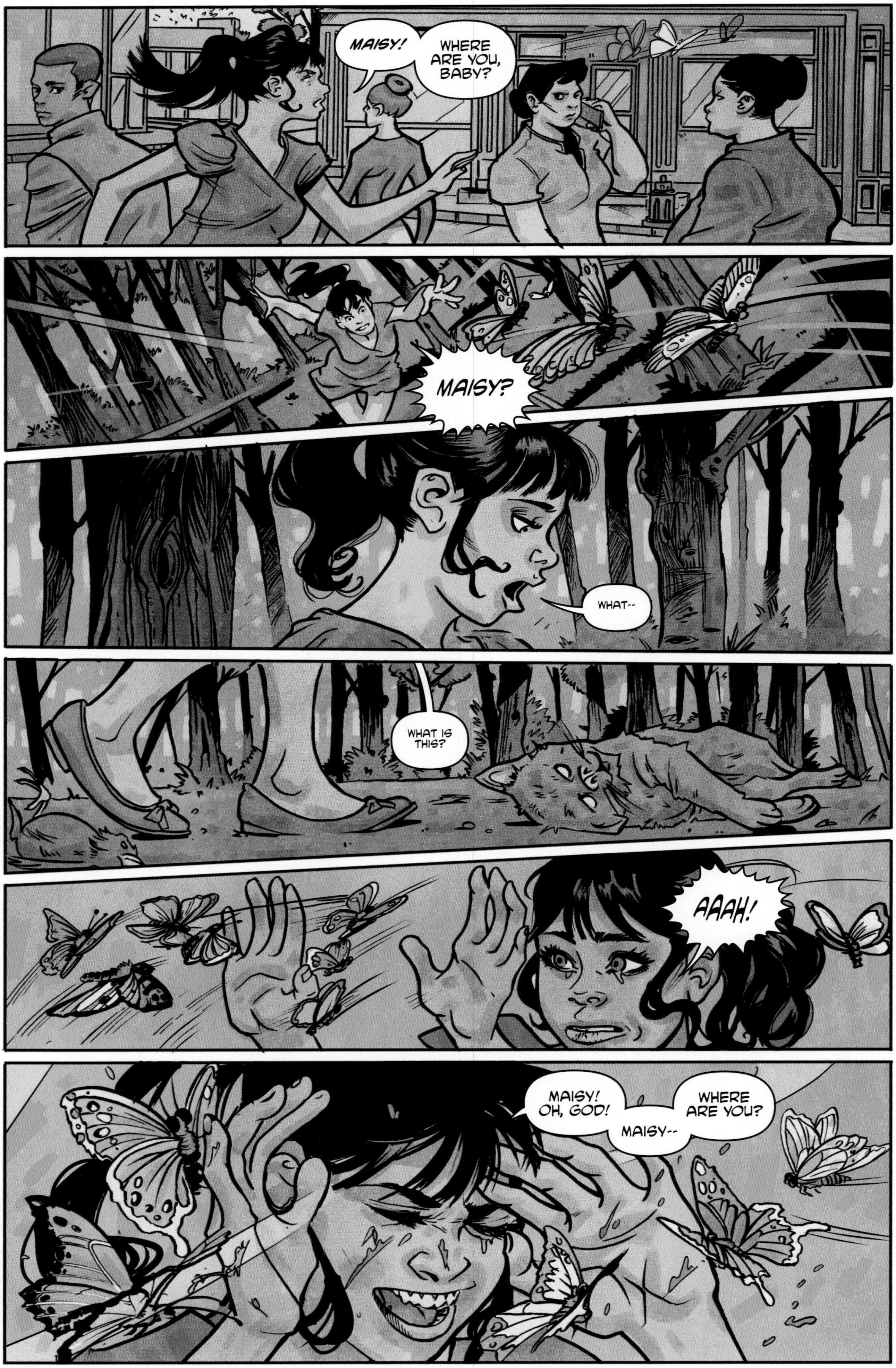
MAISY!
WHERE ARE YOU, BABY?
MAISY?
WHAT--
WHAT IS THIS?
AAAH!
MAISY! OH, GOD!
MAISY--
WHERE ARE YOU?

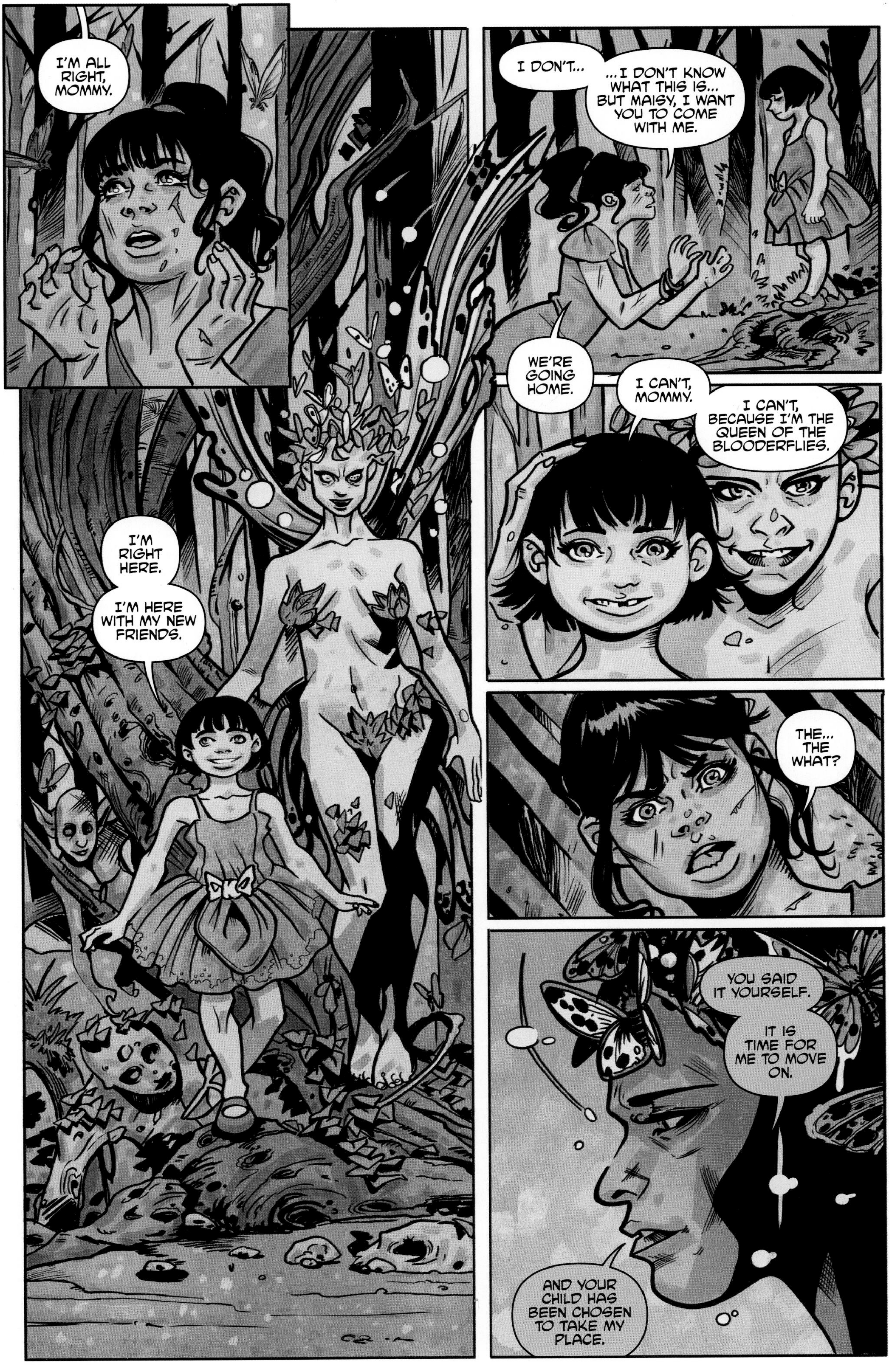
I'M ALL RIGHT, MOMMY.
I DON'T...
...I DON'T KNOW WHAT THIS IS... BUT MAISY, I WANT YOU TO COME WITH ME.
I'M RIGHT HERE.
I'M HERE WITH MY NEW FRIENDS.
WE'RE GOING HOME.
I CAN'T, MOMMY.
I CAN'T, BECAUSE I'M THE QUEEN OF THE BLOODERFLIES.
THE... THE WHAT?
YOU SAID IT YOURSELF.
IT IS TIME FOR ME TO MOVE ON.
AND YOUR CHILD HAS BEEN CHOSEN TO TAKE MY PLACE.

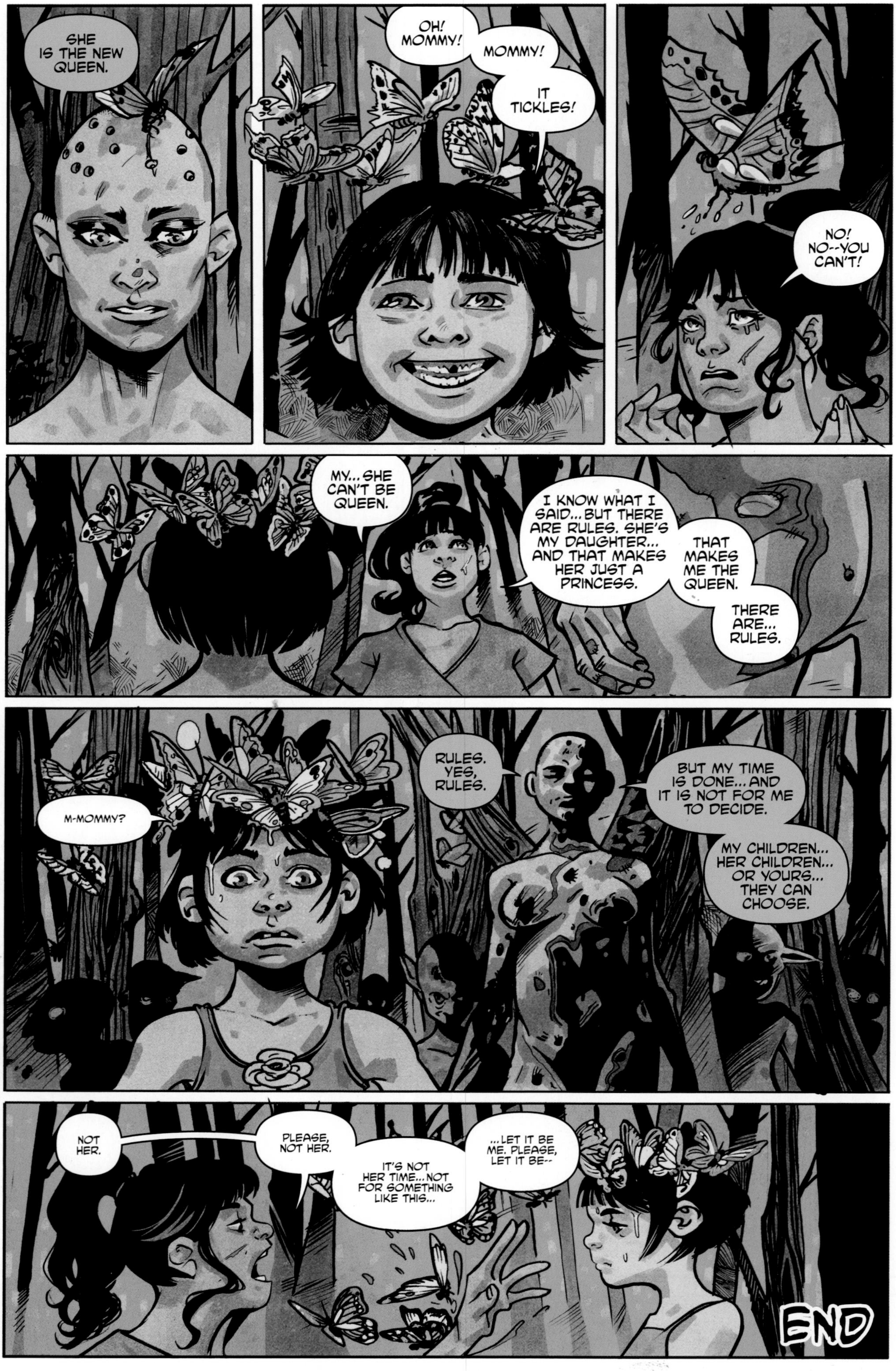
SHE IS THE NEW QUEEN.
OH! MOMMY!
MOMMY!
IT TICKLES!
NO! NO--YOU CAN'T!
MY... SHE CAN'T BE QUEEN.
I KNOW WHAT I SAID... BUT THERE ARE RULES. SHE'S MY DAUGHTER... AND THAT MAKES HER JUST A PRINCESS.
THAT MAKES ME THE QUEEN.
THERE ARE... RULES.
M-MOMMY?
RULES. YES, RULES.
BUT MY TIME IS DONE... AND IT IS NOT FOR ME TO DECIDE.
MY CHILDREN... HER CHILDREN... OR YOURS... THEY CAN CHOOSE.
NOT HER.
PLEASE, NOT HER.
IT'S NOT HER TIME... NOT FOR SOMETHING LIKE THIS...
...LET IT BE ME. PLEASE, LET IT BE--
END

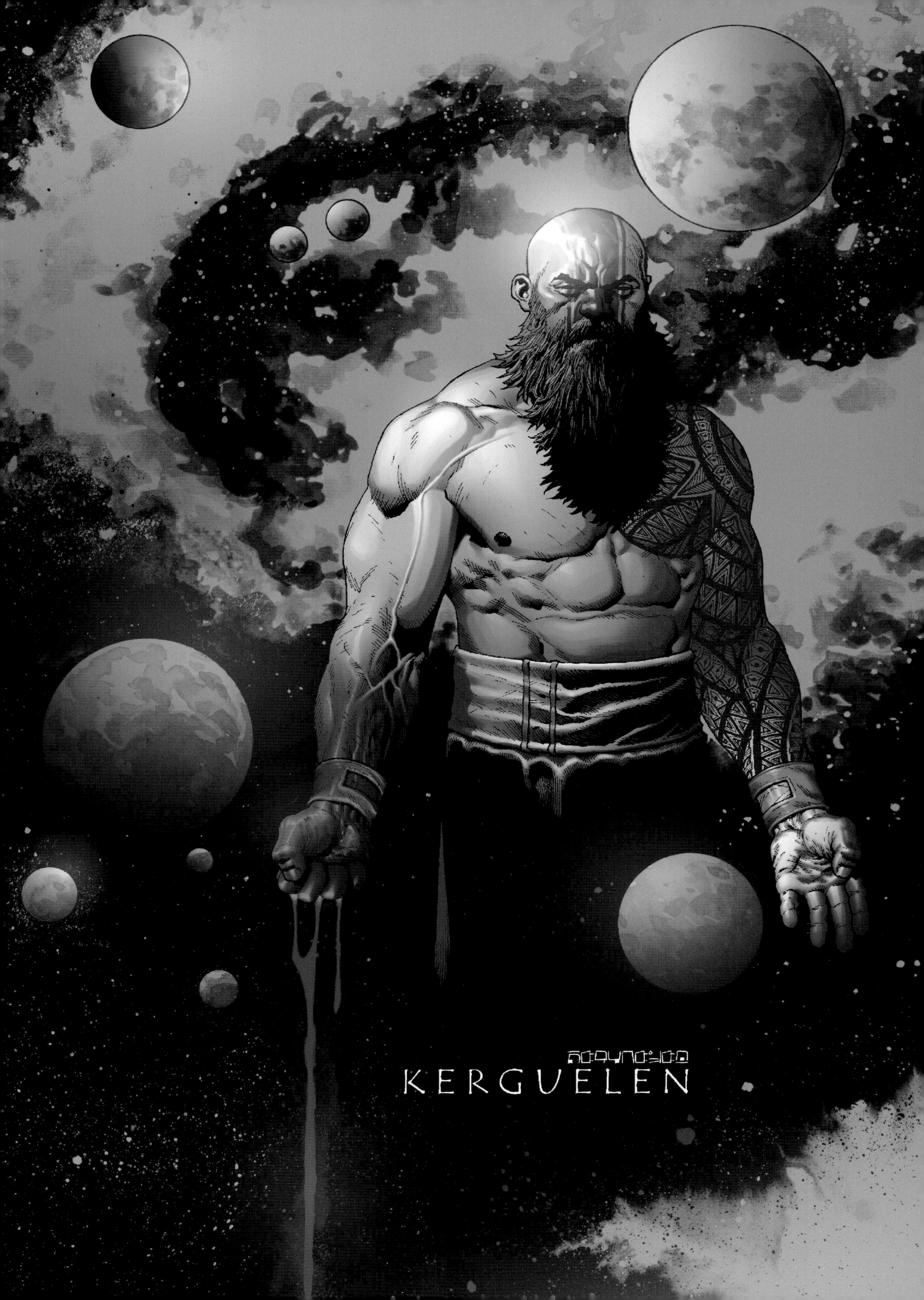
KERGUELEN

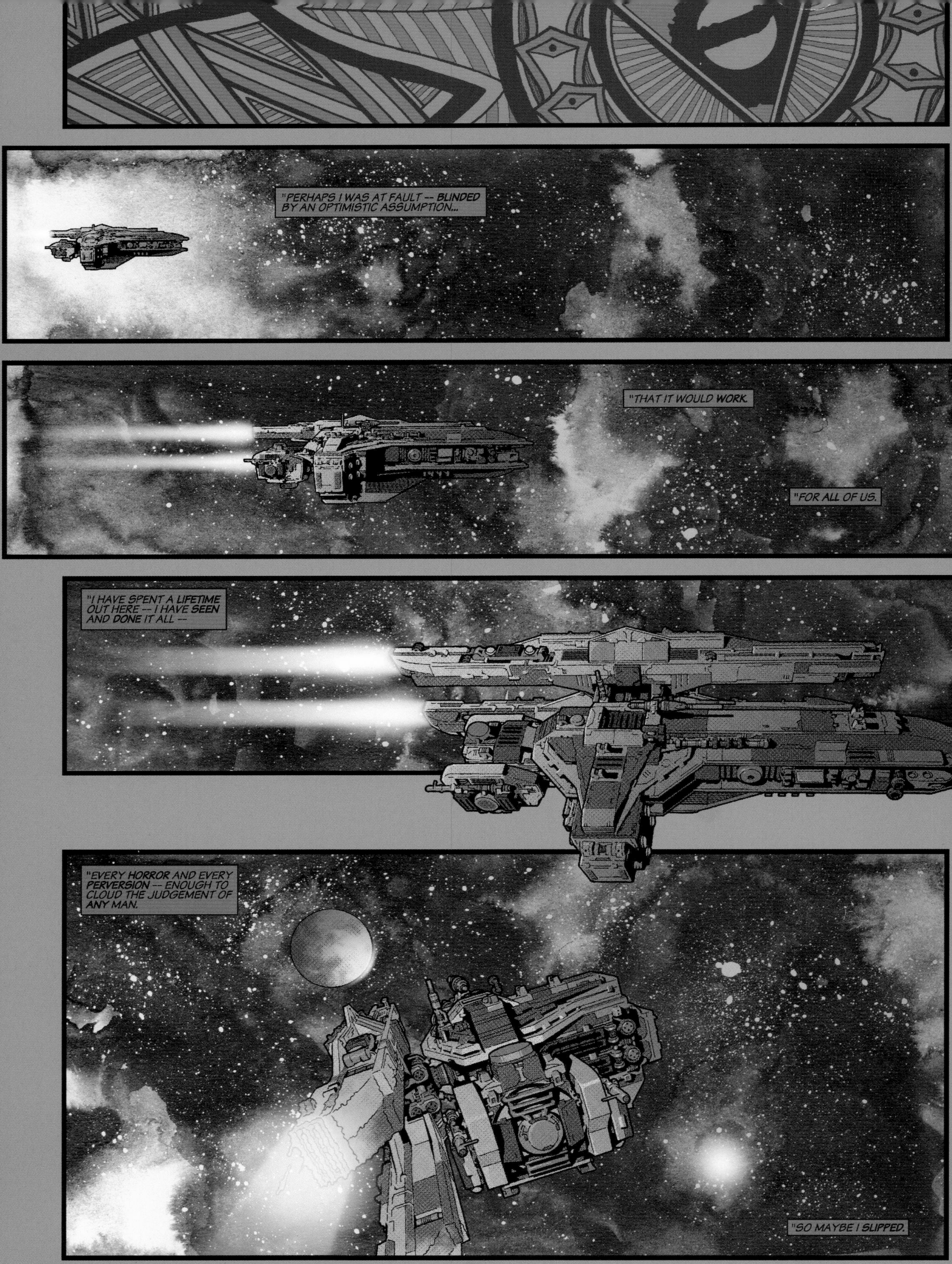
"PERHAPS I WAS AT FAULT -- BLINDED BY AN OPTIMISTIC ASSUMPTION...
"THAT IT WOULD WORK.
"FOR ALL OF US.
"I HAVE SPENT A LIFETIME OUT HERE -- I HAVE SEEN AND DONE IT ALL --
"EVERY HORROR AND EVERY PERVERSION -- ENOUGH TO CLOUD THE JUDGEMENT OF ANY MAN.
"SO MAYBE I SLIPPED.

4276 MEYER
RhELION R/

"NO. THIS IS ALL DOWN TO YOU.

"TELL ME...WHAT COULD YOU HAVE POSSIBLY HOPED TO ACHIEVE?

"YOU HAVE A RARE TALENT, MEYER -- FOR MAKING ENEMIES AT EVERY TURN. IT IS ALMOST ADMIRABLE. I AM AMAZED YOU HAVE MANAGED TO LIVE THIS LONG.

"THERE WAS A TIME WHEN THE S.E.C. WOULD HAVE CAUGHT ON TO YOU -- THEY WOULD HAVE WEEDED YOU OUT AS SOON AS YOU SIGNED UP.

"BUT WE ALL KNOW THE SERVICE IS NOT WHAT IT WAS..."

THINK HE'S STILL OUT, Ma?

HE'S FAKIN' IT, THE LITTLE pissant.

LEAKIN' ALL OVER THE DECK IS WHAT HE IS.

"THEY FAILED TO REALISE WHAT KIND OF MAN YOU TRULY ARE. SO THEY TRAINED YOU. YOU DID YOUR DUTY...

K-KK

"...FORMED THAT INDEPENDENT LITTLE BAND OF YOURS --"

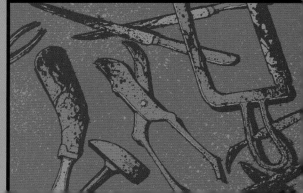

"USED THEM AS A VEIL OF LEGITIMACY —

"DECEIVING EVERYONE AROUND YOU AS YOU LED ANOTHER LIFE STEEPED IN MISDEED. COVERT AND RUTHLESS — QUALITIES WE LOOK FOR IN AN OPERATIVE...

"OH, AND THE LIVES YOU DESTROYED...

"SO EXCITING!

"YOU NEEDED THE FOCUS OF AN APPROPRIATE OUTLET. A PLACE TO GO WHERE YOU COULD BE USEFUL.

"YOU WERE SLOWLY MOVING INTO OUR ORBIT, SO WE TOOK YOU IN — TO REALISE YOUR POTENTIAL, BUT IT WAS A GAMBLE THAT COST US DEARLY...

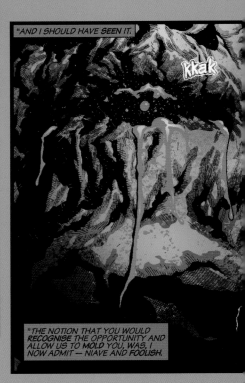

"AND I SHOULD HAVE SEEN IT.

kkak

"THE NOTION THAT YOU WOULD RECOGNISE THE OPPORTUNITY AND ALLOW US TO MOLD YOU, WAS, I NOW ADMIT — NIAVE AND FOOLISH.

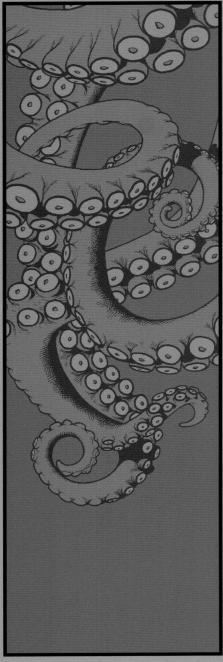

"WE GAVE YOU EVERY INCENTIVE TO SUCCEED.

"WE WENT OUT OF OUR WAY TO HELP YOU — WENT TO GREAT LENGTHS TO THROW YOUR OLD FRIENDS OFF YOUR SCENT FOLLOWING THAT BUSINESS ON TANJIER.

"WHERE IT ALL CAUGHT UP WITH YOU —

"WHERE YOU LEFT THEM TO DIE.

"YOU WERE FREE OF IT ALL AND IN A POSITION TO START ANEW."

K-CHKK

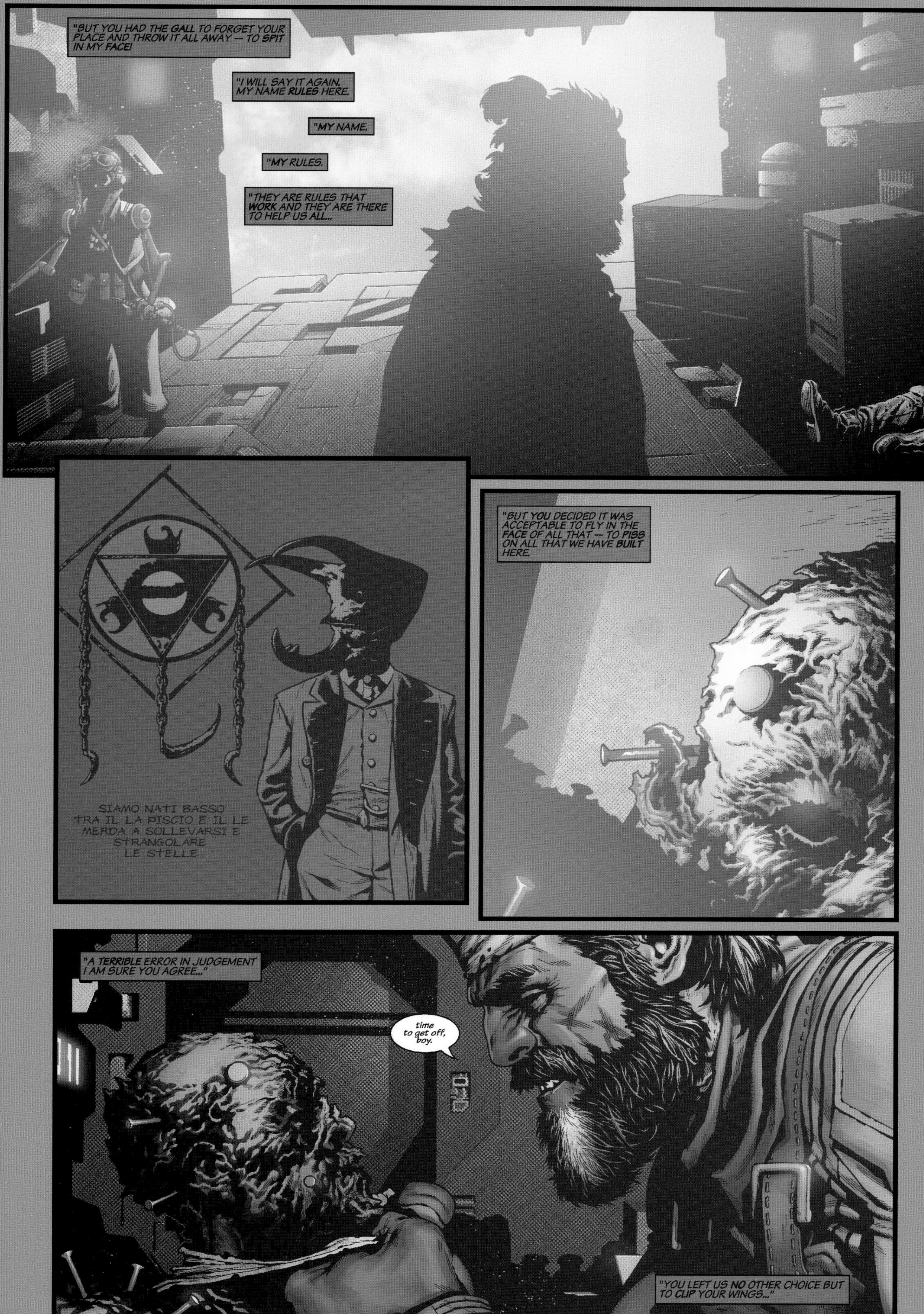
"BUT YOU HAD THE GALL TO FORGET YOUR PLACE AND THROW IT ALL AWAY -- TO SPIT IN MY FACE!
"I WILL SAY IT AGAIN. MY NAME RULES HERE.
"MY NAME.
"MY RULES.
"THEY ARE RULES THAT WORK AND THEY ARE THERE TO HELP US ALL...
SIAMO NATI BASSO TRA IL LA PISCIO E IL LE MERDA A SOLLEVARSI E STRANGOLARE LE STELLE
"BUT YOU DECIDED IT WAS ACCEPTABLE TO FLY IN THE FACE OF ALL THAT -- TO PISS ON ALL THAT WE HAVE BUILT HERE.
"A TERRIBLE ERROR IN JUDGEMENT I AM SURE YOU AGREE..."
time to get off, boy.
"YOU LEFT US NO OTHER CHOICE BUT TO CLIP YOUR WINGS..."

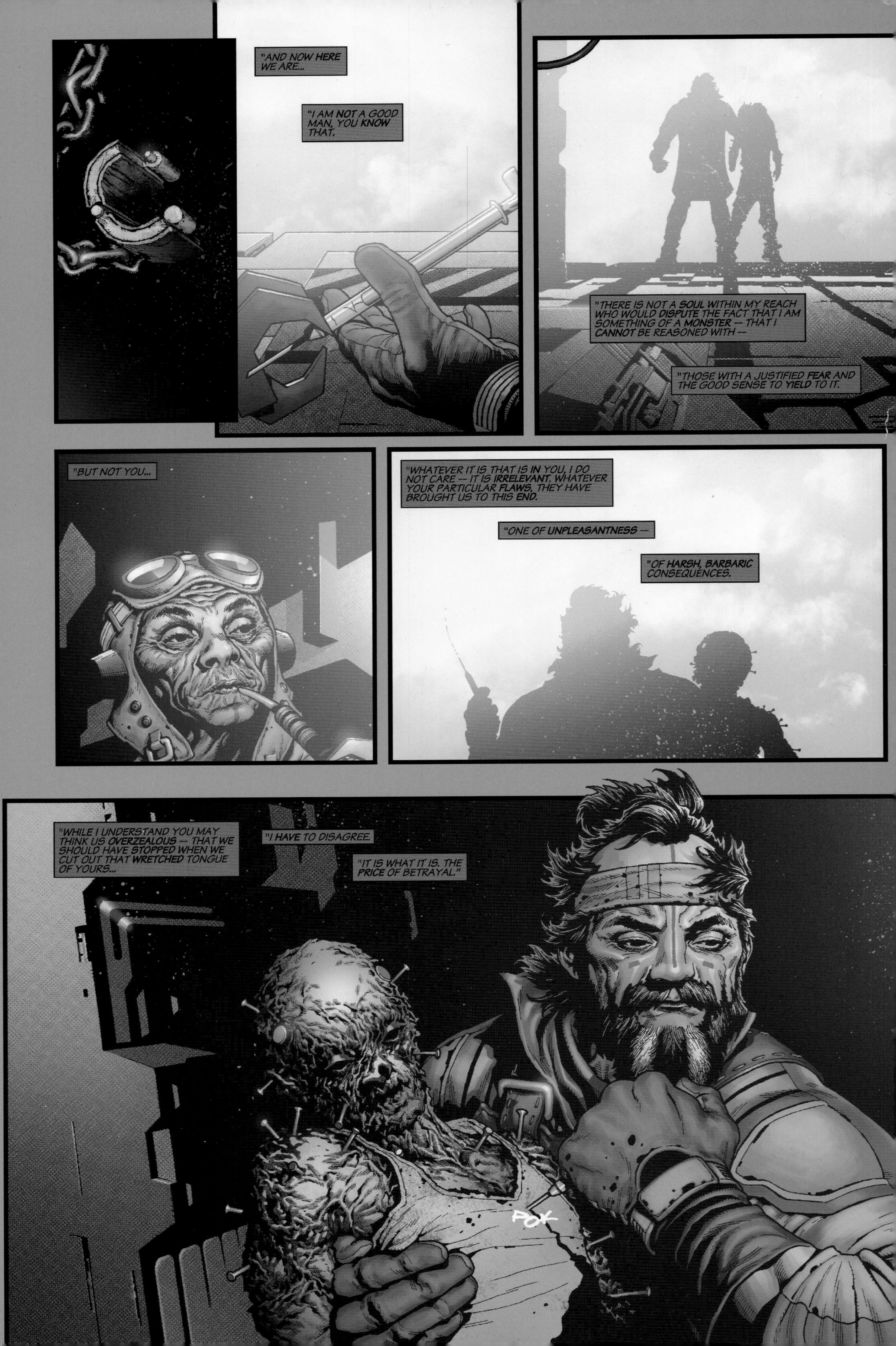
"AND NOW HERE WE ARE...
"I AM NOT A GOOD MAN, YOU KNOW THAT.
"THERE IS NOT A SOUL WITHIN MY REACH WHO WOULD DISPUTE THE FACT THAT I AM SOMETHING OF A MONSTER -- THAT I CANNOT BE REASONED WITH --
"THOSE WITH A JUSTIFIED FEAR AND THE GOOD SENSE TO YIELD TO IT.
"BUT NOT YOU...
"WHATEVER IT IS THAT IS IN YOU, I DO NOT CARE -- IT IS IRRELEVANT. WHATEVER YOUR PARTICULAR FLAWS, THEY HAVE BROUGHT US TO THIS END.
"ONE OF UNPLEASANTNESS --
"OF HARSH, BARBARIC CONSEQUENCES.
"WHILE I UNDERSTAND YOU MAY THINK US OVERZEALOUS -- THAT WE SHOULD HAVE STOPPED WHEN WE CUT OUT THAT WRETCHED TONGUE OF YOURS...
"I HAVE TO DISAGREE.
"IT IS WHAT IT IS. THE PRICE OF BETRAYAL."
POK

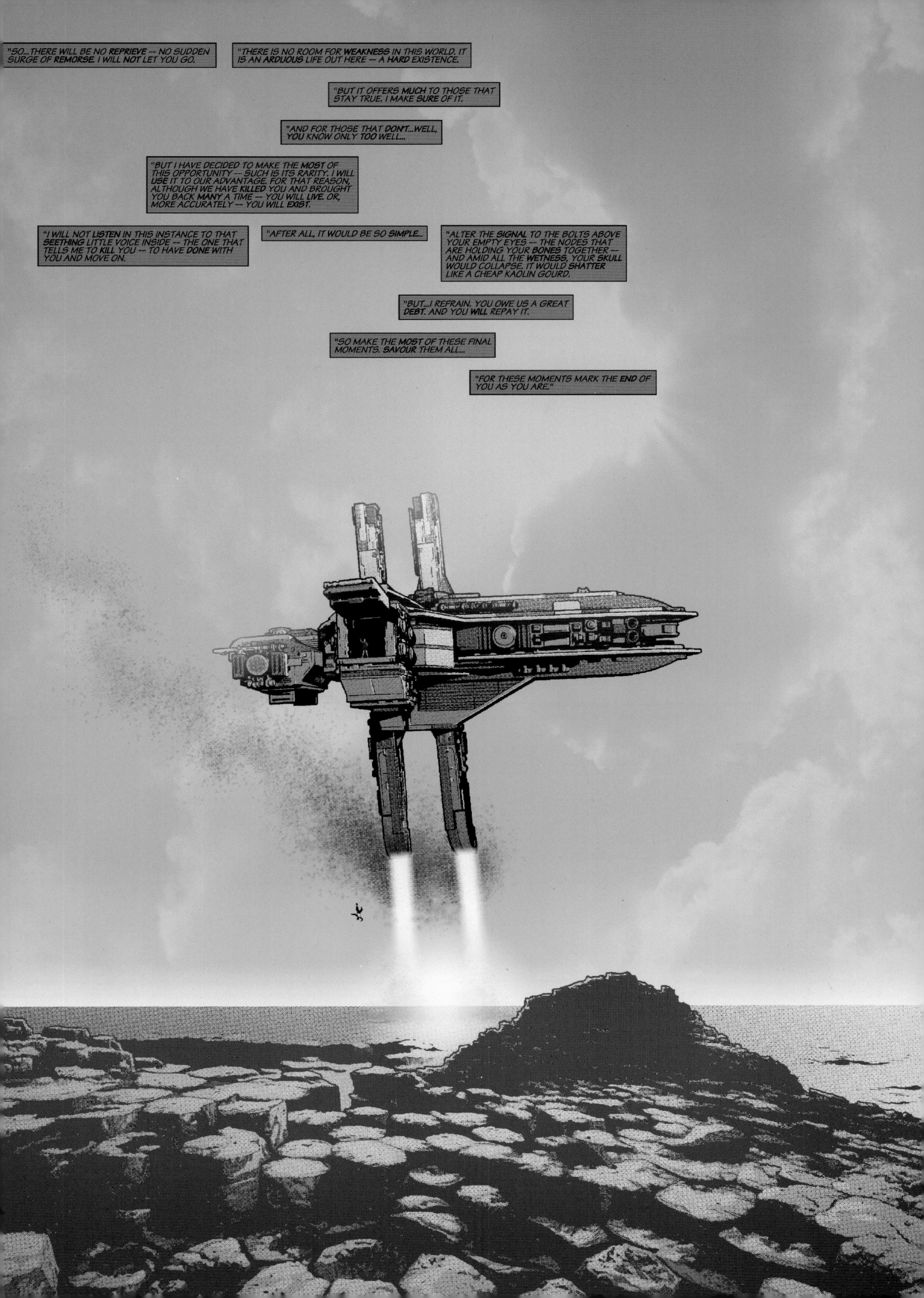
"SO...THERE WILL BE NO REPRIEVE -- NO SUDDEN SURGE OF REMORSE. I WILL NOT LET YOU GO.
"THERE IS NO ROOM FOR WEAKNESS IN THIS WORLD. IT IS AN ARDUOUS LIFE OUT HERE -- A HARD EXISTENCE.
"BUT IT OFFERS MUCH TO THOSE THAT STAY TRUE. I MAKE SURE OF IT.
"AND FOR THOSE THAT DON'T...WELL, YOU KNOW ONLY TOO WELL...
"BUT I HAVE DECIDED TO MAKE THE MOST OF THIS OPPORTUNITY -- SUCH IS ITS RARITY. I WILL USE IT TO OUR ADVANTAGE. FOR THAT REASON, ALTHOUGH WE HAVE KILLED YOU AND BROUGHT YOU BACK MANY A TIME -- YOU WILL LIVE. OR, MORE ACCURATELY -- YOU WILL EXIST.
"I WILL NOT LISTEN IN THIS INSTANCE TO THAT SEETHING LITTLE VOICE INSIDE -- THE ONE THAT TELLS ME TO KILL YOU -- TO HAVE DONE WITH YOU AND MOVE ON.
"AFTER ALL, IT WOULD BE SO SIMPLE...
"ALTER THE SIGNAL TO THE BOLTS ABOVE YOUR EMPTY EYES -- THE NODES THAT ARE HOLDING YOUR BONES TOGETHER -- AND AMID ALL THE WETNESS, YOUR SKULL WOULD COLLAPSE. IT WOULD SHATTER LIKE A CHEAP KAOLIN GOURD.
"BUT...I REFRAIN. YOU OWE US A GREAT DEBT. AND YOU WILL REPAY IT.
"SO MAKE THE MOST OF THESE FINAL MOMENTS. SAVOUR THEM ALL...
"FOR THESE MOMENTS MARK THE END OF YOU AS YOU ARE."

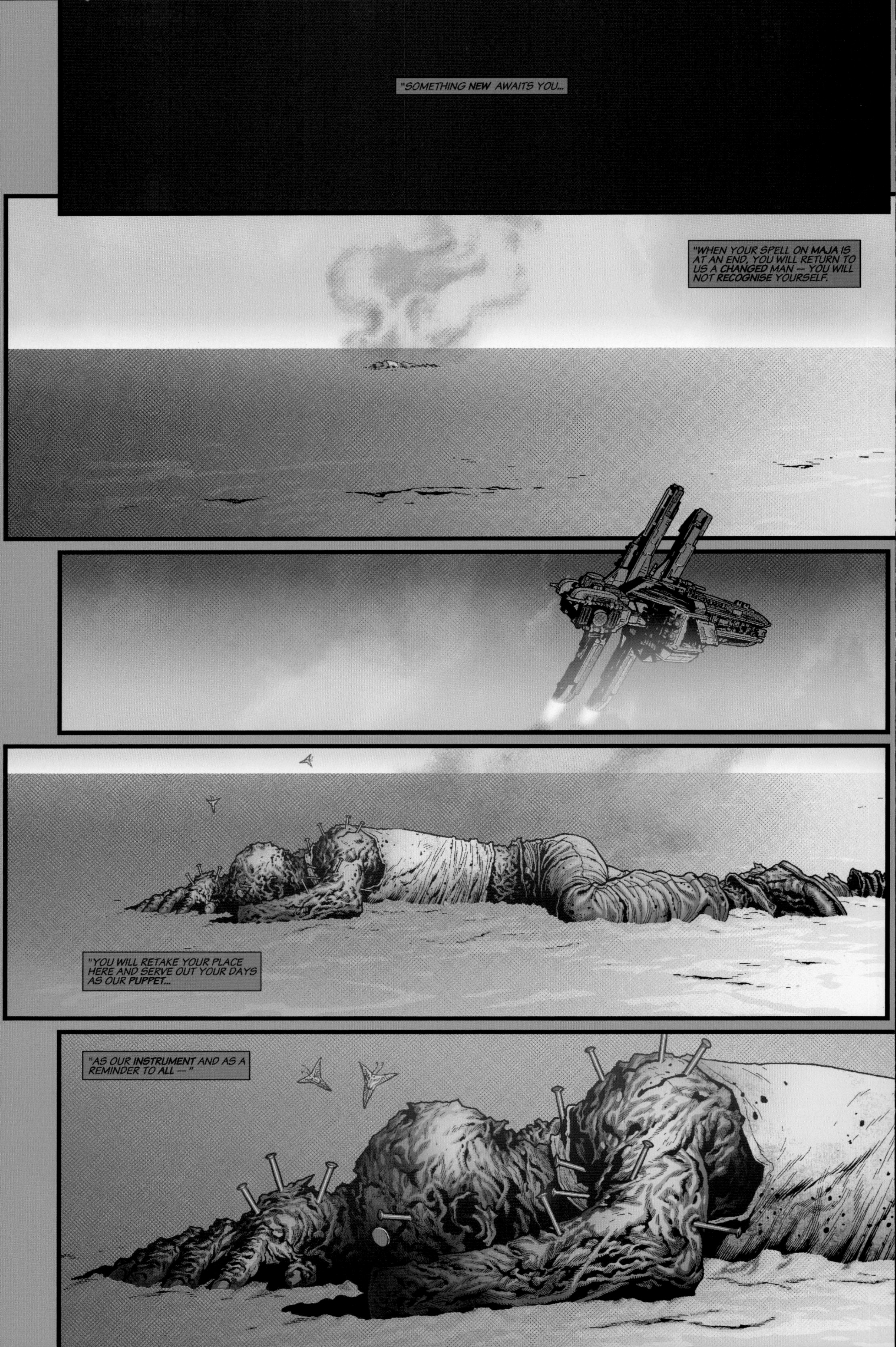
"SOMETHING NEW AWAITS YOU...
"WHEN YOUR SPELL ON MAJA IS AT AN END, YOU WILL RETURN TO US A CHANGED MAN -- YOU WILL NOT RECOGNISE YOURSELF.
"YOU WILL RETAKE YOUR PLACE HERE AND SERVE OUT YOUR DAYS AS OUR PUPPET...
"AS OUR INSTRUMENT AND AS A REMINDER TO ALL --"

"THAT NO-ONE CROSSES ME.

"IT IS JUST.

nhkk!

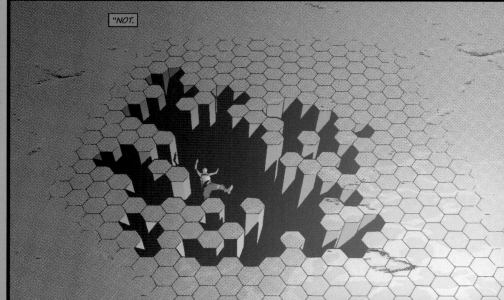
"NOT.

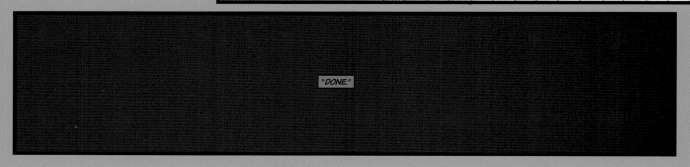
"DONE."

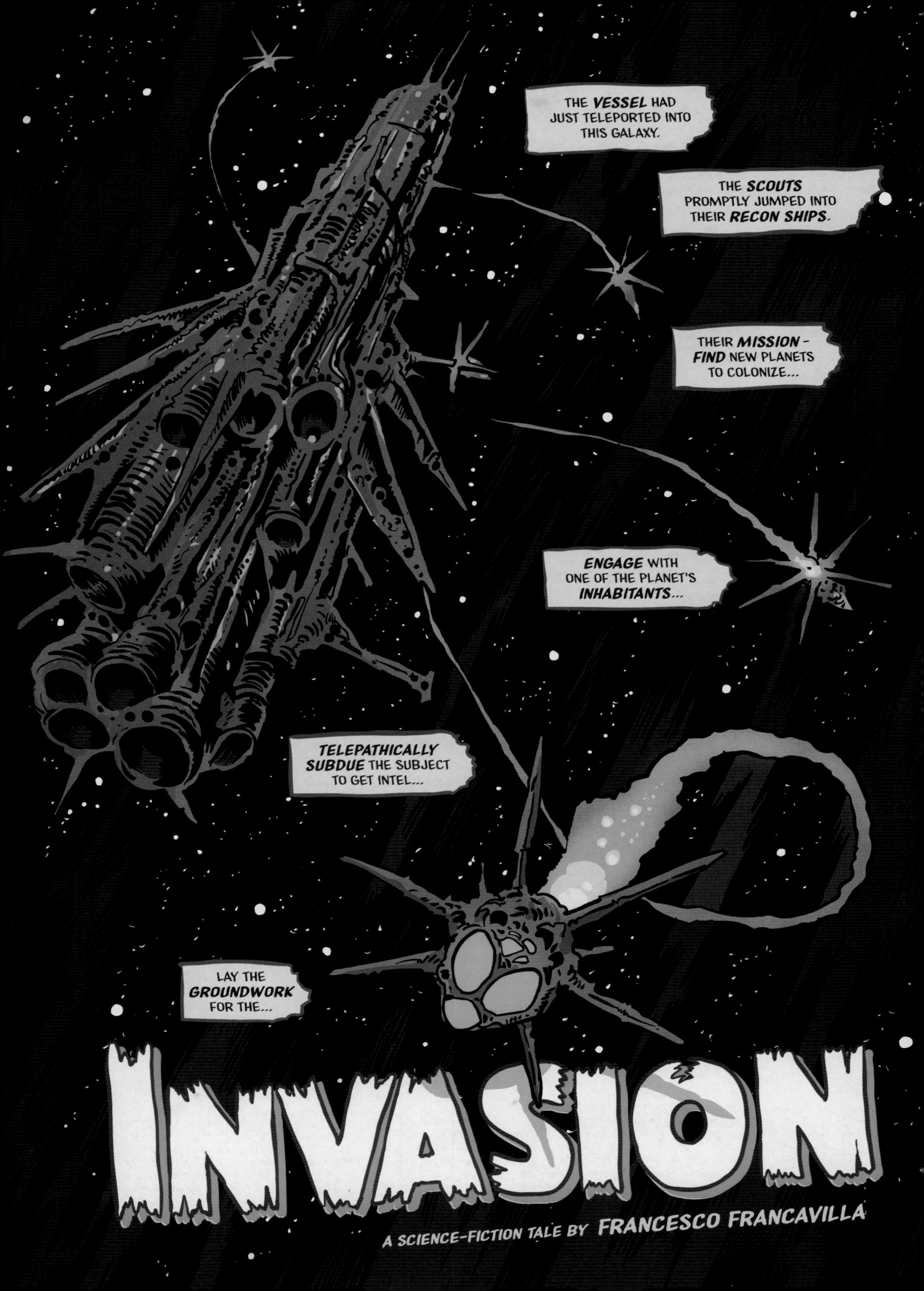
THE VESSEL HAD JUST TELEPORTED INTO THIS GALAXY.
THE SCOUTS PROMPTLY JUMPED INTO THEIR RECON SHIPS.
THEIR MISSION - FIND NEW PLANETS TO COLONIZE...
ENGAGE WITH ONE OF THE PLANET'S INHABITANTS...
TELEPATHICALLY SUBDUE THE SUBJECT TO GET INTEL...
LAY THE GROUNDWORK FOR THE...
INVASION
A SCIENCE-FICTION TALE BY FRANCESCO FRANCAVILLA

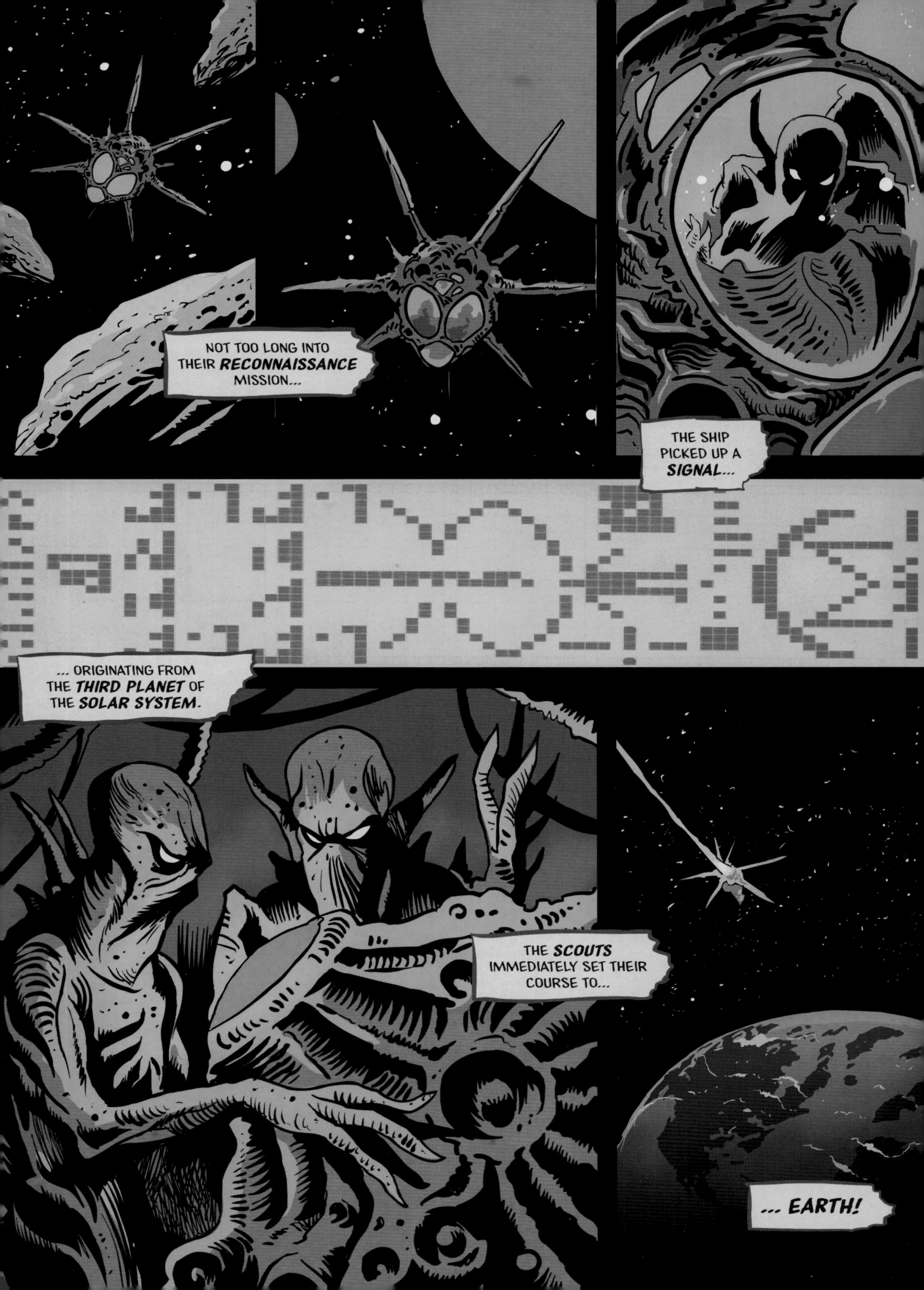
NOT TOO LONG INTO THEIR RECONNAISSANCE MISSION...
THE SHIP PICKED UP A SIGNAL...
... ORIGINATING FROM THE THIRD PLANET OF THE SOLAR SYSTEM.
THE SCOUTS IMMEDIATELY SET THEIR COURSE TO...
... EARTH!

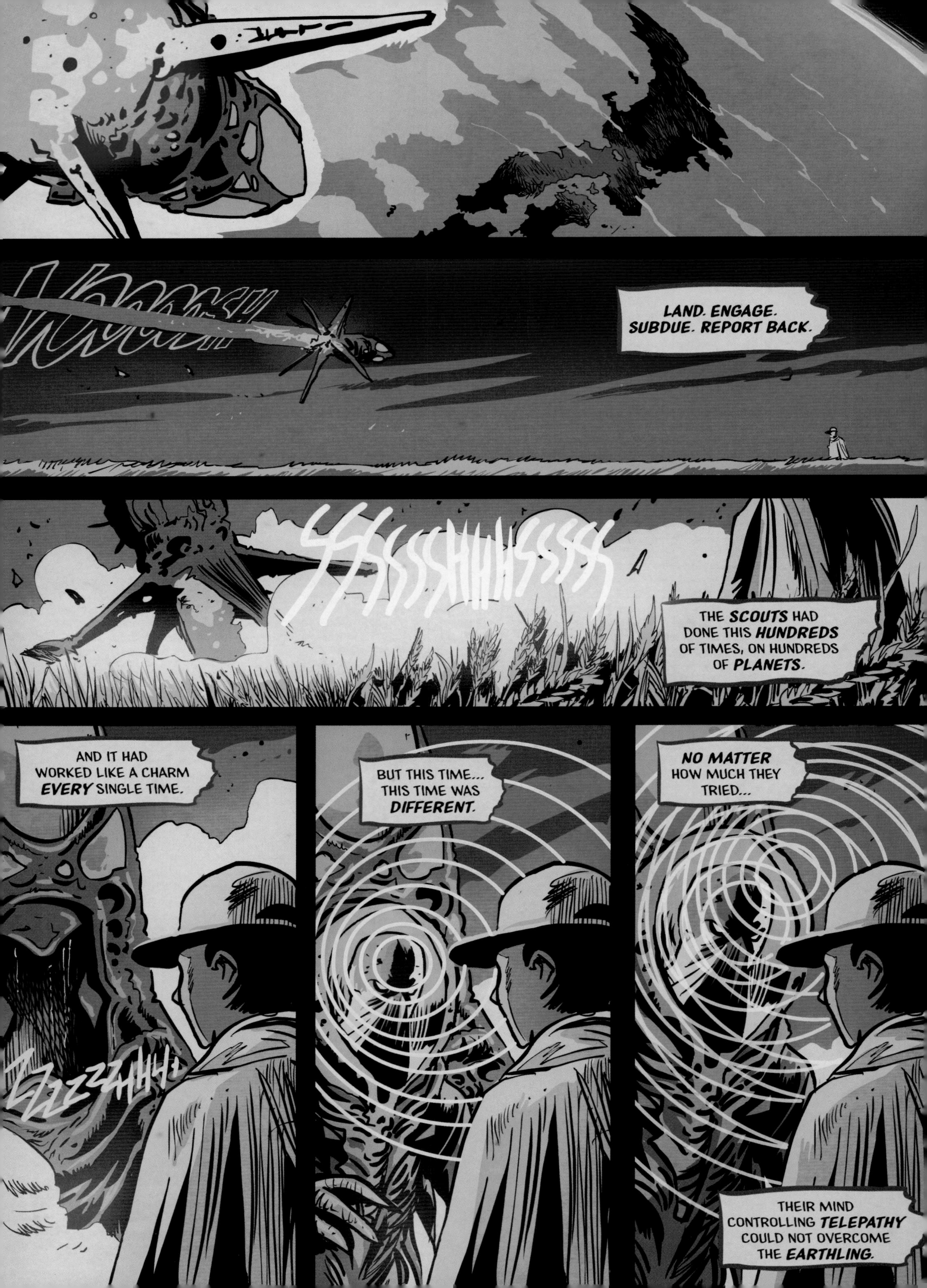
LAND. ENGAGE. SUBDUE. REPORT BACK.
THE SCOUTS HAD DONE THIS HUNDREDS OF TIMES, ON HUNDREDS OF PLANETS.
AND IT HAD WORKED LIKE A CHARM EVERY SINGLE TIME.
BUT THIS TIME... THIS TIME WAS DIFFERENT.
NO MATTER HOW MUCH THEY TRIED...
THEIR MIND CONTROLLING TELEPATHY COULD NOT OVERCOME THE EARTHLING.

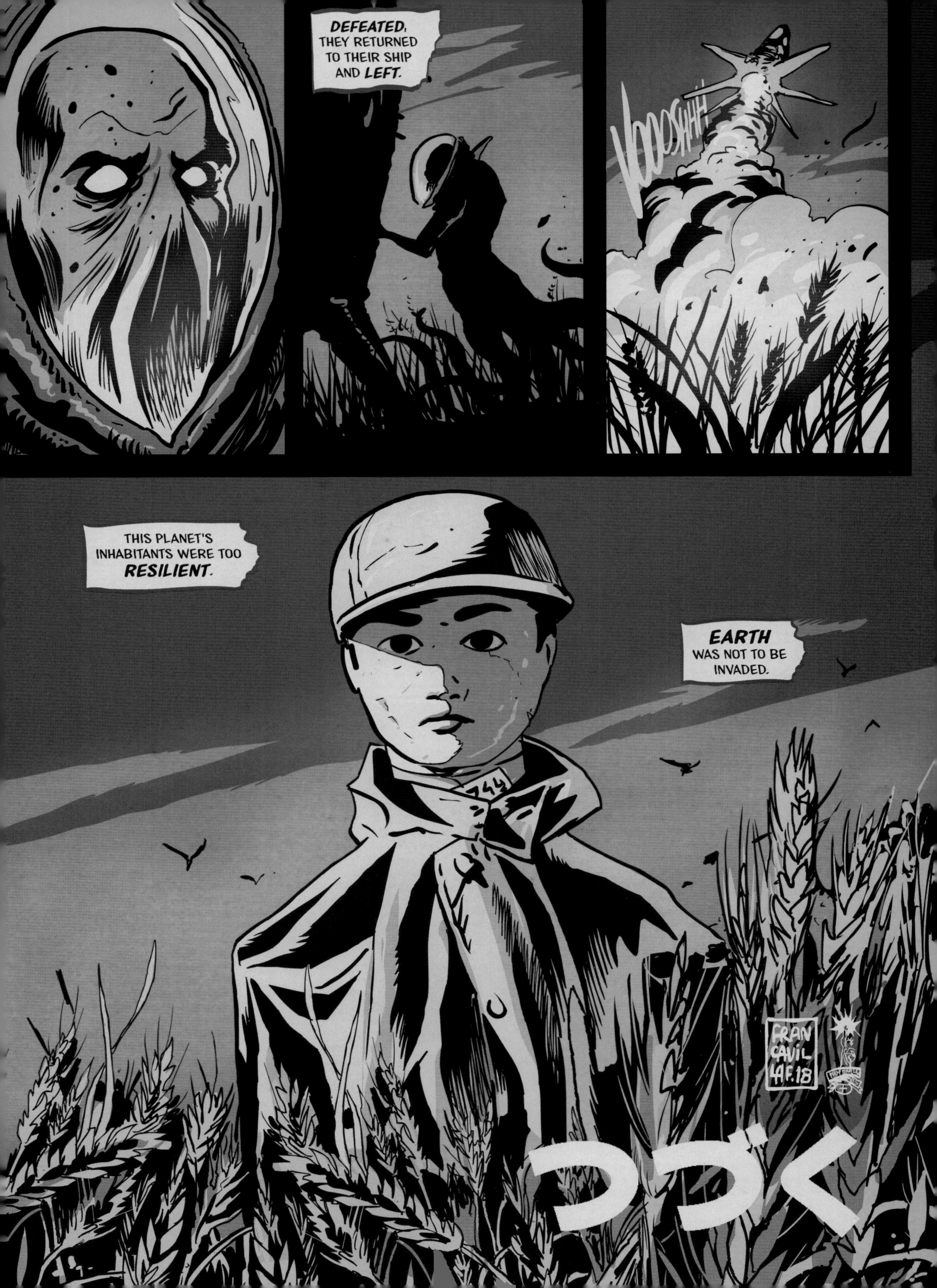
DEFEATED, THEY RETURNED TO THEIR SHIP AND LEFT.
VOOOSHHH
THIS PLANET'S INHABITANTS WERE TOO RESILIENT.
EARTH WAS NOT TO BE INVADED.
FRAN GAVIL 4F.18
つづく

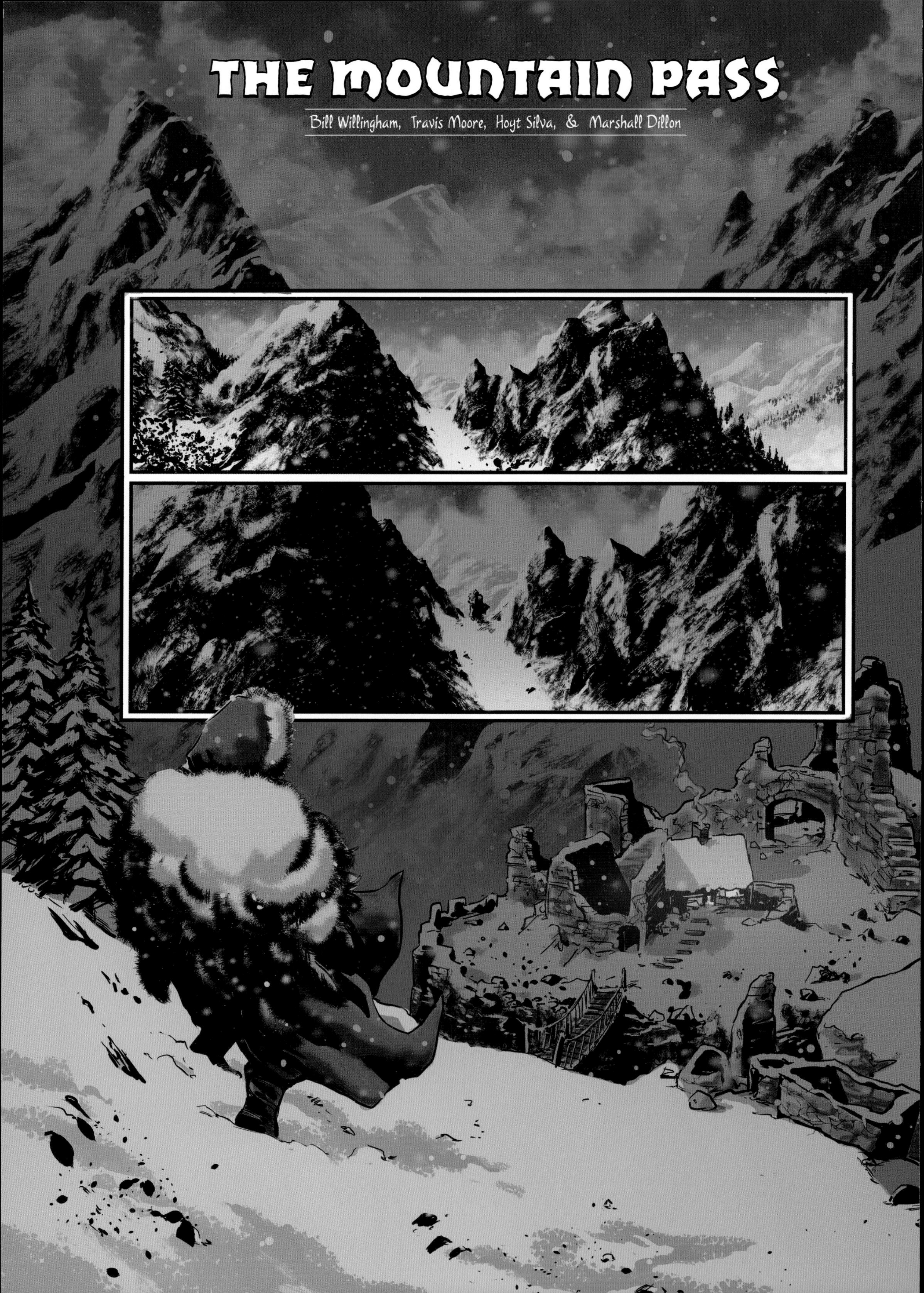
THE MOUNTAIN PASS
Bill Willingham, Travis Moore, Hoyt Silva, & Marshall Dillon

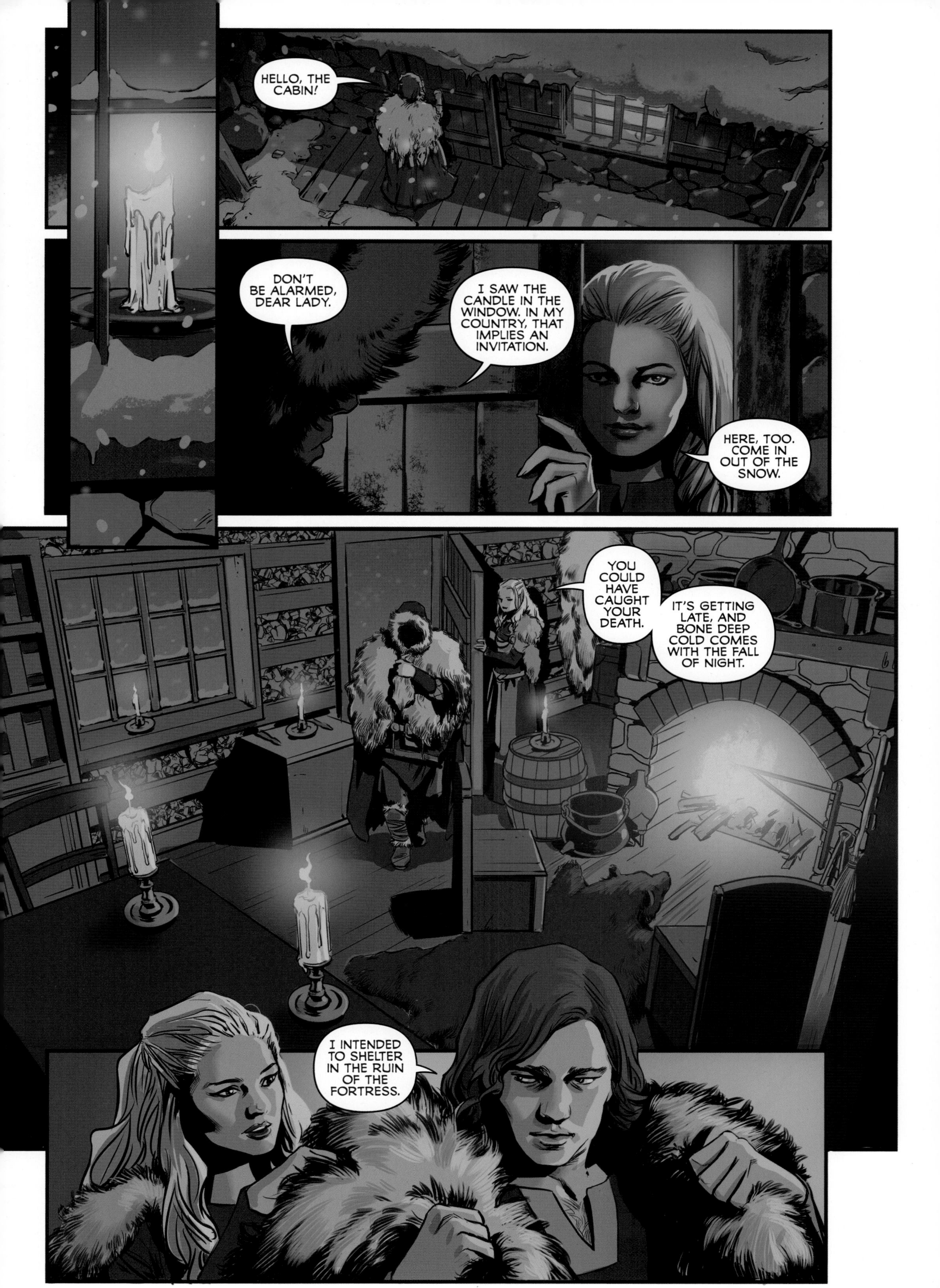

HELLO, THE CABIN!
DON'T BE ALARMED, DEAR LADY.
I SAW THE CANDLE IN THE WINDOW. IN MY COUNTRY, THAT IMPLIES AN INVITATION.
HERE, TOO. COME IN OUT OF THE SNOW.
YOU COULD HAVE CAUGHT YOUR DEATH.
IT'S GETTING LATE, AND BONE DEEP COLD COMES WITH THE FALL OF NIGHT.
I INTENDED TO SHELTER IN THE RUIN OF THE FORTRESS.

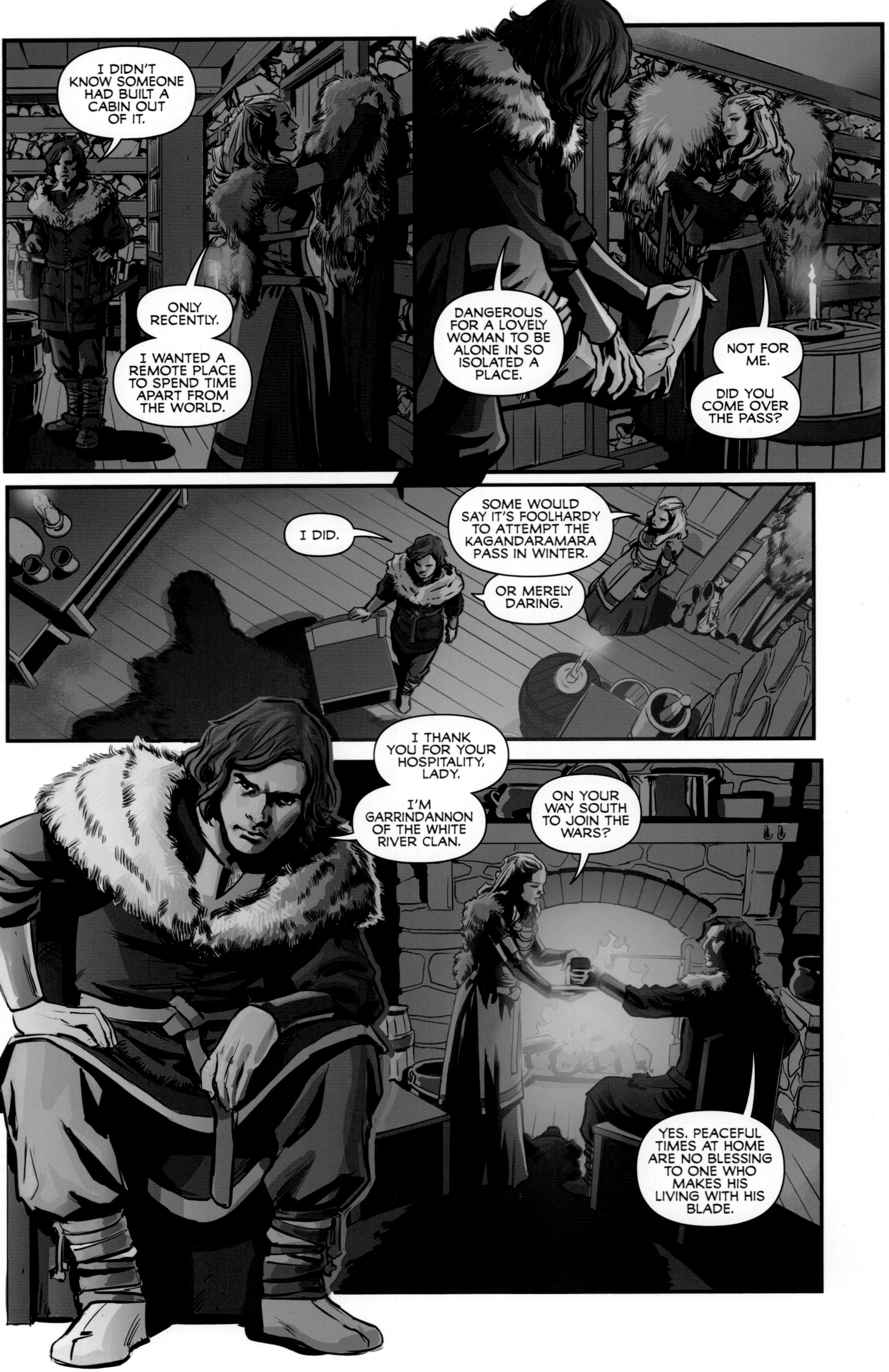
I DIDN'T KNOW SOMEONE HAD BUILT A CABIN OUT OF IT.
ONLY RECENTLY.
I WANTED A REMOTE PLACE TO SPEND TIME APART FROM THE WORLD.
DANGEROUS FOR A LOVELY WOMAN TO BE ALONE IN SO ISOLATED A PLACE.
NOT FOR ME.
DID YOU COME OVER THE PASS?
I DID.
SOME WOULD SAY IT'S FOOLHARDY TO ATTEMPT THE KAGANDARAMARA PASS IN WINTER.
OR MERELY DARING.
I THANK YOU FOR YOUR HOSPITALITY, LADY.
I'M GARRINDANNON OF THE WHITE RIVER CLAN.
ON YOUR WAY SOUTH TO JOIN THE WARS?
YES. PEACEFUL TIMES AT HOME ARE NO BLESSING TO ONE WHO MAKES HIS LIVING WITH HIS BLADE.

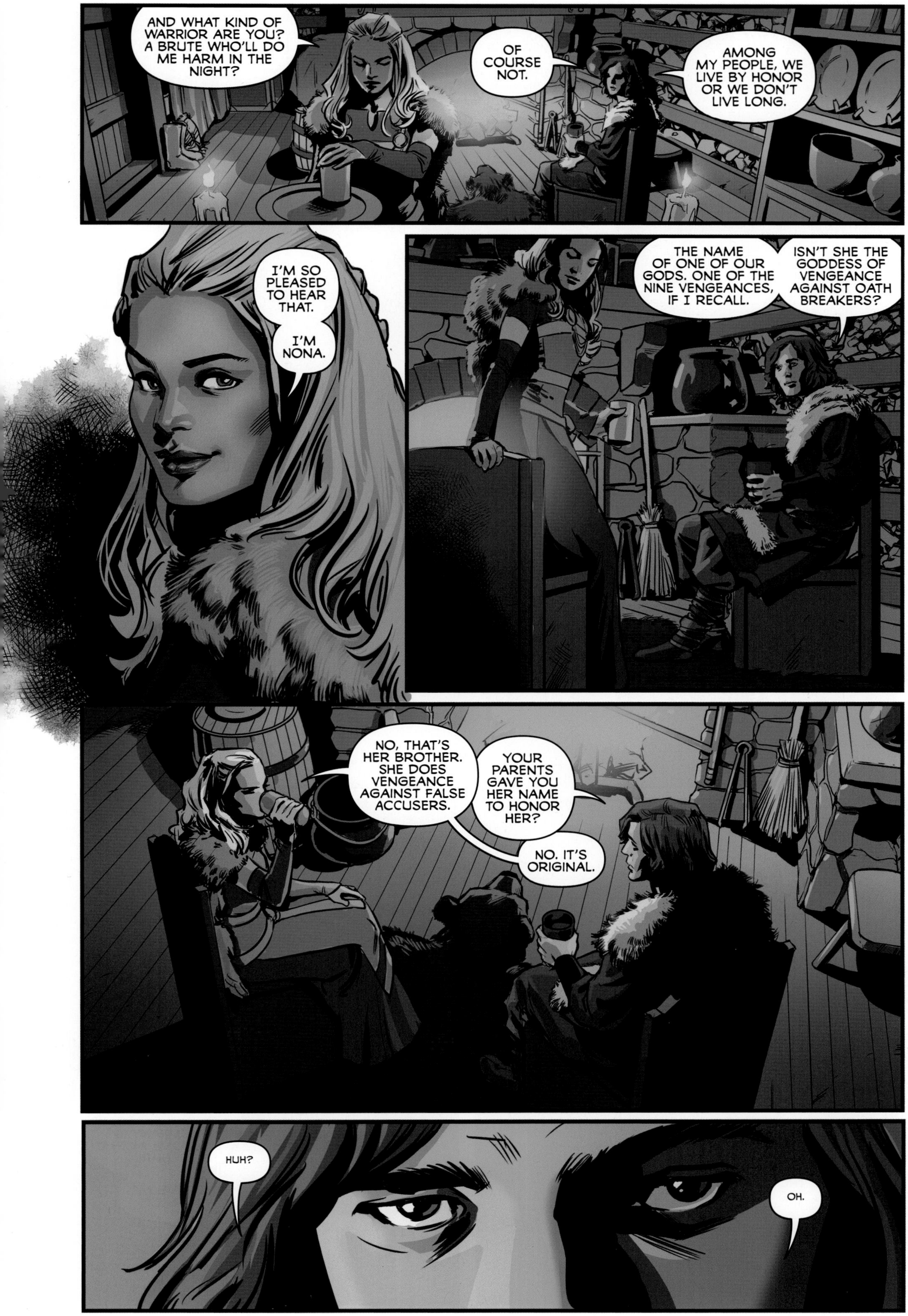
AND WHAT KIND OF WARRIOR ARE YOU? A BRUTE WHO'LL DO ME HARM IN THE NIGHT?
OF COURSE NOT.
AMONG MY PEOPLE, WE LIVE BY HONOR OR WE DON'T LIVE LONG.
I'M SO PLEASED TO HEAR THAT.
I'M NONA.
THE NAME OF ONE OF OUR GODS. ONE OF THE NINE VENGEANCES, IF I RECALL.
ISN'T SHE THE GODDESS OF VENGEANCE AGAINST OATH BREAKERS?
NO, THAT'S HER BROTHER. SHE DOES VENGEANCE AGAINST FALSE ACCUSERS.
YOUR PARENTS GAVE YOU HER NAME TO HONOR HER?
NO. IT'S ORIGINAL.
HUH?
OH.

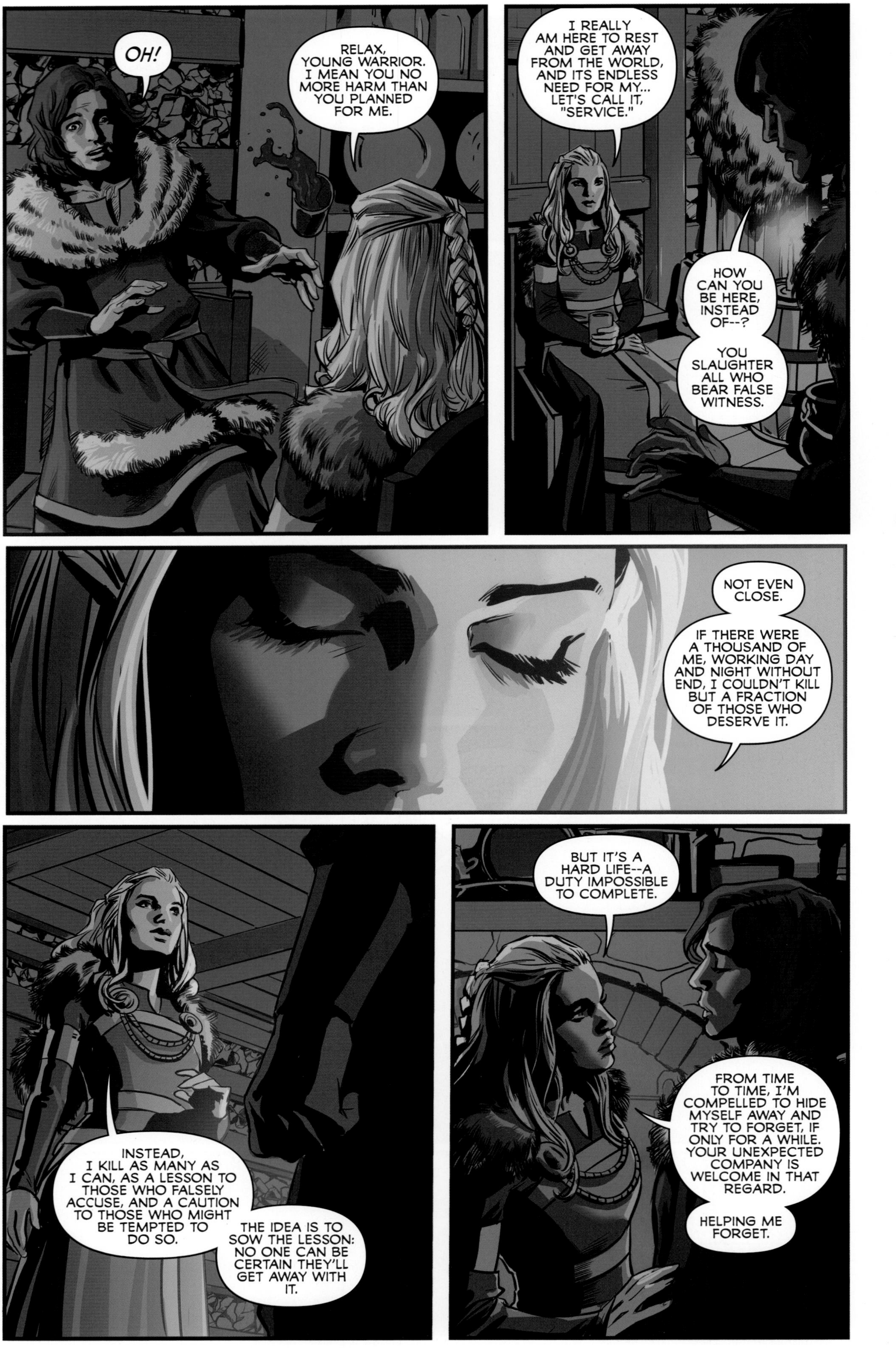
OH!
RELAX, YOUNG WARRIOR. I MEAN YOU NO MORE HARM THAN YOU PLANNED FOR ME.
I REALLY AM HERE TO REST AND GET AWAY FROM THE WORLD, AND ITS ENDLESS NEED FOR MY... LET'S CALL IT, "SERVICE."
HOW CAN YOU BE HERE, INSTEAD OF--?
YOU SLAUGHTER ALL WHO BEAR FALSE WITNESS.
NOT EVEN CLOSE.
IF THERE WERE A THOUSAND OF ME, WORKING DAY AND NIGHT WITHOUT END, I COULDN'T KILL BUT A FRACTION OF THOSE WHO DESERVE IT.
INSTEAD, I KILL AS MANY AS I CAN, AS A LESSON TO THOSE WHO FALSELY ACCUSE, AND A CAUTION TO THOSE WHO MIGHT BE TEMPTED TO DO SO.
THE IDEA IS TO SOW THE LESSON: NO ONE CAN BE CERTAIN THEY'LL GET AWAY WITH IT.
BUT IT'S A HARD LIFE--A DUTY IMPOSSIBLE TO COMPLETE.
FROM TIME TO TIME, I'M COMPELLED TO HIDE MYSELF AWAY AND TRY TO FORGET, IF ONLY FOR A WHILE. YOUR UNEXPECTED COMPANY IS WELCOME IN THAT REGARD.
HELPING ME FORGET.

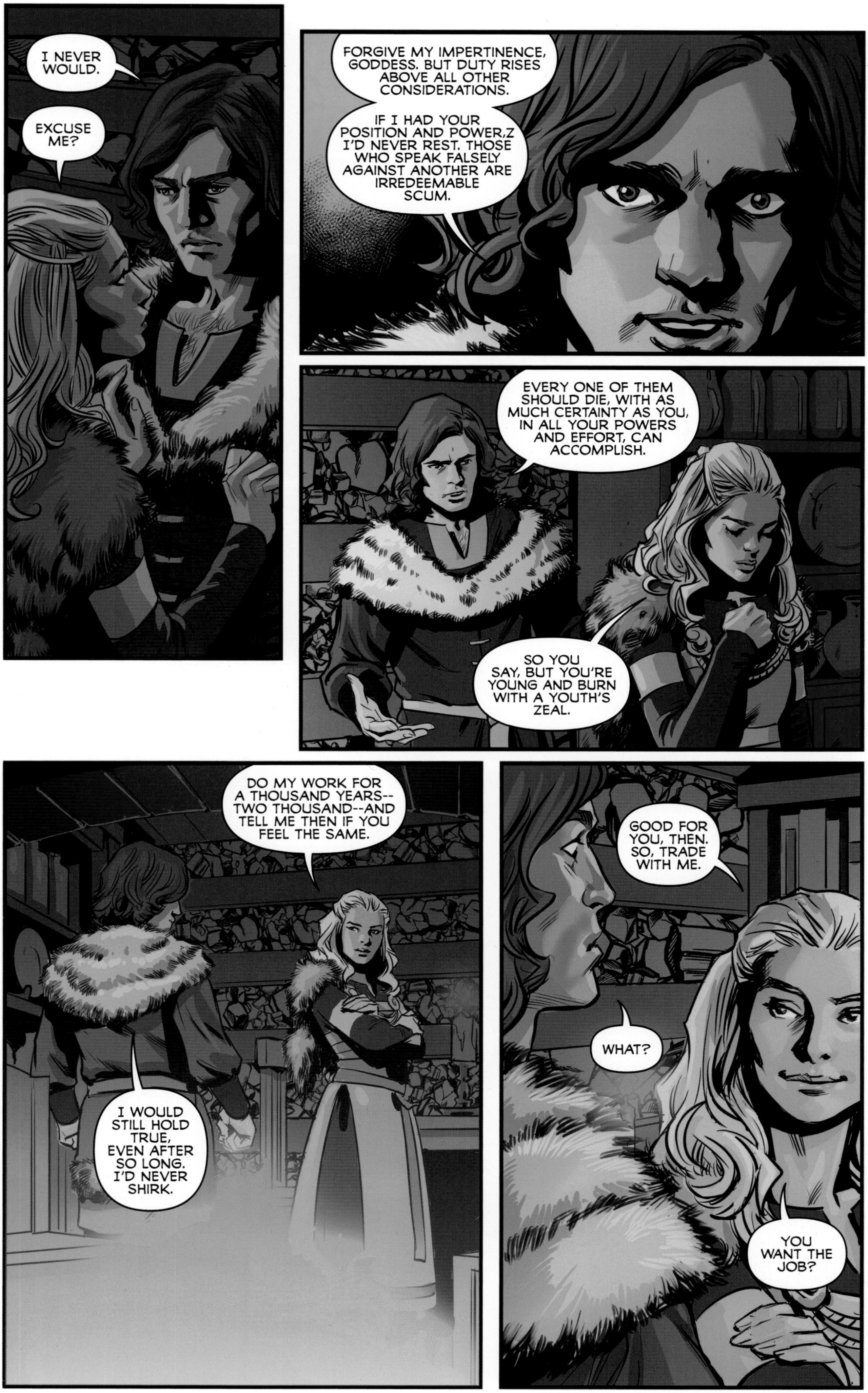
I NEVER WOULD.
EXCUSE ME?
FORGIVE MY IMPERTINENCE, GODDESS. BUT DUTY RISES ABOVE ALL OTHER CONSIDERATIONS.
IF I HAD YOUR POSITION AND POWER,Z I'D NEVER REST. THOSE WHO SPEAK FALSELY AGAINST ANOTHER ARE IRREDEEMABLE SCUM.
EVERY ONE OF THEM SHOULD DIE, WITH AS MUCH CERTAINTY AS YOU, IN ALL YOUR POWERS AND EFFORT, CAN ACCOMPLISH.
SO YOU SAY, BUT YOU'RE YOUNG AND BURN WITH A YOUTH'S ZEAL.
DO MY WORK FOR A THOUSAND YEARS-- TWO THOUSAND--AND TELL ME THEN IF YOU FEEL THE SAME.
I WOULD STILL HOLD TRUE, EVEN AFTER SO LONG. I'D NEVER SHIRK.
GOOD FOR YOU, THEN. SO, TRADE WITH ME.
WHAT?
YOU WANT THE JOB?

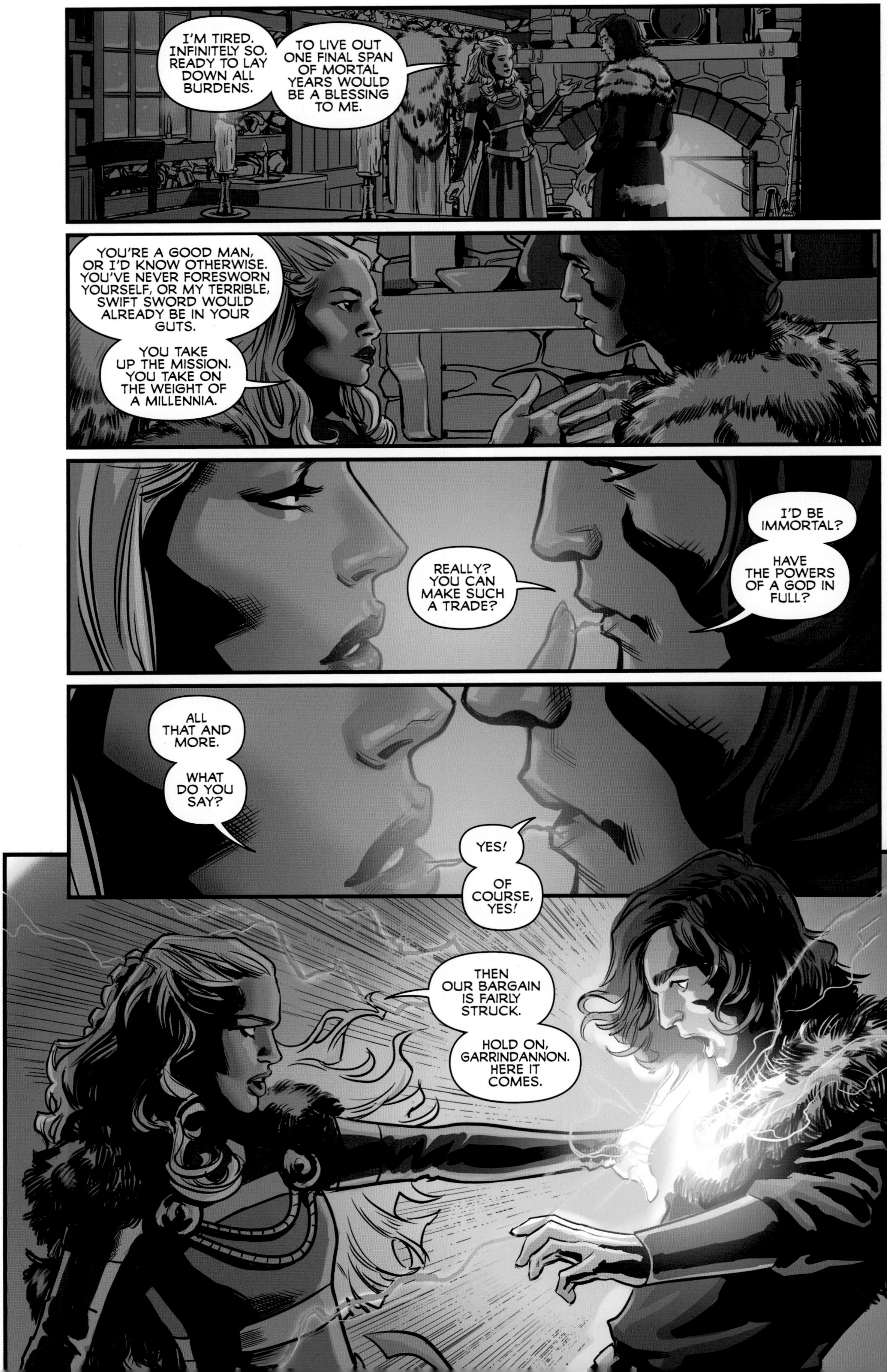
I'M TIRED. INFINITELY SO. READY TO LAY DOWN ALL BURDENS.
TO LIVE OUT ONE FINAL SPAN OF MORTAL YEARS WOULD BE A BLESSING TO ME.
YOU'RE A GOOD MAN, OR I'D KNOW OTHERWISE. YOU'VE NEVER FORESWORN YOURSELF, OR MY TERRIBLE, SWIFT SWORD WOULD ALREADY BE IN YOUR GUTS.
YOU TAKE UP THE MISSION. YOU TAKE ON THE WEIGHT OF A MILLENNIA.
REALLY? YOU CAN MAKE SUCH A TRADE?
I'D BE IMMORTAL?
HAVE THE POWERS OF A GOD IN FULL?
ALL THAT AND MORE.
WHAT DO YOU SAY?
YES!
OF COURSE, YES!
THEN OUR BARGAIN IS FAIRLY STRUCK.
HOLD ON, GARRINDANNON. HERE IT COMES.

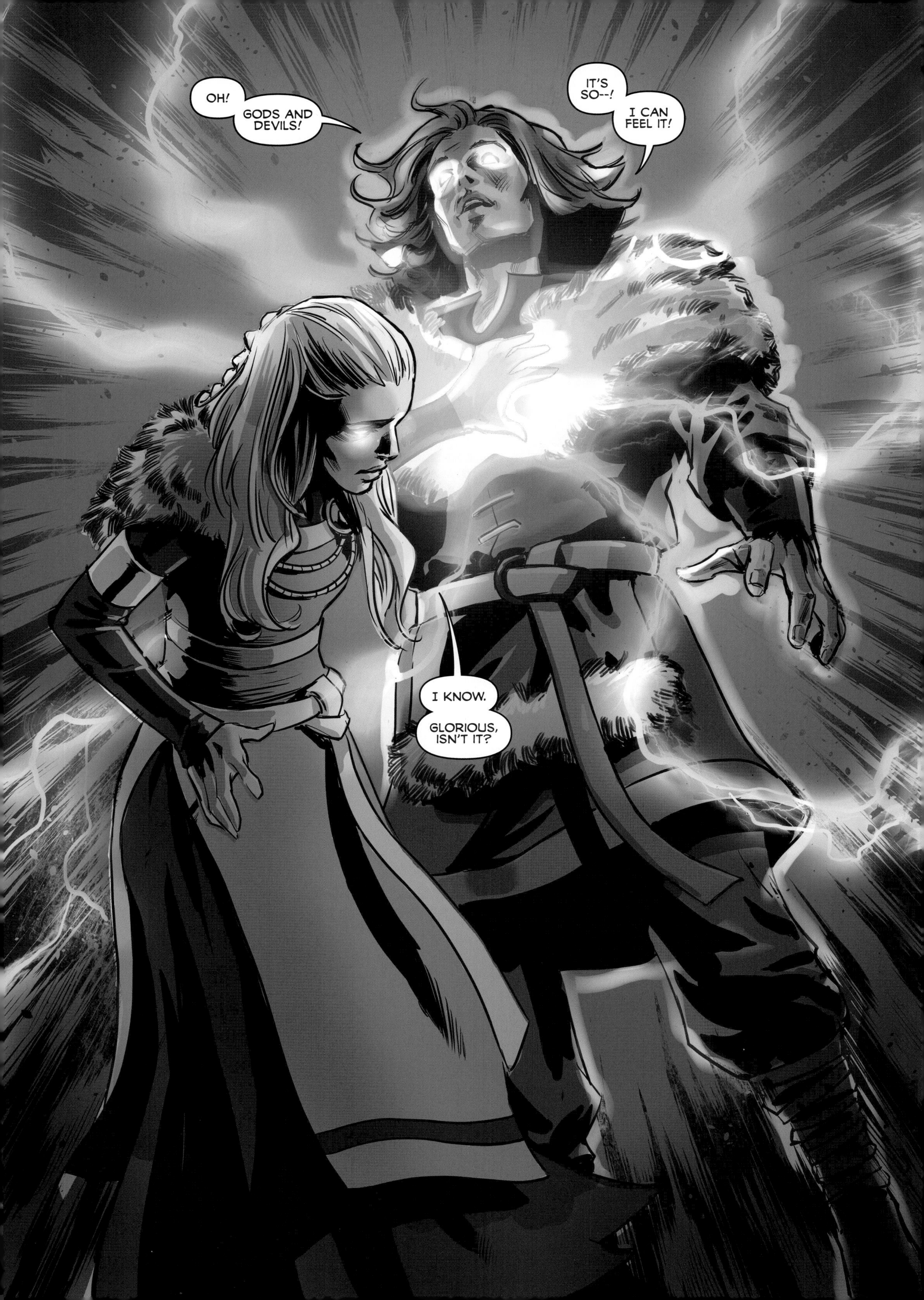
OH!
GODS AND DEVILS!
IT'S SO--!
I CAN FEEL IT!
I KNOW.
GLORIOUS, ISN'T IT?

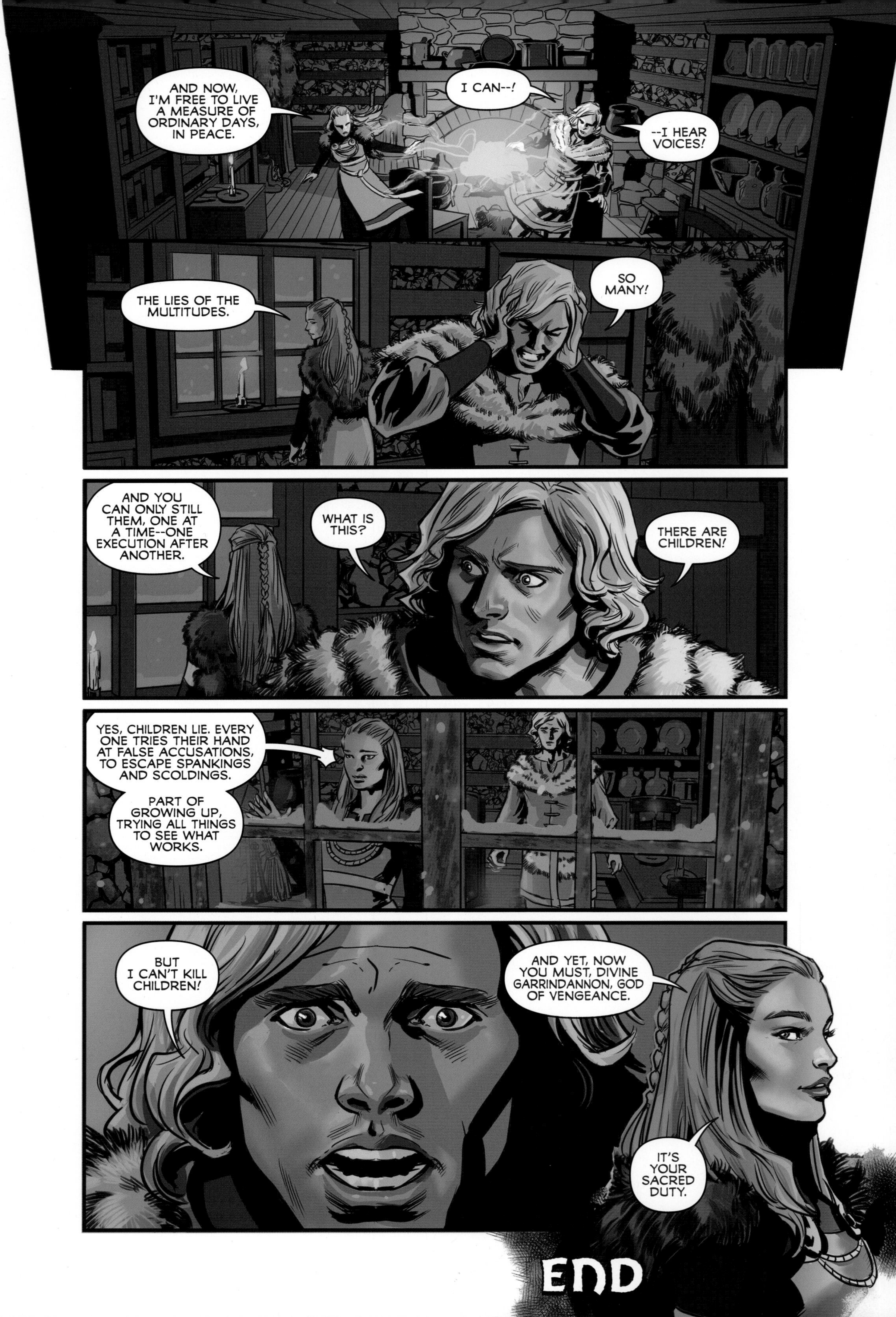
AND NOW, I'M FREE TO LIVE A MEASURE OF ORDINARY DAYS, IN PEACE.
I CAN--!
--I HEAR VOICES!
THE LIES OF THE MULTITUDES.
SO MANY!
AND YOU CAN ONLY STILL THEM, ONE AT A TIME--ONE EXECUTION AFTER ANOTHER.
WHAT IS THIS?
THERE ARE CHILDREN!
YES, CHILDREN LIE. EVERY ONE TRIES THEIR HAND AT FALSE ACCUSATIONS, TO ESCAPE SPANKINGS AND SCOLDINGS.
PART OF GROWING UP, TRYING ALL THINGS TO SEE WHAT WORKS.
BUT I CAN'T KILL CHILDREN!
AND YET, NOW YOU MUST, DIVINE GARRINDANNON, GOD OF VENGEANCE.
IT'S YOUR SACRED DUTY.
END

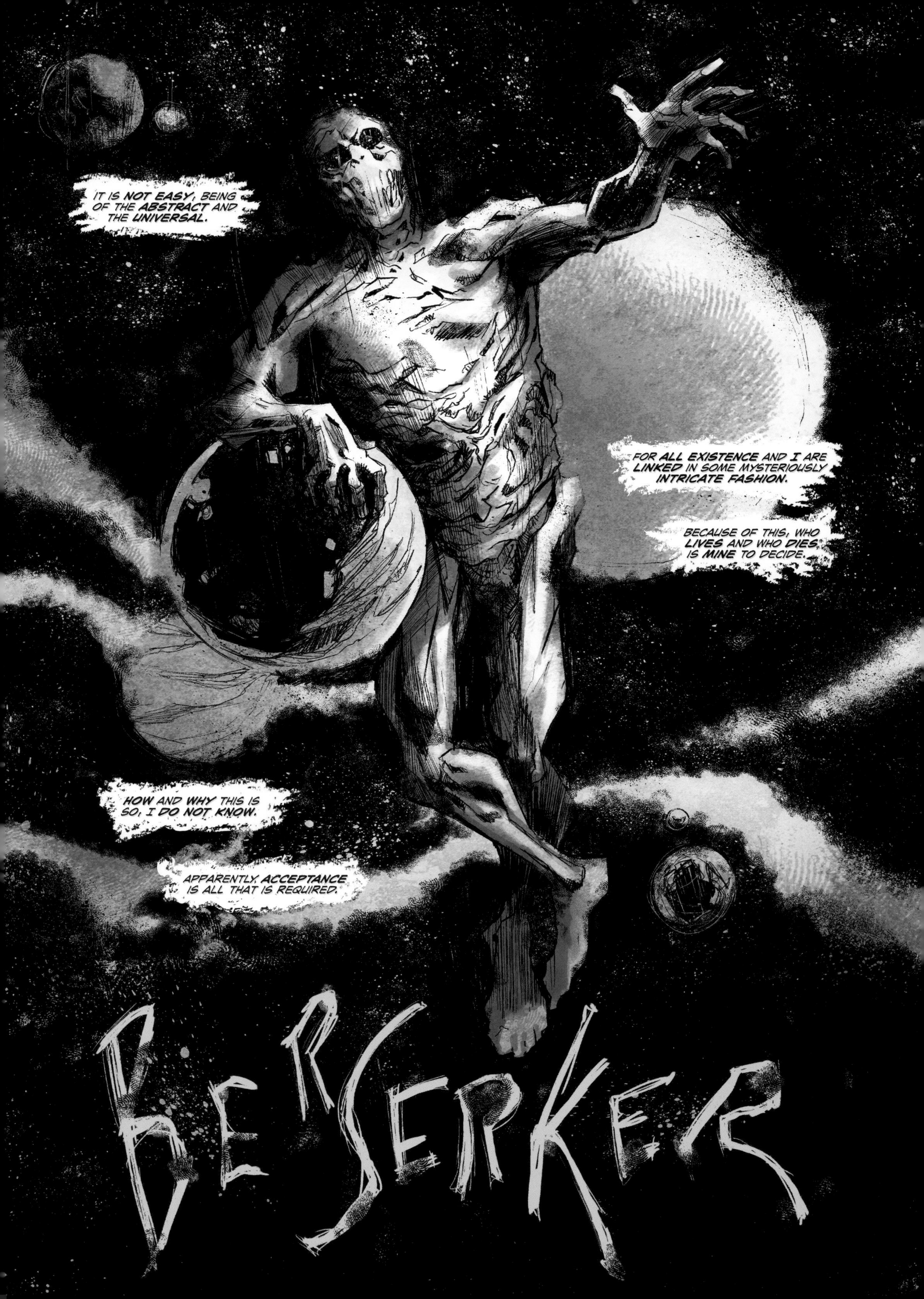
IT IS NOT EASY, BEING OF THE ABSTRACT AND THE UNIVERSAL.
FOR ALL EXISTENCE AND I ARE LINKED IN SOME MYSTERIOUSLY INTRICATE FASHION.
BECAUSE OF THIS, WHO LIVES AND WHO DIES, IS MINE TO DECIDE.
HOW AND WHY THIS IS SO, I DO NOT KNOW.
APPARENTLY, ACCEPTANCE IS ALL THAT IS REQUIRED.
BERSERKER

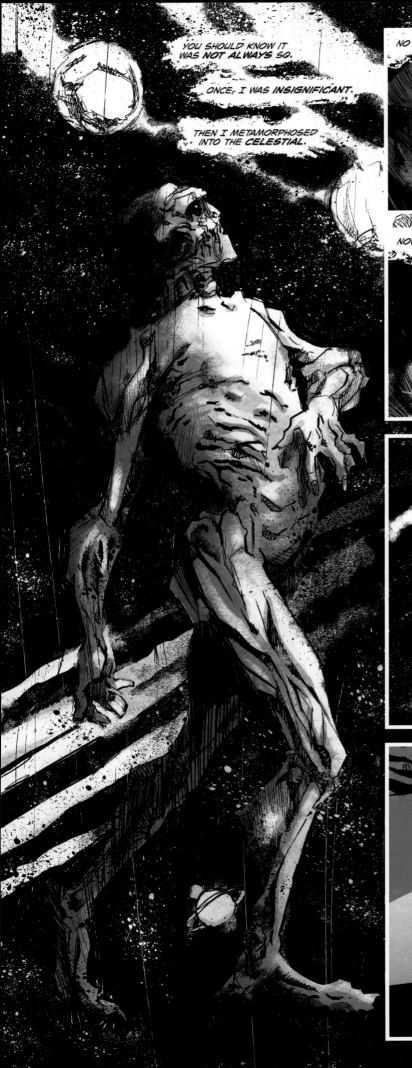

YOU SHOULD KNOW IT WAS NOT ALWAYS SO.

ONCE, I WAS INSIGNIFICANT.

THEN I METAMORPHOSED INTO THE CELESTIAL.

NO LONGER AN ANT.

NOW A TIGER.

OR PERHAPS A DRAGON.

MY HUMANITY I GLADLY ABANDONED...

...WHEN SUMMONED TO A HIGHER CALLING.

SACRIFICE WAS DEMANDED IN THIS *GRAND TRANSITION.*

DUES I WILLINGLY SURRENDERED.

AFTER ALL, THE LIFE TO BE LEFT BEHIND HAD NO MEANING.

THE SAD TRUTH IS, MOST DON'T.

THE *PETTY* RESTRAINTS FALL AWAY; THE *UNFORGIVABLE* INDIGNITIES FORGOTTEN.

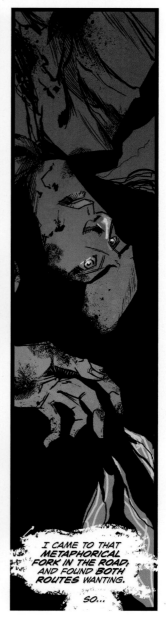

I CAME TO THAT METAPHORICAL FORK IN THE ROAD, AND FOUND *BOTH* ROUTES WANTING.

SO...

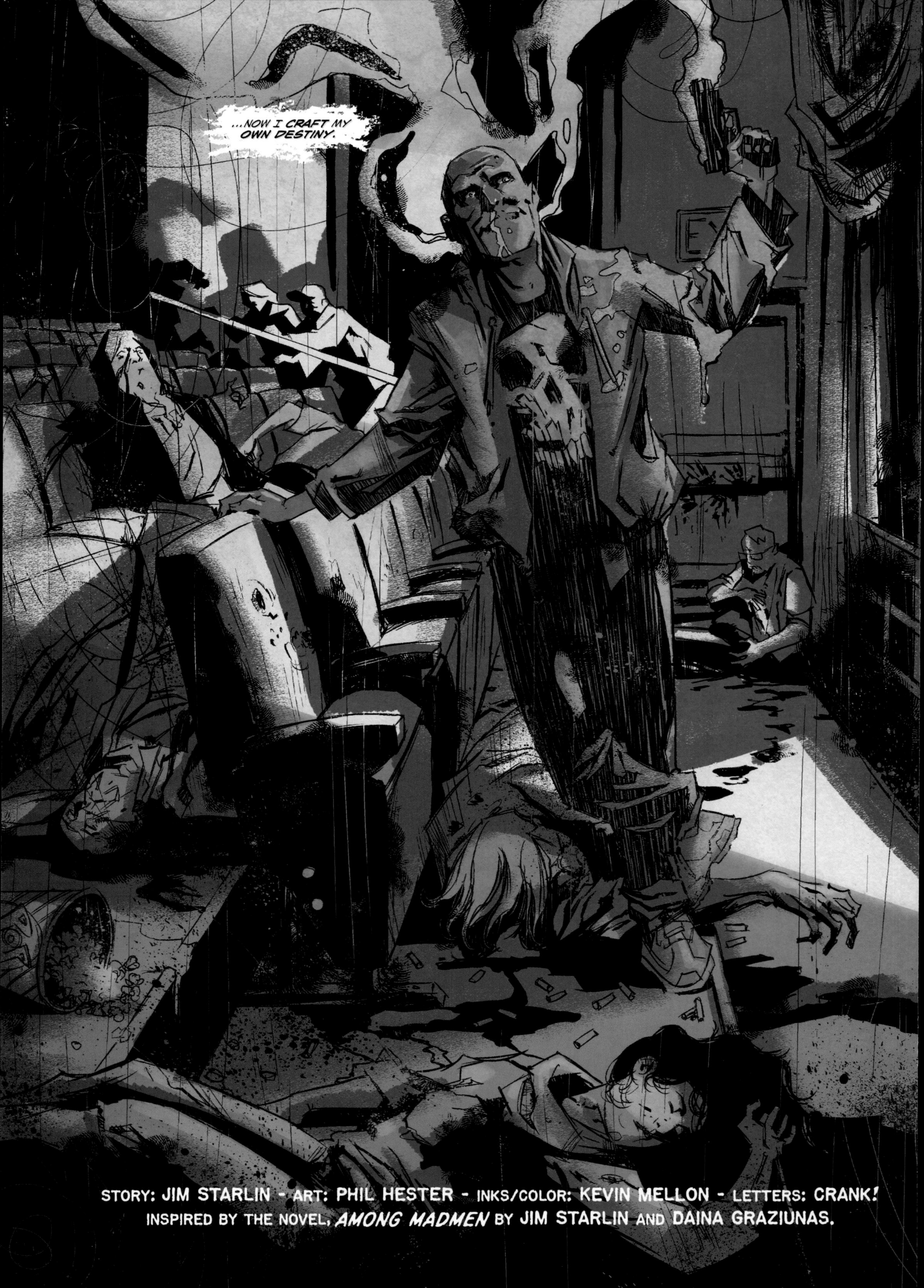
...NOW I CRAFT MY OWN DESTINY.

STORY: JIM STARLIN - ART: PHIL HESTER - INKS/COLOR: KEVIN MELLON - LETTERS: CRANK!
INSPIRED BY THE NOVEL, *AMONG MADMEN* BY JIM STARLIN AND DAINA GRAZIUNAS.

LAREDO, TEXAS. MONDAY.

I KNOW IT'S A BIT ECCENTRIC, BUT I LOVE **UNLOVABLE** THINGS.

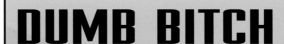

DUMB BITCH

Marguerite Bennett, Hoyt Silva & Marshall Dillon

THE CHIPPED **HUMMEL FIGURINES** FROM THE FLEA MARKET--*OOH*, OR THE CRACKED **STAFFORD-SHIRE CHINA** FROM YARD SALES--

--MY **TEDDY**, NO ONE WANTED HIM, HE GOT LEFT AT THE BOTTOM OF THE BASKET AT CHRISTMAS, AND I FELT SO **SORRY** FOR HIM--

OR POOR **ROXIE**. DID YOU KNOW THAT WHEN THEY FOUND HER WANDERING BY THE RIVER, THEY SAID SHE WAS **TOO UGLY** TO BE ADOPTED?

I-I NEVER THOUGHT OF YOUR HUSBAND AS AN **ANIMAL LOVER**, ROSA--

--I REMEMBER HIM WHEN HE WAS A BOY, BEFORE HE, *UH*, **MADE SOMETHING OF HIMSELF**--

YES, HE, HA, HE HAS A BIT OF A TEMPER, BUT WHEN WE MOVED IN LAST MONTH, I SAID TO MYSELF, "A SHELTER DOG WILL BE **HEALTHY** FOR HIM," AND ROXIE IS SUCH A **GOOD** GIRL--

--SHE BRINGS US PRESENTS FROM THE JUNK HEAP, SOMETIMES--

--HERE'S WHAT SHE BROUGHT ME **THIS MORNING**, IT'S A--

VROOOOM

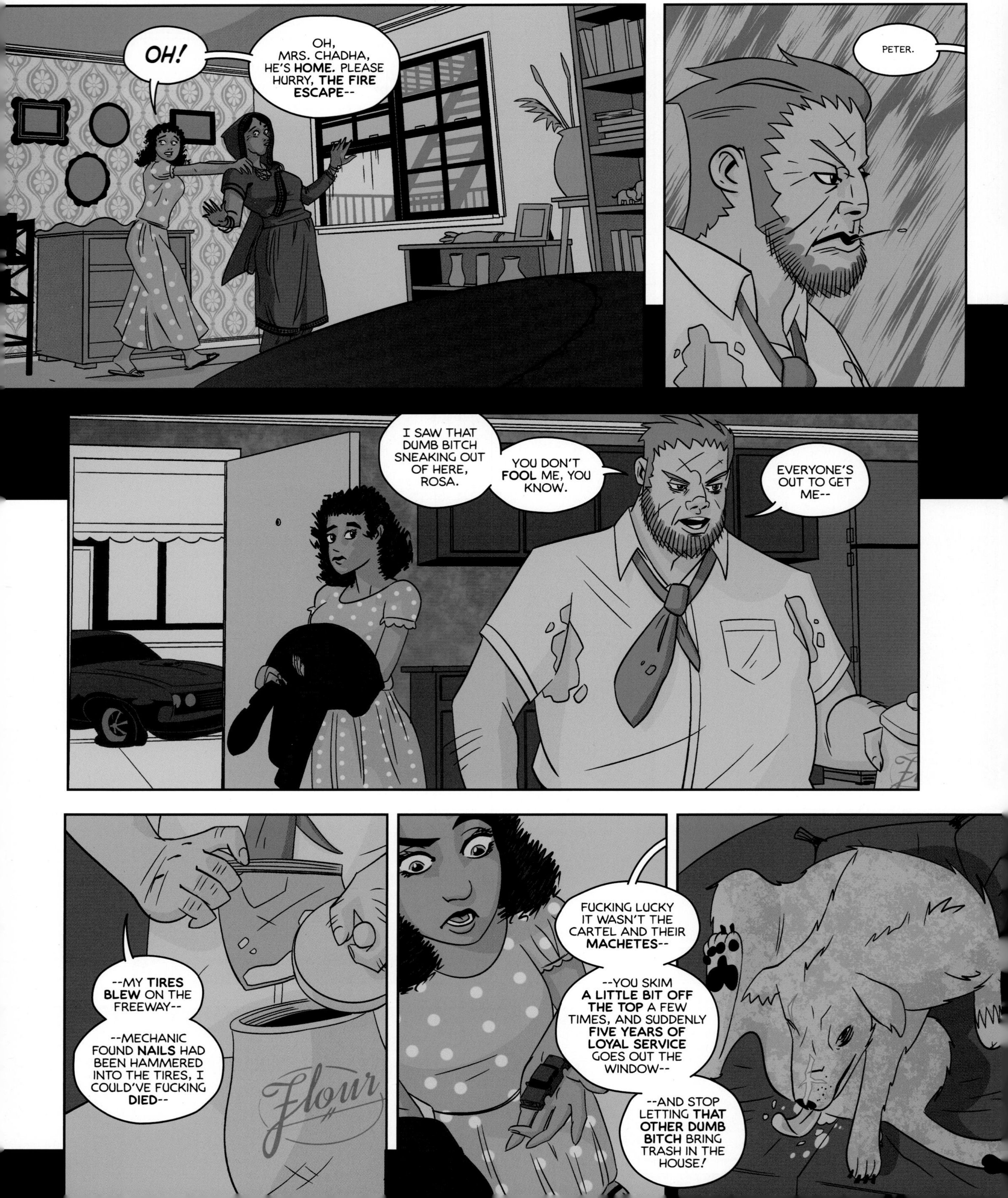
OH!
OH, MRS. CHADHA, HE'S HOME. PLEASE HURRY, THE FIRE ESCAPE--
PETER.
I SAW THAT DUMB BITCH SNEAKING OUT OF HERE, ROSA.
YOU DON'T FOOL ME, YOU KNOW.
EVERYONE'S OUT TO GET ME--
--MY TIRES BLEW ON THE FREEWAY--
--MECHANIC FOUND NAILS HAD BEEN HAMMERED INTO THE TIRES, I COULD'VE FUCKING DIED--
Flour
FUCKING LUCKY IT WASN'T THE CARTEL AND THEIR MACHETES--
--YOU SKIM A LITTLE BIT OFF THE TOP A FEW TIMES, AND SUDDENLY FIVE YEARS OF LOYAL SERVICE GOES OUT THE WINDOW--
--AND STOP LETTING THAT OTHER DUMB BITCH BRING TRASH IN THE HOUSE!

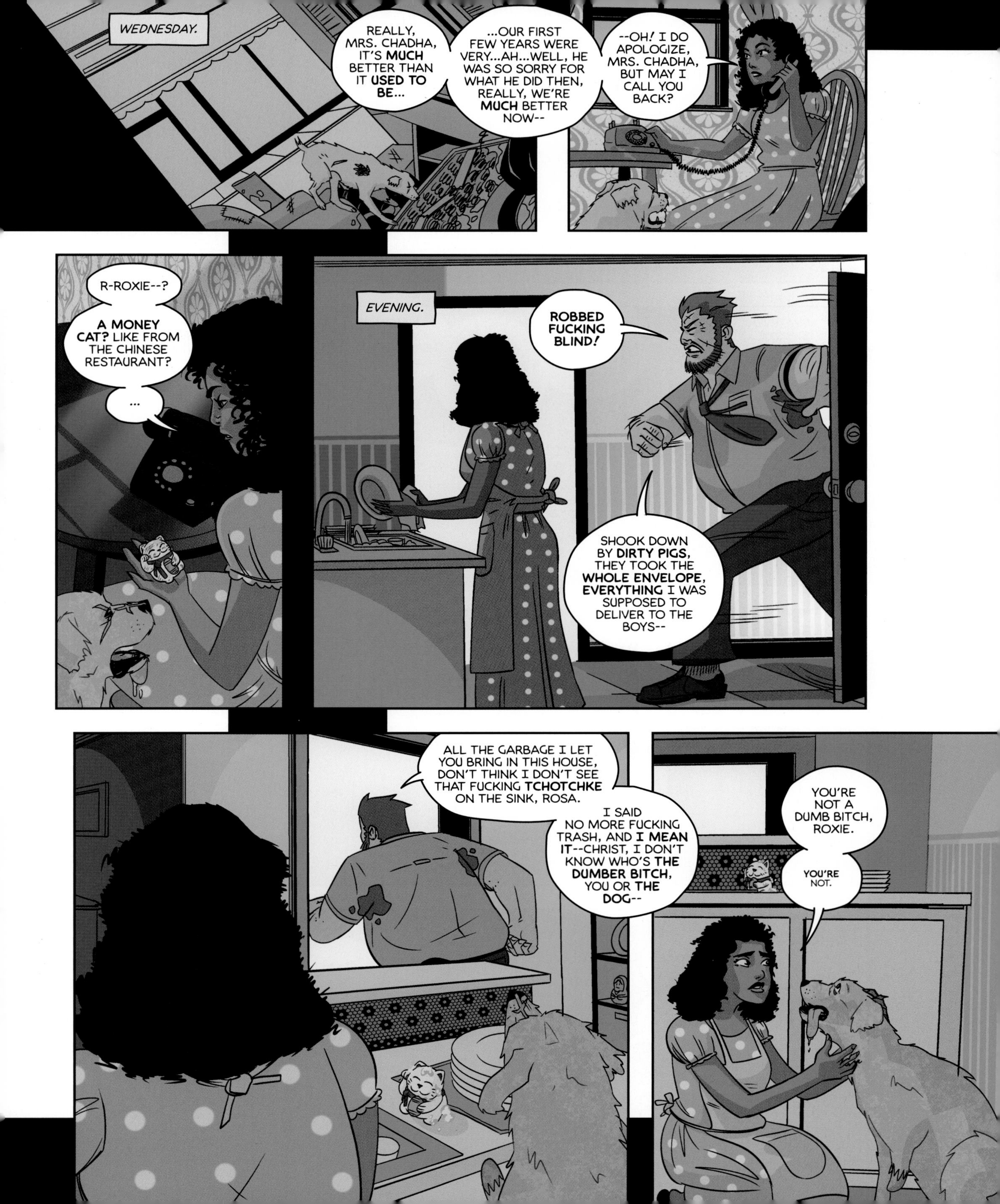
WEDNESDAY.
REALLY, MRS. CHADHA, IT'S MUCH BETTER THAN IT USED TO BE...
...OUR FIRST FEW YEARS WERE VERY...AH...WELL, HE WAS SO SORRY FOR WHAT HE DID THEN, REALLY, WE'RE MUCH BETTER NOW--
--OH! I DO APOLOGIZE, MRS. CHADHA, BUT MAY I CALL YOU BACK?
R-ROXIE--?
A MONEY CAT? LIKE FROM THE CHINESE RESTAURANT?
...
EVENING.
ROBBED FUCKING BLIND!
SHOOK DOWN BY DIRTY PIGS, THEY TOOK THE WHOLE ENVELOPE, EVERYTHING I WAS SUPPOSED TO DELIVER TO THE BOYS--
ALL THE GARBAGE I LET YOU BRING IN THIS HOUSE, DON'T THINK I DON'T SEE THAT FUCKING TCHOTCHKE ON THE SINK, ROSA.
I SAID NO MORE FUCKING TRASH, AND I MEAN IT--CHRIST, I DON'T KNOW WHO'S THE DUMBER BITCH, YOU OR THE DOG--
YOU'RE NOT A DUMB BITCH, ROXIE.
YOU'RE NOT.

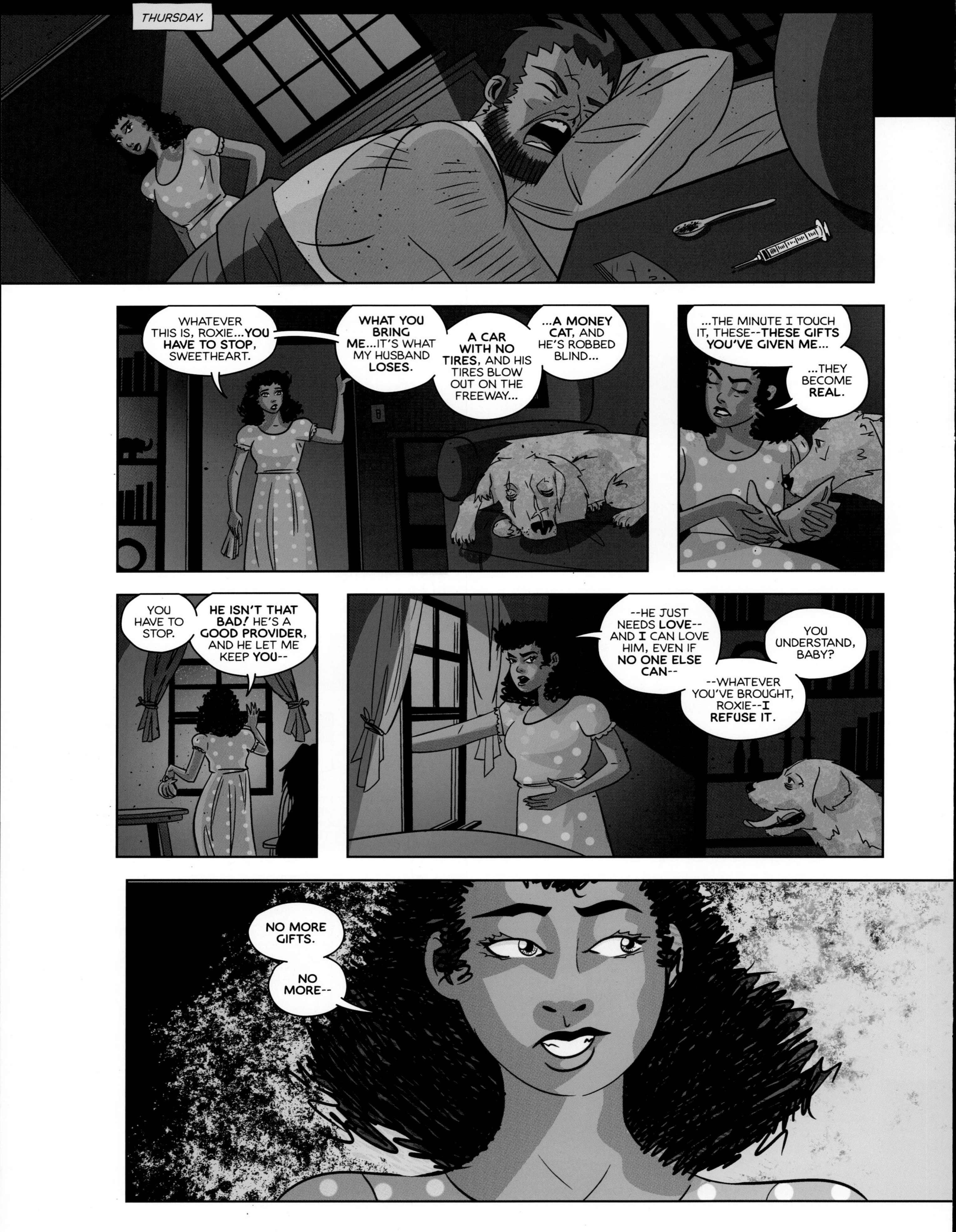
THURSDAY.
WHATEVER THIS IS, ROXIE...YOU HAVE TO STOP, SWEETHEART.
WHAT YOU BRING ME...IT'S WHAT MY HUSBAND LOSES.
A CAR WITH NO TIRES, AND HIS TIRES BLOW OUT ON THE FREEWAY...
...A MONEY CAT, AND HE'S ROBBED BLIND...
...THE MINUTE I TOUCH IT, THESE--THESE GIFTS YOU'VE GIVEN ME...
...THEY BECOME REAL.
YOU HAVE TO STOP.
HE ISN'T THAT BAD! HE'S A GOOD PROVIDER, AND HE LET ME KEEP YOU--
--HE JUST NEEDS LOVE--AND I CAN LOVE HIM, EVEN IF NO ONE ELSE CAN--
YOU UNDERSTAND, BABY?
--WHATEVER YOU'VE BROUGHT, ROXIE--I REFUSE IT.
NO MORE GIFTS.
NO MORE--

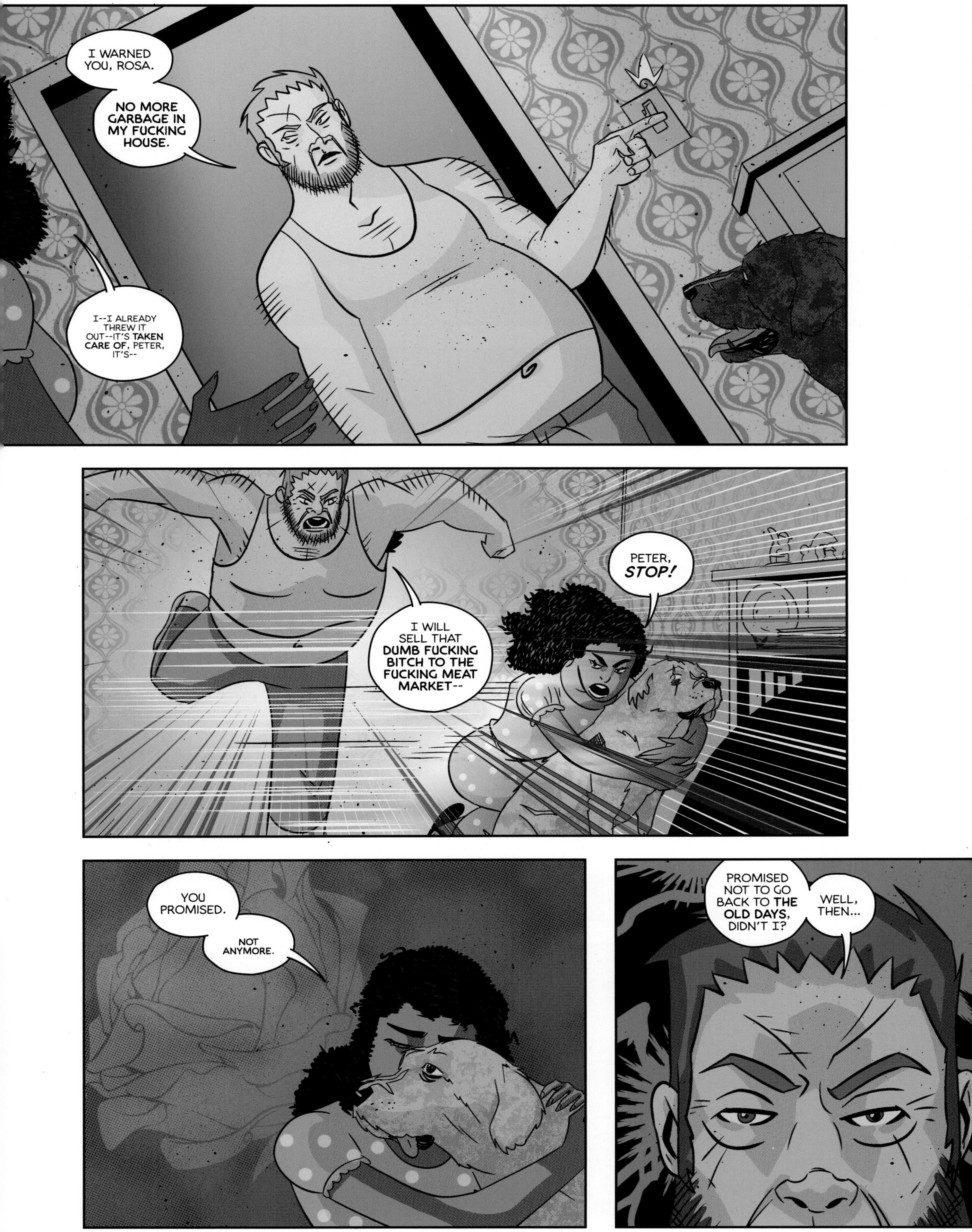
I WARNED YOU, ROSA.
NO MORE GARBAGE IN MY FUCKING HOUSE.
I--I ALREADY THREW IT OUT--IT'S TAKEN CARE OF, PETER, IT'S--
I WILL SELL THAT DUMB FUCKING BITCH TO THE FUCKING MEAT MARKET--
PETER, STOP!
YOU PROMISED.
NOT ANYMORE.
PROMISED NOT TO GO BACK TO THE OLD DAYS, DIDN'T I?
WELL, THEN...

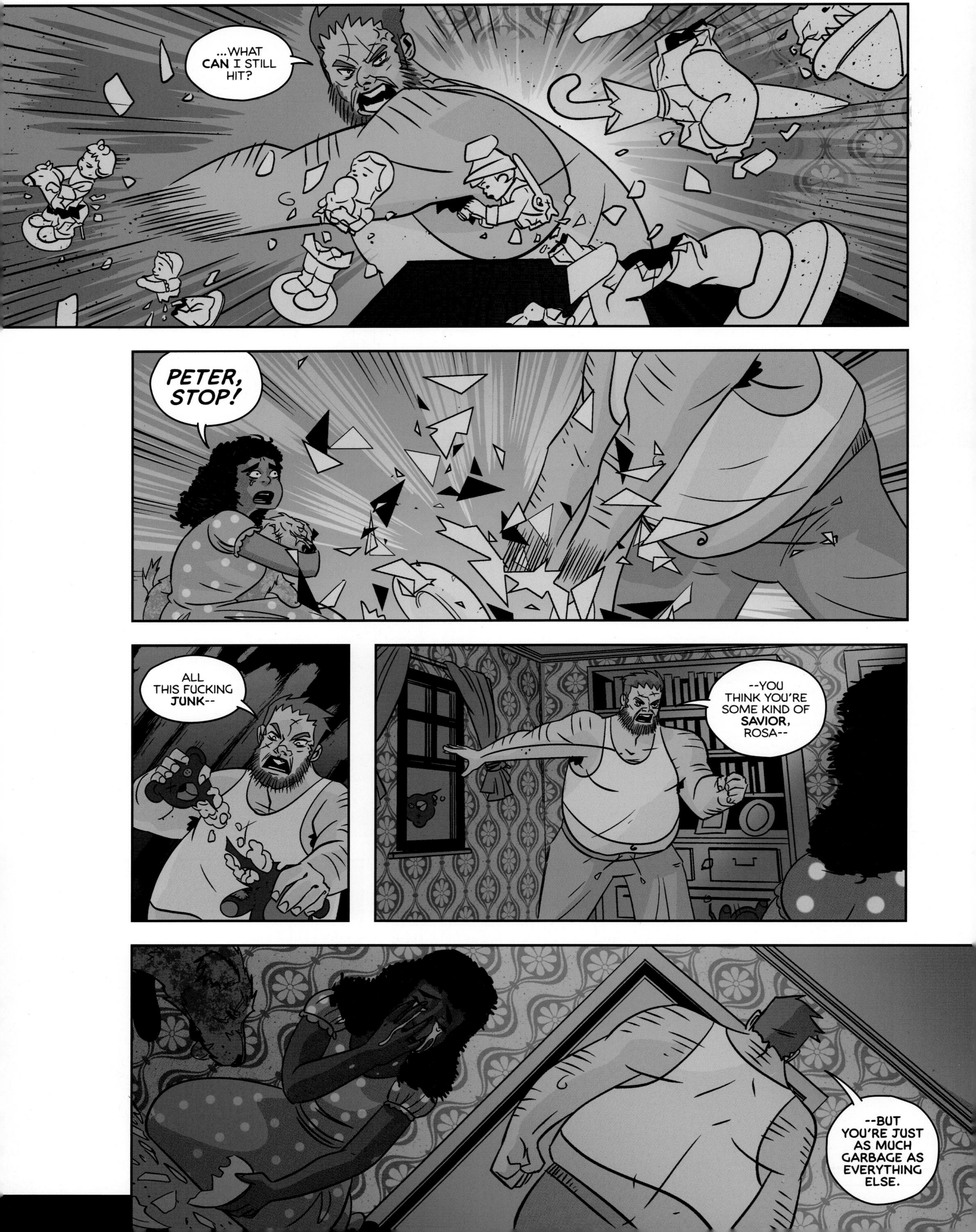
...WHAT CAN I STILL HIT?
PETER, STOP!
ALL THIS FUCKING JUNK--
--YOU THINK YOU'RE SOME KIND OF SAVIOR, ROSA--
--BUT YOU'RE JUST AS MUCH GARBAGE AS EVERYTHING ELSE.

FRIDAY.

ROSA! ROSA!

I NEED TO TALK TO YOU--!

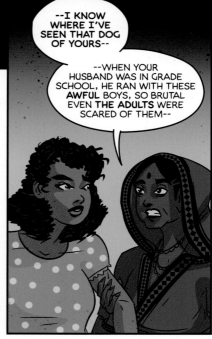

--I KNOW WHERE I'VE SEEN THAT DOG OF YOURS--

--WHEN YOUR HUSBAND WAS IN GRADE SCHOOL, HE RAN WITH THESE AWFUL BOYS, SO BRUTAL EVEN THE ADULTS WERE SCARED OF THEM--

"THEY GOT A HOLD OF A DOG WITH A BEAUTIFUL COAT OF FUR-- TORTURED IT, SET IT AFIRE, THREW IT IN THE CANAL--

"--I COULDN'T SEE IT AT FIRST... FIFTEEN, TWENTY YEARS AGO--

"--BUT IT'S THE SAME DOG.

"LIKE SHE KNEW SOMEONE WOULD FINALLY LOVE HER...

"...AND WHEN YOU MOVED IN, SHE CAME BACK HOME..."

R-ROXIE...?

WHAT'VE...WHAT'VE YOU BROUGHT ME, SWEETHEART?

WHAT'S MY HUSBAND GOING TO LOSE TODAY?

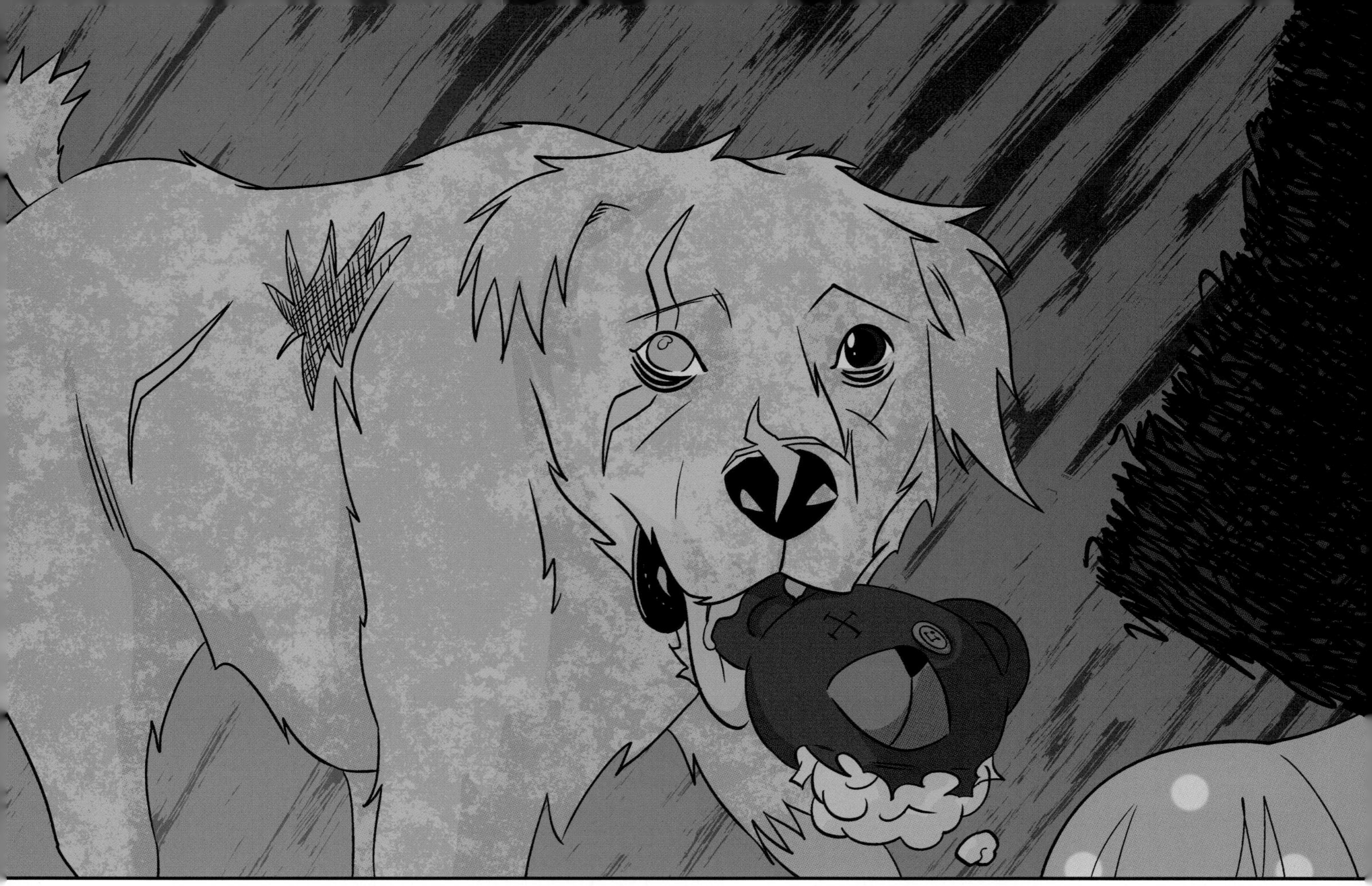

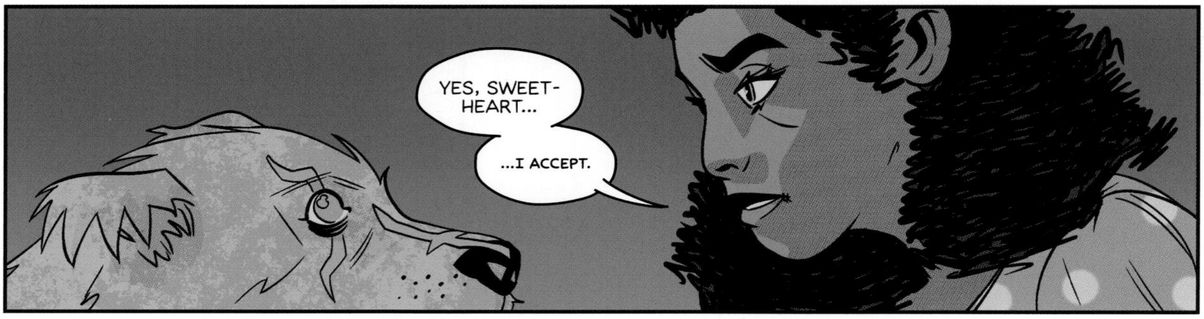
YES, SWEET-HEART...
...I ACCEPT.

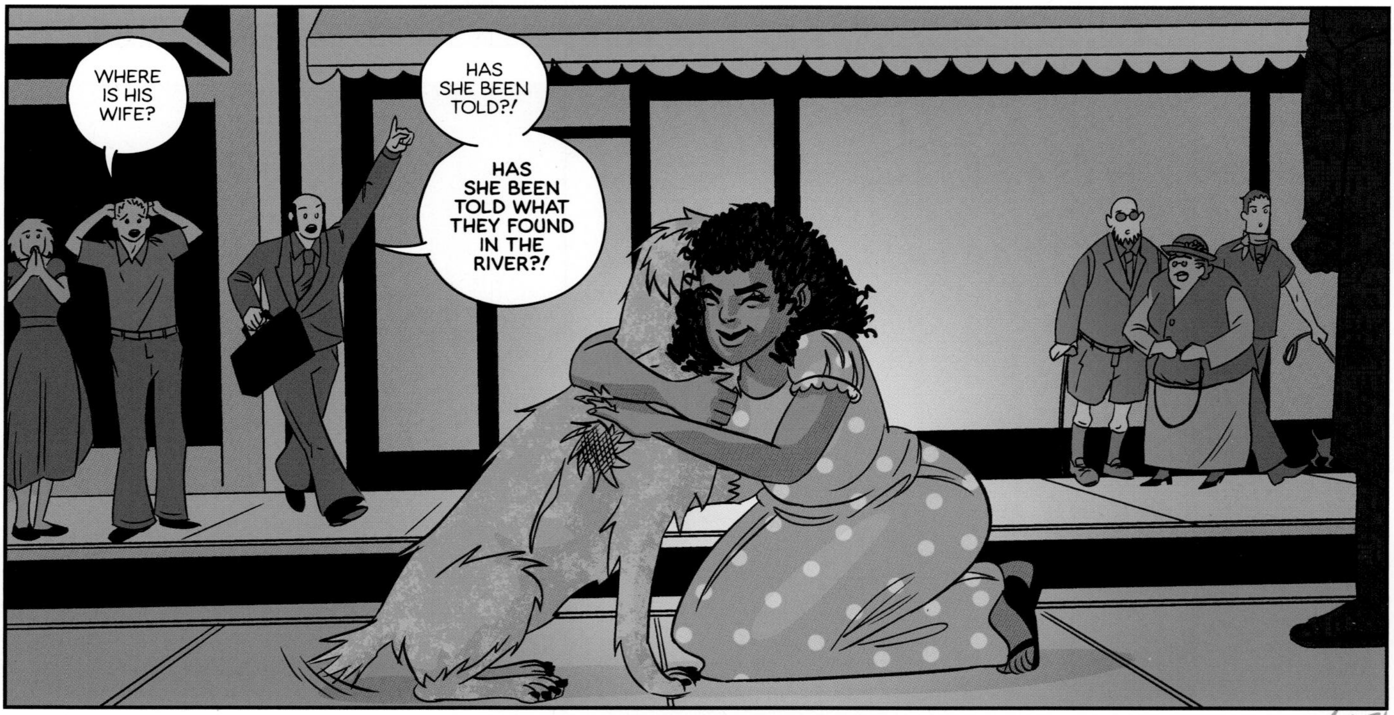
WHERE IS HIS WIFE?
HAS SHE BEEN TOLD?!
HAS SHE BEEN TOLD WHAT THEY FOUND IN THE RIVER?!
WOOF!

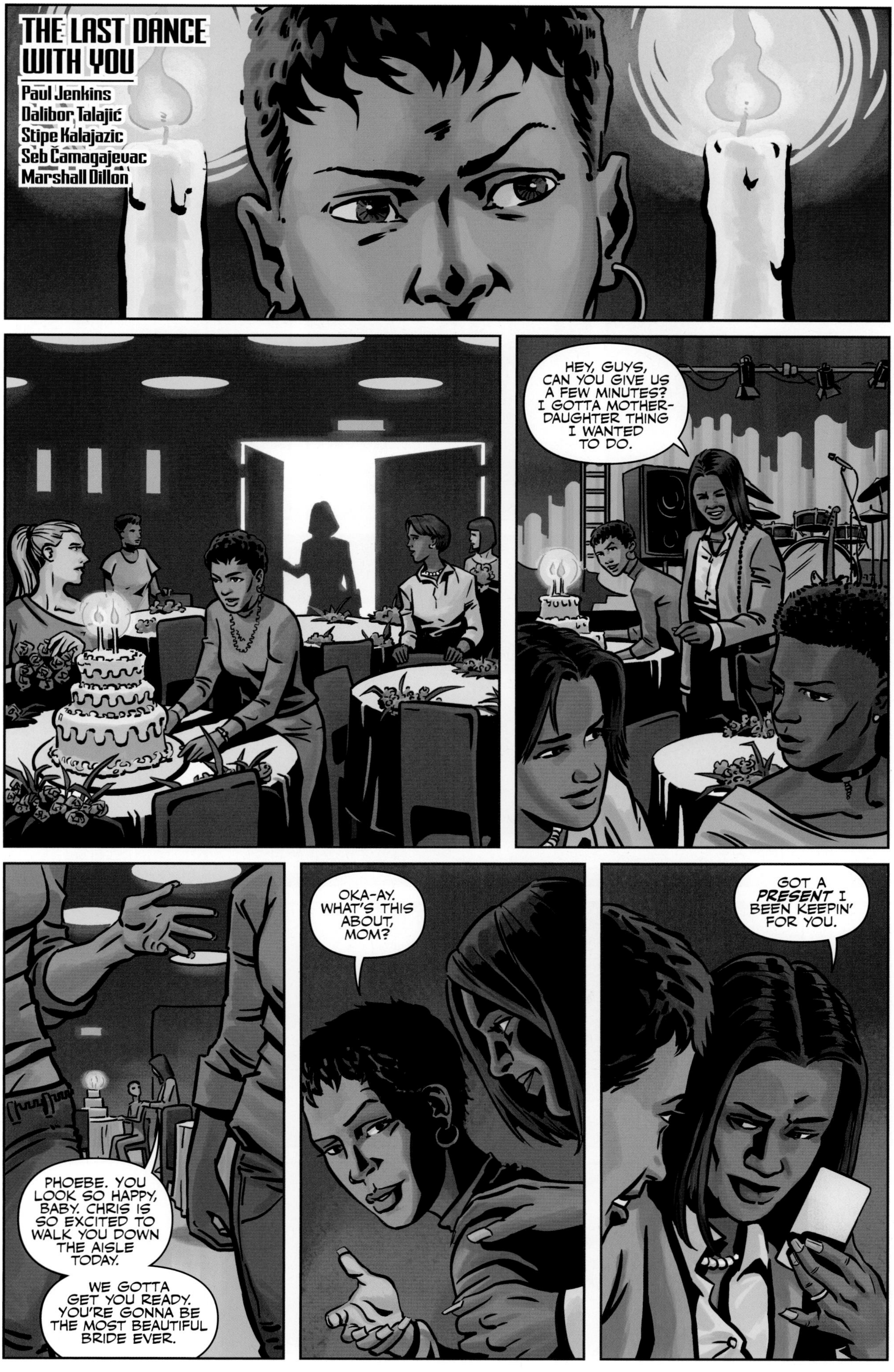
THE LAST DANCE WITH YOU
Paul Jenkins
Dalibor Talajić
Stipe Kalajazic
Seb Čamagajevac
Marshall Dillon
HEY, GUYS, CAN YOU GIVE US A FEW MINUTES? I GOTTA MOTHER-DAUGHTER THING I WANTED TO DO.
PHOEBE. YOU LOOK SO HAPPY, BABY. CHRIS IS SO EXCITED TO WALK YOU DOWN THE AISLE TODAY.
WE GOTTA GET YOU READY. YOU'RE GONNA BE THE MOST BEAUTIFUL BRIDE EVER.
OKA-AY. WHAT'S THIS ABOUT, MOM?
GOT A *PRESENT* I BEEN KEEPIN' FOR YOU.

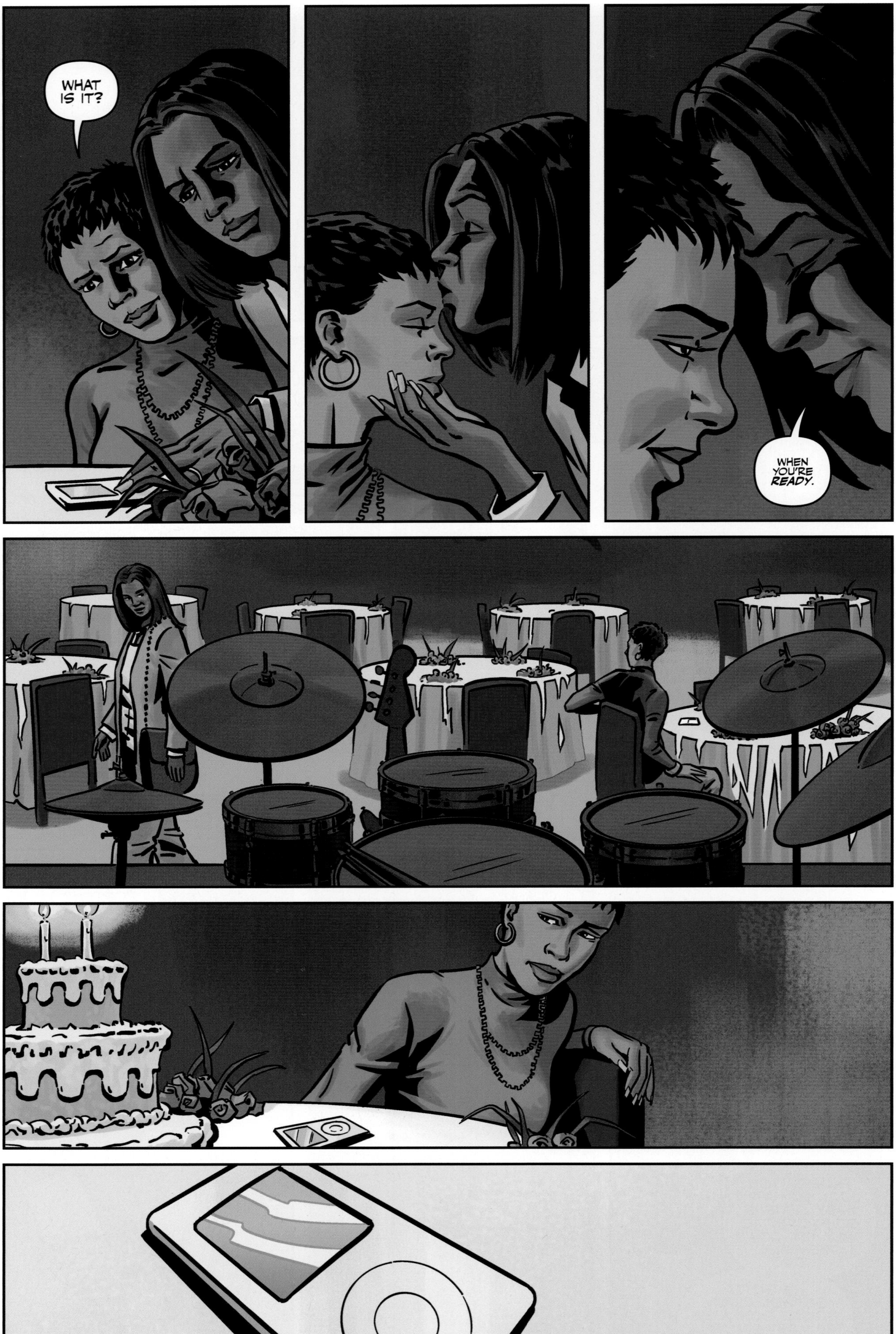
WHAT IS IT?
WHEN YOU'RE *READY*.

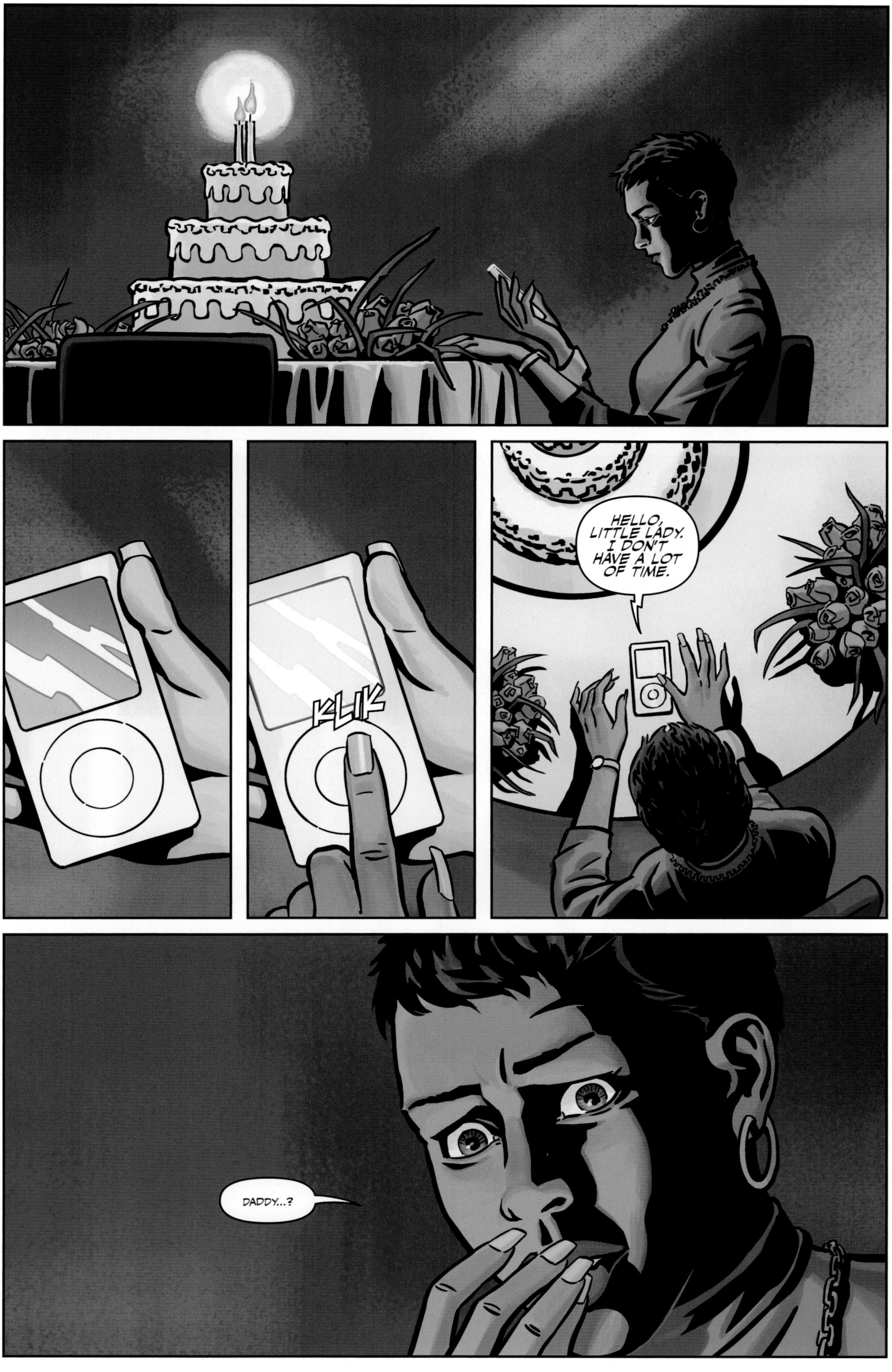
KLIK
HELLO, LITTLE LADY. I DON'T HAVE A LOT OF TIME.
DADDY...?

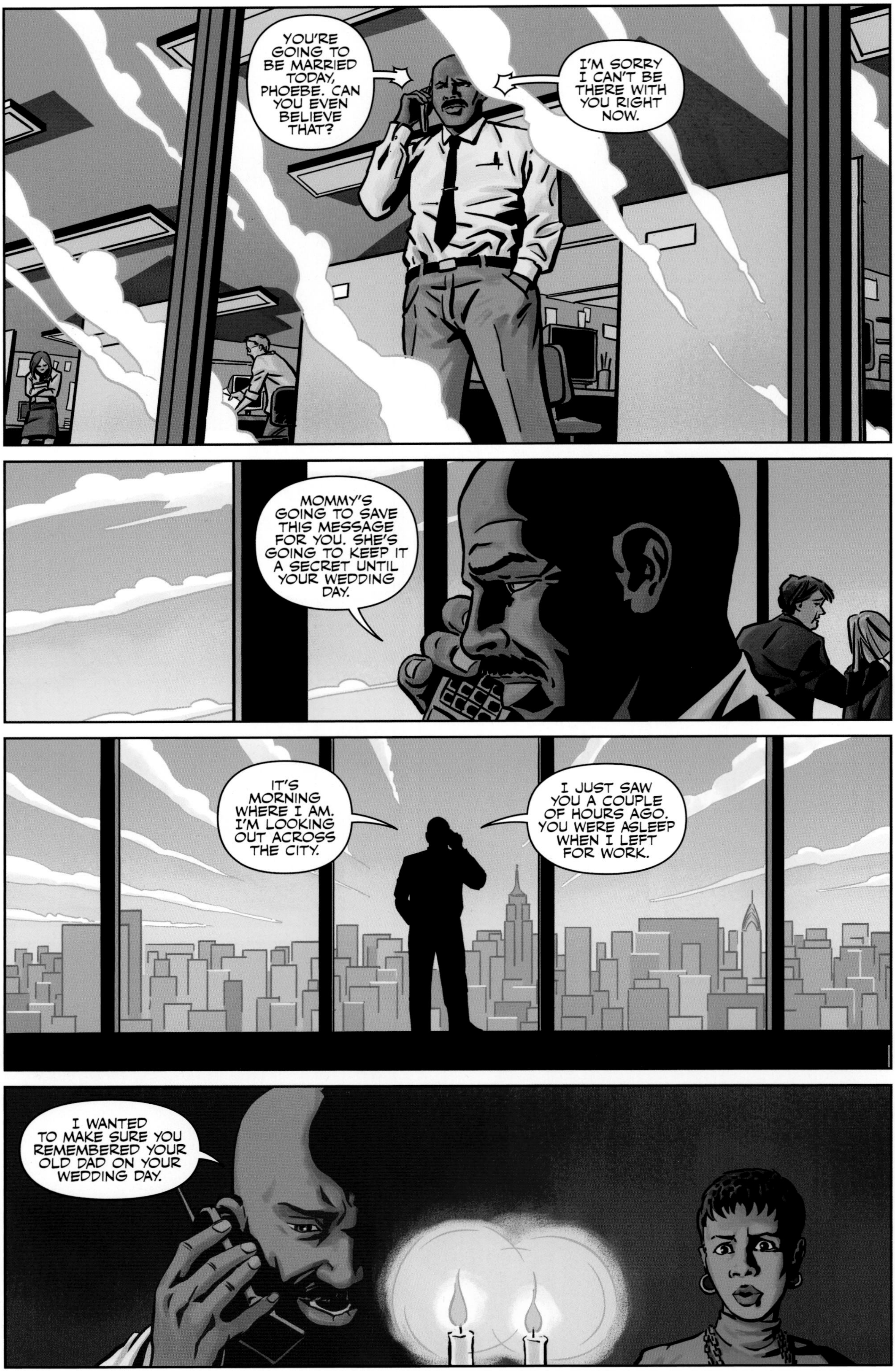
YOU'RE GOING TO BE MARRIED TODAY, PHOEBE. CAN YOU EVEN BELIEVE THAT?
I'M SORRY I CAN'T BE THERE WITH YOU RIGHT NOW.
MOMMY'S GOING TO SAVE THIS MESSAGE FOR YOU. SHE'S GOING TO KEEP IT A SECRET UNTIL YOUR WEDDING DAY.
IT'S MORNING WHERE I AM. I'M LOOKING OUT ACROSS THE CITY.
I JUST SAW YOU A COUPLE OF HOURS AGO. YOU WERE ASLEEP WHEN I LEFT FOR WORK.
I WANTED TO MAKE SURE YOU REMEMBERED YOUR OLD DAD ON YOUR WEDDING DAY.

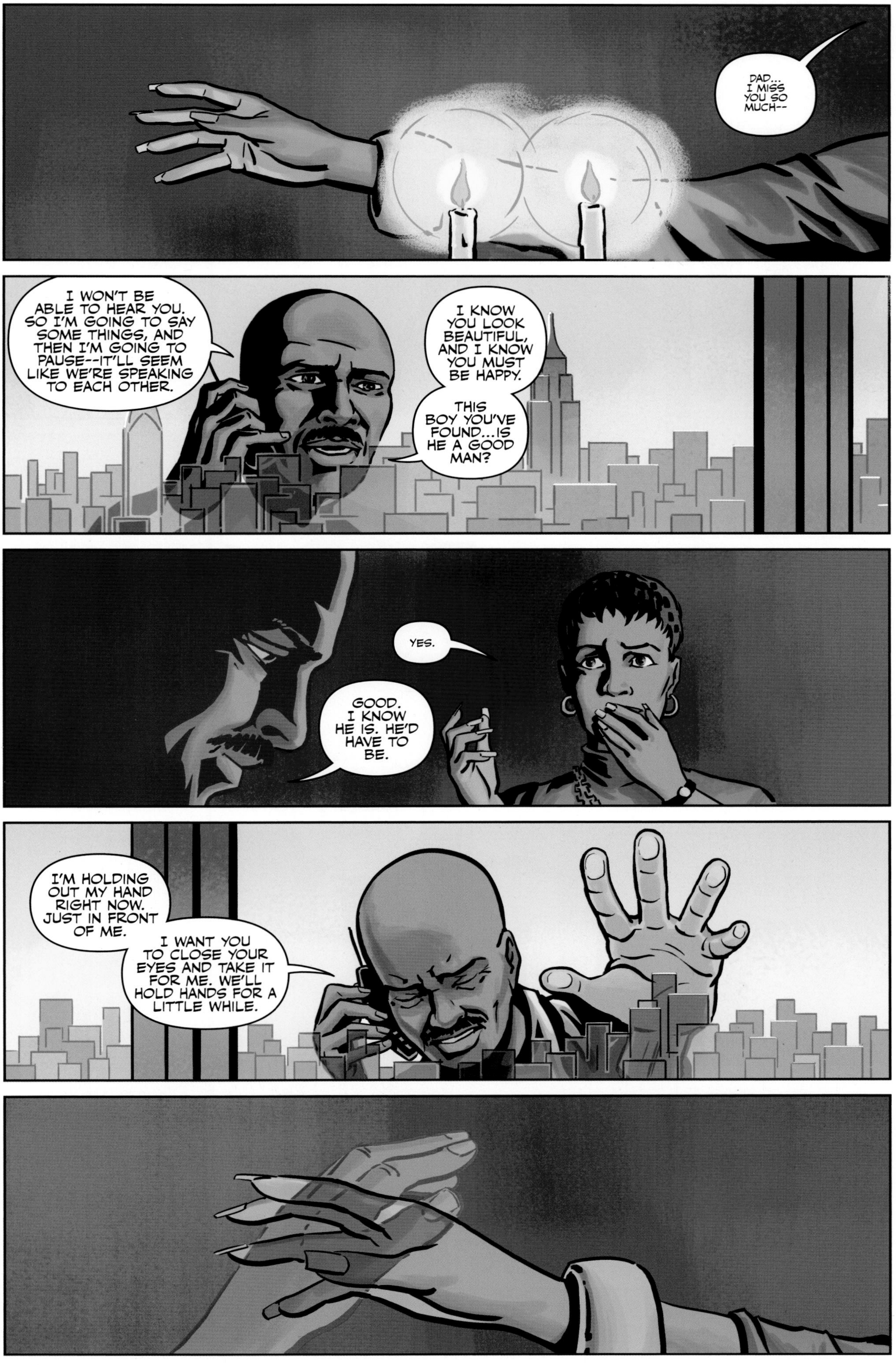
DAD... I MISS YOU SO MUCH--
I WON'T BE ABLE TO HEAR YOU. SO I'M GOING TO SAY SOME THINGS, AND THEN I'M GOING TO PAUSE--IT'LL SEEM LIKE WE'RE SPEAKING TO EACH OTHER.
I KNOW YOU LOOK BEAUTIFUL, AND I KNOW YOU MUST BE HAPPY.
THIS BOY YOU'VE FOUND...IS HE A GOOD MAN?
YES.
GOOD. I KNOW HE IS. HE'D HAVE TO BE.
I'M HOLDING OUT MY HAND RIGHT NOW. JUST IN FRONT OF ME.
I WANT YOU TO CLOSE YOUR EYES AND TAKE IT FOR ME. WE'LL HOLD HANDS FOR A LITTLE WHILE.

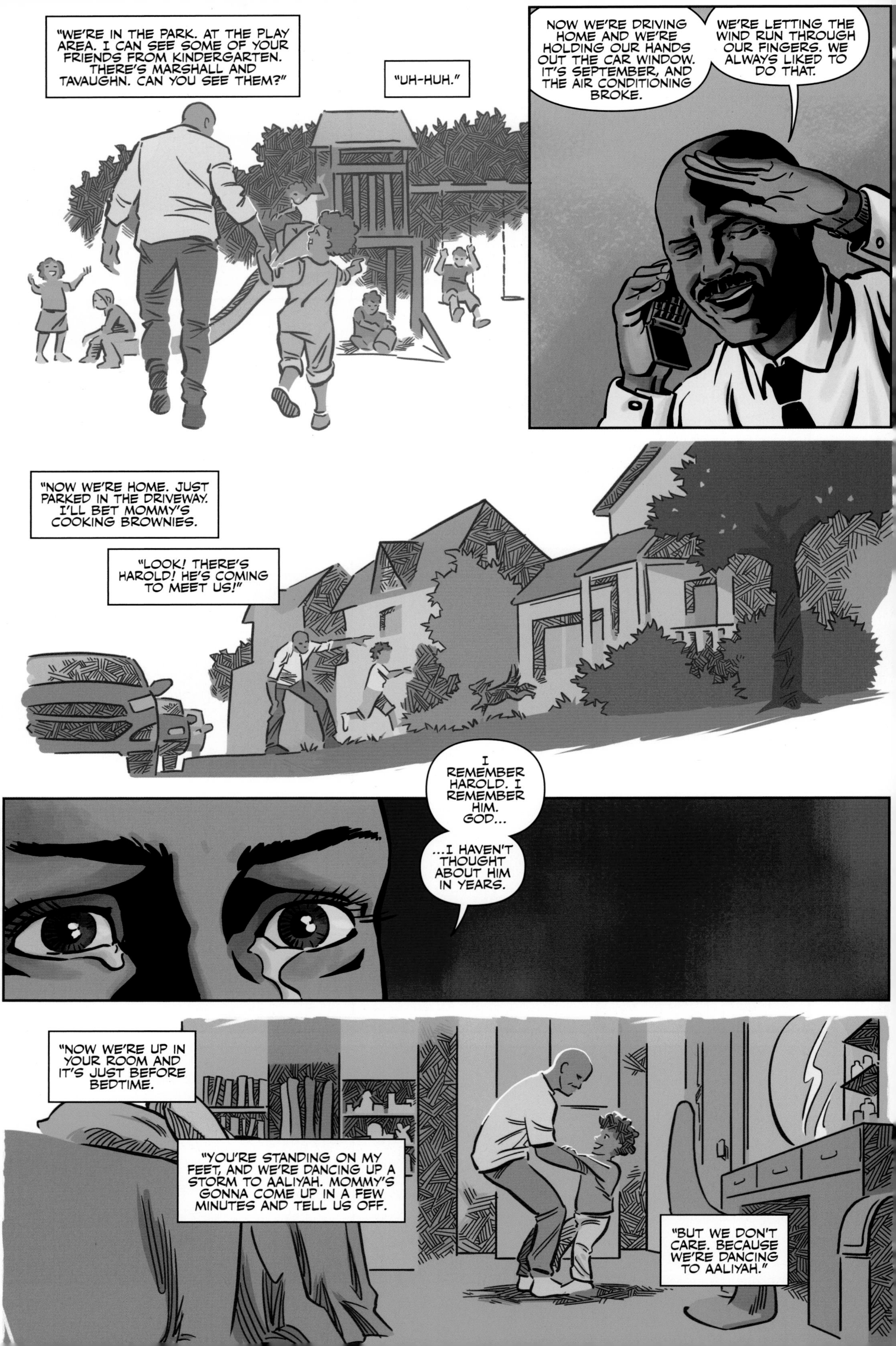
"WE'RE IN THE PARK. AT THE PLAY AREA. I CAN SEE SOME OF YOUR FRIENDS FROM KINDERGARTEN. THERE'S MARSHALL AND TAVAUGHN. CAN YOU SEE THEM?"
"UH-HUH."
NOW WE'RE DRIVING HOME AND WE'RE HOLDING OUR HANDS OUT THE CAR WINDOW. IT'S SEPTEMBER, AND THE AIR CONDITIONING BROKE.
WE'RE LETTING THE WIND RUN THROUGH OUR FINGERS. WE ALWAYS LIKED TO DO THAT.
"NOW WE'RE HOME. JUST PARKED IN THE DRIVEWAY. I'LL BET MOMMY'S COOKING BROWNIES.
"LOOK! THERE'S HAROLD! HE'S COMING TO MEET US!"
I REMEMBER HAROLD. I REMEMBER HIM. GOD...
...I HAVEN'T THOUGHT ABOUT HIM IN YEARS.
"NOW WE'RE UP IN YOUR ROOM AND IT'S JUST BEFORE BEDTIME.
"YOU'RE STANDING ON MY FEET, AND WE'RE DANCING UP A STORM TO AALIYAH. MOMMY'S GONNA COME UP IN A FEW MINUTES AND TELL US OFF.
"BUT WE DON'T CARE. BECAUSE WE'RE DANCING TO AALIYAH."

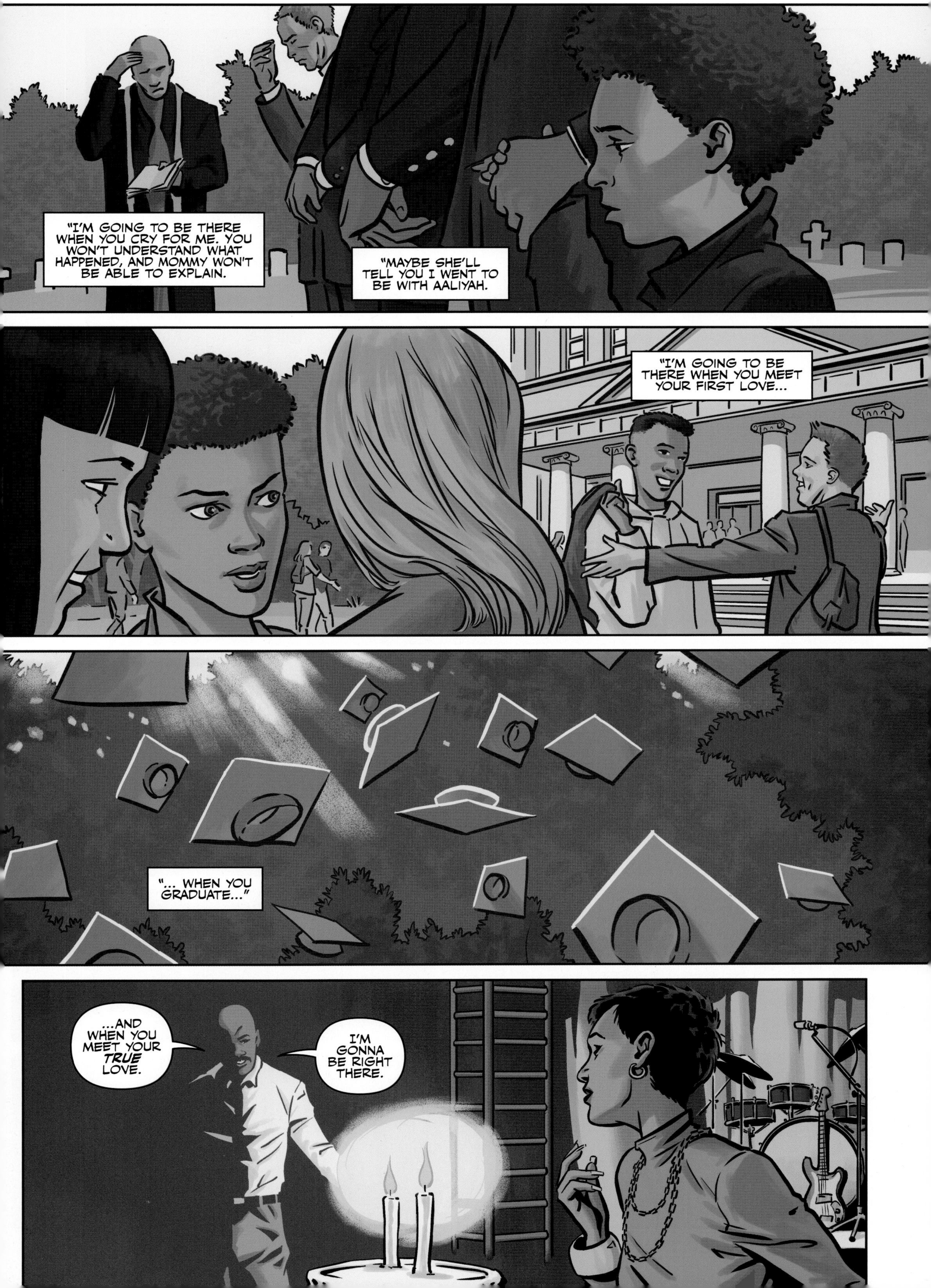
"I'M GOING TO BE THERE WHEN YOU CRY FOR ME. YOU WON'T UNDERSTAND WHAT HAPPENED, AND MOMMY WON'T BE ABLE TO EXPLAIN.
"MAYBE SHE'LL TELL YOU I WENT TO BE WITH AALIYAH.
"I'M GOING TO BE THERE WHEN YOU MEET YOUR FIRST LOVE...
"... WHEN YOU GRADUATE..."
...AND WHEN YOU MEET YOUR *TRUE* LOVE.
I'M GONNA BE RIGHT THERE.

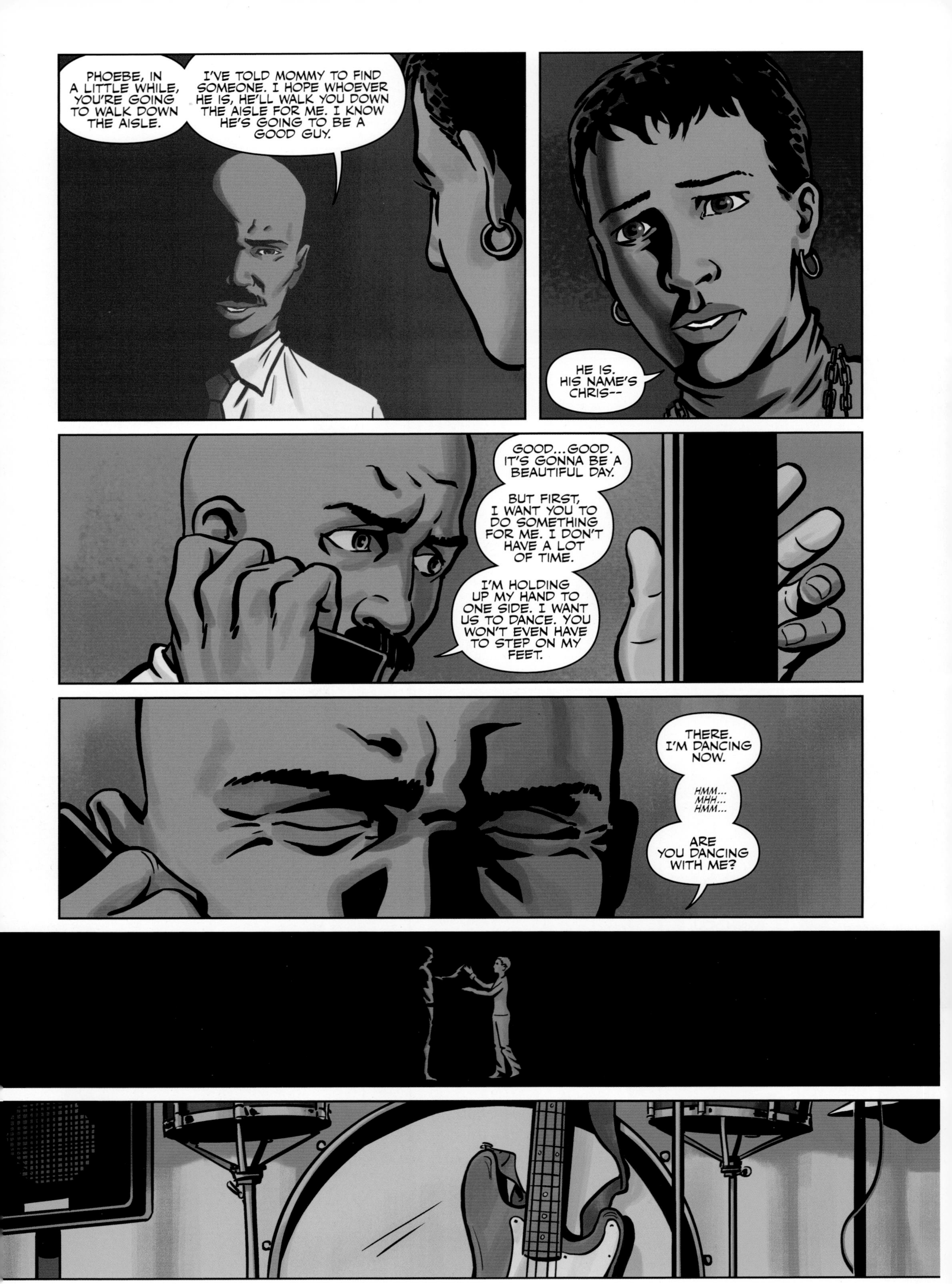
PHOEBE, IN A LITTLE WHILE, YOU'RE GOING TO WALK DOWN THE AISLE.
I'VE TOLD MOMMY TO FIND SOMEONE. I HOPE WHOEVER HE IS, HE'LL WALK YOU DOWN THE AISLE FOR ME. I KNOW HE'S GOING TO BE A GOOD GUY.
HE IS. HIS NAME'S CHRIS--
GOOD...GOOD. IT'S GONNA BE A BEAUTIFUL DAY.
BUT FIRST, I WANT YOU TO DO SOMETHING FOR ME. I DON'T HAVE A LOT OF TIME.
I'M HOLDING UP MY HAND TO ONE SIDE. I WANT US TO DANCE. YOU WON'T EVEN HAVE TO STEP ON MY FEET.
THERE. I'M DANCING NOW.
HMM... MHH... HMM...
ARE YOU DANCING WITH ME?

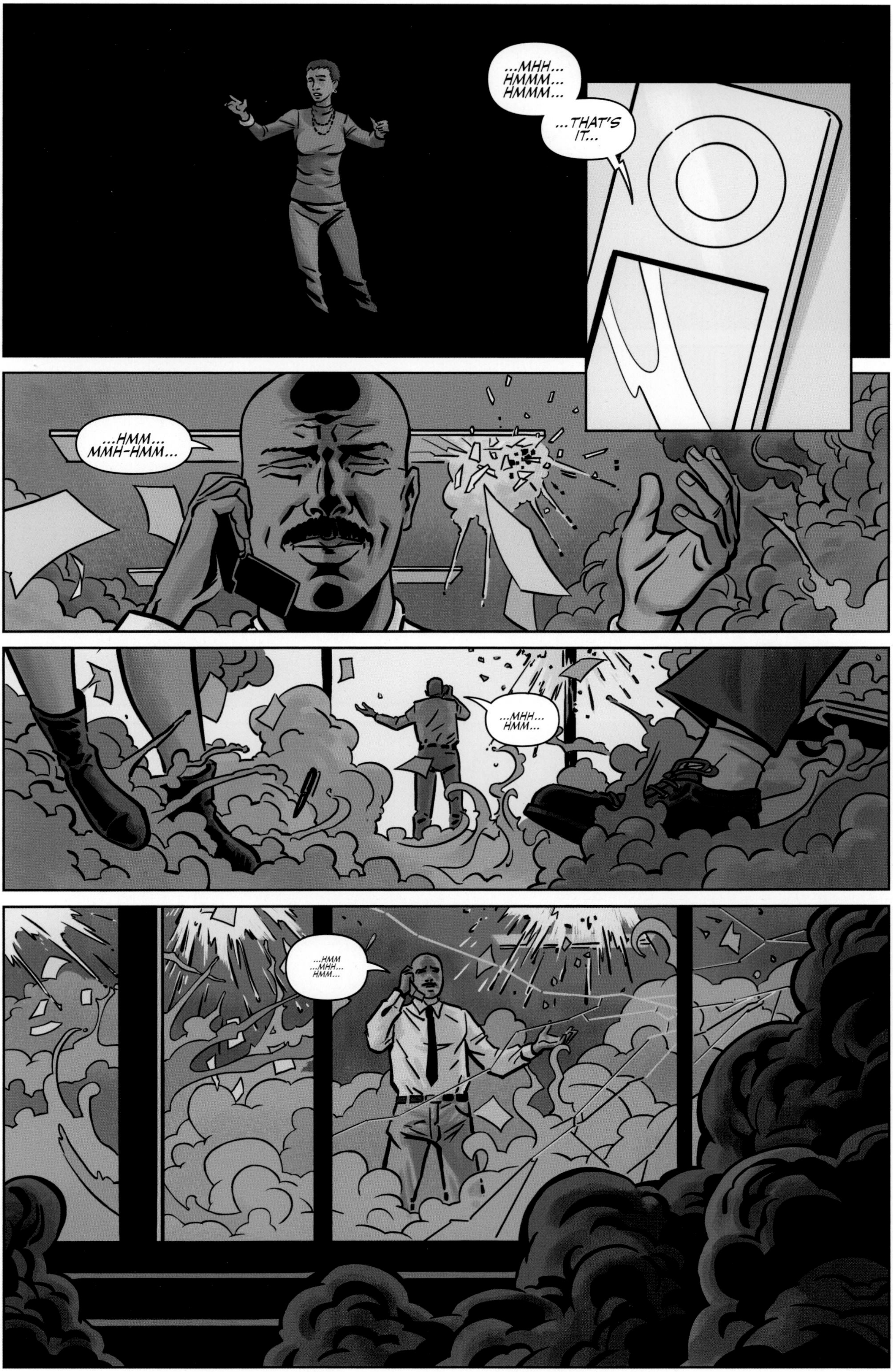
...MHH... HMMM... HMMM...
...THAT'S IT...
...HMM... MMH-HMM...
...MHH... HMM...
...HMM ...MHH... HMM...

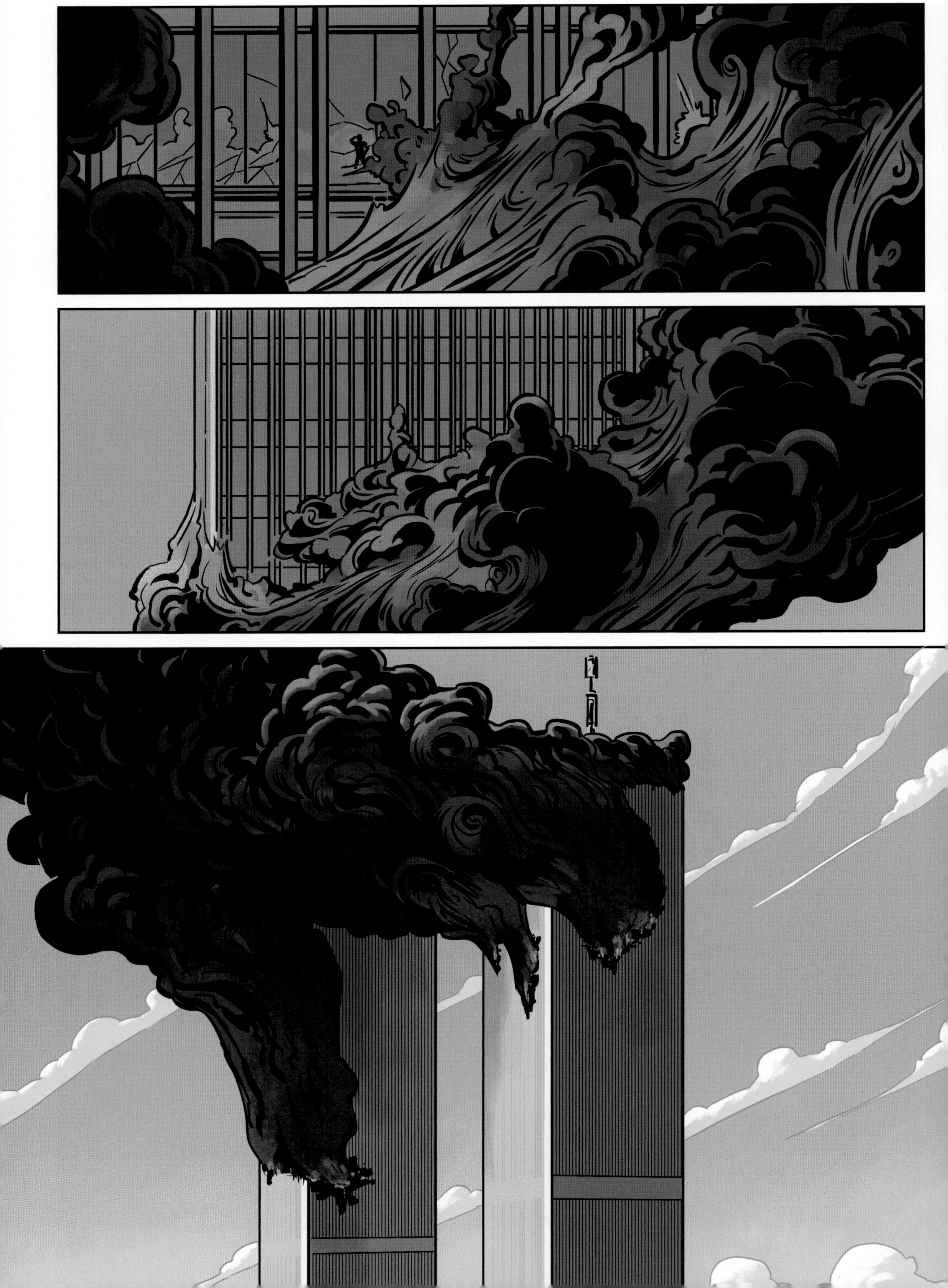

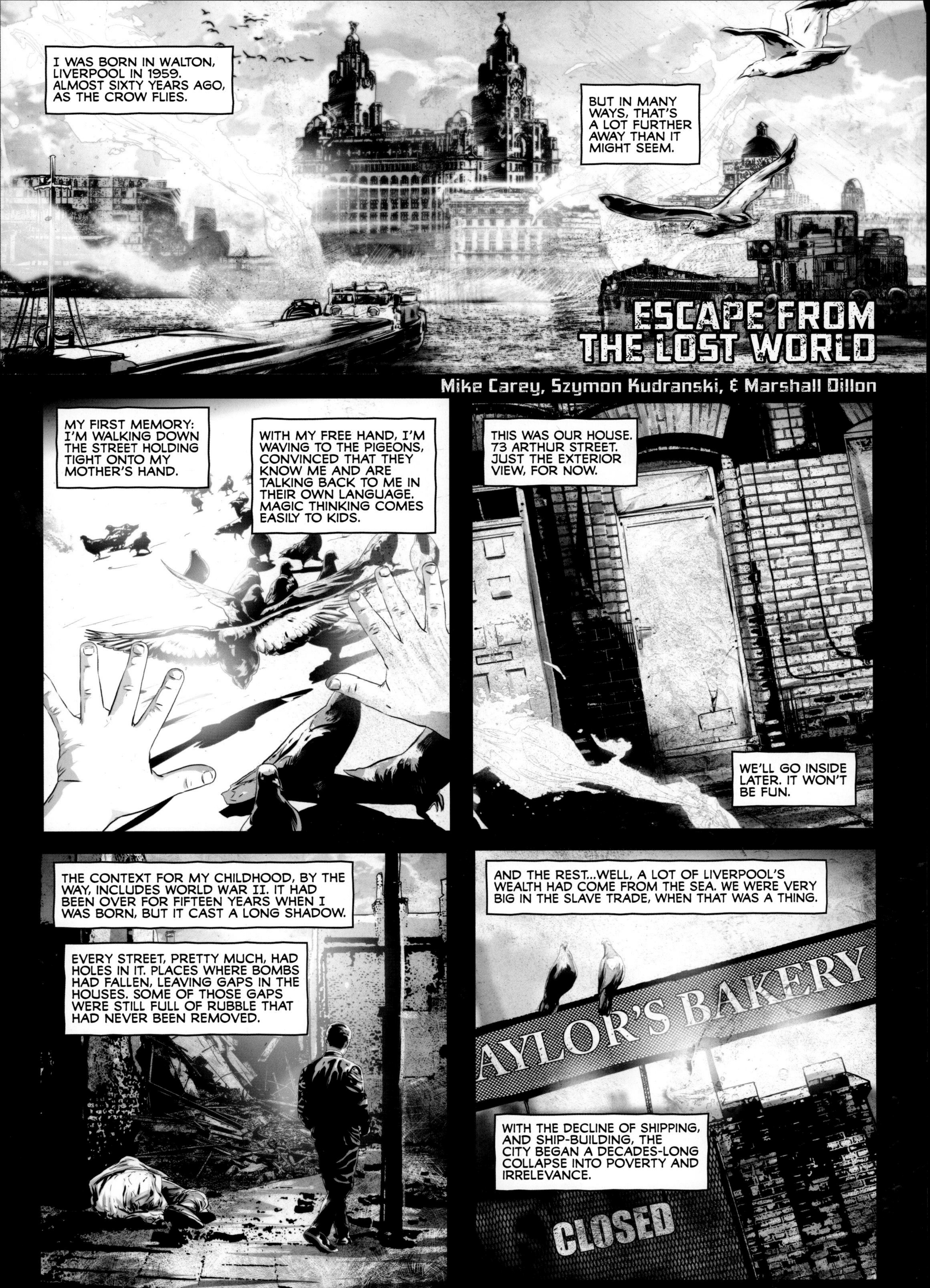
I WAS BORN IN WALTON, LIVERPOOL IN 1959. ALMOST SIXTY YEARS AGO, AS THE CROW FLIES.
BUT IN MANY WAYS, THAT'S A LOT FURTHER AWAY THAN IT MIGHT SEEM.
ESCAPE FROM THE LOST WORLD
Mike Carey, Szymon Kudranski, & Marshall Dillon
MY FIRST MEMORY: I'M WALKING DOWN THE STREET HOLDING TIGHT ONTO MY MOTHER'S HAND.
WITH MY FREE HAND, I'M WAVING TO THE PIGEONS, CONVINCED THAT THEY KNOW ME AND ARE TALKING BACK TO ME IN THEIR OWN LANGUAGE. MAGIC THINKING COMES EASILY TO KIDS.
THIS WAS OUR HOUSE. 73 ARTHUR STREET. JUST THE EXTERIOR VIEW, FOR NOW.
WE'LL GO INSIDE LATER. IT WON'T BE FUN.
THE CONTEXT FOR MY CHILDHOOD, BY THE WAY, INCLUDES WORLD WAR II. IT HAD BEEN OVER FOR FIFTEEN YEARS WHEN I WAS BORN, BUT IT CAST A LONG SHADOW.
EVERY STREET, PRETTY MUCH, HAD HOLES IN IT. PLACES WHERE BOMBS HAD FALLEN, LEAVING GAPS IN THE HOUSES. SOME OF THOSE GAPS WERE STILL FULL OF RUBBLE THAT HAD NEVER BEEN REMOVED.
AND THE REST...WELL, A LOT OF LIVERPOOL'S WEALTH HAD COME FROM THE SEA. WE WERE VERY BIG IN THE SLAVE TRADE, WHEN THAT WAS A THING.
AYLOR'S BAKERY
WITH THE DECLINE OF SHIPPING, AND SHIP-BUILDING, THE CITY BEGAN A DECADES-LONG COLLAPSE INTO POVERTY AND IRRELEVANCE.
CLOSED

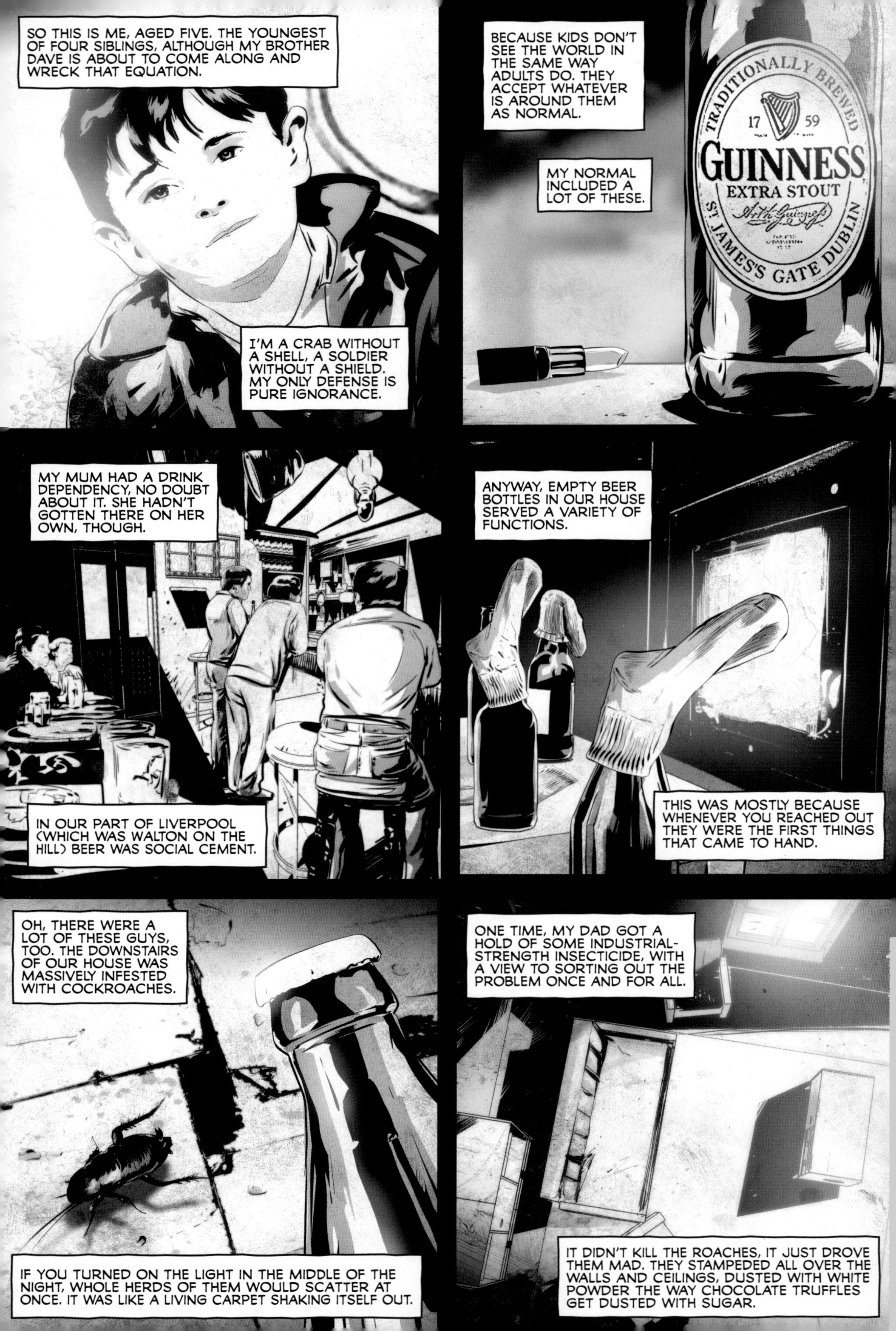
SO THIS IS ME, AGED FIVE. THE YOUNGEST OF FOUR SIBLINGS, ALTHOUGH MY BROTHER DAVE IS ABOUT TO COME ALONG AND WRECK THAT EQUATION.
I'M A CRAB WITHOUT A SHELL, A SOLDIER WITHOUT A SHIELD. MY ONLY DEFENSE IS PURE IGNORANCE.
BECAUSE KIDS DON'T SEE THE WORLD IN THE SAME WAY ADULTS DO. THEY ACCEPT WHATEVER IS AROUND THEM AS NORMAL.
MY NORMAL INCLUDED A LOT OF THESE.
TRADITIONALLY BREWED
17 59
GUINNESS
EXTRA STOUT
ST JAMES'S GATE DUBLIN
MY MUM HAD A DRINK DEPENDENCY, NO DOUBT ABOUT IT. SHE HADN'T GOTTEN THERE ON HER OWN, THOUGH.
IN OUR PART OF LIVERPOOL (WHICH WAS WALTON ON THE HILL) BEER WAS SOCIAL CEMENT.
ANYWAY, EMPTY BEER BOTTLES IN OUR HOUSE SERVED A VARIETY OF FUNCTIONS.
THIS WAS MOSTLY BECAUSE WHENEVER YOU REACHED OUT THEY WERE THE FIRST THINGS THAT CAME TO HAND.
OH, THERE WERE A LOT OF THESE GUYS, TOO. THE DOWNSTAIRS OF OUR HOUSE WAS MASSIVELY INFESTED WITH COCKROACHES.
IF YOU TURNED ON THE LIGHT IN THE MIDDLE OF THE NIGHT, WHOLE HERDS OF THEM WOULD SCATTER AT ONCE. IT WAS LIKE A LIVING CARPET SHAKING ITSELF OUT.
ONE TIME, MY DAD GOT A HOLD OF SOME INDUSTRIAL-STRENGTH INSECTICIDE, WITH A VIEW TO SORTING OUT THE PROBLEM ONCE AND FOR ALL.
IT DIDN'T KILL THE ROACHES, IT JUST DROVE THEM MAD. THEY STAMPEDED ALL OVER THE WALLS AND CEILINGS, DUSTED WITH WHITE POWDER THE WAY CHOCOLATE TRUFFLES GET DUSTED WITH SUGAR.

WE ALMOST NEVER SAW ROACHES UPSTAIRS, THOUGH. THERE WAS A STRICT DEMARCATION GOING ON.

BEFORE FEEDING, A BED BUG LOOKS LIKE THIS.

WHEN YOU WAKE UP IN THE NIGHT AND YOU FIND THEM SUCKING ON YOUR CHEST OR THE INSIDE OF YOUR ARM, THEY'RE SWOLLEN UP LIKE TINY BALLOONS, TAUT AND BULGING WITH STOLEN BLOOD.

UPSTAIRS BELONGED TO THE BED BUGS. ON SUMMER NIGHTS, I'D LIE AWAKE AND WAIT FOR THEM TO DIVE-BOMB ME FROM THE CEILING.

OTHER THINGS I REMEMBER. IF I PUT UP POSTERS ON THE WALL, THE CORNERS WOULD QUICKLY BECOME SPOTTED WITH BED BUG SHIT.

AND THE STENCH! BITTER ALMOND, THE WAY CYANIDE IS SUPPOSED TO SMELL. FAINTLY PRESENT, ALWAYS, OVERPOWERING IF YOU KILLED ONE.

THIS IS MY BED, BY THE WAY. CIRCA 1971, WHEN I'M TWELVE YEARS OLD. THE OLD COATS SERVE AS BLANKETS. MY YOUNGER BROTHER, AGED SEVEN, SLEEPS AT THE BOTTOM END.

ATOM SPACE

STAR INVASION

AND OUR TEENAGED SISTER, PAULINE, HAS THE ROOM'S OTHER BED. PRIVACY ISN'T A CONCEPT WE UNDERSTAND.

WHEN MY DAD'S ON NIGHTS, THOUGH, DAVE AND I MIGRATE TO MUM'S BED. SHE HAS TERRIBLE INSOMNIA AND KEEPS THE LIGHT ON ALL NIGHT.

BUY THIS GUN! BB

SMASH

WE READ UNTIL TWO OR THREE A.M. ENID BLYTON. RUDYARD KIPLING. MARY NORTON. WHATEVER WE CAN GET OUR HANDS ON.

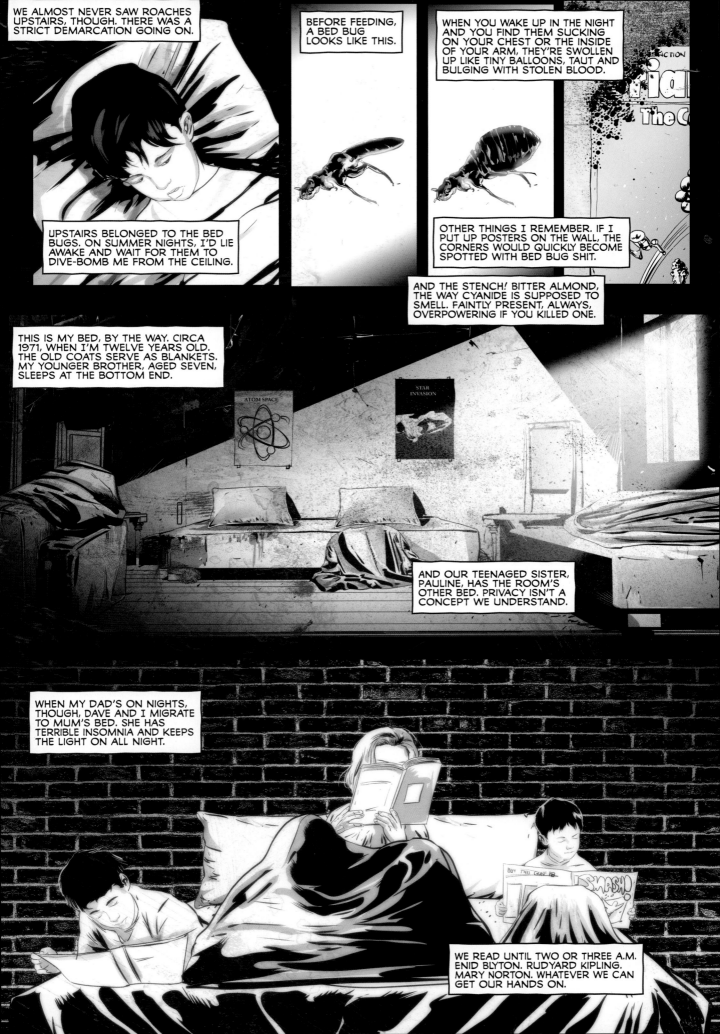

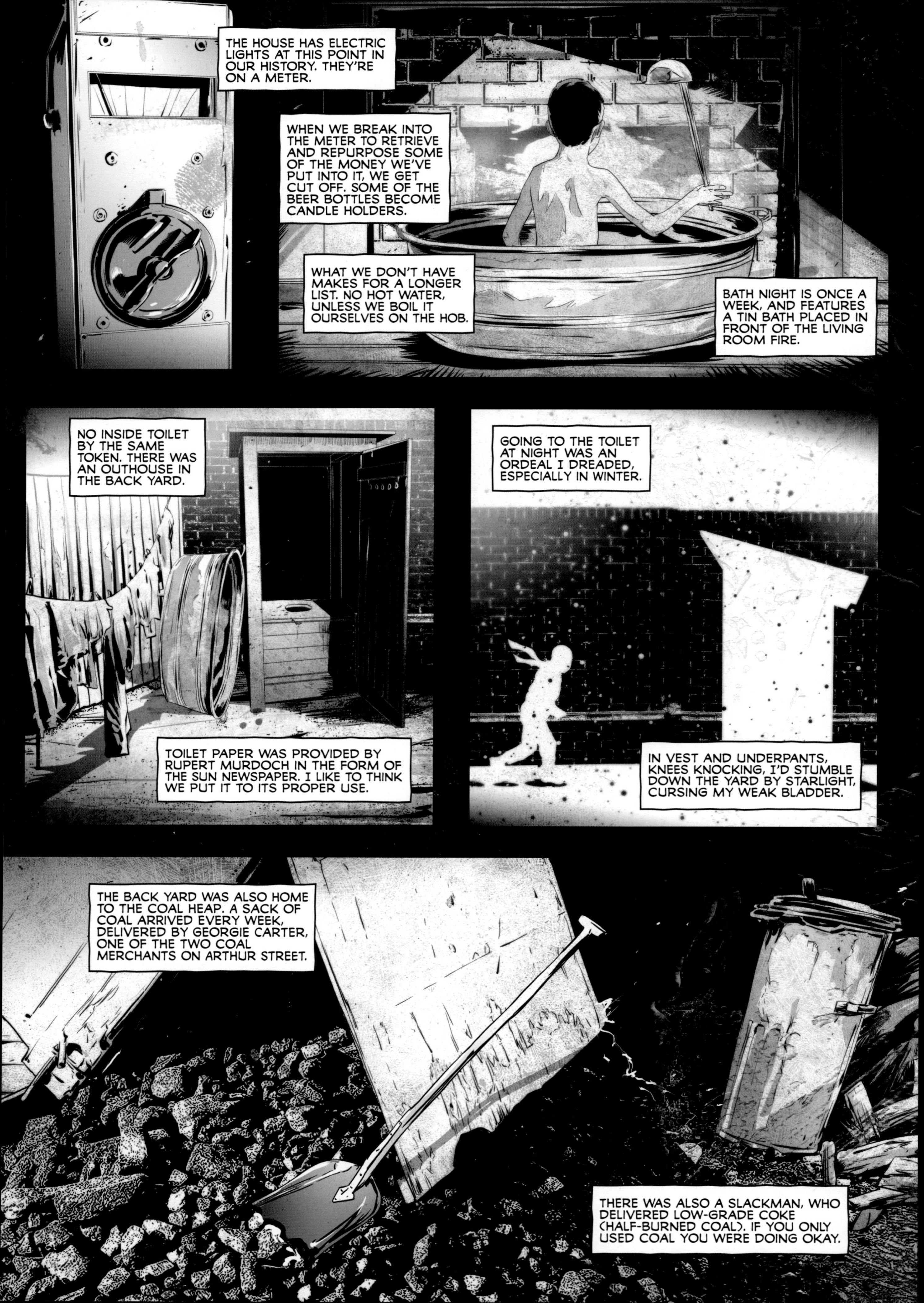
THE HOUSE HAS ELECTRIC LIGHTS AT THIS POINT IN OUR HISTORY. THEY'RE ON A METER.
WHEN WE BREAK INTO THE METER TO RETRIEVE AND REPURPOSE SOME OF THE MONEY WE'VE PUT INTO IT, WE GET CUT OFF. SOME OF THE BEER BOTTLES BECOME CANDLE HOLDERS.
WHAT WE DON'T HAVE MAKES FOR A LONGER LIST. NO HOT WATER, UNLESS WE BOIL IT OURSELVES ON THE HOB.
BATH NIGHT IS ONCE A WEEK, AND FEATURES A TIN BATH PLACED IN FRONT OF THE LIVING ROOM FIRE.
NO INSIDE TOILET BY THE SAME TOKEN. THERE WAS AN OUTHOUSE IN THE BACK YARD.
TOILET PAPER WAS PROVIDED BY RUPERT MURDOCH IN THE FORM OF THE SUN NEWSPAPER. I LIKE TO THINK WE PUT IT TO ITS PROPER USE.
GOING TO THE TOILET AT NIGHT WAS AN ORDEAL I DREADED, ESPECIALLY IN WINTER.
IN VEST AND UNDERPANTS, KNEES KNOCKING, I'D STUMBLE DOWN THE YARD BY STARLIGHT, CURSING MY WEAK BLADDER.
THE BACK YARD WAS ALSO HOME TO THE COAL HEAP. A SACK OF COAL ARRIVED EVERY WEEK, DELIVERED BY GEORGIE CARTER, ONE OF THE TWO COAL MERCHANTS ON ARTHUR STREET.
THERE WAS ALSO A SLACKMAN, WHO DELIVERED LOW-GRADE COKE (HALF-BURNED COAL). IF YOU ONLY USED COAL YOU WERE DOING OKAY.

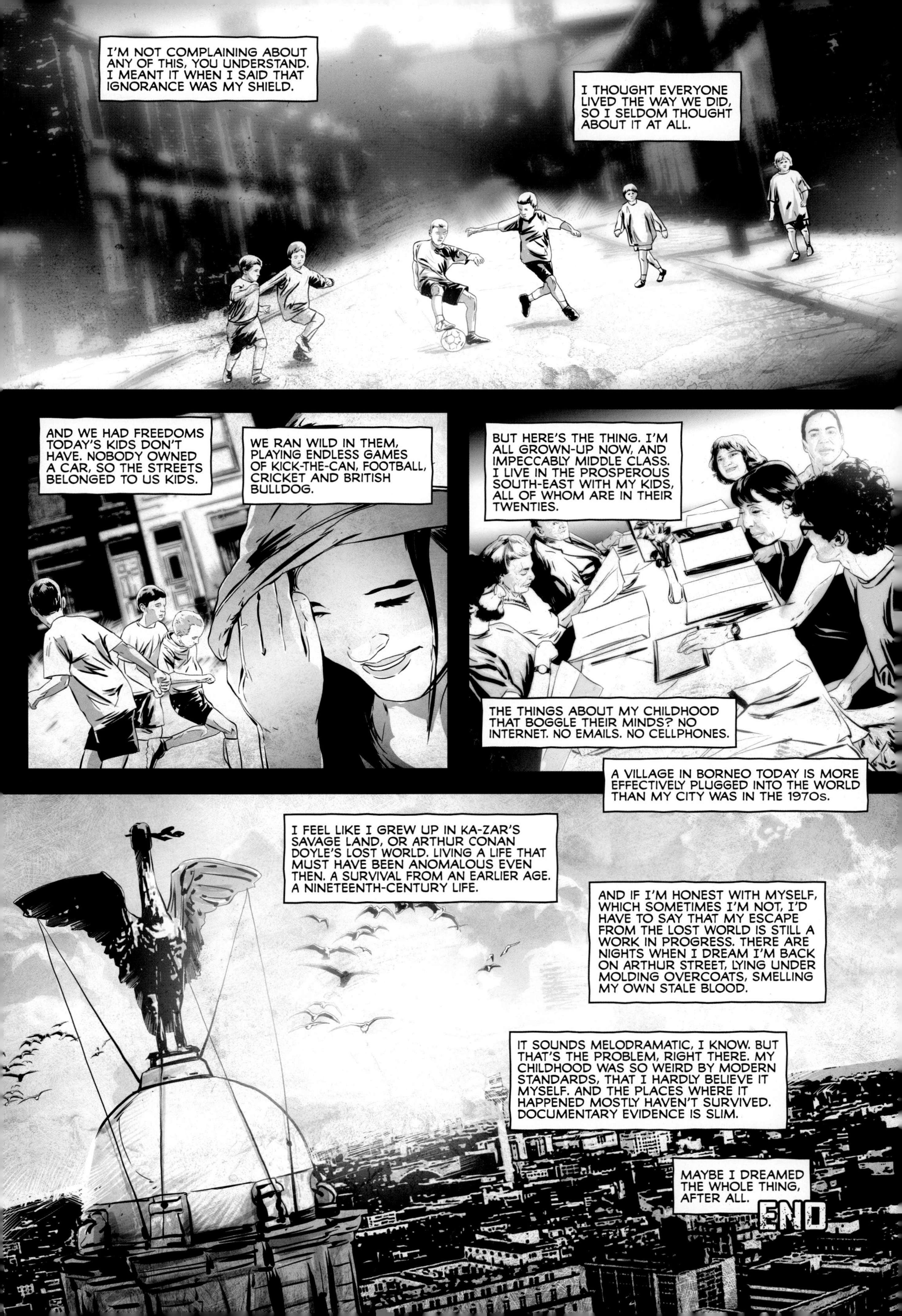
I'M NOT COMPLAINING ABOUT ANY OF THIS, YOU UNDERSTAND. I MEANT IT WHEN I SAID THAT IGNORANCE WAS MY SHIELD.
I THOUGHT EVERYONE LIVED THE WAY WE DID, SO I SELDOM THOUGHT ABOUT IT AT ALL.
AND WE HAD FREEDOMS TODAY'S KIDS DON'T HAVE. NOBODY OWNED A CAR, SO THE STREETS BELONGED TO US KIDS.
WE RAN WILD IN THEM, PLAYING ENDLESS GAMES OF KICK-THE-CAN, FOOTBALL, CRICKET AND BRITISH BULLDOG.
BUT HERE'S THE THING. I'M ALL GROWN-UP NOW, AND IMPECCABLY MIDDLE CLASS. I LIVE IN THE PROSPEROUS SOUTH-EAST WITH MY KIDS, ALL OF WHOM ARE IN THEIR TWENTIES.
THE THINGS ABOUT MY CHILDHOOD THAT BOGGLE THEIR MINDS? NO INTERNET. NO EMAILS. NO CELLPHONES.
A VILLAGE IN BORNEO TODAY IS MORE EFFECTIVELY PLUGGED INTO THE WORLD THAN MY CITY WAS IN THE 1970s.
I FEEL LIKE I GREW UP IN KA-ZAR'S SAVAGE LAND, OR ARTHUR CONAN DOYLE'S LOST WORLD. LIVING A LIFE THAT MUST HAVE BEEN ANOMALOUS EVEN THEN. A SURVIVAL FROM AN EARLIER AGE. A NINETEENTH-CENTURY LIFE.
AND IF I'M HONEST WITH MYSELF, WHICH SOMETIMES I'M NOT, I'D HAVE TO SAY THAT MY ESCAPE FROM THE LOST WORLD IS STILL A WORK IN PROGRESS. THERE ARE NIGHTS WHEN I DREAM I'M BACK ON ARTHUR STREET, LYING UNDER MOLDING OVERCOATS, SMELLING MY OWN STALE BLOOD.
IT SOUNDS MELODRAMATIC, I KNOW. BUT THAT'S THE PROBLEM, RIGHT THERE. MY CHILDHOOD WAS SO WEIRD BY MODERN STANDARDS, THAT I HARDLY BELIEVE IT MYSELF. AND THE PLACES WHERE IT HAPPENED MOSTLY HAVEN'T SURVIVED. DOCUMENTARY EVIDENCE IS SLIM.
MAYBE I DREAMED THE WHOLE THING, AFTER ALL.
END

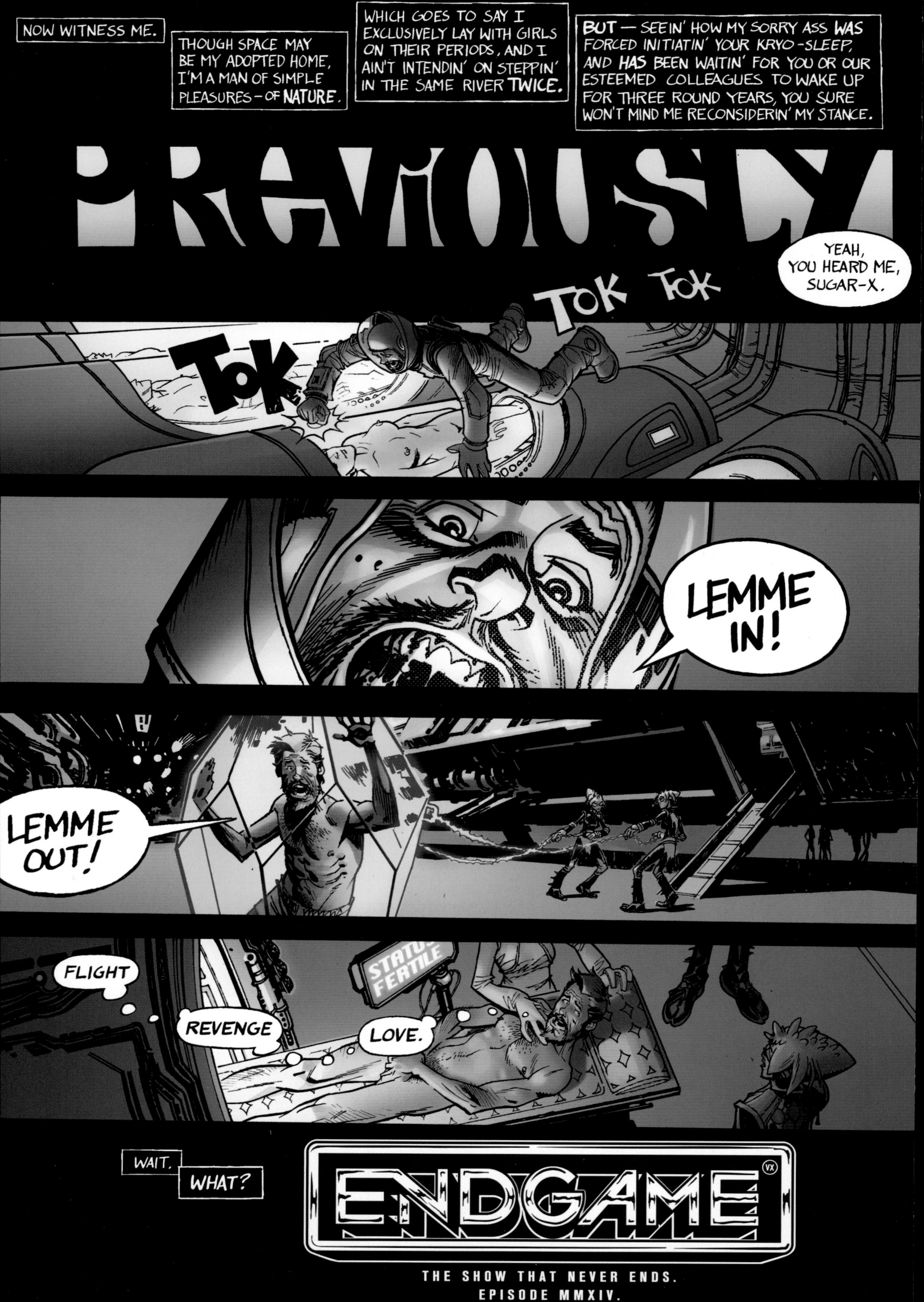
NOW WITNESS ME.
THOUGH SPACE MAY BE MY ADOPTED HOME, I'M A MAN OF SIMPLE PLEASURES – OF NATURE.
WHICH GOES TO SAY I EXCLUSIVELY LAY WITH GIRLS ON THEIR PERIODS, AND I AIN'T INTENDIN' ON STEPPIN' IN THE SAME RIVER TWICE.
BUT – SEEIN' HOW MY SORRY ASS WAS FORCED INITIATIN' YOUR KRYO-SLEEP, AND HAS BEEN WAITIN' FOR YOU OR OUR ESTEEMED COLLEAGUES TO WAKE UP FOR THREE ROUND YEARS, YOU SURE WON'T MIND ME RECONSIDERIN' MY STANCE.
PREVIOUSLY
YEAH, YOU HEARD ME, SUGAR-X.
TOK TOK
TOK
LEMME IN!
LEMME OUT!
STATUS FERTILE
FLIGHT
REVENGE
LOVE.
WAIT.
WHAT?
ENDGAME
THE SHOW THAT NEVER ENDS.
EPISODE MMXIV.

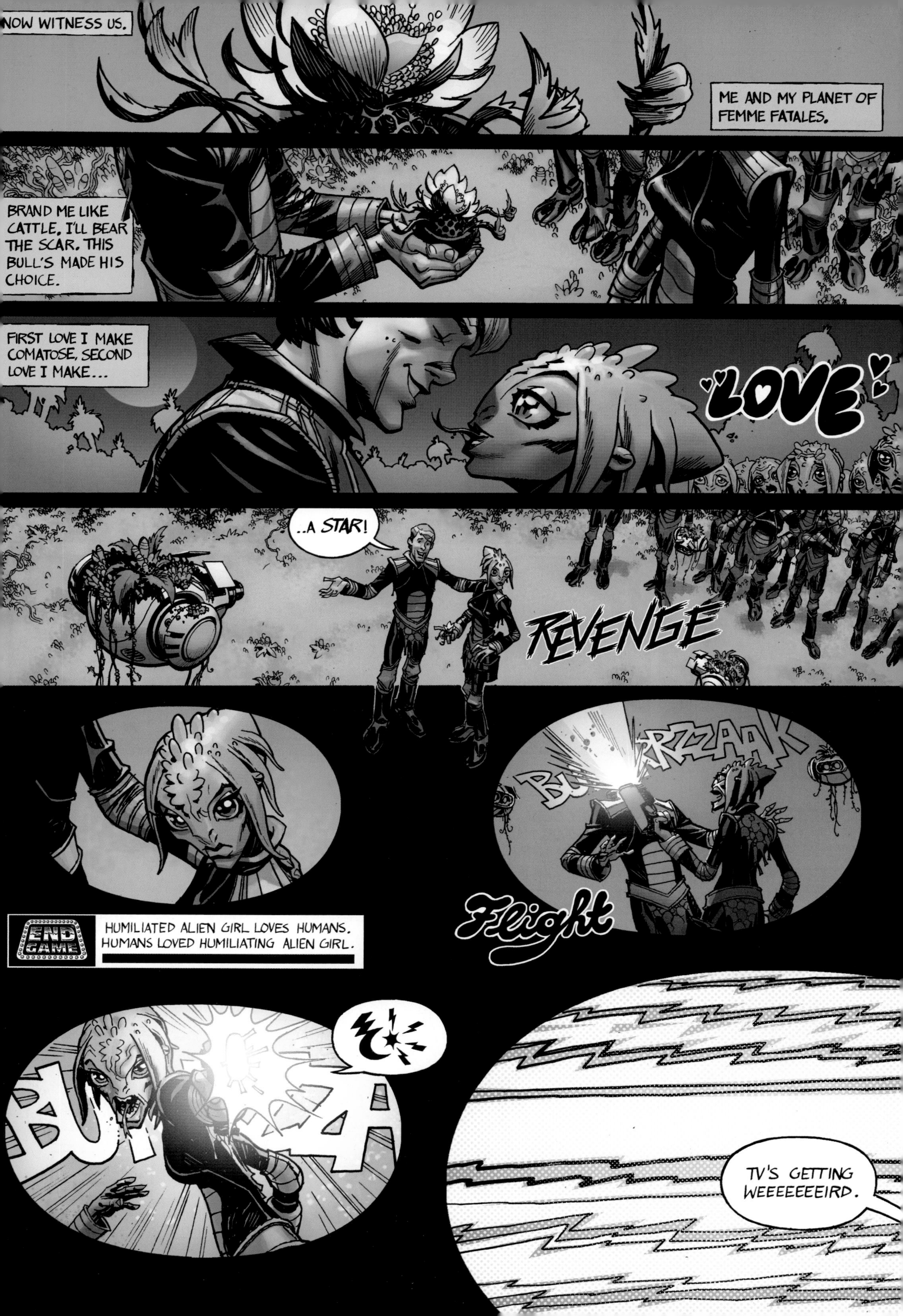
NOW WITNESS US.
ME AND MY PLANET OF FEMME FATALES.
BRAND ME LIKE CATTLE. I'LL BEAR THE SCAR. THIS BULL'S MADE HIS CHOICE.
FIRST LOVE I MAKE COMATOSE, SECOND LOVE I MAKE...
LOVE
..A STAR!
REVENGE
RZZAAK
Flight
END GAME
HUMILIATED ALIEN GIRL LOVES HUMANS.
HUMANS LOVED HUMILIATING ALIEN GIRL.
TV'S GETTING WEEEEEEEIRD.

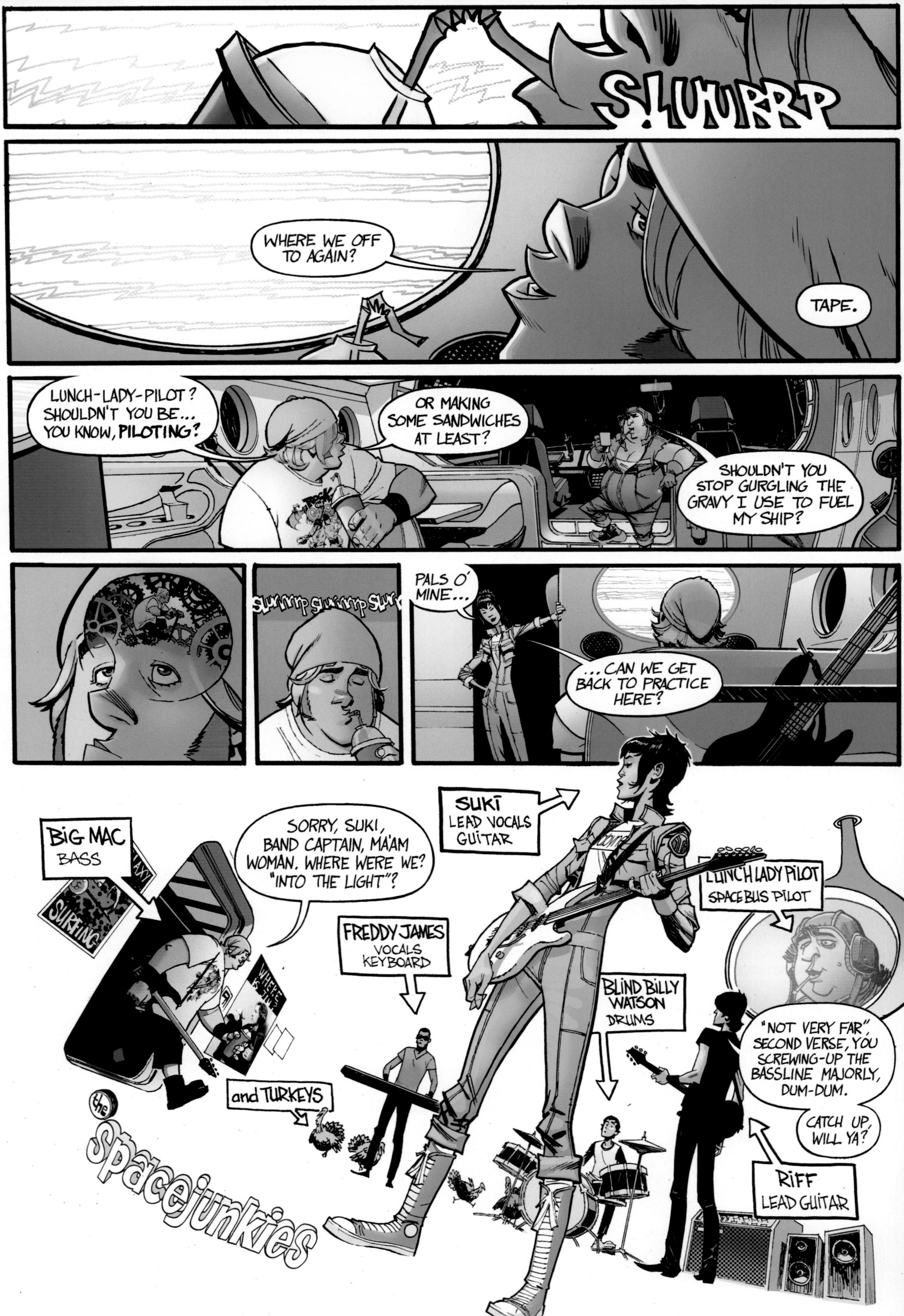

SLUURRP
WHERE WE OFF TO AGAIN?
TAPE.
LUNCH-LADY-PILOT? SHOULDN'T YOU BE... YOU KNOW, PILOTING?
OR MAKING SOME SANDWICHES AT LEAST?
SHOULDN'T YOU STOP GURGLING THE GRAVY I USE TO FUEL MY SHIP?
PALS O' MINE...
...CAN WE GET BACK TO PRACTICE HERE?
BIG MAC
BASS
SORRY, SUKI, BAND CAPTAIN, MA'AM WOMAN. WHERE WERE WE? "INTO THE LIGHT"?
SUKI
LEAD VOCALS
GUITAR
LUNCH LADY PILOT
SPACE BUS PILOT
SURFING
FREDDY JAMES
VOCALS
KEYBOARD
BLIND BILLY WATSON
DRUMS
"NOT VERY FAR", SECOND VERSE, YOU SCREWING-UP THE BASSLINE MAJORLY, DUM-DUM.
CATCH UP, WILL YA?
and TURKEYS
the spacejunkies
RIFF
LEAD GUITAR

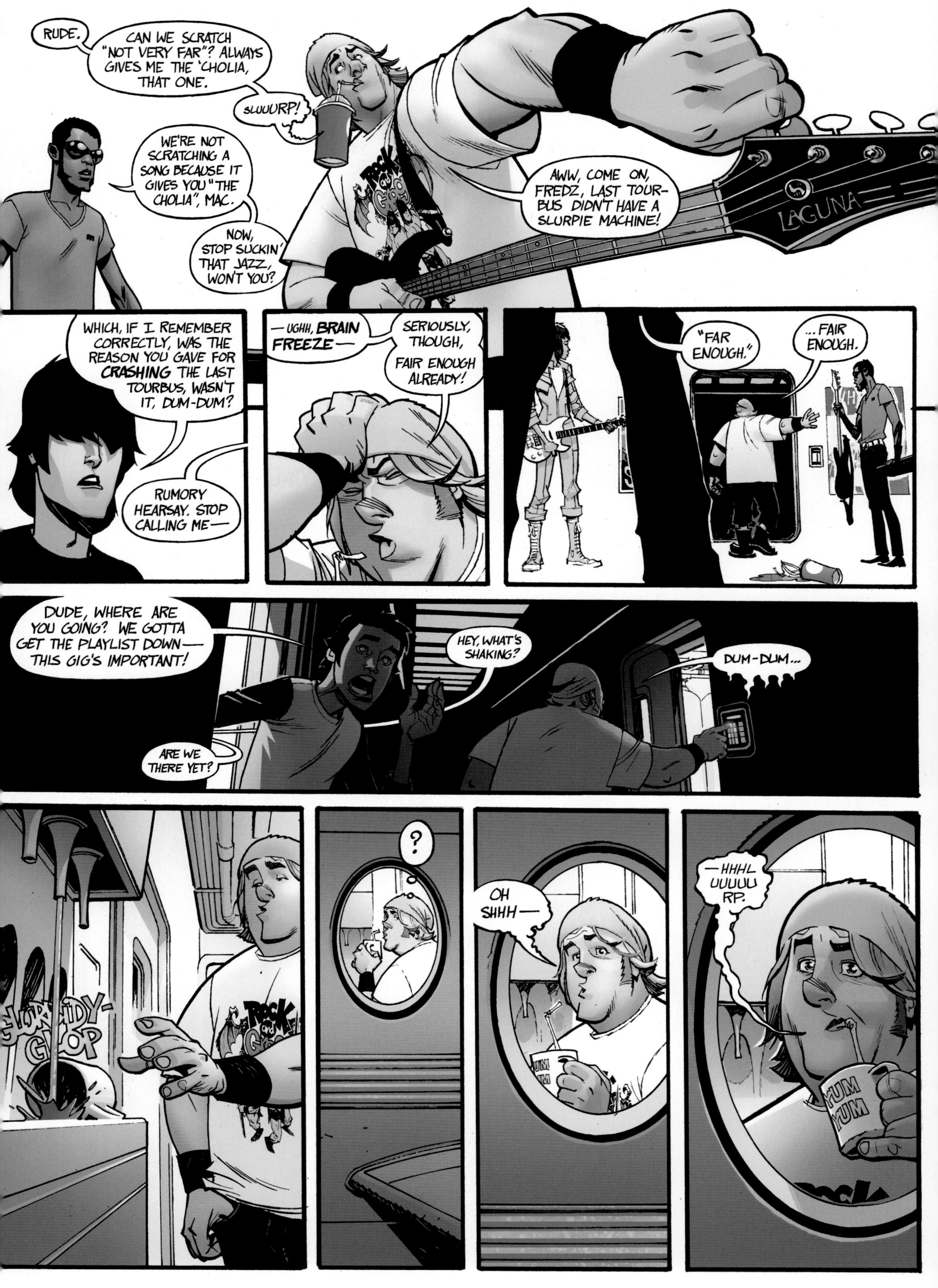
RUDE.
CAN WE SCRATCH "NOT VERY FAR"? ALWAYS GIVES ME THE 'CHOLIA, THAT ONE.
SLUUURP!
WE'RE NOT SCRATCHING A SONG BECAUSE IT GIVES YOU "THE CHOLIA", MAC.
NOW, STOP SUCKIN' THAT JAZZ, WON'T YOU?
AWW, COME ON, FREDZ, LAST TOUR-BUS DIDN'T HAVE A SLURPIE MACHINE!
LAGUNA
WHICH, IF I REMEMBER CORRECTLY, WAS THE REASON YOU GAVE FOR CRASHING THE LAST TOURBUS, WASN'T IT, DUM-DUM?
RUMORY HEARSAY. STOP CALLING ME—
—UGHH, BRAIN FREEZE—
SERIOUSLY, THOUGH,
FAIR ENOUGH ALREADY!
"FAR ENOUGH."
...FAIR ENOUGH.
DUDE, WHERE ARE YOU GOING? WE GOTTA GET THE PLAYLIST DOWN— THIS GIG'S IMPORTANT!
HEY, WHAT'S SHAKING?
ARE WE THERE YET?
DUM-DUM...
GLURRIDY-GLOP
?
OH SHHH—
YUM YUM
—HHHL UUUUU RP.
YUM YUM

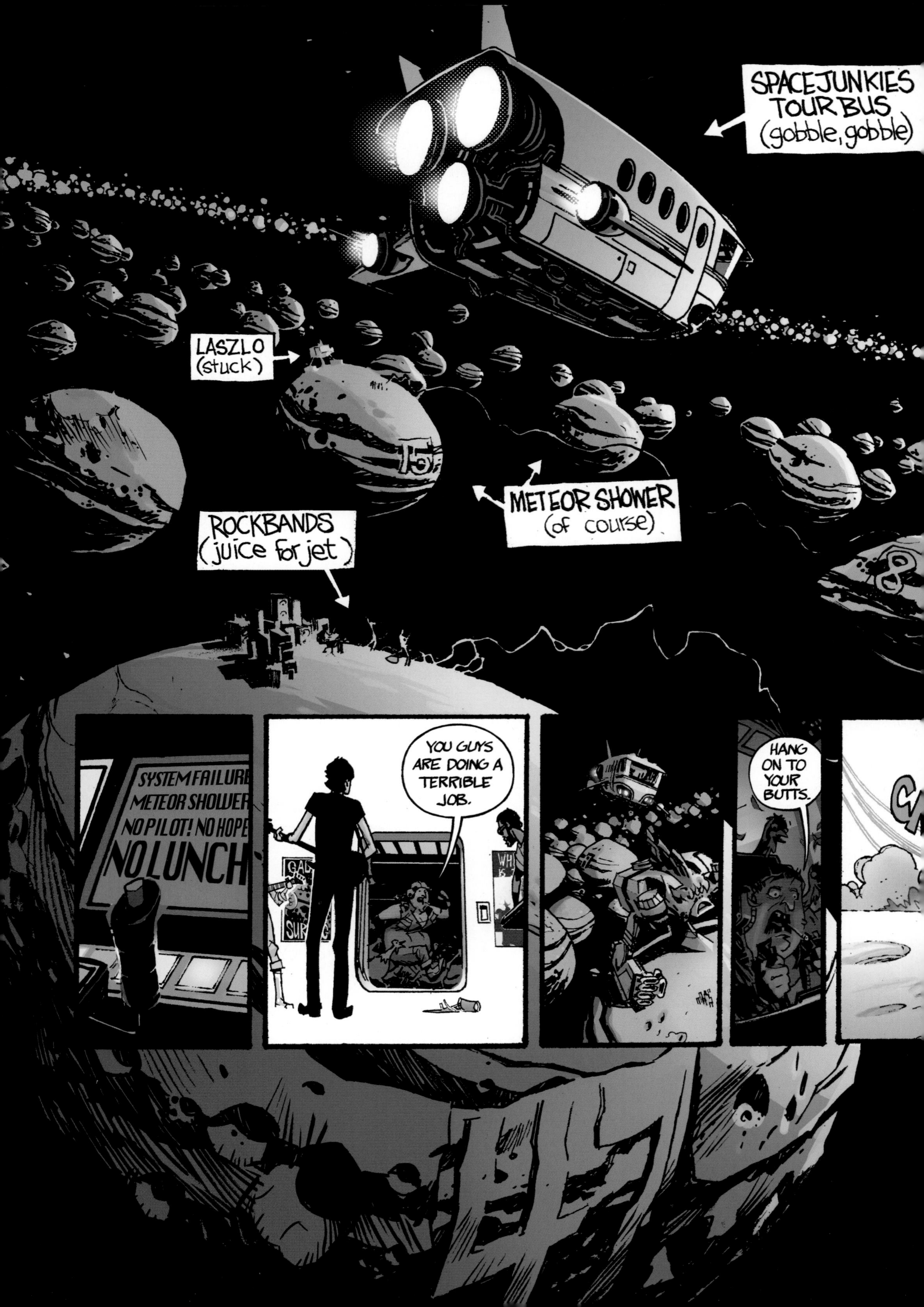

SPACEJUNKIES TOUR BUS (gobble, gobble)
LASZLO (stuck)
METEOR SHOWER (of course)
ROCKBANDS (juice for jet)
SYSTEM FAILURE
METEOR SHOWER
NO PILOT! NO HOPE
NO LUNCH
YOU GUYS ARE DOING A TERRIBLE JOB.
HANG ON TO YOUR BUTTS.

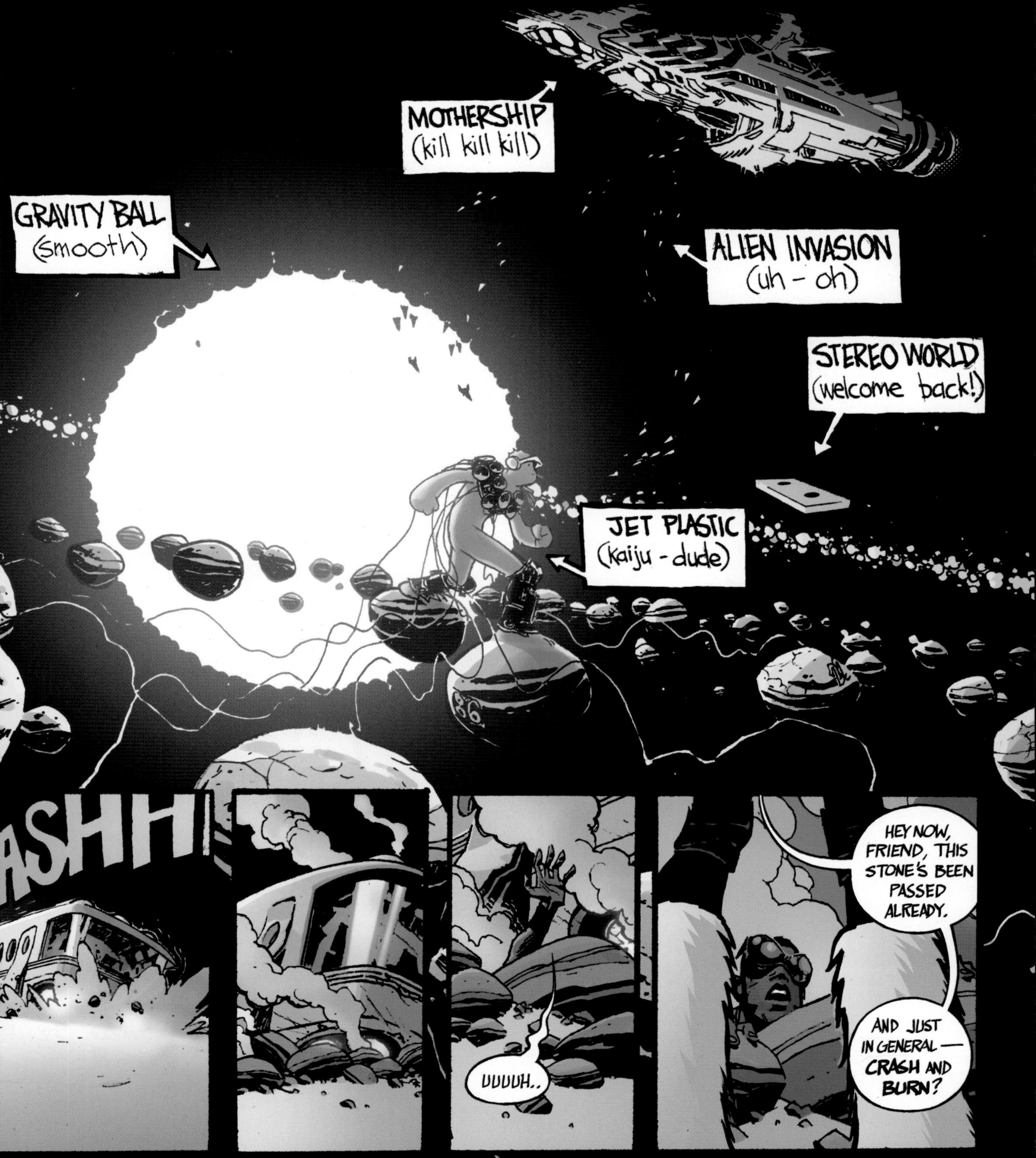
MOTHERSHIP
(kill kill kill)
GRAVITY BALL
(smooth)
ALIEN INVASION
(uh - oh)
STEREO WORLD
(welcome back!)
JET PLASTIC
(kaiju - dude)
ASHH
UUUUH..
HEY NOW, FRIEND, THIS STONE'S BEEN PASSED ALREADY.
AND JUST IN GENERAL — CRASH AND BURN?

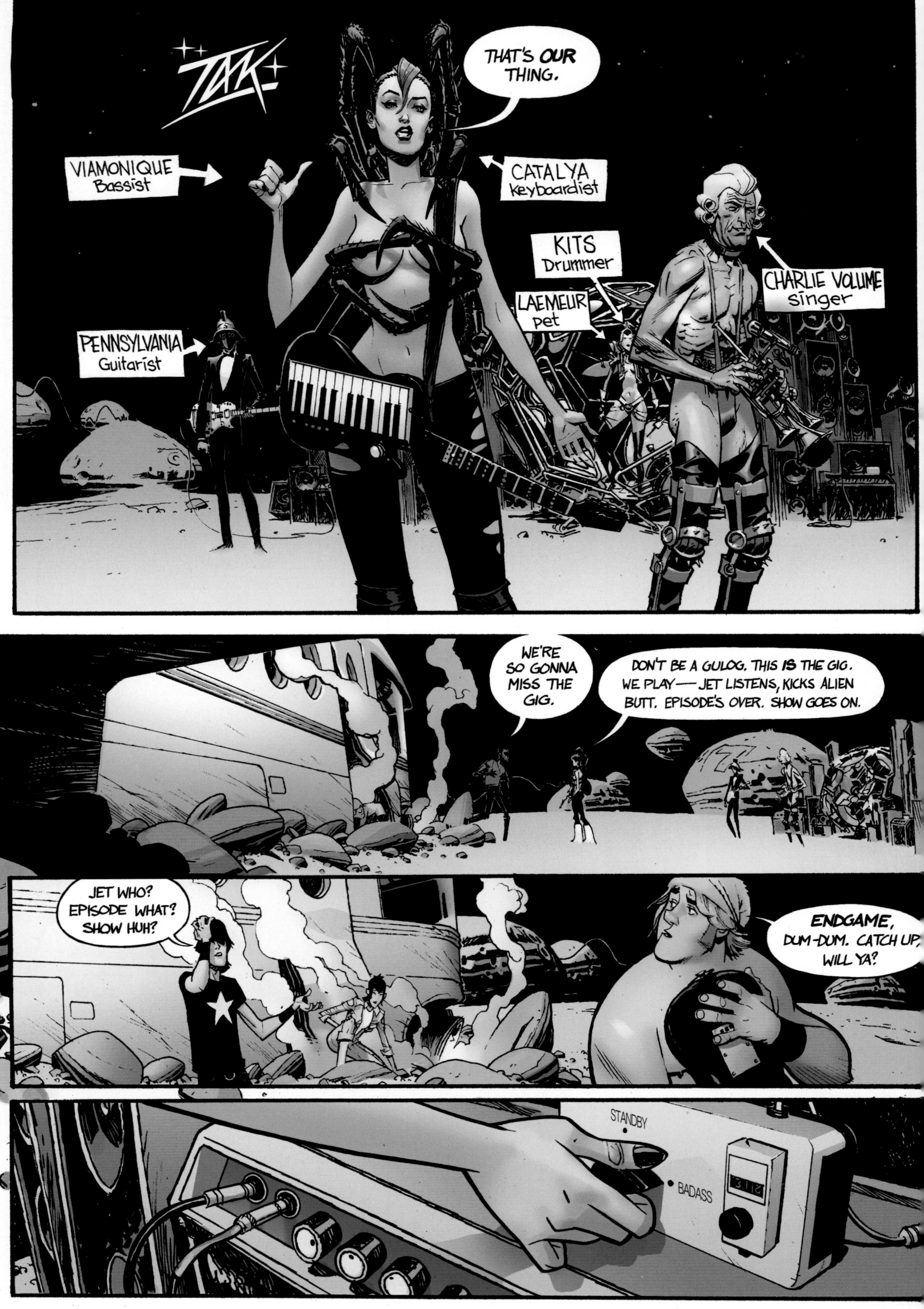
TAK
THAT'S OUR THING.
VIAMONIQUE
Bassist
CATALYA
Keyboardist
KITS
Drummer
LAEMEUR
pet
CHARLIE VOLUME
singer
PENNSYLVANIA
Guitarist
WE'RE SO GONNA MISS THE GIG.
DON'T BE A GULOG. THIS IS THE GIG. WE PLAY— JET LISTENS, KICKS ALIEN BUTT. EPISODE'S OVER. SHOW GOES ON.
JET WHO? EPISODE WHAT? SHOW HUH?
ENDGAME, DUM-DUM. CATCH UP, WILL YA?
STANDBY
BADASS

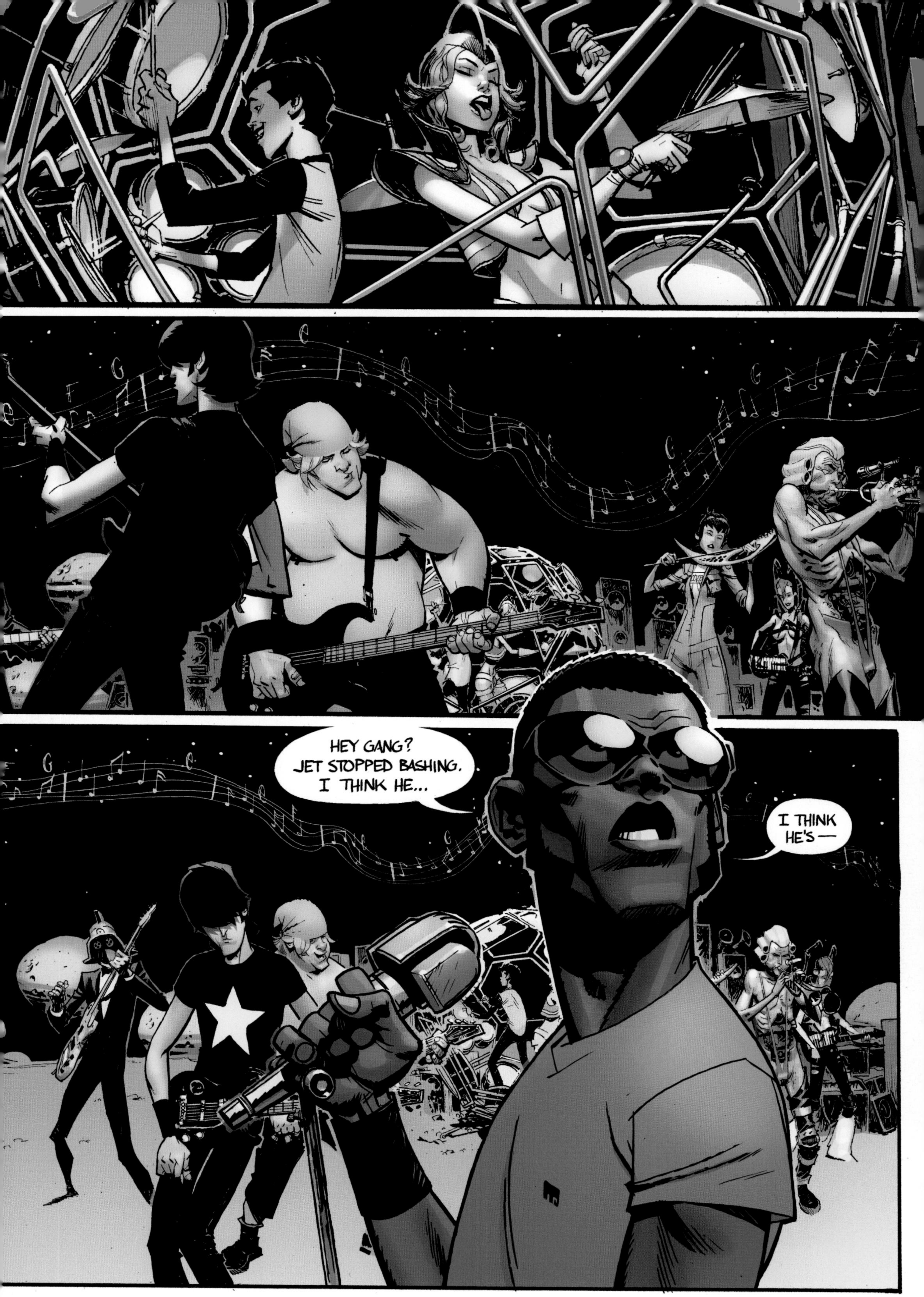
HEY GANG?
JET STOPPED BASHING.
I THINK HE...
I THINK HE'S—

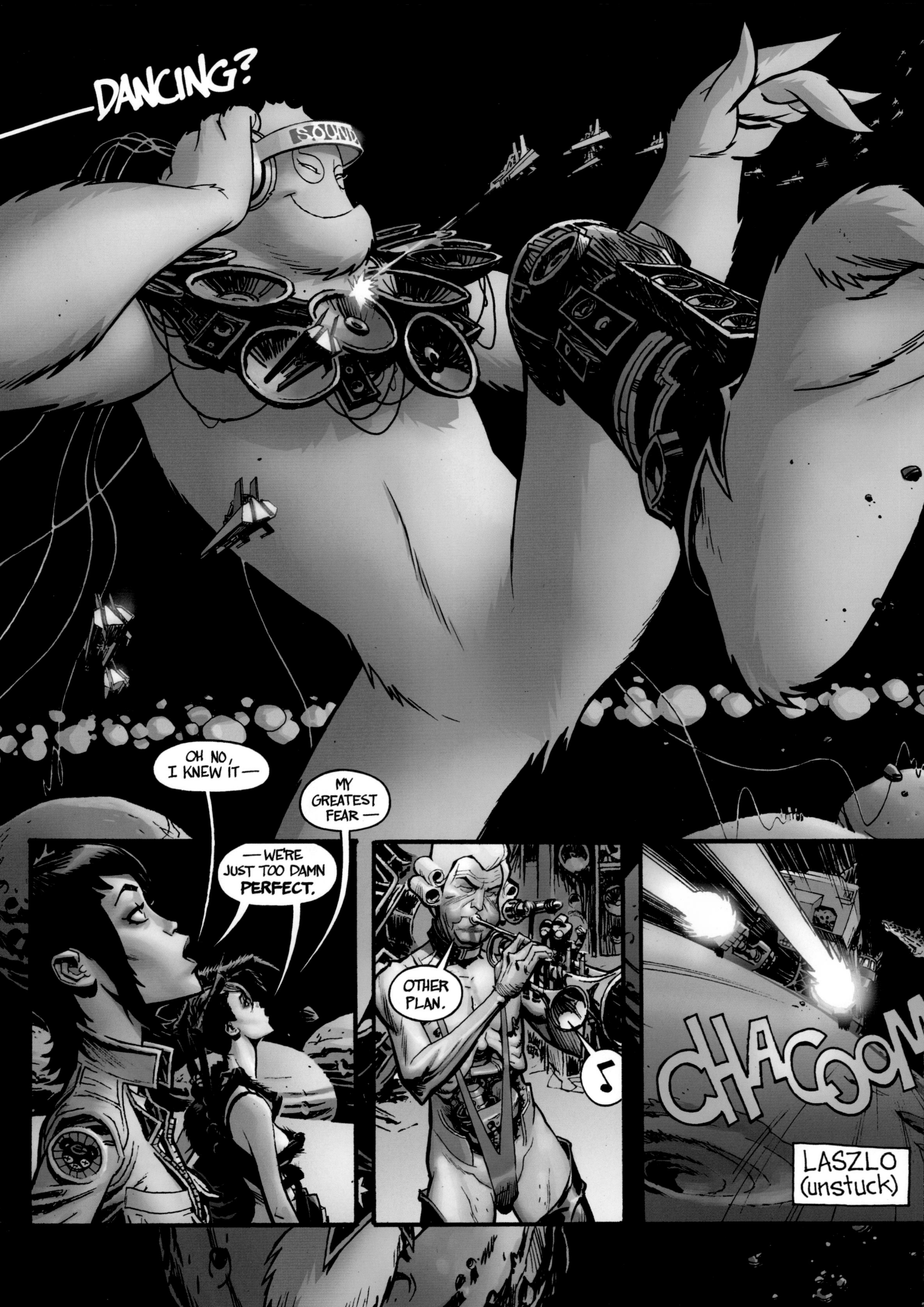
DANCING?
OH NO, I KNEW IT—
MY GREATEST FEAR—
—WE'RE JUST TOO DAMN PERFECT.
OTHER PLAN.
♪
CHACOOM
LASZLO (unstuck)

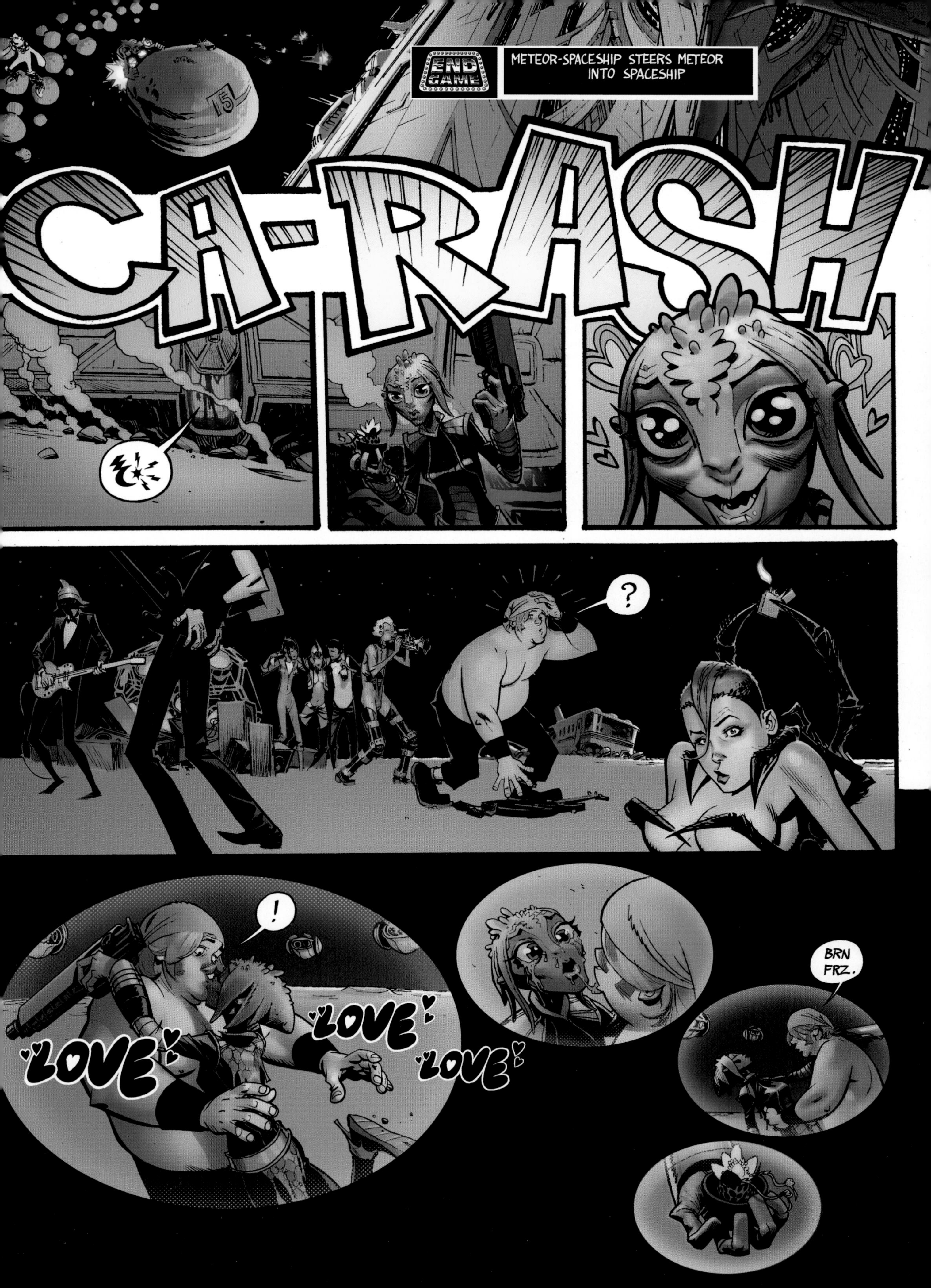
END GAME
METEOR-SPACESHIP STEERS METEOR INTO SPACESHIP
15
CA-RASH
?
!
LOVE
LOVE
LOVE
BRN FRZ.

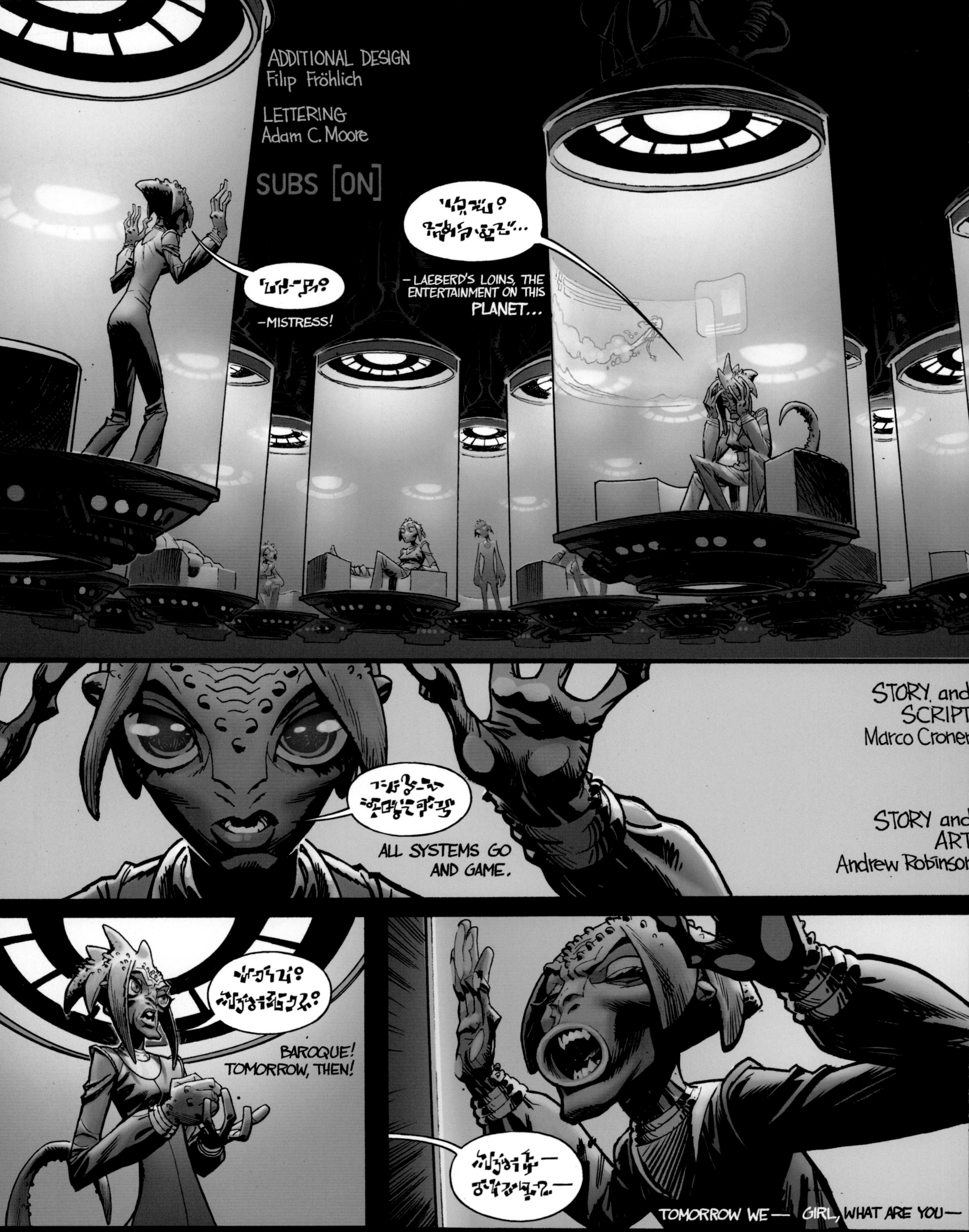
ADDITIONAL DESIGN
Filip Fröhlich
LETTERING
Adam C. Moore
SUBS [ON]
—MISTRESS!
—LAEBERD'S LOINS, THE ENTERTAINMENT ON THIS PLANET...
STORY and SCRIPT
Marco Croner
ALL SYSTEMS GO AND GAME.
STORY and ART
Andrew Robinson
BAROQUE! TOMORROW, THEN!
TOMORROW WE— GIRL, WHAT ARE YOU—

The ANCIENT KINKY
CREATED BY
Marco Croner
with Adam C. Moore

ENDGAME

THE SHOW THAT NEVER ENDS.

Spacejunkies
CREATED BY
Andrew Robinson

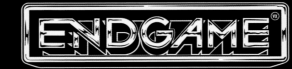

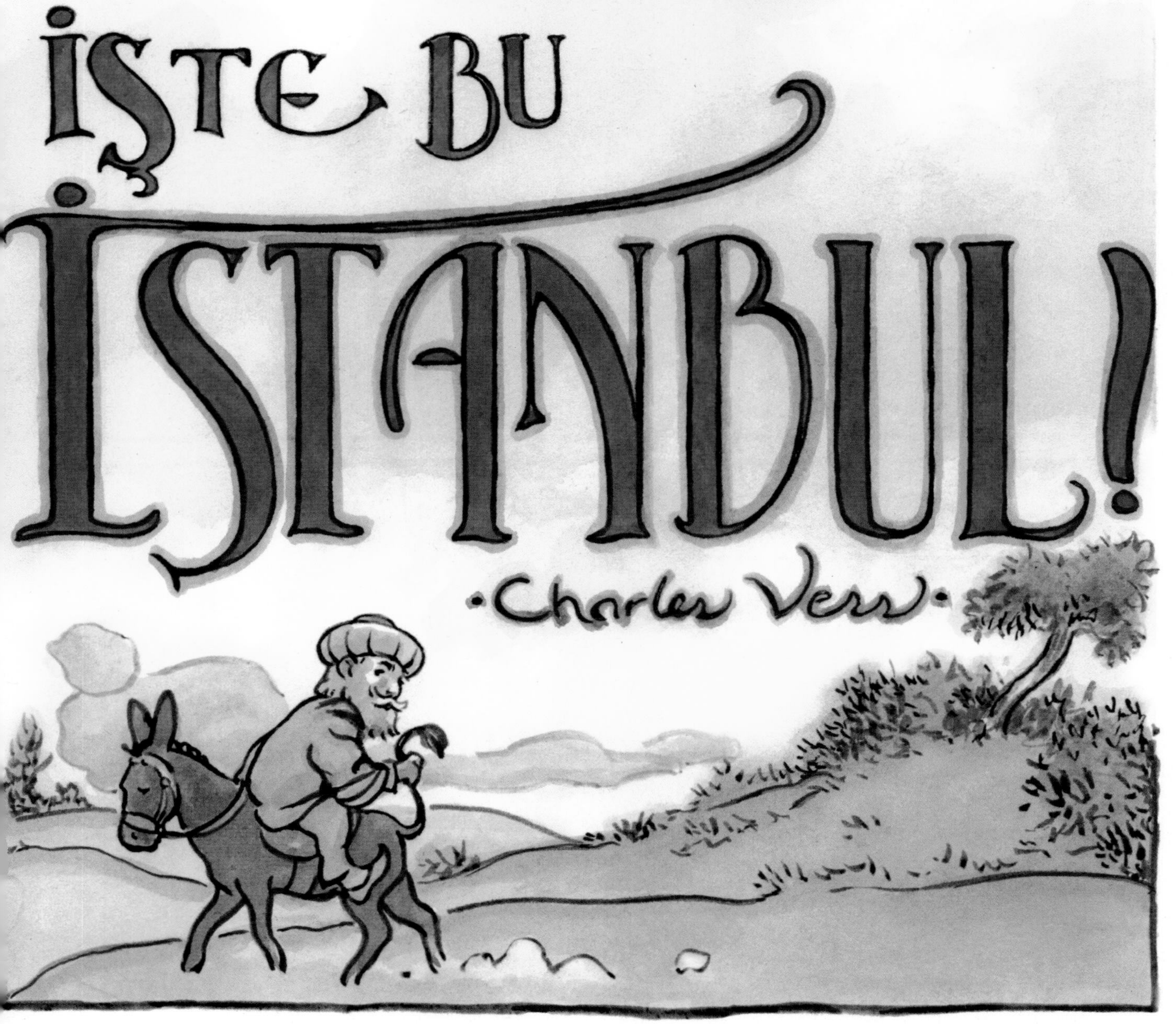
İŞTE BU
İSTANBUL!
·Charles Vess·

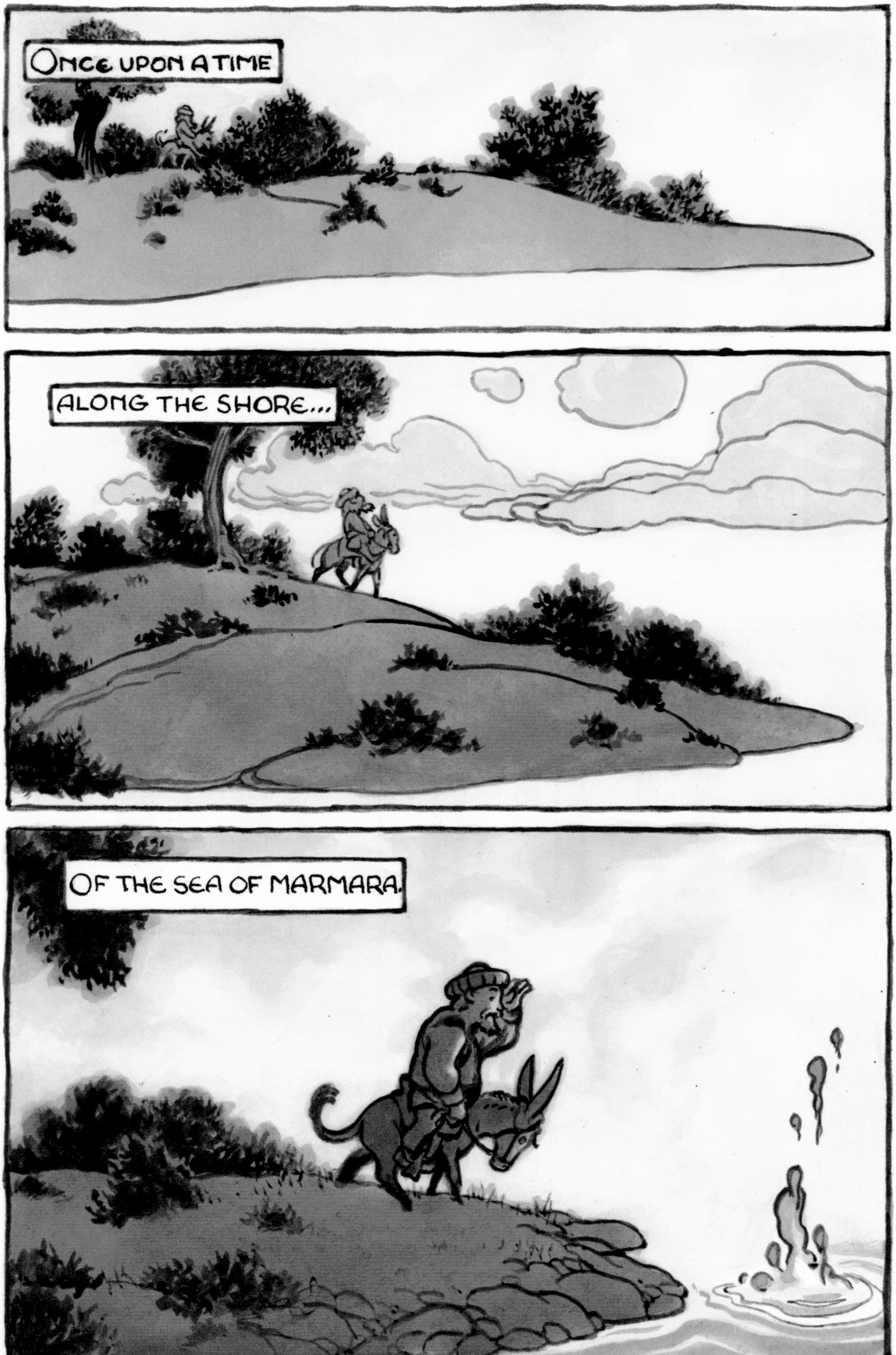
ONCE UPON A TIME
ALONG THE SHORE...
OF THE SEA OF MARMARA.

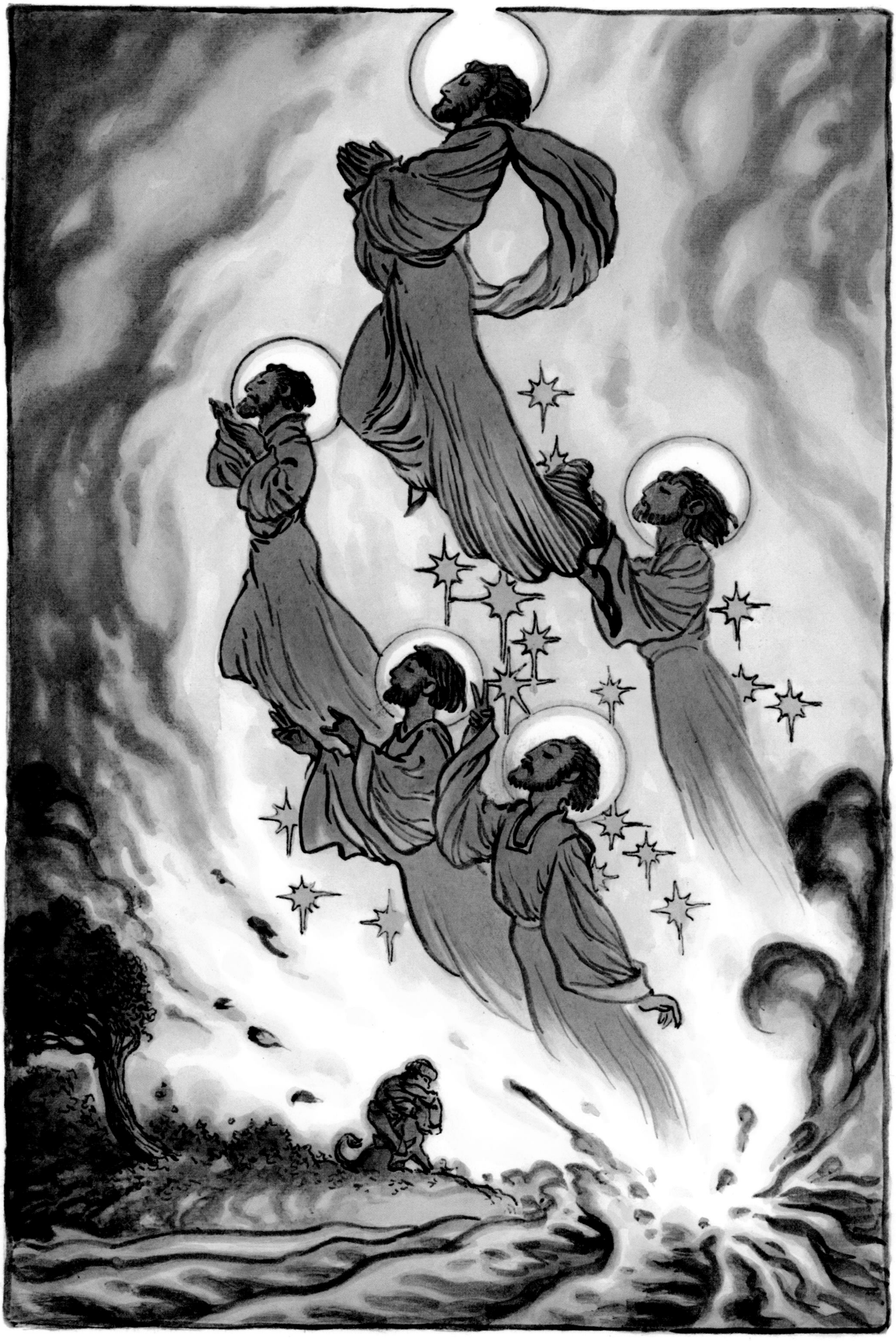

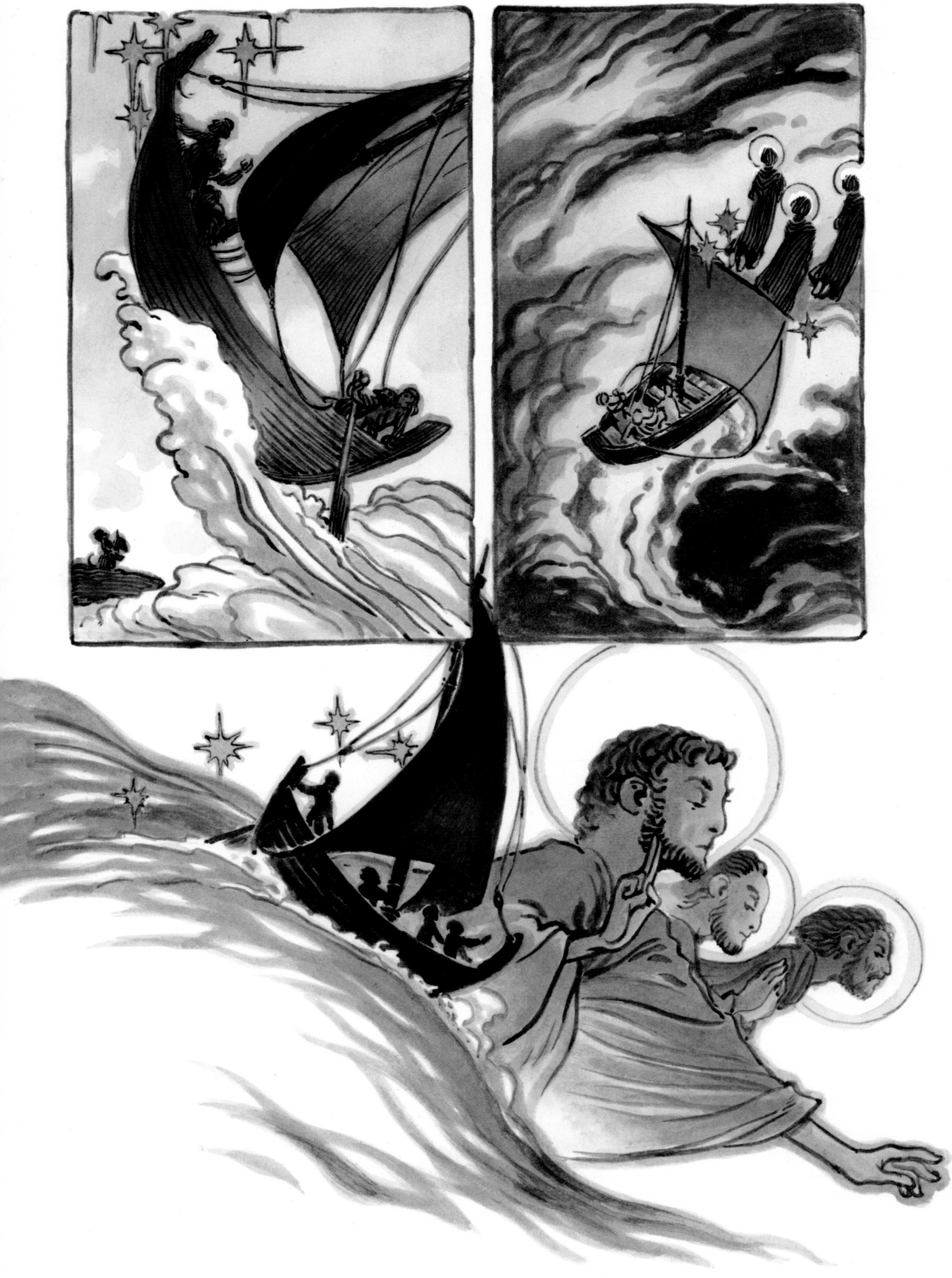

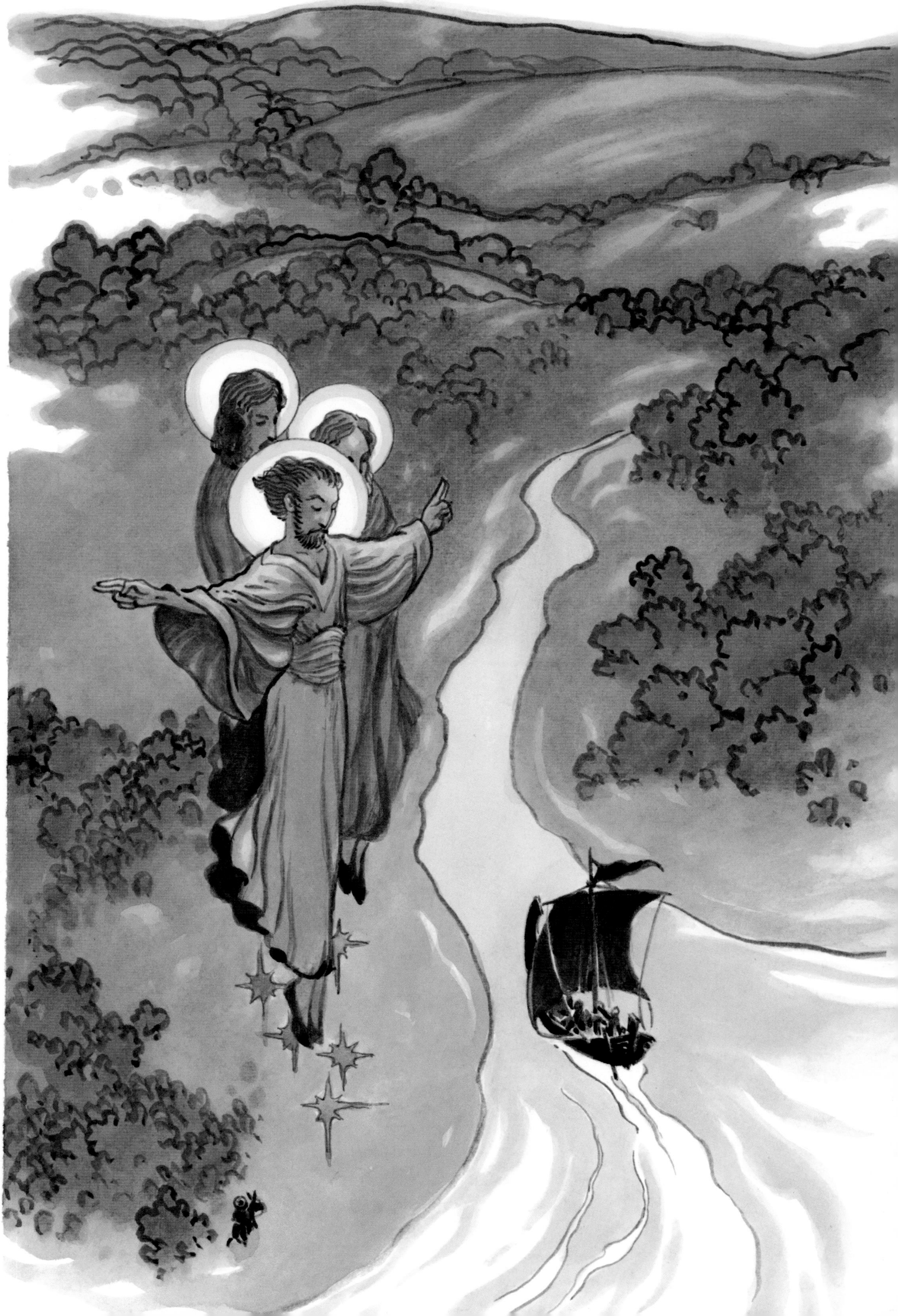

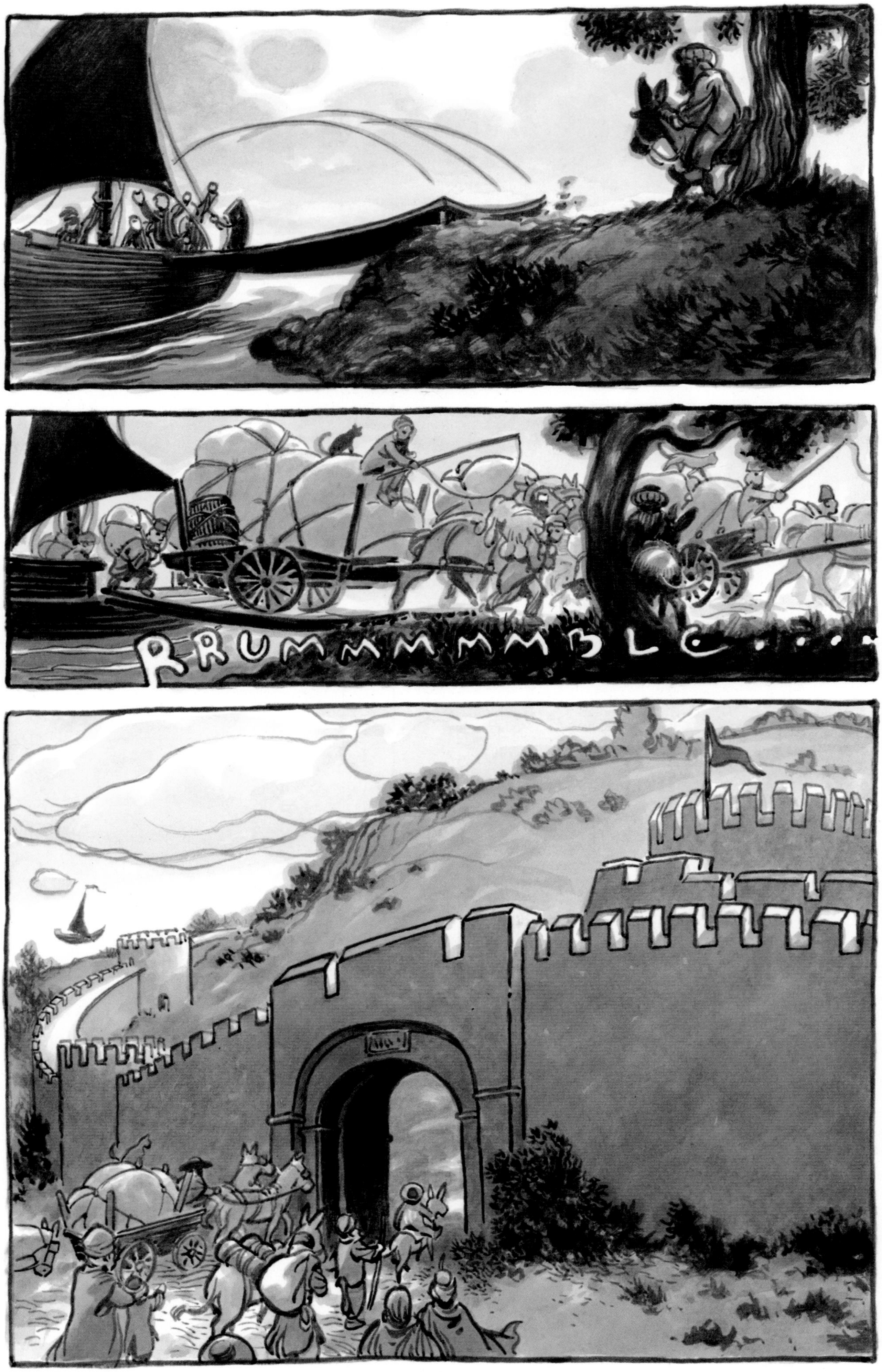
RRUMMMMMBLE....

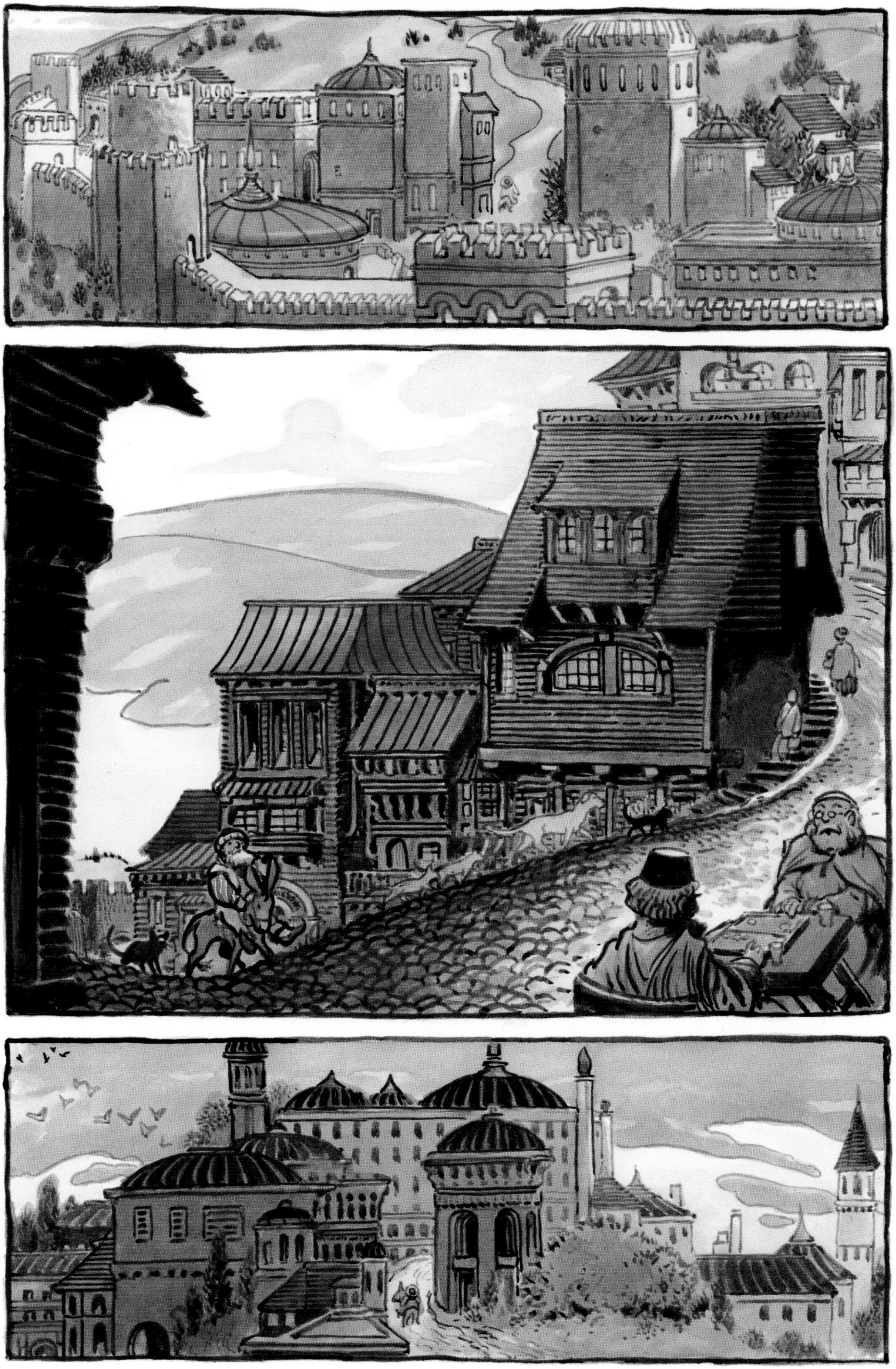

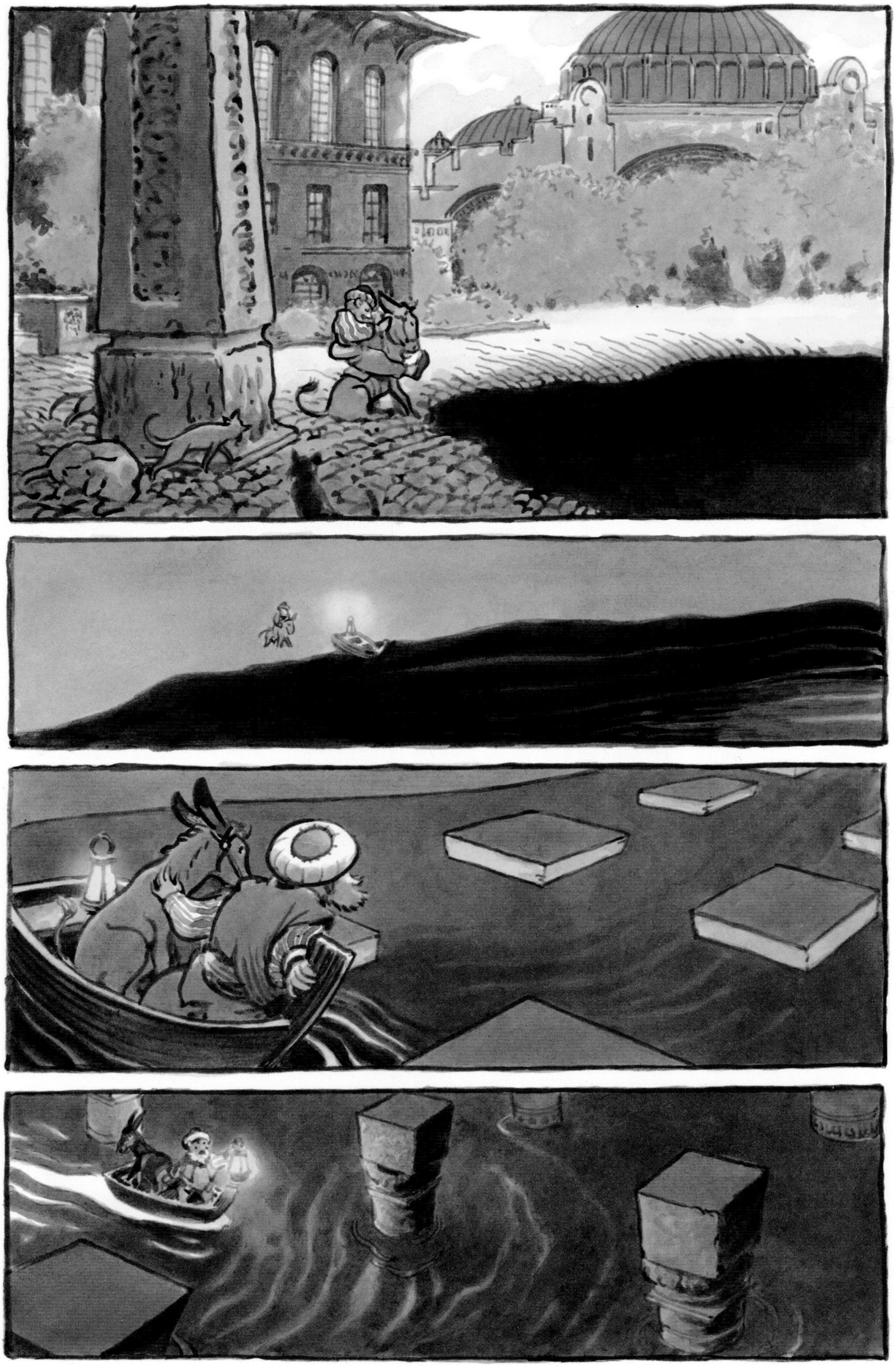

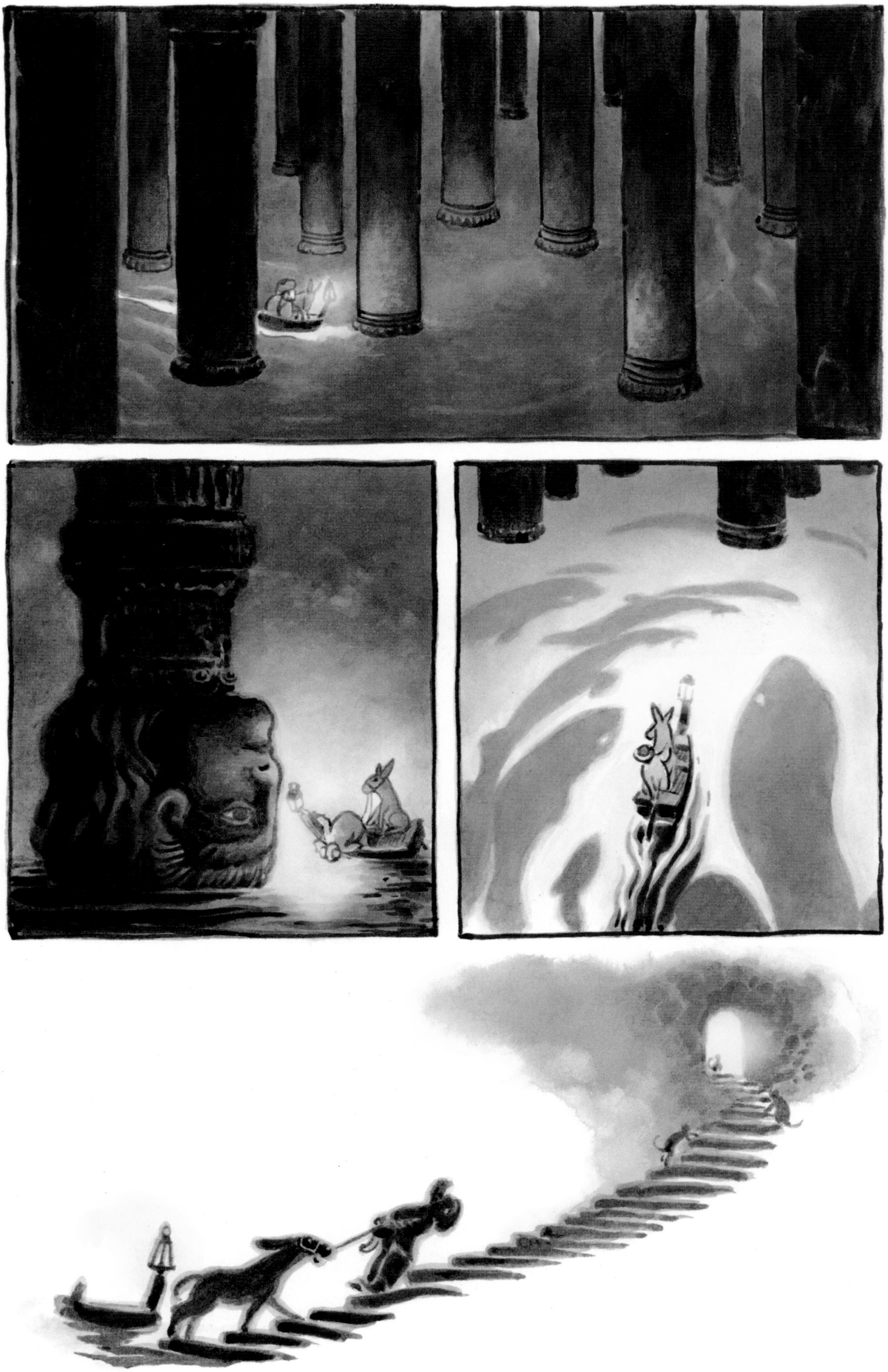

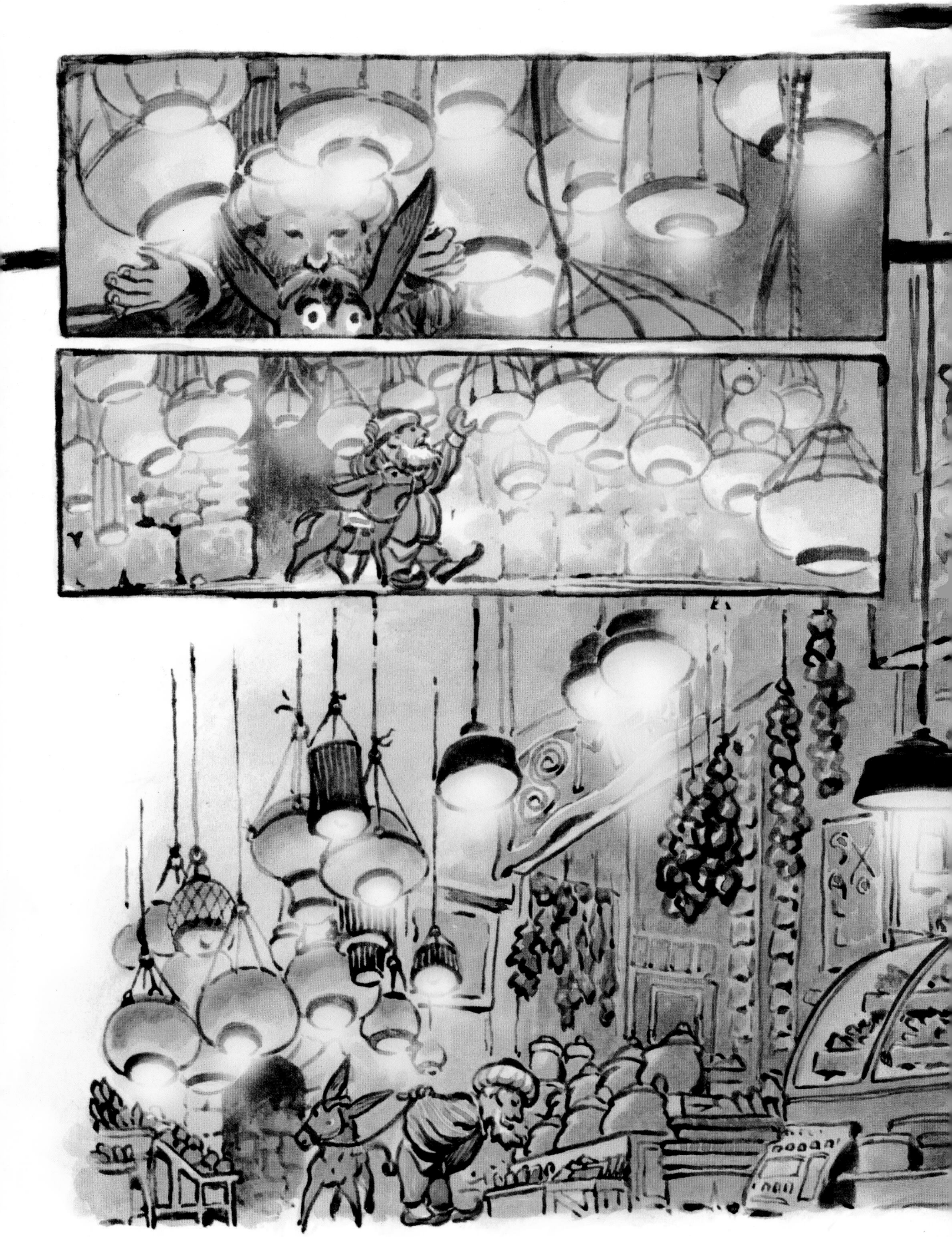

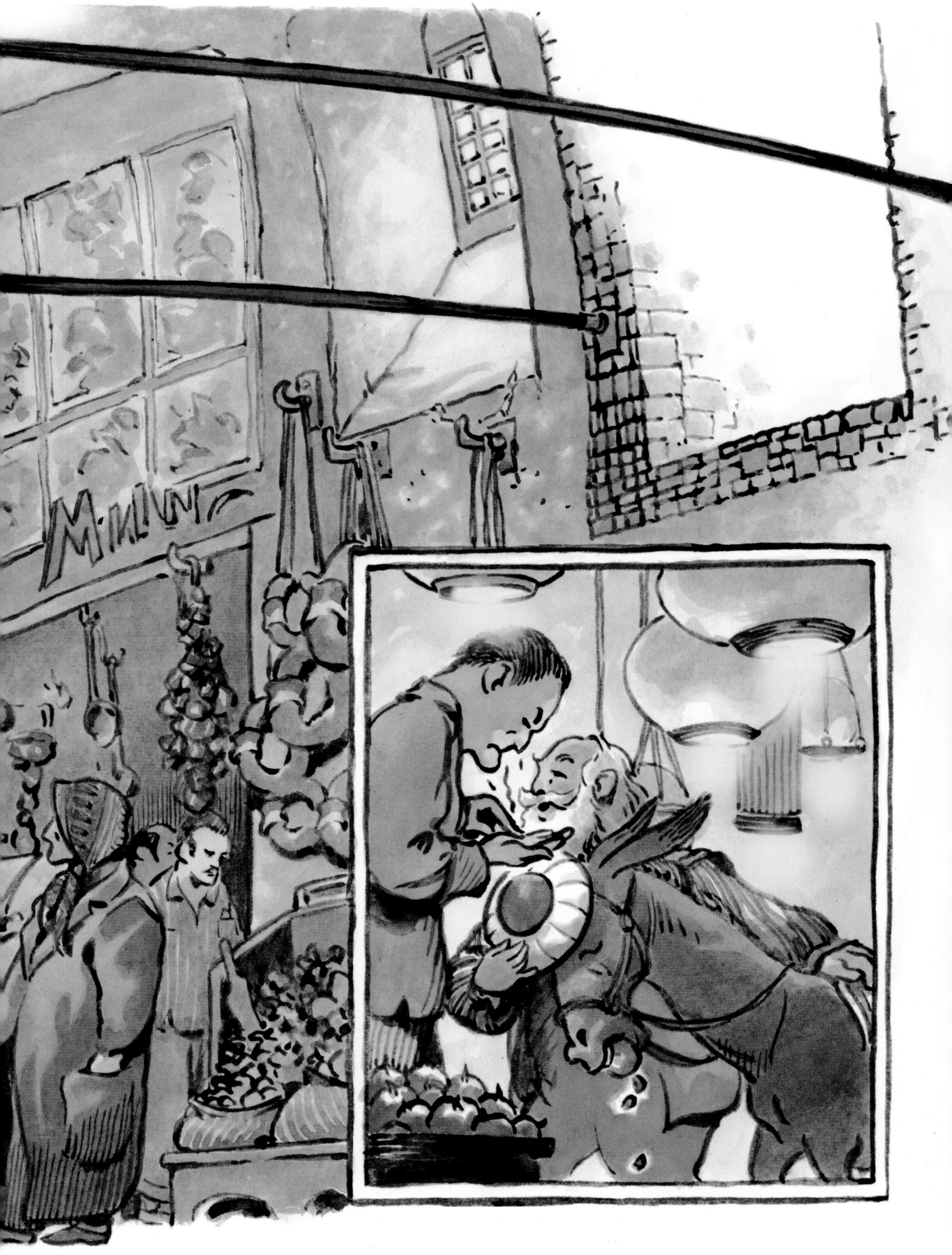

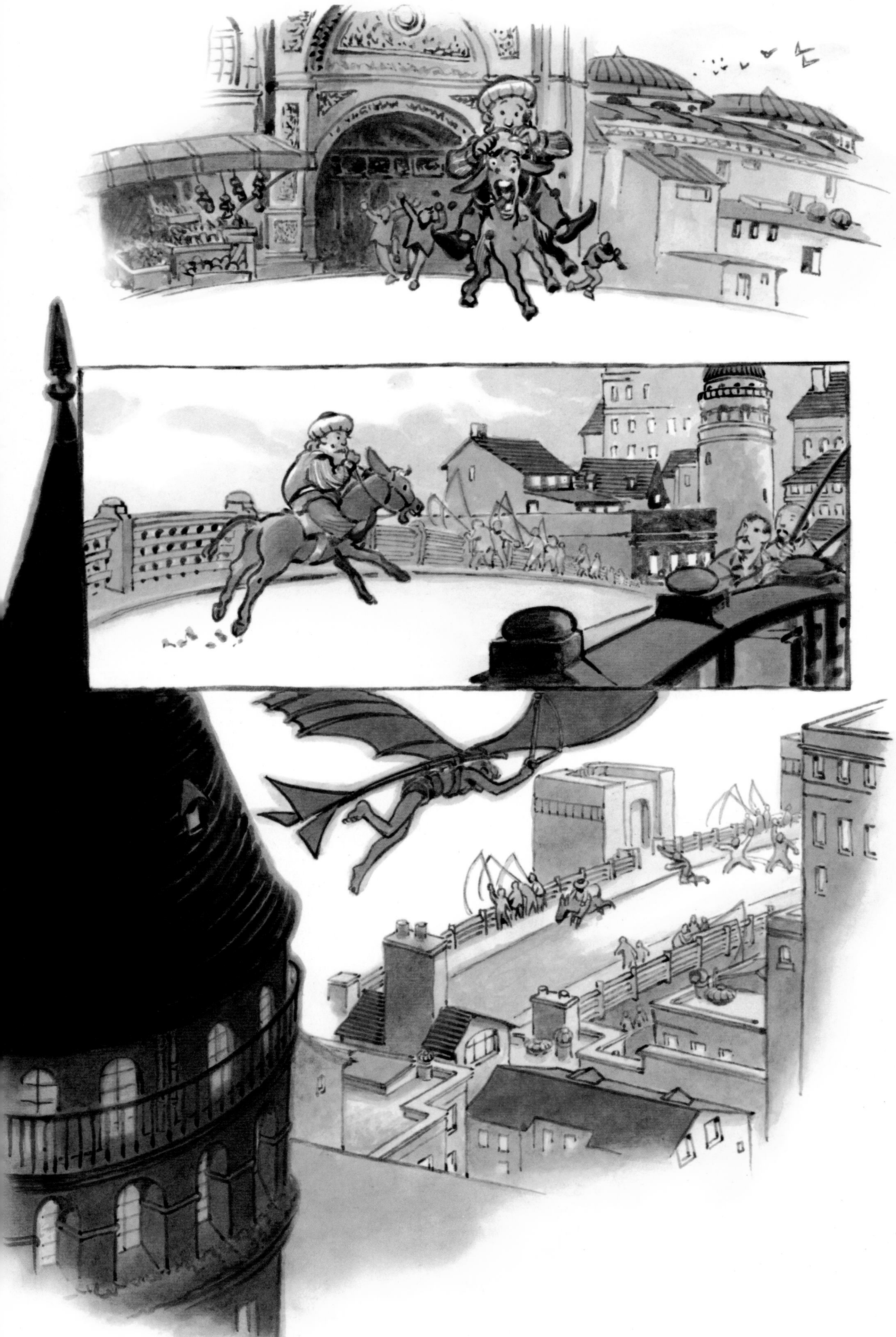

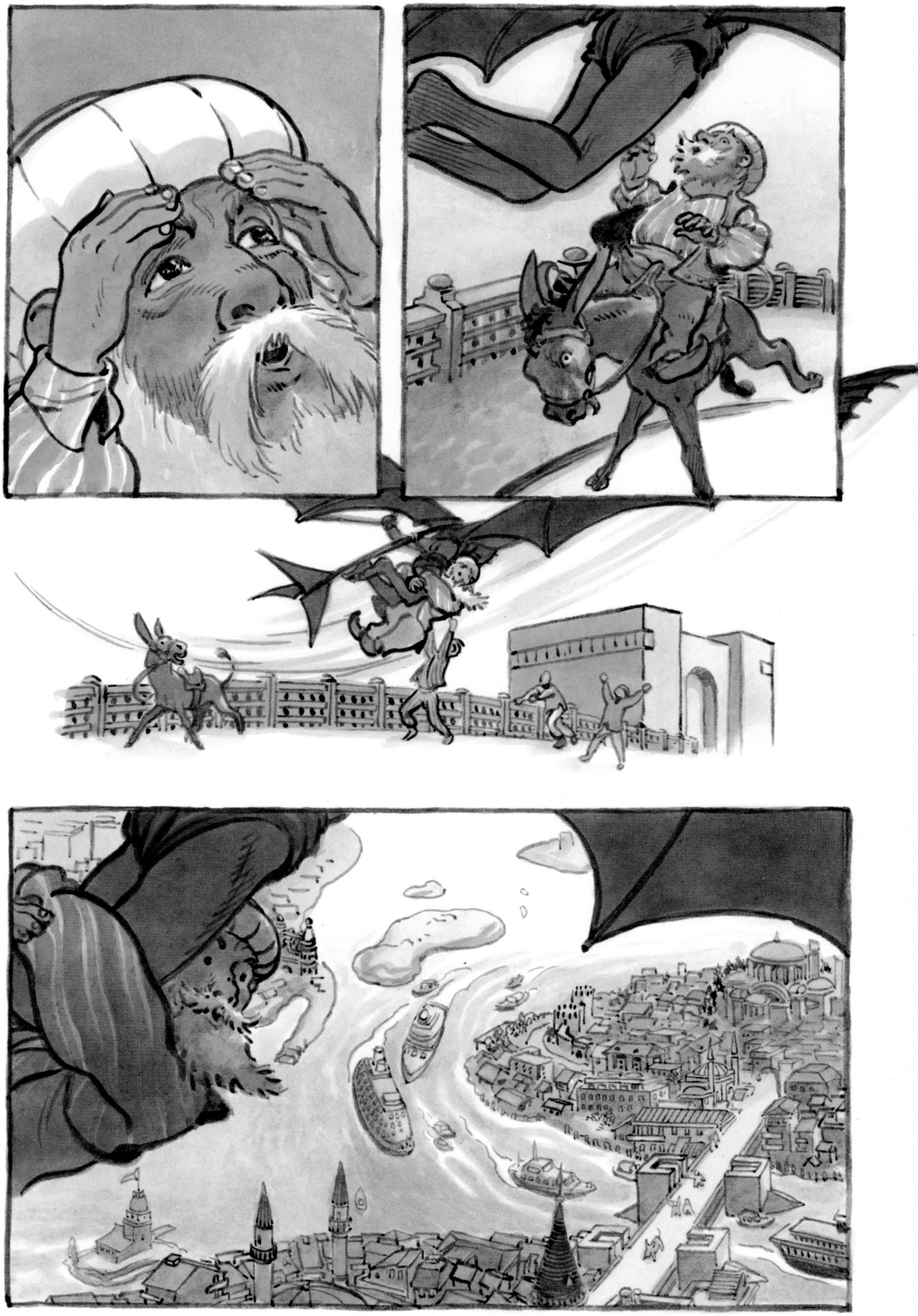

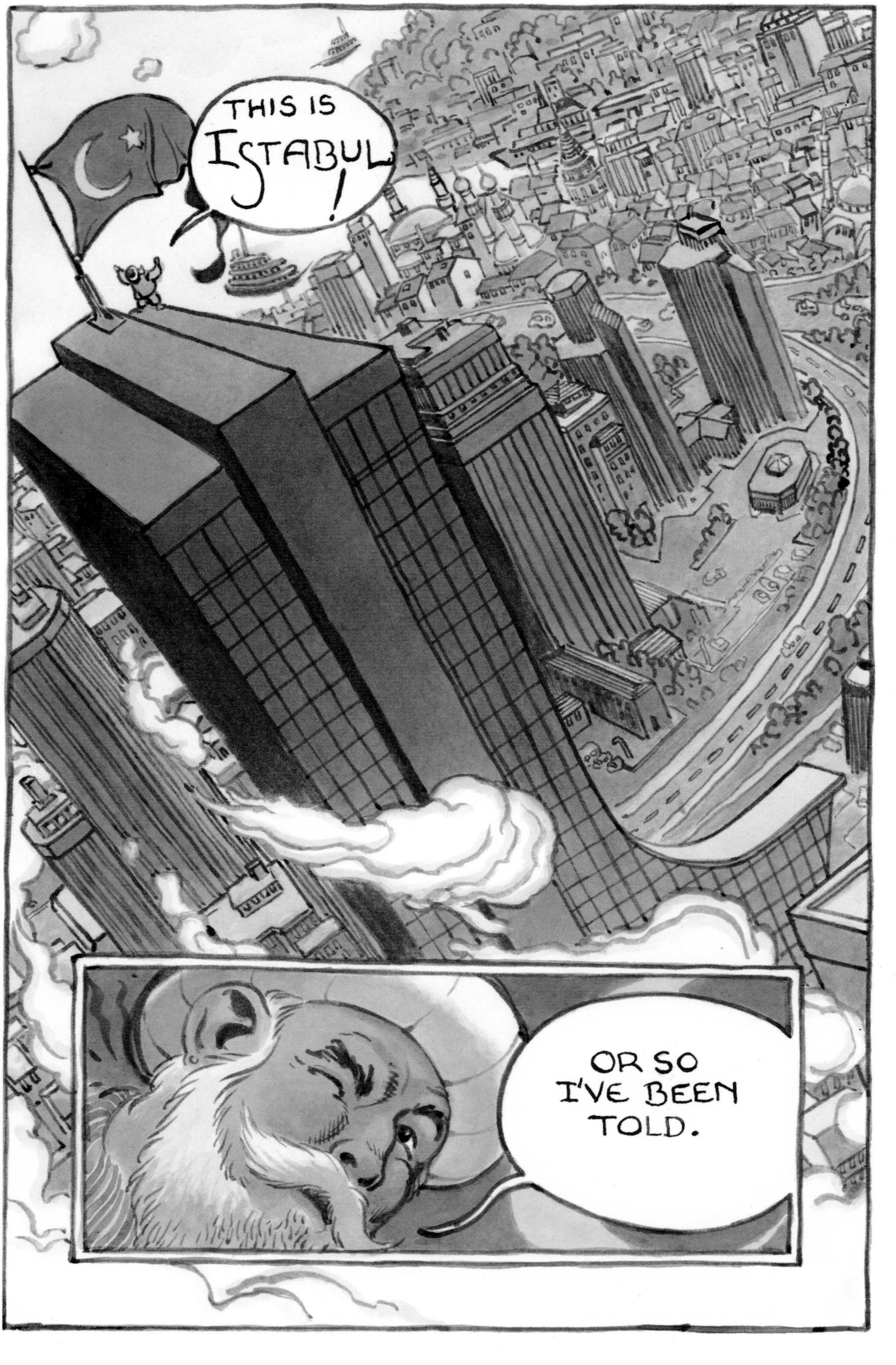
THIS IS ISTABUL!
OR SO I'VE BEEN TOLD.

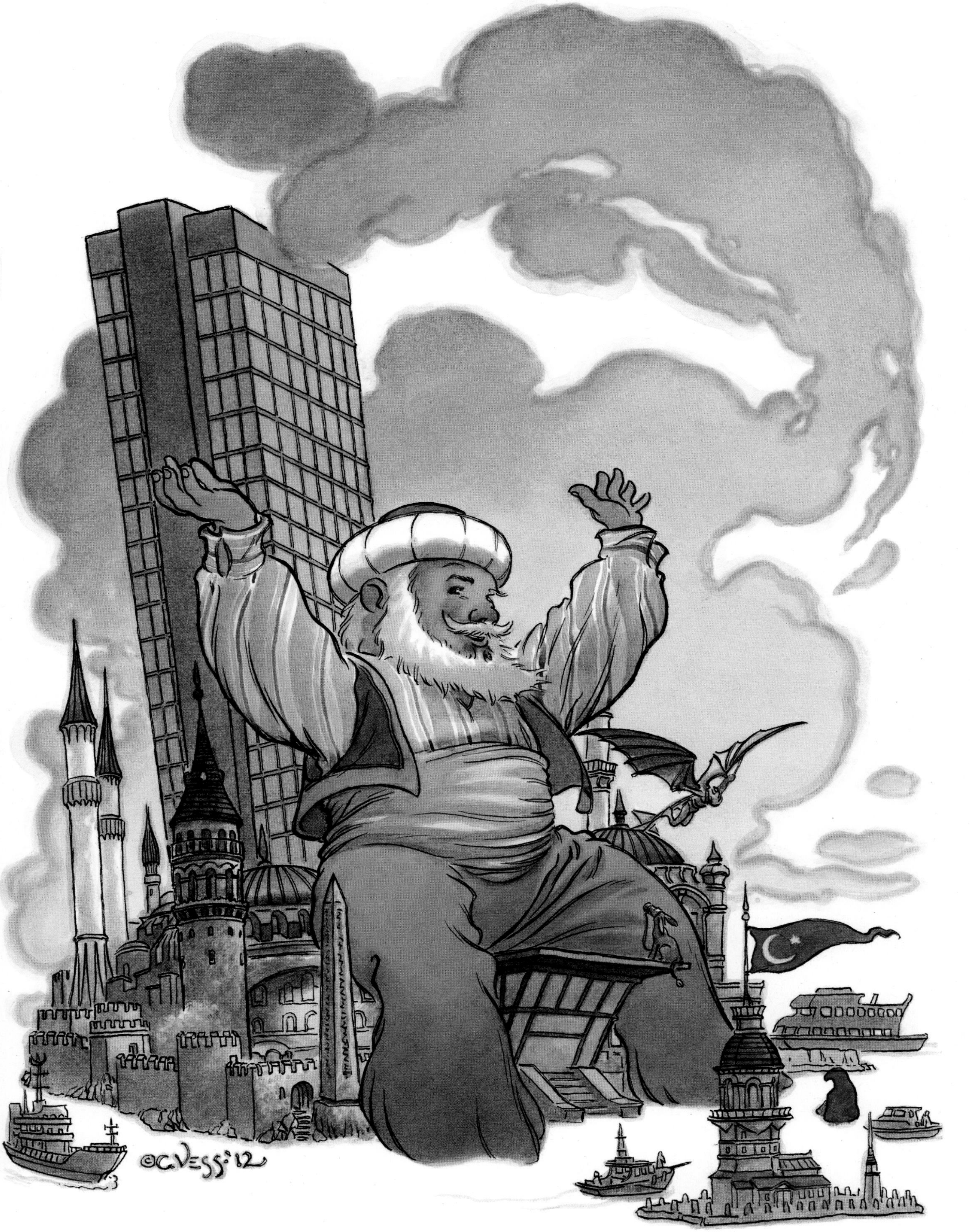
©C.VESS '12

BASED ON A TRUE STORY

WHO IS SHE HOLDING?

ME.

REALLY? GEEZ, YOU WERE CUTE ONCE.

JUST SAYIN'.

YEAH, WELL, THANKS AGAIN FOR HELPING ME SORT THROUGH THIS.

HELPING? THE DEAL IS, IT GOES THROUGH ME BEFORE IT GOES IN THE DUMPSTER-- WHICH, BY THE BY, JUDGING FROM ALL THIS STUFF--

--YOUR AUNT NEVER USED ONE.

I GET IT. THANKS AGAIN, AGIAN. I KNOW IT'S A PAIN IN THE ASS.

By Brian Azzarello, Toni Fejezula & Marshall Dillon

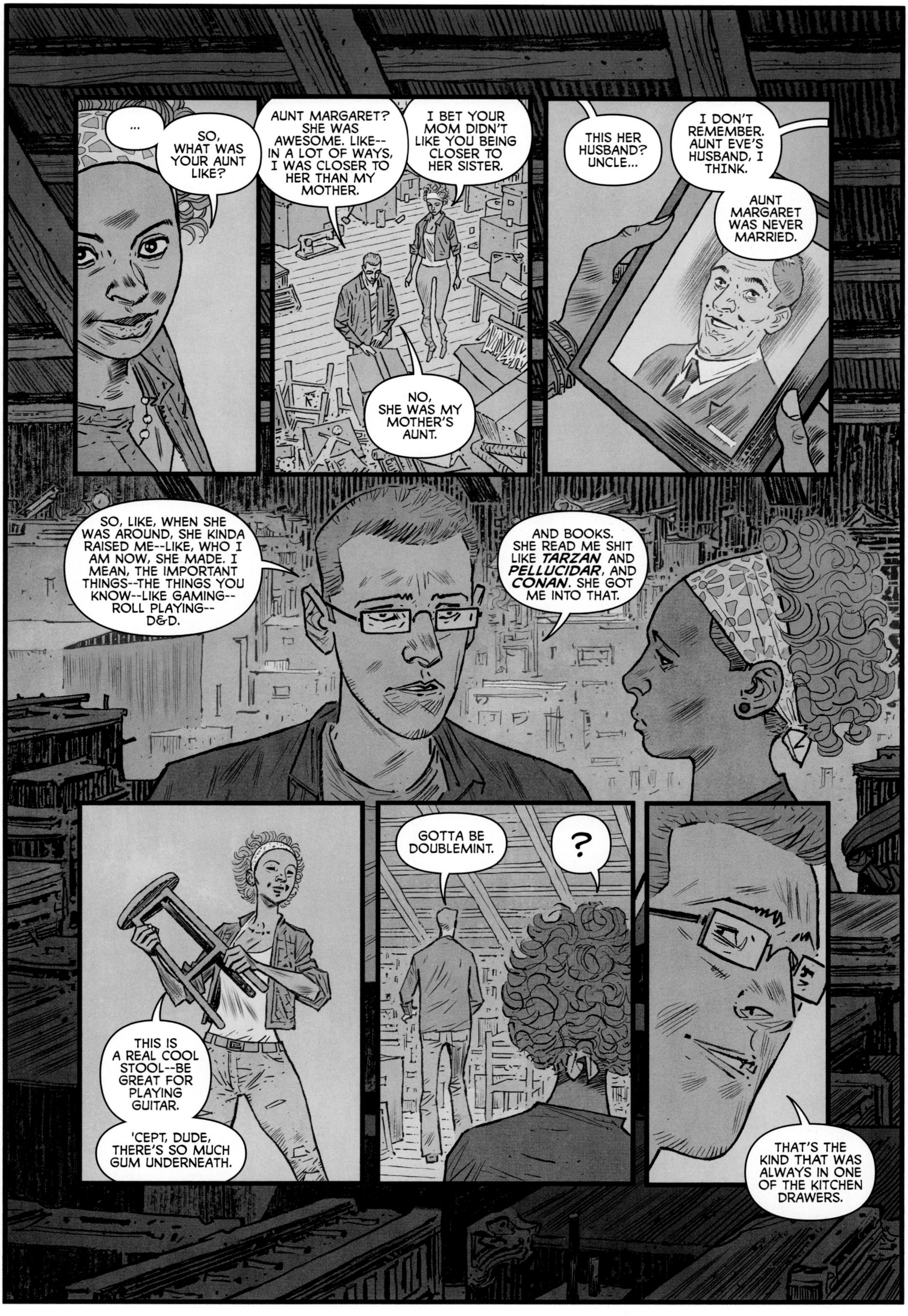
...
SO, WHAT WAS YOUR AUNT LIKE?
AUNT MARGARET? SHE WAS AWESOME. LIKE-- IN A LOT OF WAYS, I WAS CLOSER TO HER THAN MY MOTHER.
I BET YOUR MOM DIDN'T LIKE YOU BEING CLOSER TO HER SISTER.
NO, SHE WAS MY MOTHER'S AUNT.
THIS HER HUSBAND? UNCLE...
I DON'T REMEMBER. AUNT EVE'S HUSBAND, I THINK.
AUNT MARGARET WAS NEVER MARRIED.
SO, LIKE, WHEN SHE WAS AROUND, SHE KINDA RAISED ME--LIKE, WHO I AM NOW, SHE MADE. I MEAN, THE IMPORTANT THINGS--THE THINGS YOU KNOW--LIKE GAMING--ROLL PLAYING--D&D.
AND BOOKS. SHE READ ME SHIT LIKE TARZAN AND PELLUCIDAR, AND CONAN. SHE GOT ME INTO THAT.
THIS IS A REAL COOL STOOL--BE GREAT FOR PLAYING GUITAR.
'CEPT, DUDE, THERE'S SO MUCH GUM UNDERNEATH.
GOTTA BE DOUBLEMINT.
?
THAT'S THE KIND THAT WAS ALWAYS IN ONE OF THE KITCHEN DRAWERS.

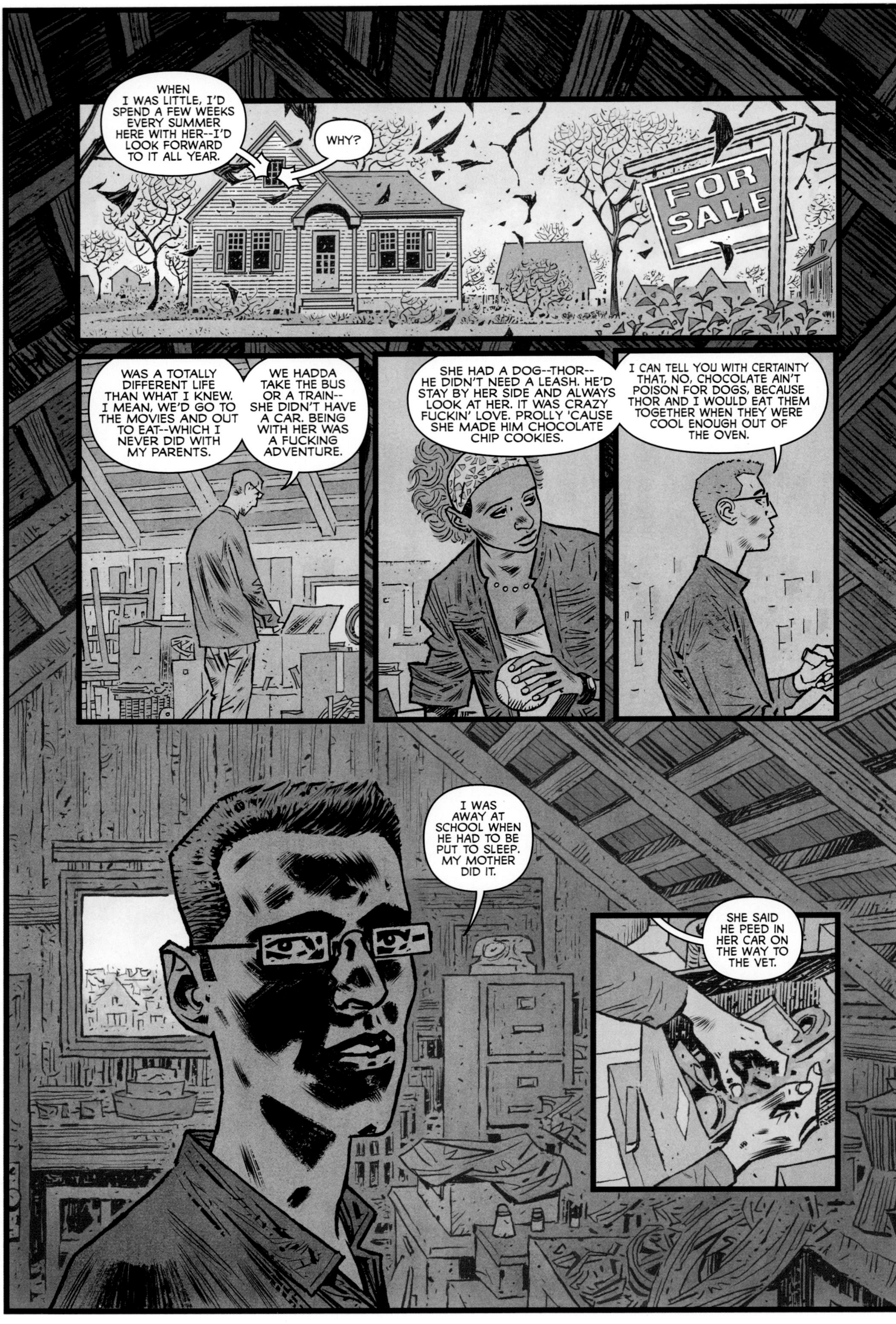
WHEN I WAS LITTLE, I'D SPEND A FEW WEEKS EVERY SUMMER HERE WITH HER--I'D LOOK FORWARD TO IT ALL YEAR.
WHY?
FOR SALE
WAS A TOTALLY DIFFERENT LIFE THAN WHAT I KNEW. I MEAN, WE'D GO TO THE MOVIES AND OUT TO EAT--WHICH I NEVER DID WITH MY PARENTS.
WE HADDA TAKE THE BUS OR A TRAIN--SHE DIDN'T HAVE A CAR. BEING WITH HER WAS A FUCKING ADVENTURE.
SHE HAD A DOG--THOR--HE DIDN'T NEED A LEASH. HE'D STAY BY HER SIDE AND ALWAYS LOOK AT HER. IT WAS CRAZY FUCKIN' LOVE. PROLLY 'CAUSE SHE MADE HIM CHOCOLATE CHIP COOKIES.
I CAN TELL YOU WITH CERTAINTY THAT, NO, CHOCOLATE AIN'T POISON FOR DOGS, BECAUSE THOR AND I WOULD EAT THEM TOGETHER WHEN THEY WERE COOL ENOUGH OUT OF THE OVEN.
I WAS AWAY AT SCHOOL WHEN HE HAD TO BE PUT TO SLEEP. MY MOTHER DID IT.
SHE SAID HE PEED IN HER CAR ON THE WAY TO THE VET.

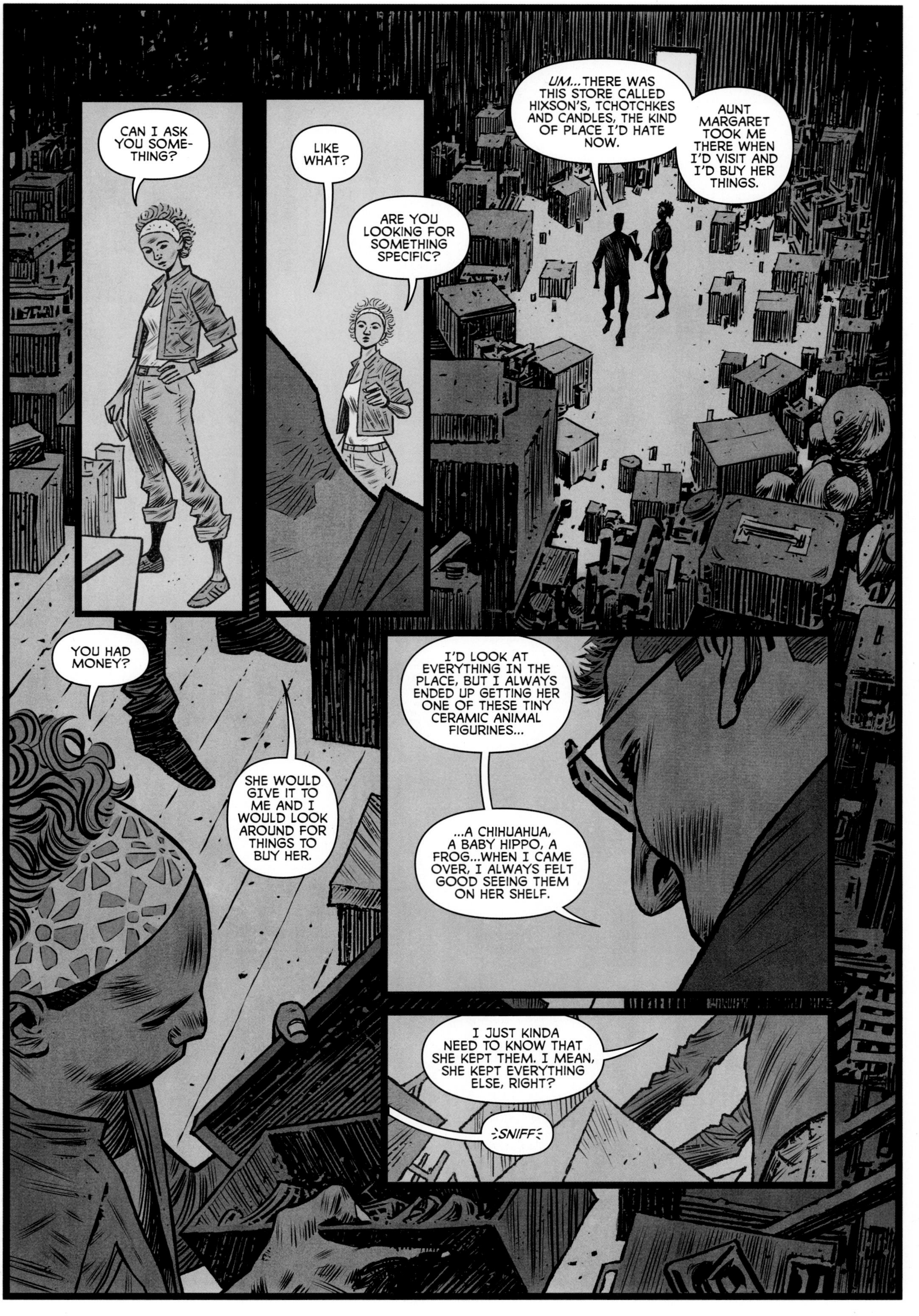
CAN I ASK YOU SOME-THING?
LIKE WHAT?
ARE YOU LOOKING FOR SOMETHING SPECIFIC?
UM... THERE WAS THIS STORE CALLED HIXSON'S, TCHOTCHKES AND CANDLES, THE KIND OF PLACE I'D HATE NOW.
AUNT MARGARET TOOK ME THERE WHEN I'D VISIT AND I'D BUY HER THINGS.
YOU HAD MONEY?
SHE WOULD GIVE IT TO ME AND I WOULD LOOK AROUND FOR THINGS TO BUY HER.
I'D LOOK AT EVERYTHING IN THE PLACE, BUT I ALWAYS ENDED UP GETTING HER ONE OF THESE TINY CERAMIC ANIMAL FIGURINES...
...A CHIHUAHUA, A BABY HIPPO, A FROG...WHEN I CAME OVER, I ALWAYS FELT GOOD SEEING THEM ON HER SHELF.
I JUST KINDA NEED TO KNOW THAT SHE KEPT THEM. I MEAN, SHE KEPT EVERYTHING ELSE, RIGHT?
SNIFF

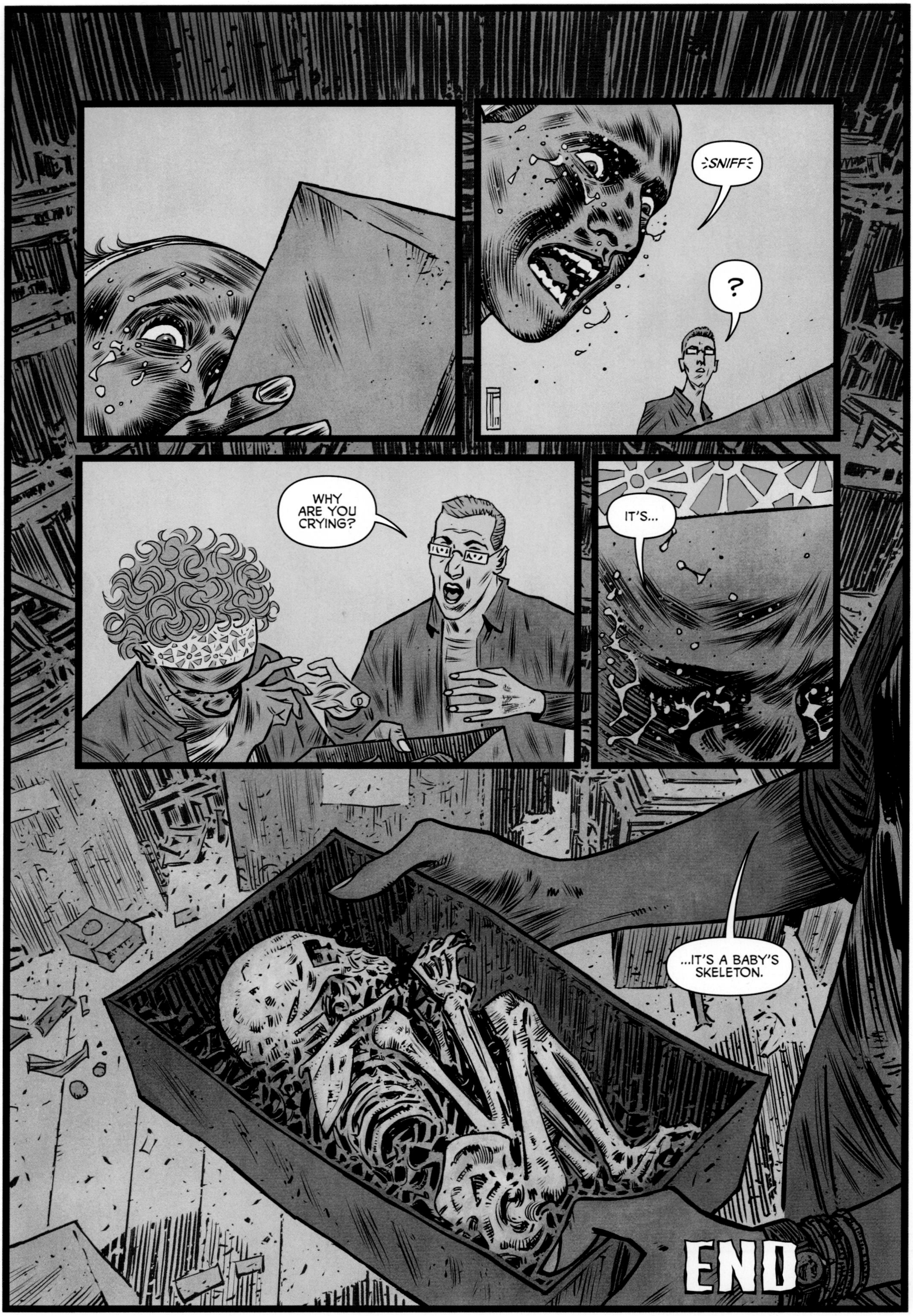
SNIFF
?
WHY ARE YOU CRYING?
IT'S...
...IT'S A BABY'S SKELETON.
END

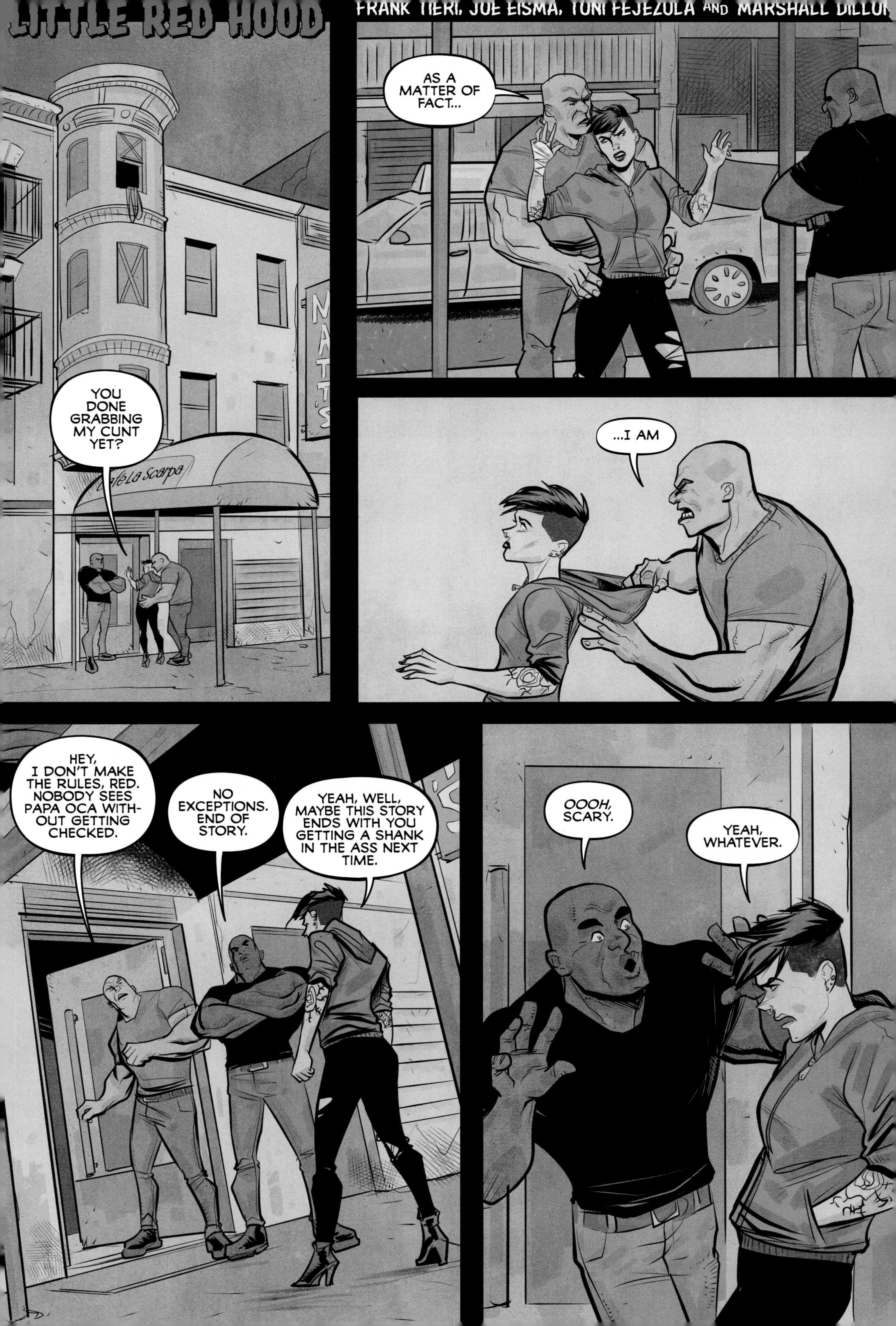
LITTLE RED HOOD
FRANK TIERI, JOE EISMA, TONI FEJEZULA AND MARSHALL DILLON
YOU DONE GRABBING MY CUNT YET?
AS A MATTER OF FACT...
...I AM
HEY, I DON'T MAKE THE RULES, RED. NOBODY SEES PAPA OCA WITHOUT GETTING CHECKED.
NO EXCEPTIONS. END OF STORY.
YEAH, WELL, MAYBE THIS STORY ENDS WITH YOU GETTING A SHANK IN THE ASS NEXT TIME.
OOOH, SCARY.
YEAH, WHATEVER.

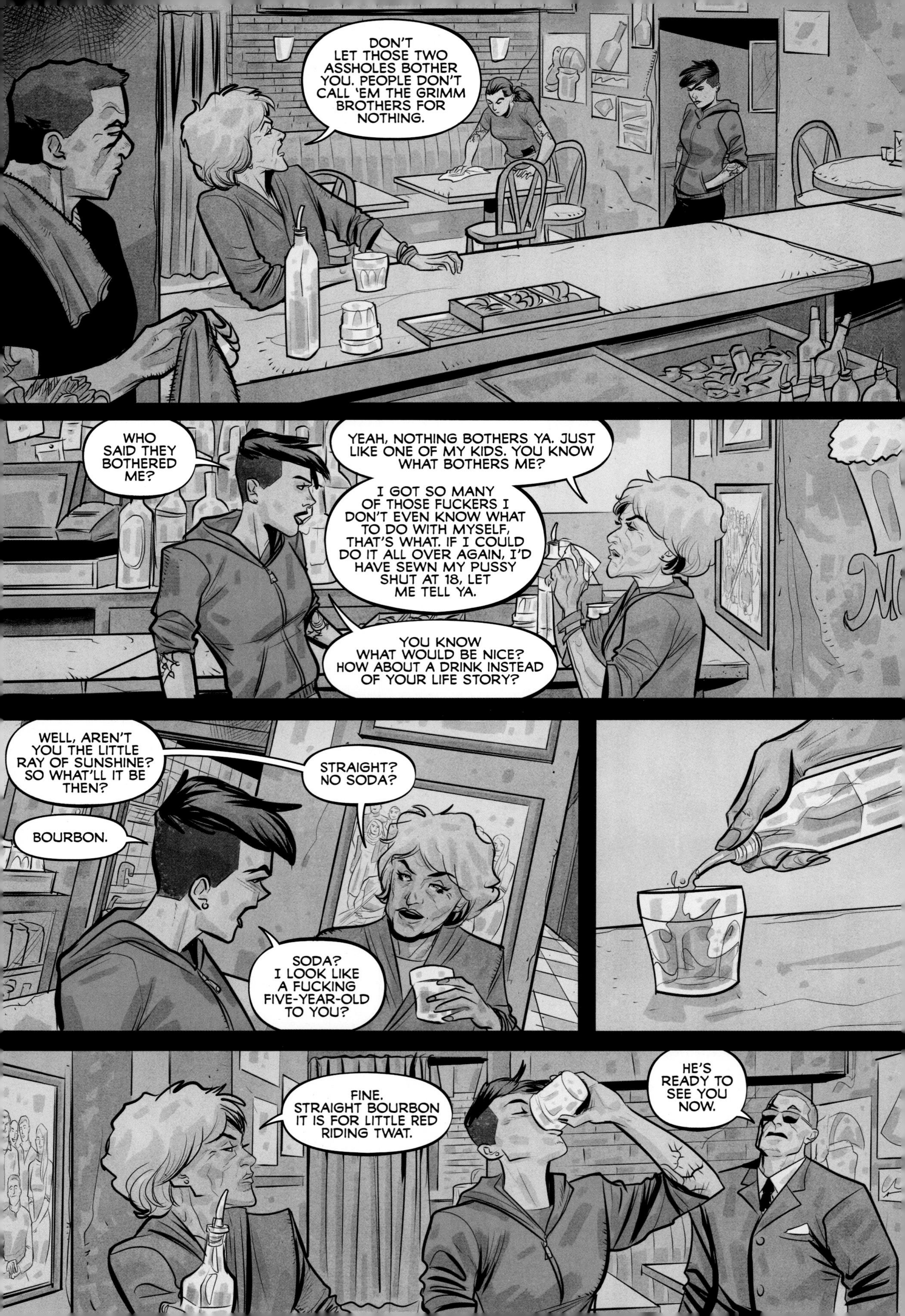
DON'T LET THOSE TWO ASSHOLES BOTHER YOU. PEOPLE DON'T CALL 'EM THE GRIMM BROTHERS FOR NOTHING.
WHO SAID THEY BOTHERED ME?
YEAH, NOTHING BOTHERS YA. JUST LIKE ONE OF MY KIDS. YOU KNOW WHAT BOTHERS ME?
I GOT SO MANY OF THOSE FUCKERS I DON'T EVEN KNOW WHAT TO DO WITH MYSELF, THAT'S WHAT. IF I COULD DO IT ALL OVER AGAIN, I'D HAVE SEWN MY PUSSY SHUT AT 18, LET ME TELL YA.
YOU KNOW WHAT WOULD BE NICE? HOW ABOUT A DRINK INSTEAD OF YOUR LIFE STORY?
WELL, AREN'T YOU THE LITTLE RAY OF SUNSHINE? SO WHAT'LL IT BE THEN?
BOURBON.
STRAIGHT? NO SODA?
SODA? I LOOK LIKE A FUCKING FIVE-YEAR-OLD TO YOU?
FINE. STRAIGHT BOURBON IT IS FOR LITTLE RED RIDING TWAT.
HE'S READY TO SEE YOU NOW.

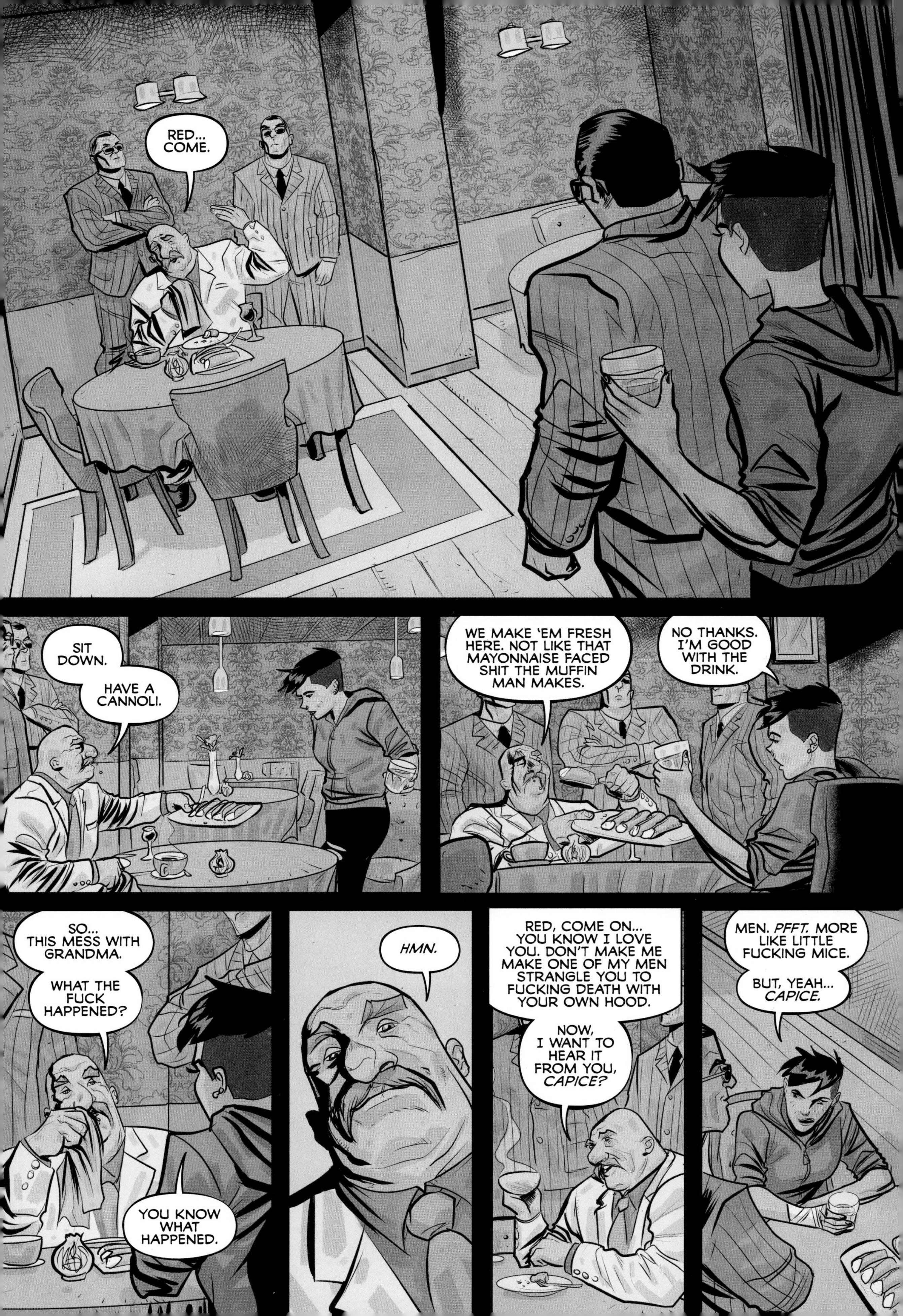
RED... COME.
SIT DOWN.
HAVE A CANNOLI.
WE MAKE 'EM FRESH HERE. NOT LIKE THAT MAYONNAISE FACED SHIT THE MUFFIN MAN MAKES.
NO THANKS. I'M GOOD WITH THE DRINK.
SO... THIS MESS WITH GRANDMA.
WHAT THE FUCK HAPPENED?
YOU KNOW WHAT HAPPENED.
HMN.
RED, COME ON... YOU KNOW I LOVE YOU. DON'T MAKE ME MAKE ONE OF MY MEN STRANGLE YOU TO FUCKING DEATH WITH YOUR OWN HOOD.
NOW, I WANT TO HEAR IT FROM YOU, CAPICE?
MEN. PFFT. MORE LIKE LITTLE FUCKING MICE.
BUT, YEAH... CAPICE.

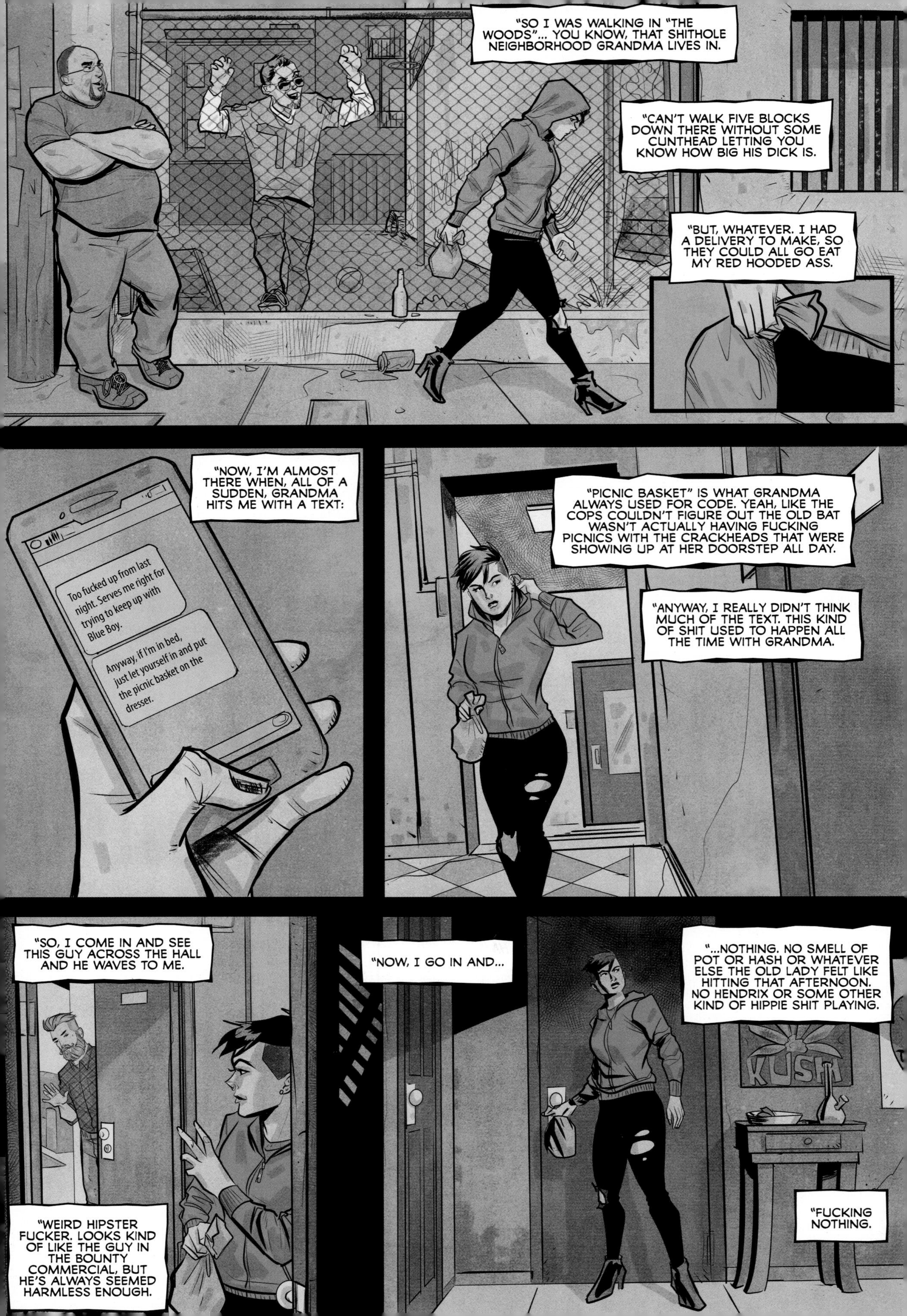
"SO I WAS WALKING IN "THE WOODS"... YOU KNOW, THAT SHITHOLE NEIGHBORHOOD GRANDMA LIVES IN.
"CAN'T WALK FIVE BLOCKS DOWN THERE WITHOUT SOME CUNTHEAD LETTING YOU KNOW HOW BIG HIS DICK IS.
"BUT, WHATEVER. I HAD A DELIVERY TO MAKE, SO THEY COULD ALL GO EAT MY RED HOODED ASS.
"NOW, I'M ALMOST THERE WHEN, ALL OF A SUDDEN, GRANDMA HITS ME WITH A TEXT:
Too fucked up from last night. Serves me right for trying to keep up with Blue Boy.
Anyway, if I'm in bed, just let yourself in and put the picnic basket on the dresser.
"PICNIC BASKET" IS WHAT GRANDMA ALWAYS USED FOR CODE. YEAH, LIKE THE COPS COULDN'T FIGURE OUT THE OLD BAT WASN'T ACTUALLY HAVING FUCKING PICNICS WITH THE CRACKHEADS THAT WERE SHOWING UP AT HER DOORSTEP ALL DAY.
"ANYWAY, I REALLY DIDN'T THINK MUCH OF THE TEXT. THIS KIND OF SHIT USED TO HAPPEN ALL THE TIME WITH GRANDMA.
"SO, I COME IN AND SEE THIS GUY ACROSS THE HALL AND HE WAVES TO ME.
"WEIRD HIPSTER FUCKER. LOOKS KIND OF LIKE THE GUY IN THE BOUNTY COMMERCIAL, BUT HE'S ALWAYS SEEMED HARMLESS ENOUGH.
"NOW, I GO IN AND...
"...NOTHING. NO SMELL OF POT OR HASH OR WHATEVER ELSE THE OLD LADY FELT LIKE HITTING THAT AFTERNOON. NO HENDRIX OR SOME OTHER KIND OF HIPPIE SHIT PLAYING.
KUSH
"FUCKING NOTHING.

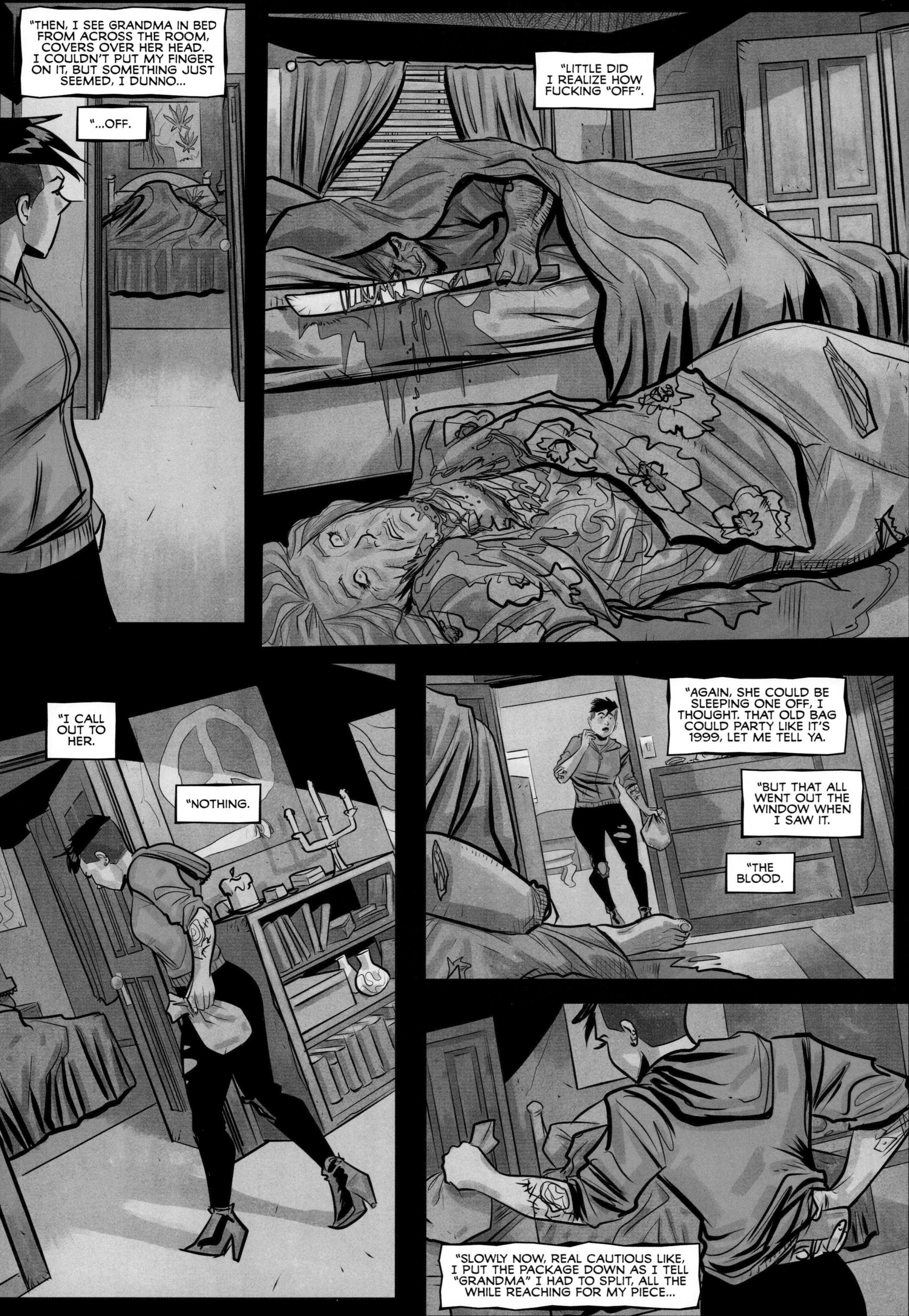
"THEN, I SEE GRANDMA IN BED FROM ACROSS THE ROOM, COVERS OVER HER HEAD. I COULDN'T PUT MY FINGER ON IT, BUT SOMETHING JUST SEEMED, I DUNNO...
"...OFF.
"LITTLE DID I REALIZE HOW FUCKING "OFF".
"I CALL OUT TO HER.
"NOTHING.
"AGAIN, SHE COULD BE SLEEPING ONE OFF, I THOUGHT. THAT OLD BAG COULD PARTY LIKE IT'S 1999, LET ME TELL YA.
"BUT THAT ALL WENT OUT THE WINDOW WHEN I SAW IT.
"THE BLOOD.
"SLOWLY NOW, REAL CAUTIOUS LIKE, I PUT THE PACKAGE DOWN AS I TELL "GRANDMA" I HAD TO SPLIT, ALL THE WHILE REACHING FOR MY PIECE...

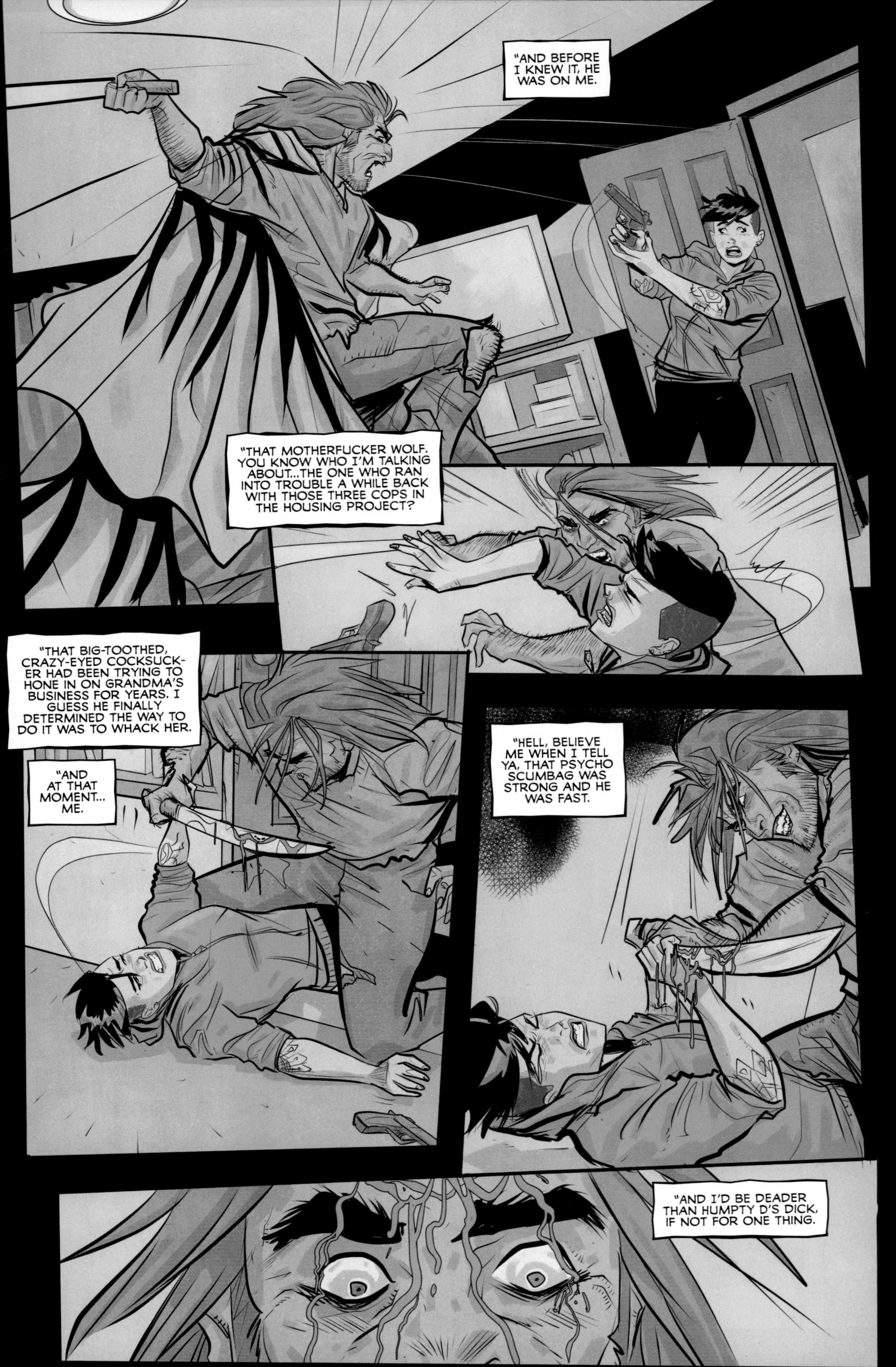
"AND BEFORE I KNEW IT, HE WAS ON ME.
"THAT MOTHERFUCKER WOLF. YOU KNOW WHO I'M TALKING ABOUT...THE ONE WHO RAN INTO TROUBLE A WHILE BACK WITH THOSE THREE COPS IN THE HOUSING PROJECT?
"THAT BIG-TOOTHED, CRAZY-EYED COCKSUCKER HAD BEEN TRYING TO HONE IN ON GRANDMA'S BUSINESS FOR YEARS. I GUESS HE FINALLY DETERMINED THE WAY TO DO IT WAS TO WHACK HER.
"AND AT THAT MOMENT... ME.
"HELL, BELIEVE ME WHEN I TELL YA, THAT PSYCHO SCUMBAG WAS STRONG AND HE WAS FAST.
"AND I'D BE DEADER THAN HUMPTY D'S DICK, IF NOT FOR ONE THING.

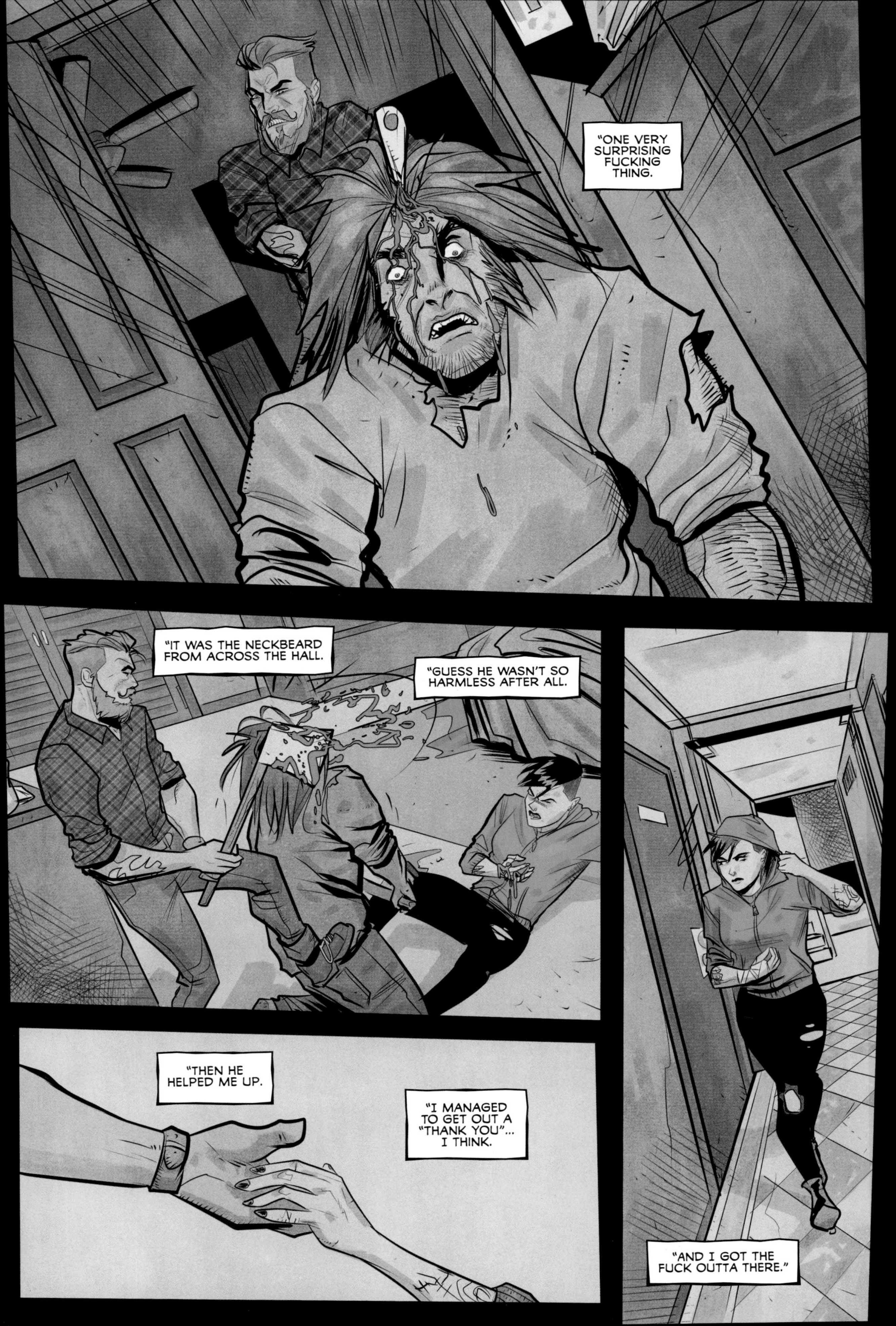
"ONE VERY SURPRISING FUCKING THING.
"IT WAS THE NECKBEARD FROM ACROSS THE HALL.
"GUESS HE WASN'T SO HARMLESS AFTER ALL.
"THEN HE HELPED ME UP.
"I MANAGED TO GET OUT A "THANK YOU"... I THINK.
"AND I GOT THE FUCK OUTTA THERE."

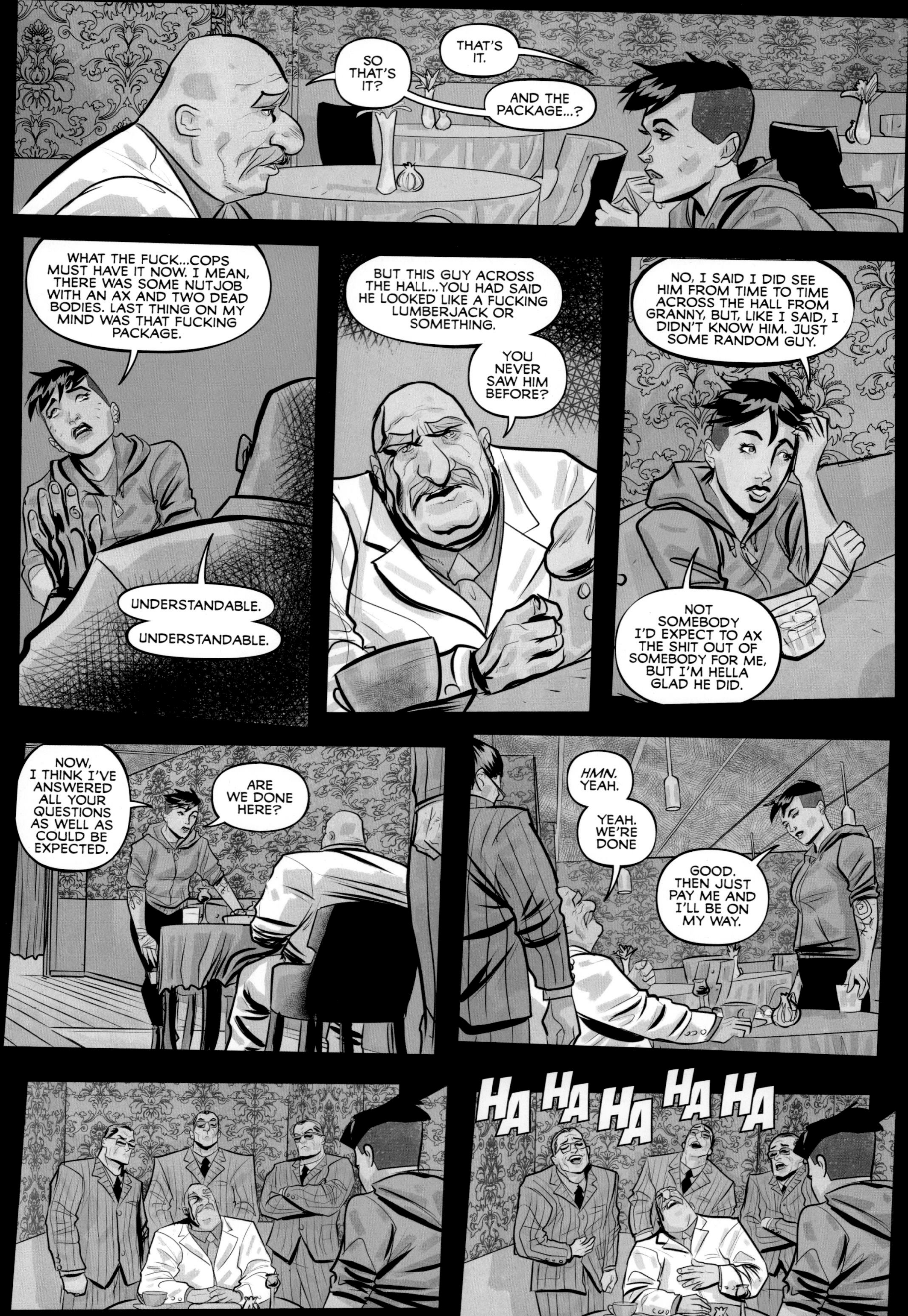
THAT'S IT.
SO THAT'S IT?
AND THE PACKAGE...?
WHAT THE FUCK...COPS MUST HAVE IT NOW. I MEAN, THERE WAS SOME NUTJOB WITH AN AX AND TWO DEAD BODIES. LAST THING ON MY MIND WAS THAT FUCKING PACKAGE.
UNDERSTANDABLE.
UNDERSTANDABLE.
BUT THIS GUY ACROSS THE HALL...YOU HAD SAID HE LOOKED LIKE A FUCKING LUMBERJACK OR SOMETHING.
YOU NEVER SAW HIM BEFORE?
NO, I SAID I DID SEE HIM FROM TIME TO TIME ACROSS THE HALL FROM GRANNY, BUT, LIKE I SAID, I DIDN'T KNOW HIM. JUST SOME RANDOM GUY.
NOT SOMEBODY I'D EXPECT TO AX THE SHIT OUT OF SOMEBODY FOR ME, BUT I'M HELLA GLAD HE DID.
NOW, I THINK I'VE ANSWERED ALL YOUR QUESTIONS AS WELL AS COULD BE EXPECTED.
ARE WE DONE HERE?
HMN. YEAH.
YEAH. WE'RE DONE
GOOD. THEN JUST PAY ME AND I'LL BE ON MY WAY.
HA HA HA HA HA HA

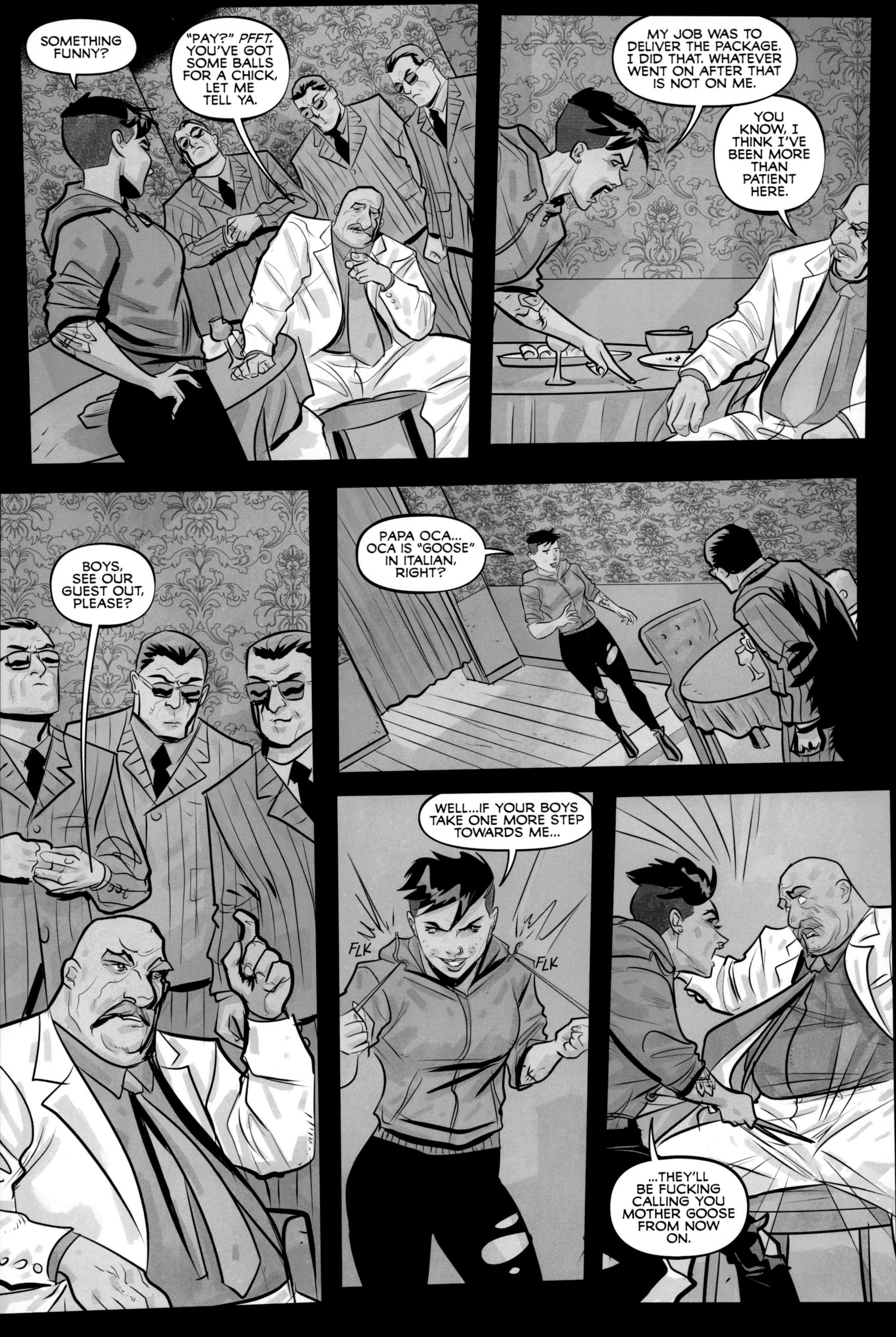
SOMETHING FUNNY?
"PAY?" PFFT. YOU'VE GOT SOME BALLS FOR A CHICK, LET ME TELL YA.
MY JOB WAS TO DELIVER THE PACKAGE. I DID THAT. WHATEVER WENT ON AFTER THAT IS NOT ON ME.
YOU KNOW, I THINK I'VE BEEN MORE THAN PATIENT HERE.
BOYS, SEE OUR GUEST OUT, PLEASE?
PAPA OCA... OCA IS "GOOSE" IN ITALIAN, RIGHT?
WELL...IF YOUR BOYS TAKE ONE MORE STEP TOWARDS ME...
FLK
FLK
...THEY'LL BE FUCKING CALLING YOU MOTHER GOOSE FROM NOW ON.

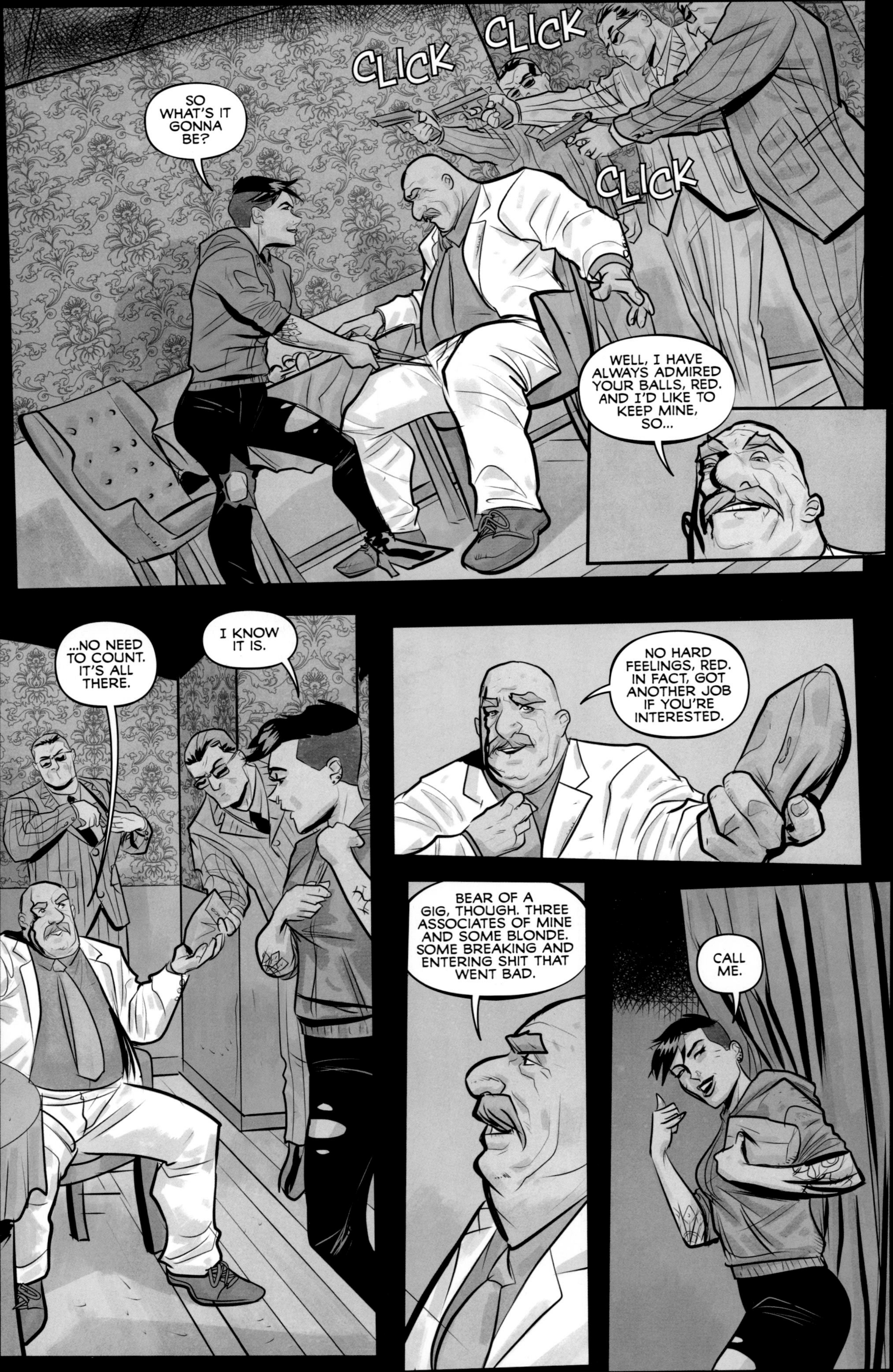
SO WHAT'S IT GONNA BE?
CLICK
CLICK
CLICK
WELL, I HAVE ALWAYS ADMIRED YOUR BALLS, RED. AND I'D LIKE TO KEEP MINE, SO...
...NO NEED TO COUNT. IT'S ALL THERE.
I KNOW IT IS.
NO HARD FEELINGS, RED. IN FACT, GOT ANOTHER JOB IF YOU'RE INTERESTED.
BEAR OF A GIG, THOUGH. THREE ASSOCIATES OF MINE AND SOME BLONDE. SOME BREAKING AND ENTERING SHIT THAT WENT BAD.
CALL ME.

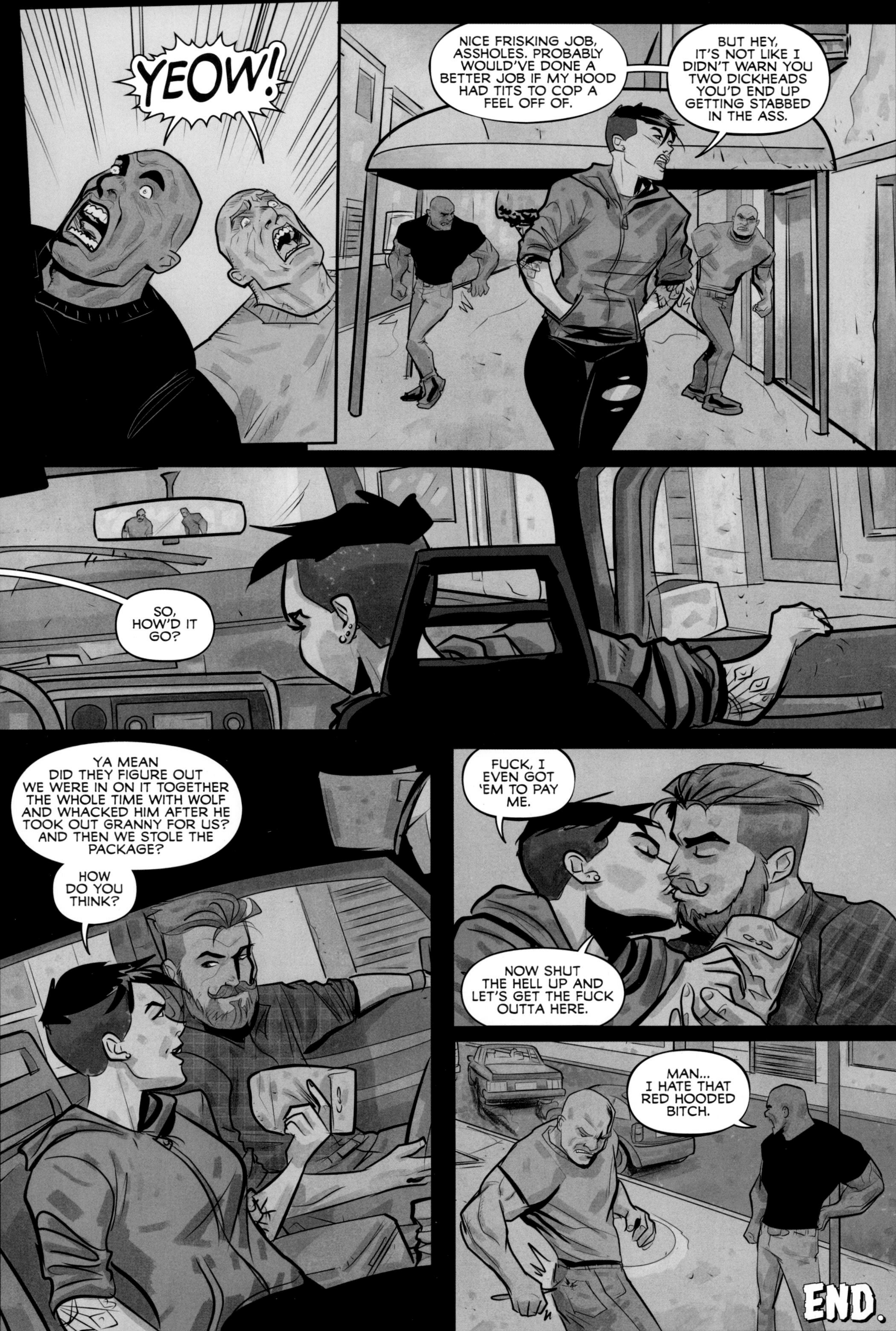
YEOW!
NICE FRISKING JOB, ASSHOLES. PROBABLY WOULD'VE DONE A BETTER JOB IF MY HOOD HAD TITS TO COP A FEEL OFF OF.
BUT HEY, IT'S NOT LIKE I DIDN'T WARN YOU TWO DICKHEADS YOU'D END UP GETTING STABBED IN THE ASS.
SO, HOW'D IT GO?
YA MEAN DID THEY FIGURE OUT WE WERE IN ON IT TOGETHER THE WHOLE TIME WITH WOLF AND WHACKED HIM AFTER HE TOOK OUT GRANNY FOR US? AND THEN WE STOLE THE PACKAGE?
HOW DO YOU THINK?
FUCK, I EVEN GOT 'EM TO PAY ME.
NOW SHUT THE HELL UP AND LET'S GET THE FUCK OUTTA HERE.
MAN... I HATE THAT RED HOODED BITCH.
END.

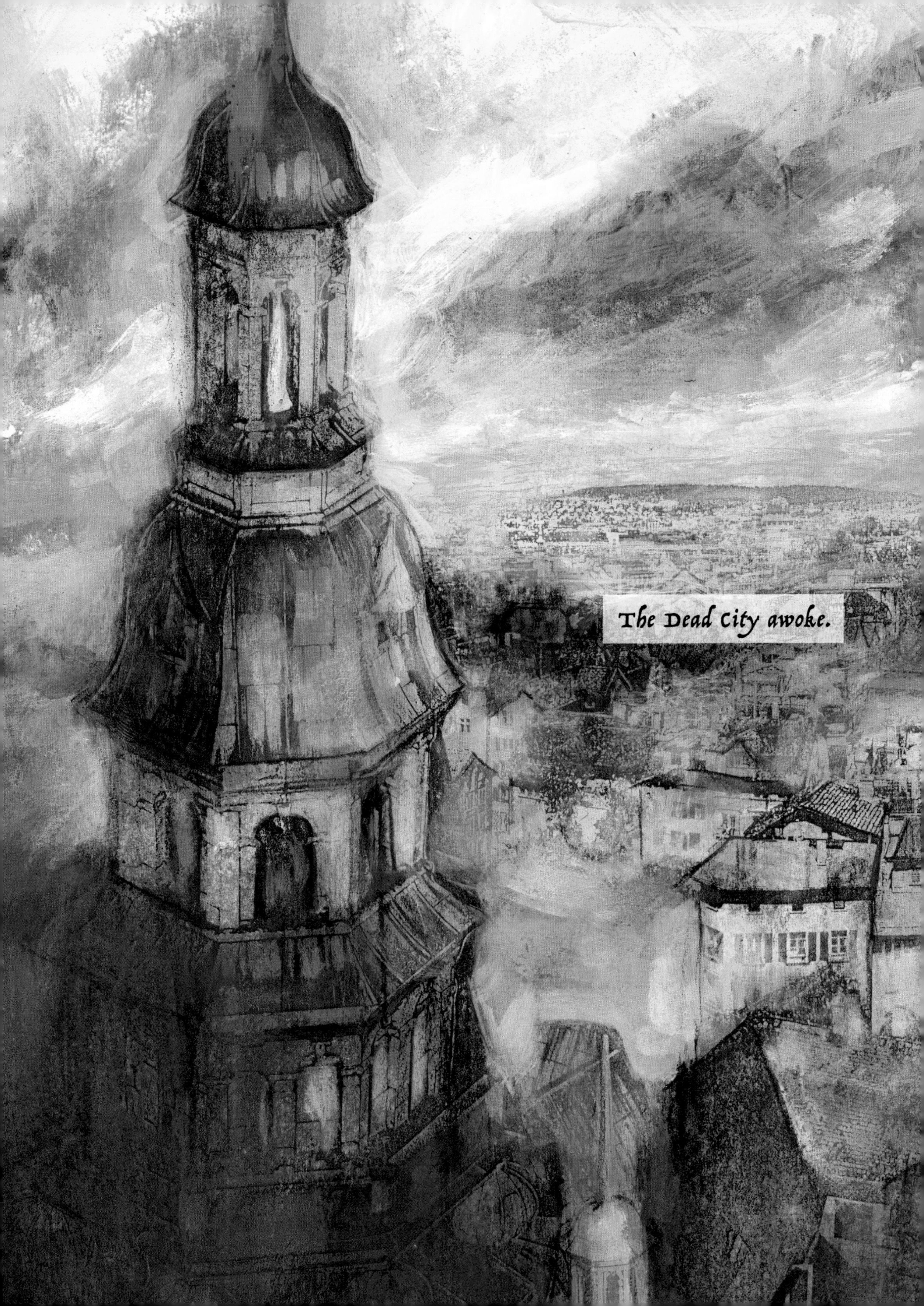
The Dead City awoke.

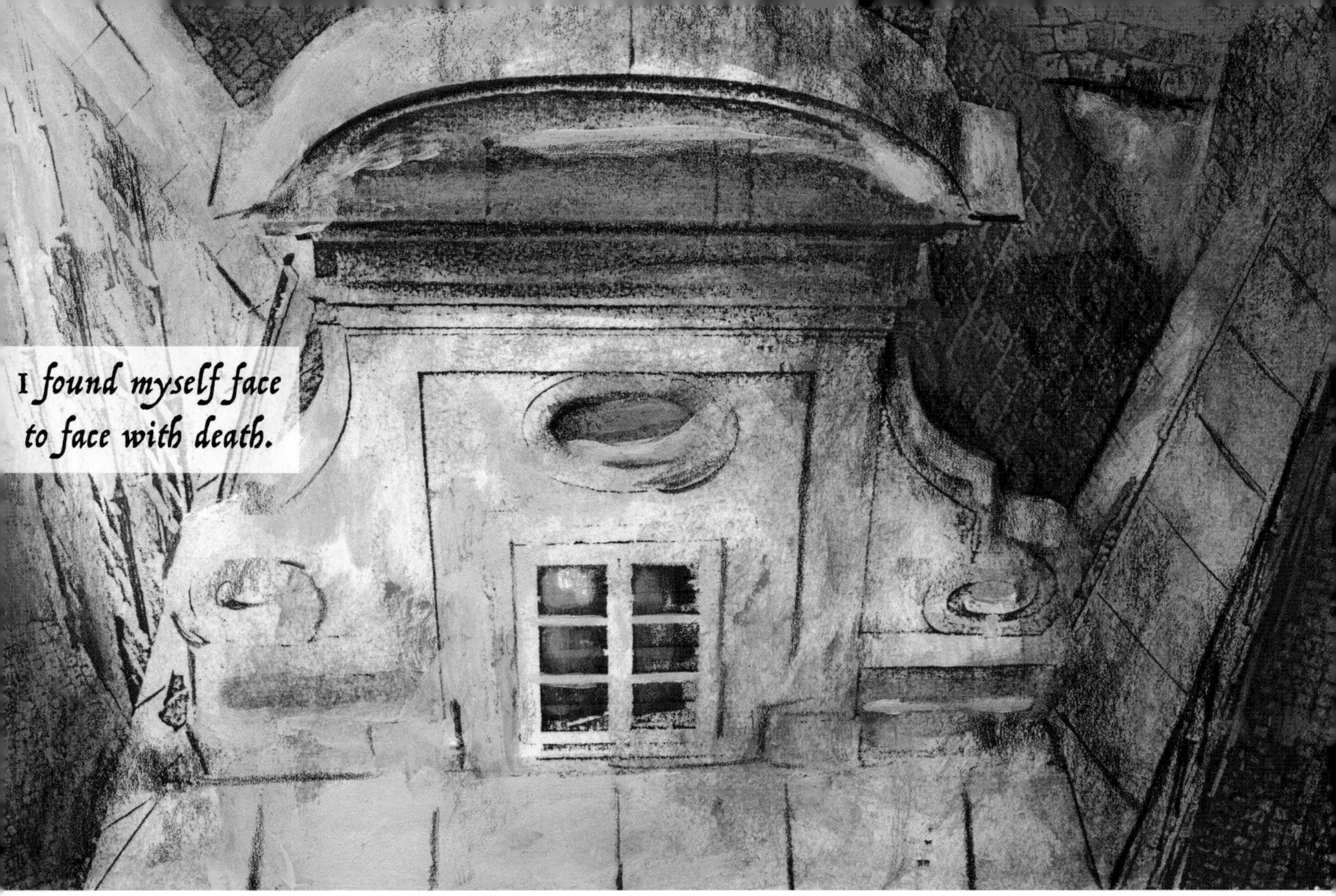
I found myself face to face with death.

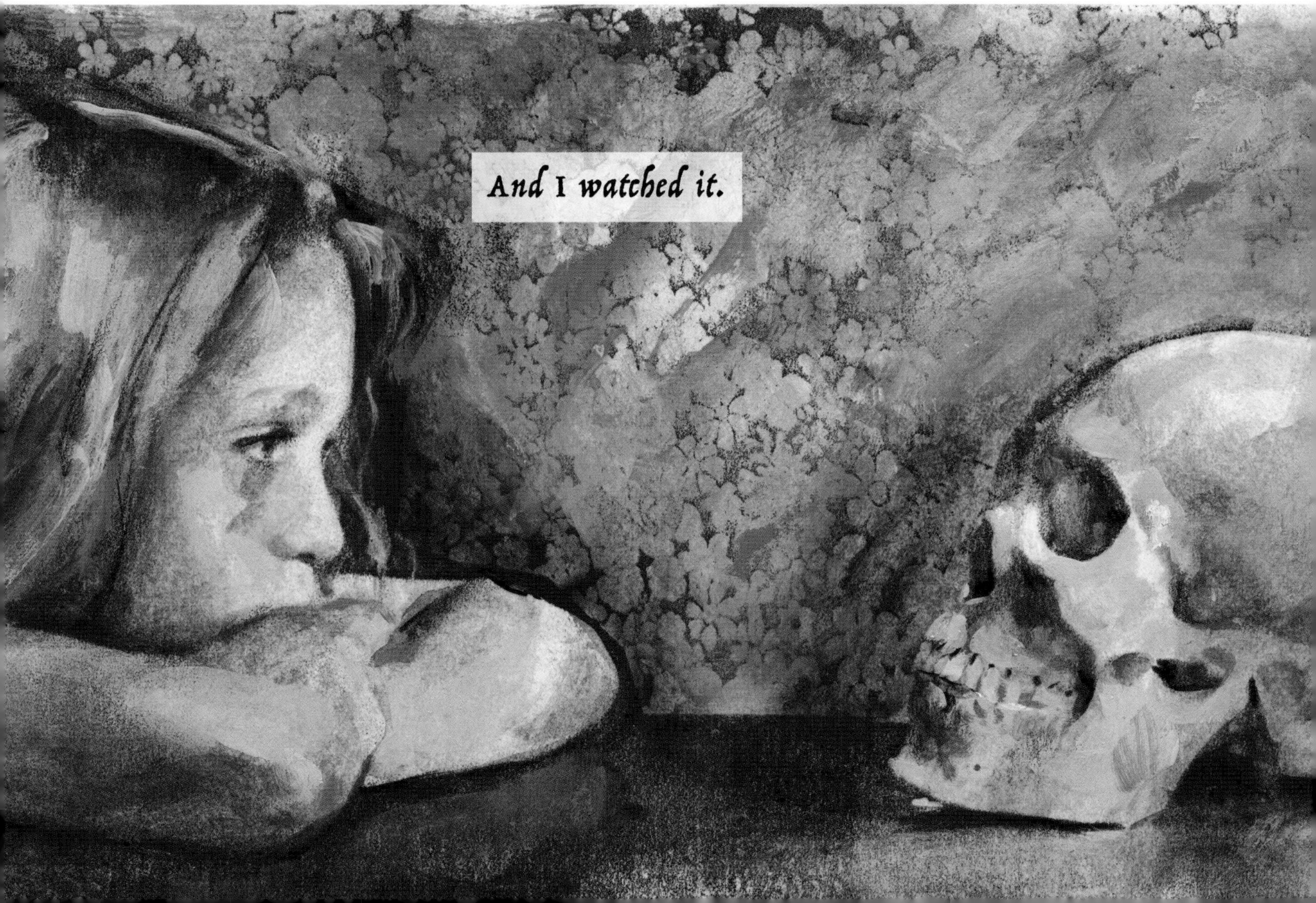
And I watched it.

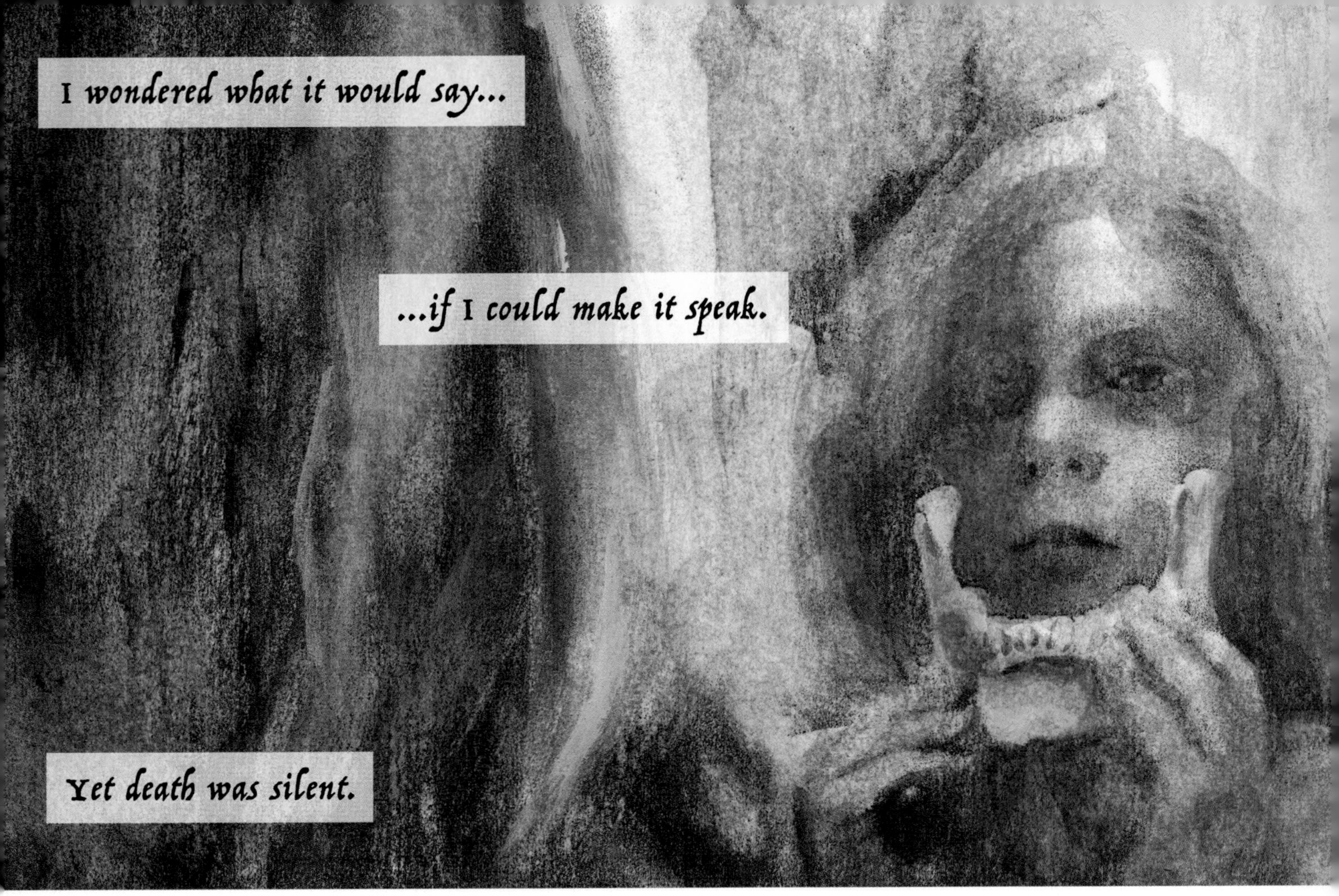
I wondered what it would say...
...if I could make it speak.
Yet death was silent.

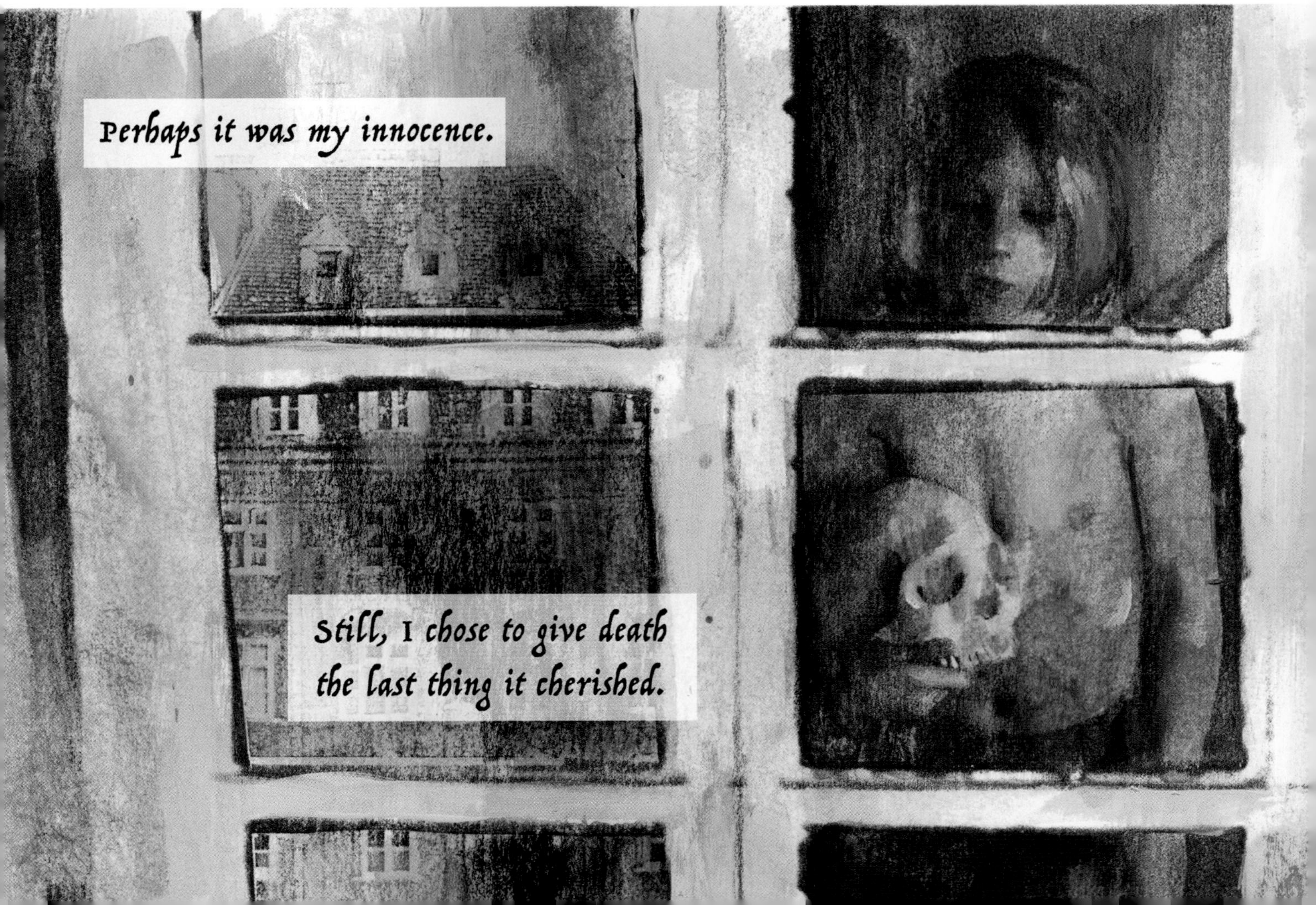
Perhaps it was my innocence.
Still, I chose to give death the last thing it cherished.

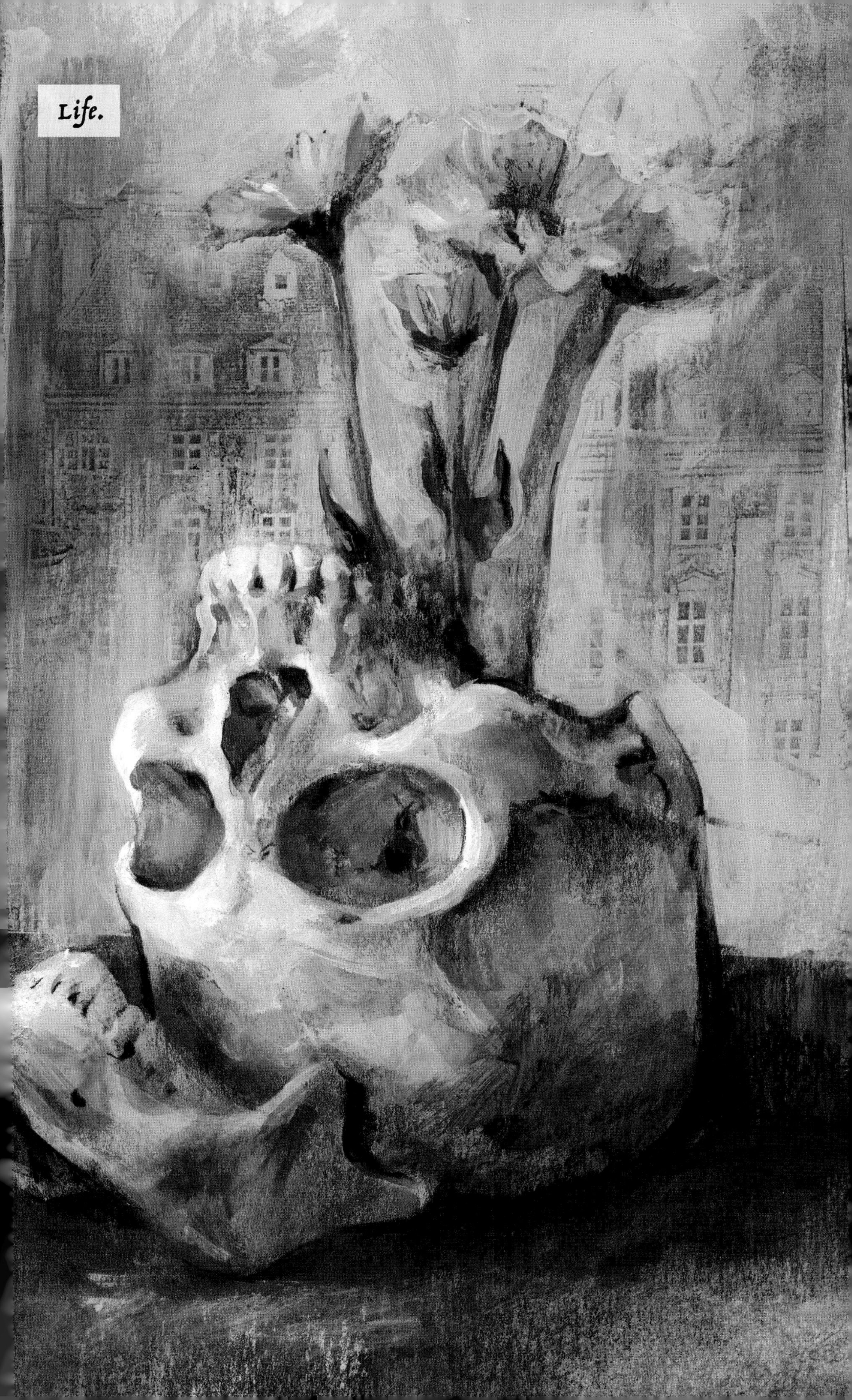
Life.

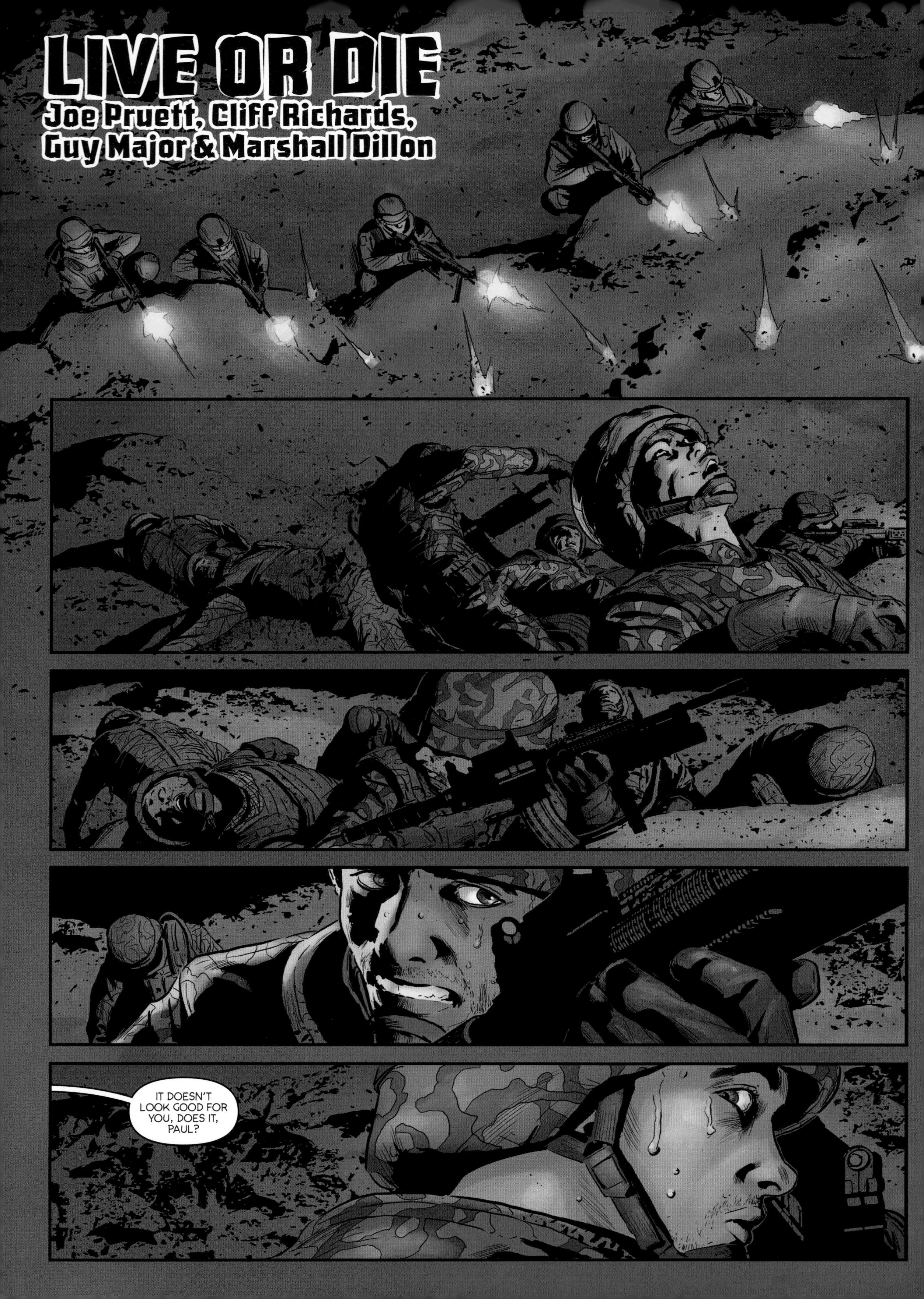

LIVE OR DIE
Joe Pruett, Cliff Richards, Guy Major & Marshall Dillon
IT DOESN'T LOOK GOOD FOR YOU, DOES IT, PAUL?

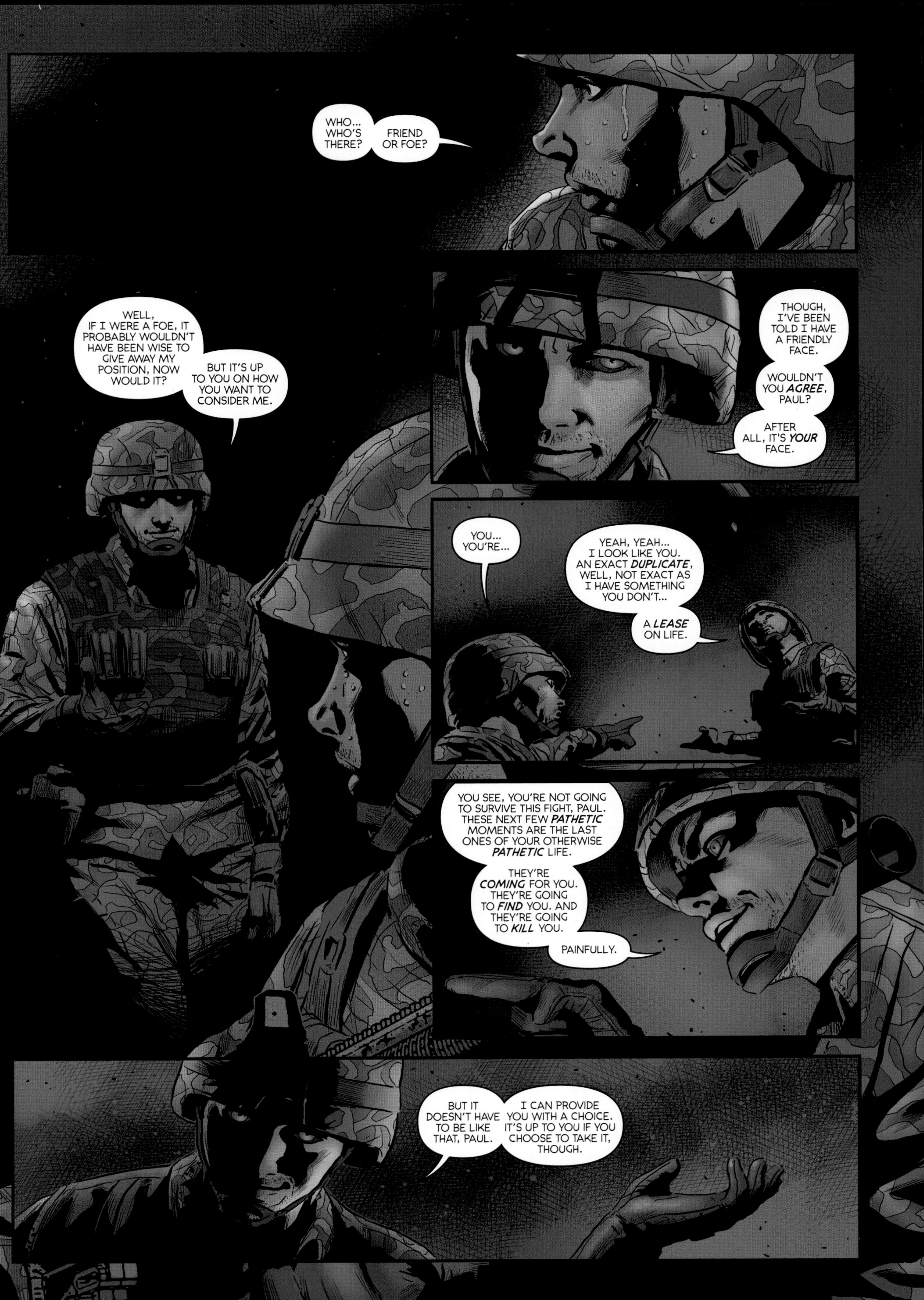
WHO... WHO'S THERE?
FRIEND OR FOE?
WELL, IF I WERE A FOE, IT PROBABLY WOULDN'T HAVE BEEN WISE TO GIVE AWAY MY POSITION, NOW WOULD IT?
BUT IT'S UP TO YOU ON HOW YOU WANT TO CONSIDER ME.
THOUGH, I'VE BEEN TOLD I HAVE A FRIENDLY FACE.
WOULDN'T YOU *AGREE*, PAUL?
AFTER ALL, IT'S *YOUR* FACE.
YOU... YOU'RE...
YEAH, YEAH... I LOOK LIKE YOU. AN EXACT *DUPLICATE*, WELL, NOT EXACT AS I HAVE SOMETHING YOU DON'T...
A *LEASE* ON LIFE.
YOU SEE, YOU'RE NOT GOING TO SURVIVE THIS FIGHT, PAUL. THESE NEXT FEW *PATHETIC* MOMENTS ARE THE LAST ONES OF YOUR OTHERWISE *PATHETIC* LIFE.
THEY'RE *COMING* FOR YOU. THEY'RE GOING TO *FIND* YOU. AND THEY'RE GOING TO *KILL* YOU.
PAINFULLY.
BUT IT DOESN'T HAVE TO BE LIKE THAT, PAUL.
I CAN PROVIDE YOU WITH A CHOICE. IT'S UP TO YOU IF YOU CHOOSE TO TAKE IT, THOUGH.

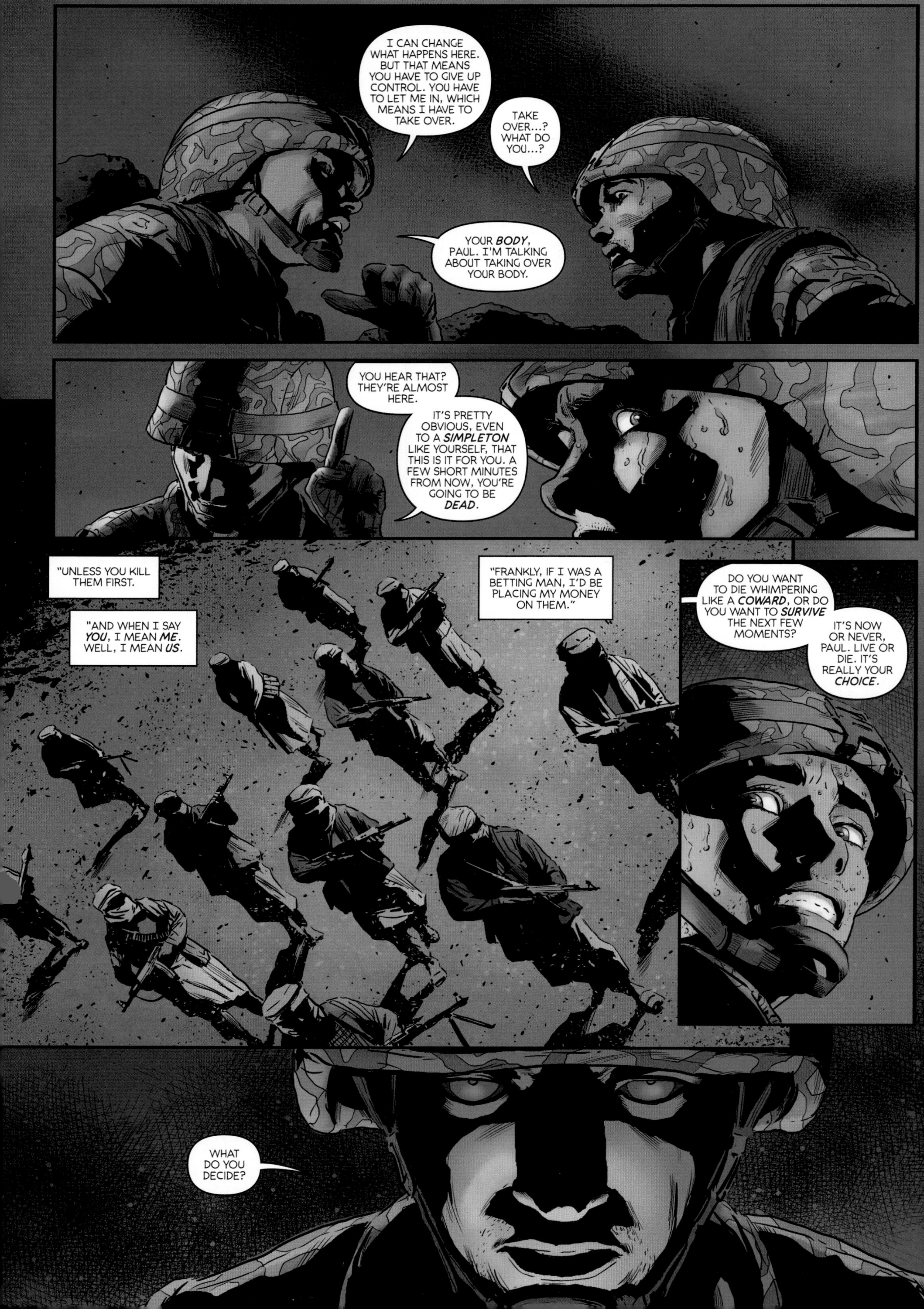
I CAN CHANGE WHAT HAPPENS HERE. BUT THAT MEANS YOU HAVE TO GIVE UP CONTROL. YOU HAVE TO LET ME IN, WHICH MEANS I HAVE TO TAKE OVER.
TAKE OVER...? WHAT DO YOU...?
YOUR BODY, PAUL. I'M TALKING ABOUT TAKING OVER YOUR BODY.
YOU HEAR THAT? THEY'RE ALMOST HERE.
IT'S PRETTY OBVIOUS, EVEN TO A SIMPLETON LIKE YOURSELF, THAT THIS IS IT FOR YOU. A FEW SHORT MINUTES FROM NOW, YOU'RE GOING TO BE DEAD.
"UNLESS YOU KILL THEM FIRST.
"AND WHEN I SAY YOU, I MEAN ME. WELL, I MEAN US.
"FRANKLY, IF I WAS A BETTING MAN, I'D BE PLACING MY MONEY ON THEM."
DO YOU WANT TO DIE WHIMPERING LIKE A COWARD, OR DO YOU WANT TO SURVIVE THE NEXT FEW MOMENTS?
IT'S NOW OR NEVER, PAUL. LIVE OR DIE. IT'S REALLY YOUR CHOICE.
WHAT DO YOU DECIDE?

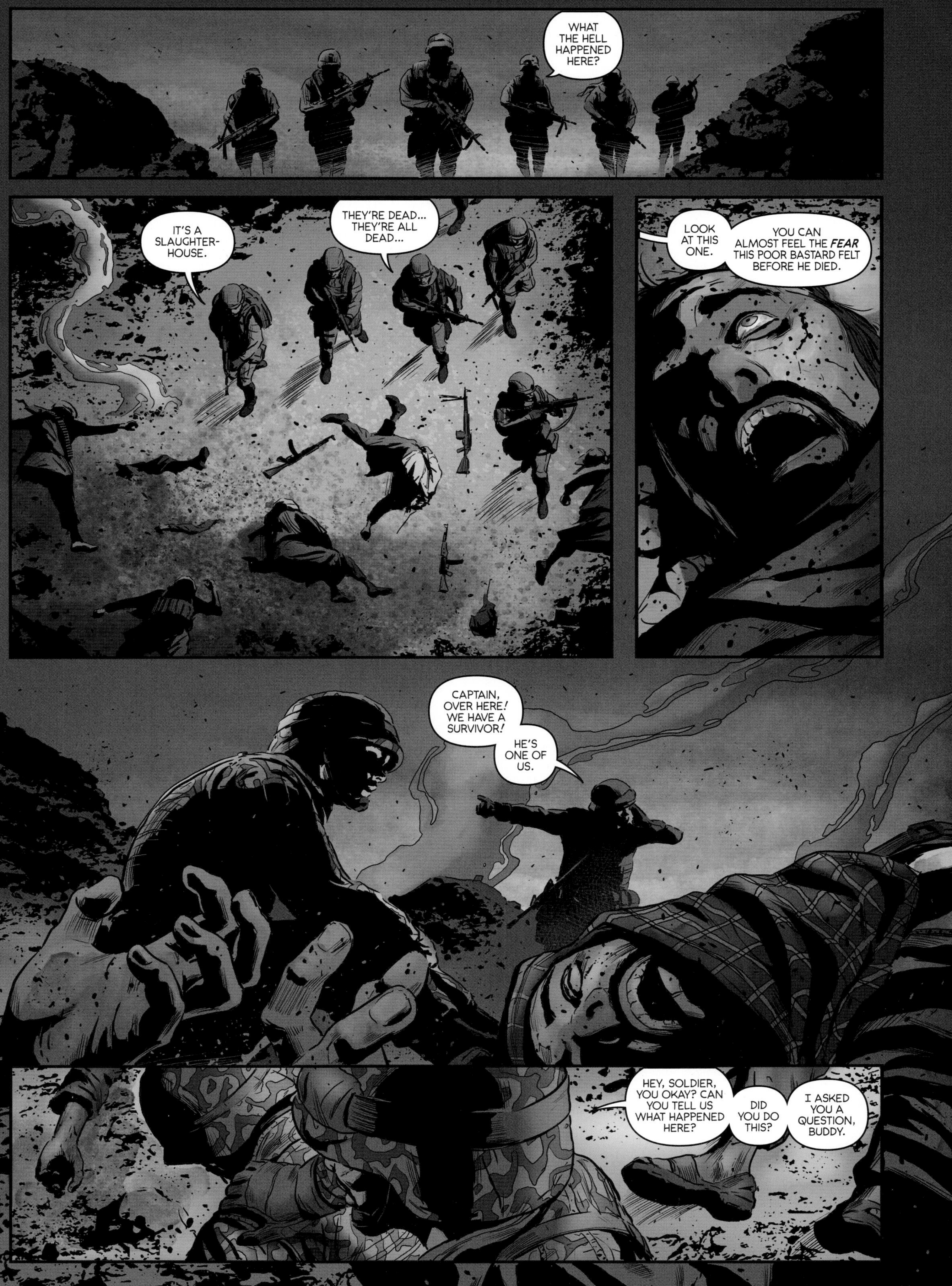
WHAT THE HELL HAPPENED HERE?
IT'S A SLAUGHTER-HOUSE.
THEY'RE DEAD... THEY'RE ALL DEAD...
LOOK AT THIS ONE.
YOU CAN ALMOST FEEL THE ***FEAR*** THIS POOR BASTARD FELT BEFORE HE DIED.
CAPTAIN, OVER HERE! WE HAVE A SURVIVOR!
HE'S ONE OF US.
HEY, SOLDIER, YOU OKAY? CAN YOU TELL US WHAT HAPPENED HERE?
DID YOU DO THIS?
I ASKED YOU A QUESTION, BUDDY.

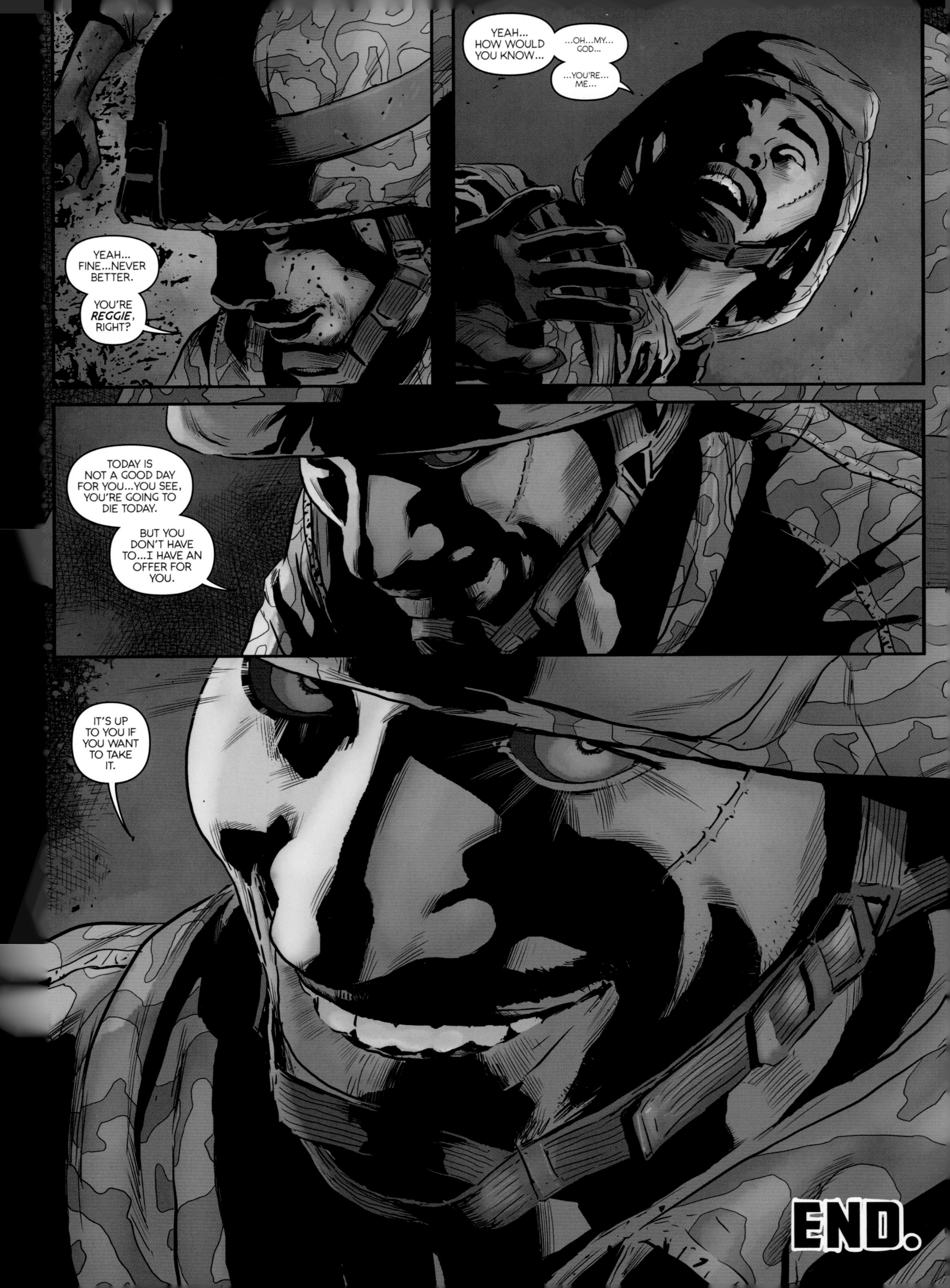
YEAH... FINE...NEVER BETTER.
YOU'RE *REGGIE*, RIGHT?
YEAH... HOW WOULD YOU KNOW...
...OH...MY... GOD...
...YOU'RE... ME...
TODAY IS NOT A GOOD DAY FOR YOU...YOU SEE, YOU'RE GOING TO DIE TODAY.
BUT YOU DON'T HAVE TO...I HAVE AN OFFER FOR YOU.
IT'S UP TO YOU IF YOU WANT TO TAKE IT.
END.

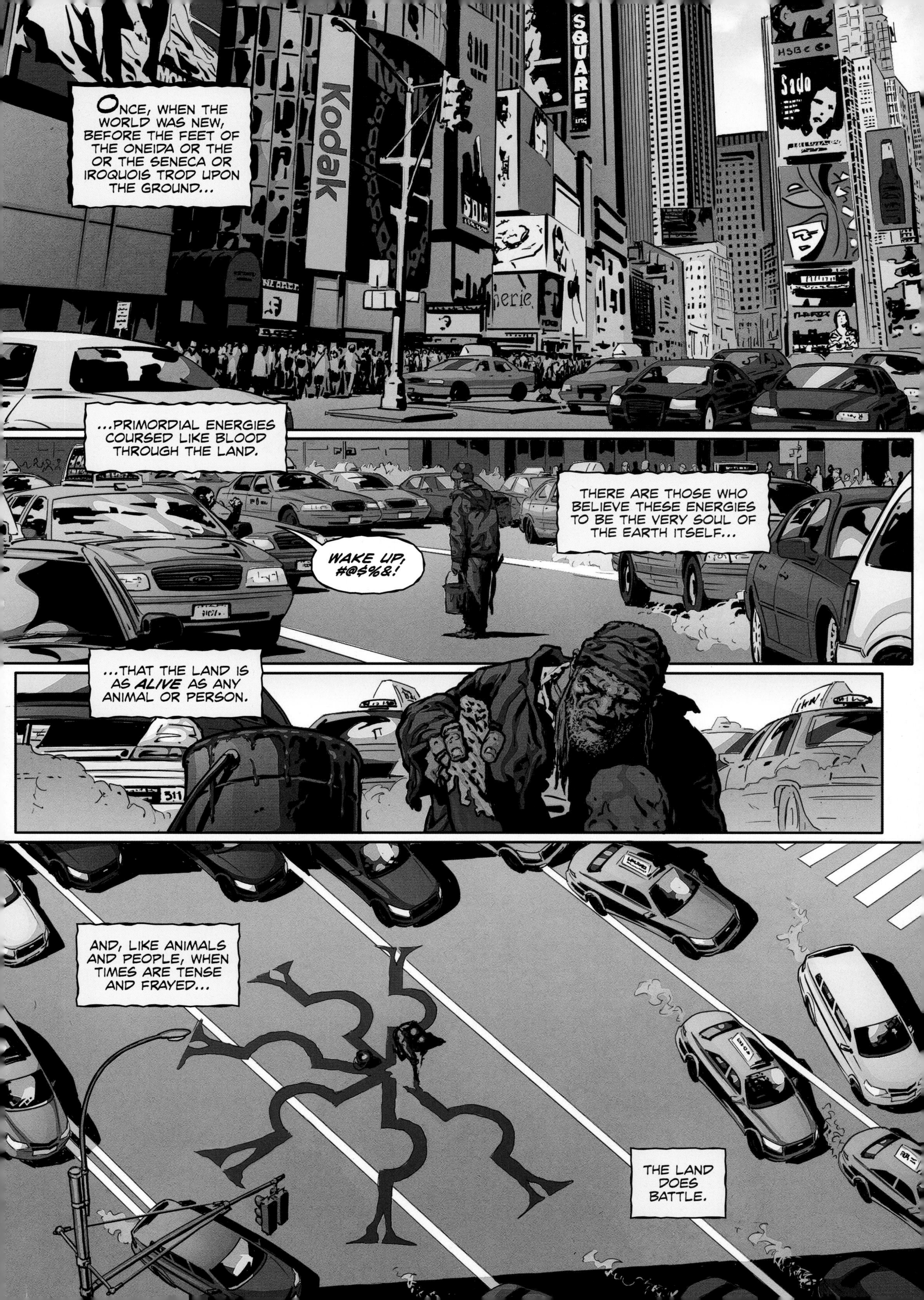

ONCE, WHEN THE WORLD WAS NEW, BEFORE THE FEET OF THE ONEIDA OR THE OR THE SENECA OR IROQUOIS TROD UPON THE GROUND...
...PRIMORDIAL ENERGIES COURSED LIKE BLOOD THROUGH THE LAND.
THERE ARE THOSE WHO BELIEVE THESE ENERGIES TO BE THE VERY SOUL OF THE EARTH ITSELF...
WAKE UP, #@$%&!
...THAT THE LAND IS AS ALIVE AS ANY ANIMAL OR PERSON.
AND, LIKE ANIMALS AND PEOPLE, WHEN TIMES ARE TENSE AND FRAYED...
THE LAND DOES BATTLE.

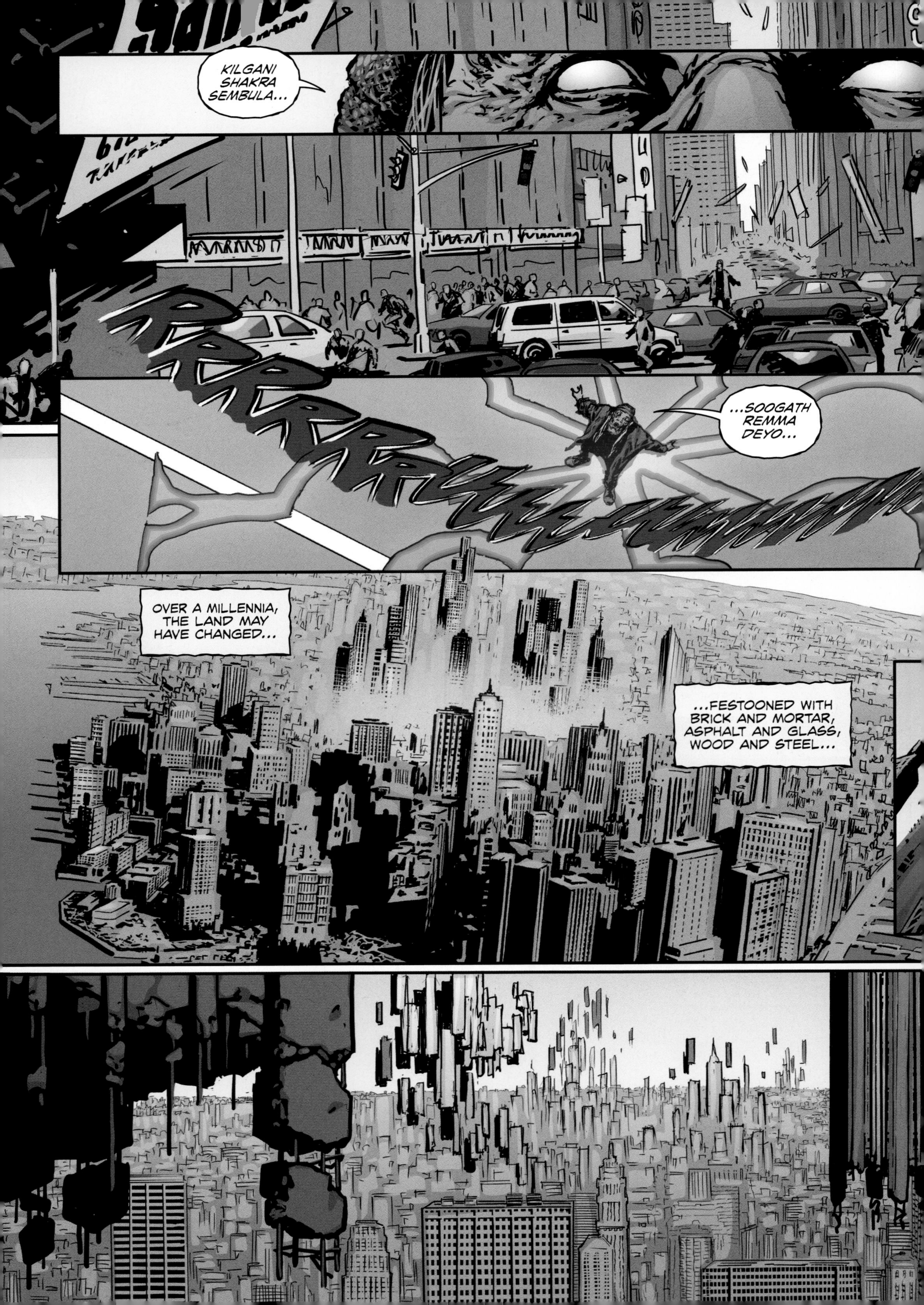
KILGANI SHAKRA SEMBULA...
RRRRRRRRRUMMMMMMMMMMMMM
...SOOGATH REMMA DEYO...
OVER A MILLENNIA, THE LAND MAY HAVE CHANGED...
...FESTOONED WITH BRICK AND MORTAR, ASPHALT AND GLASS, WOOD AND STEEL...

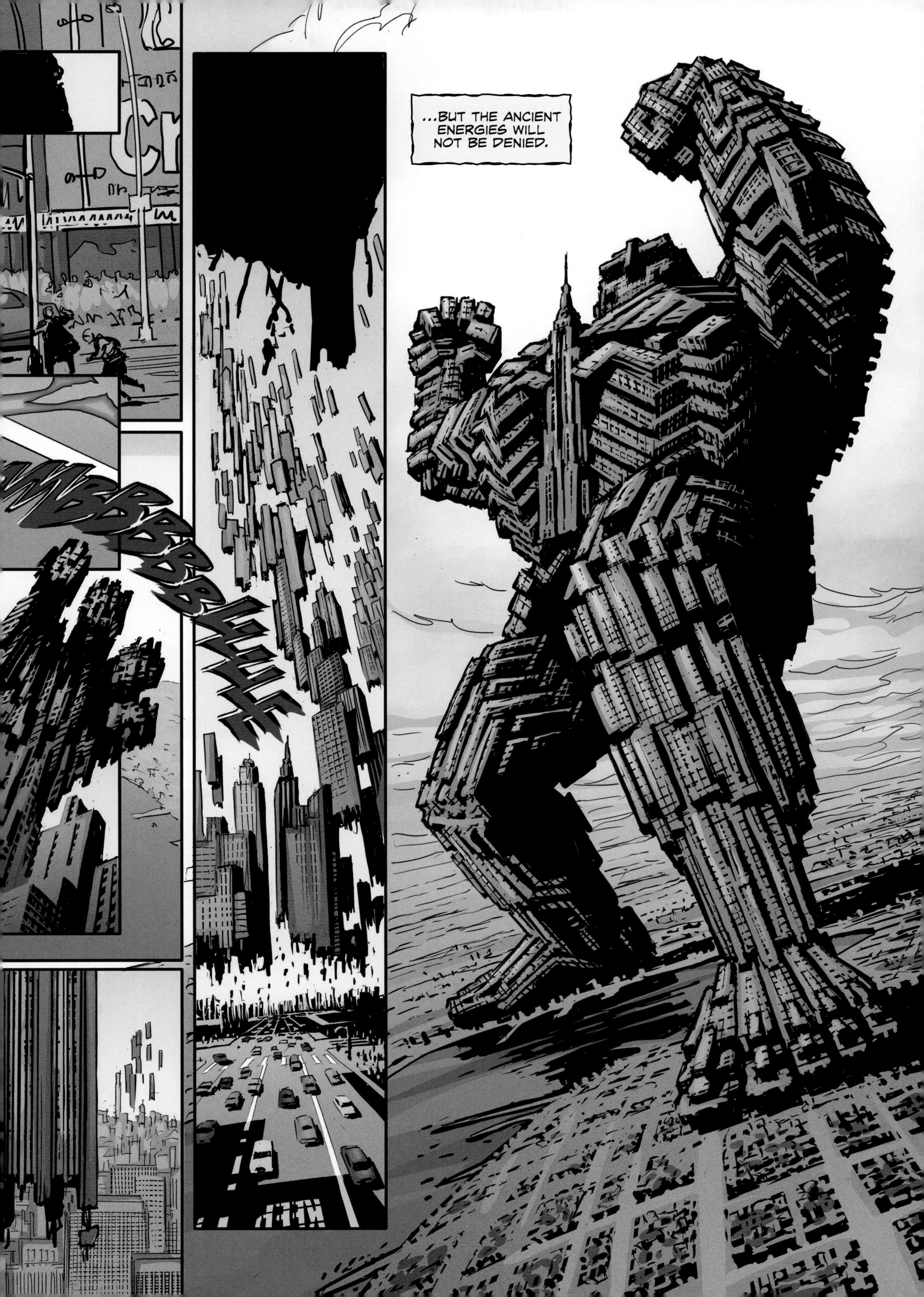
...BUT THE ANCIENT ENERGIES WILL NOT BE DENIED.

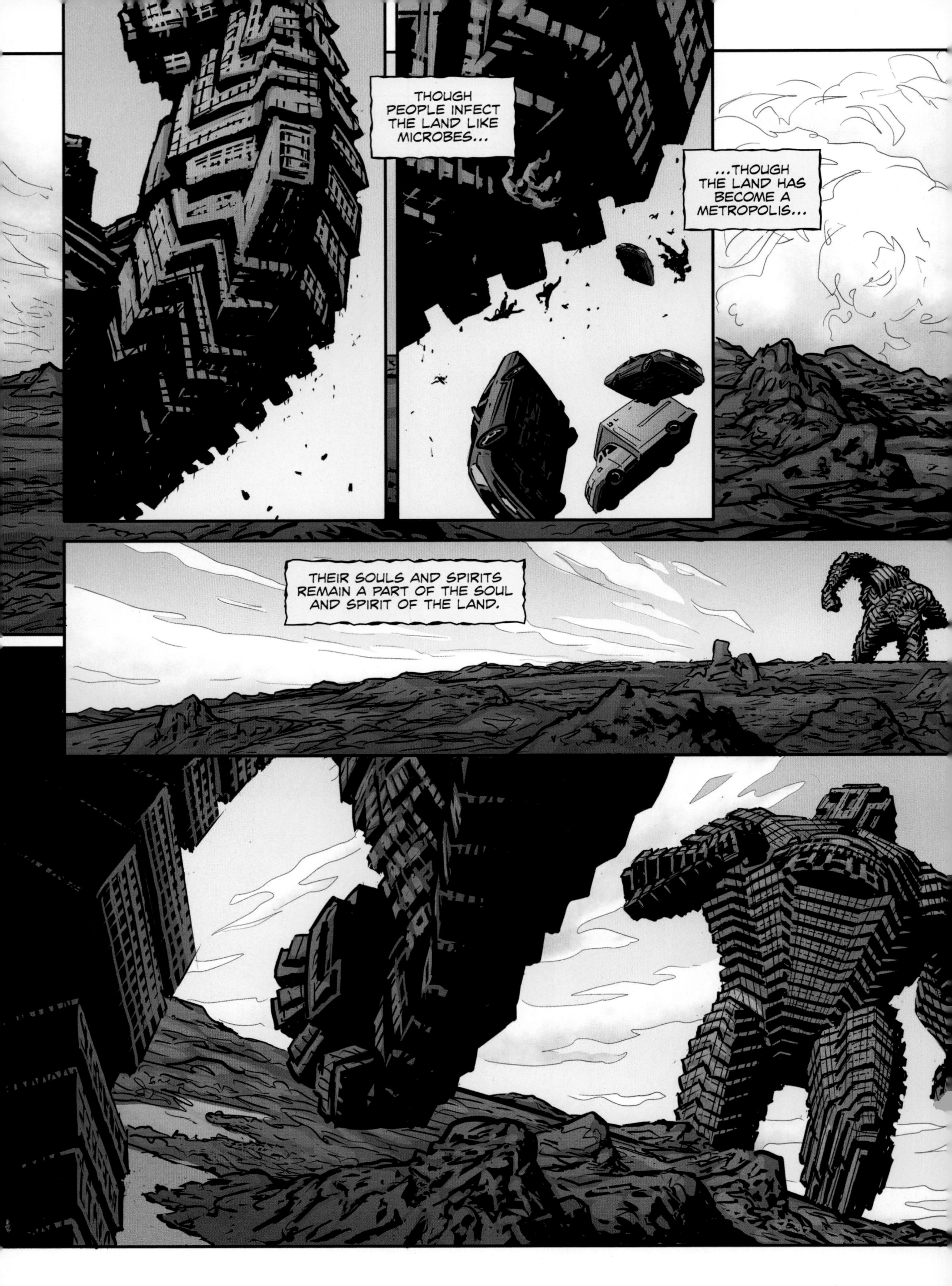
THOUGH PEOPLE INFECT THE LAND LIKE MICROBES...
...THOUGH THE LAND HAS BECOME A METROPOLIS...
THEIR SOULS AND SPIRITS REMAIN A PART OF THE SOUL AND SPIRIT OF THE LAND.

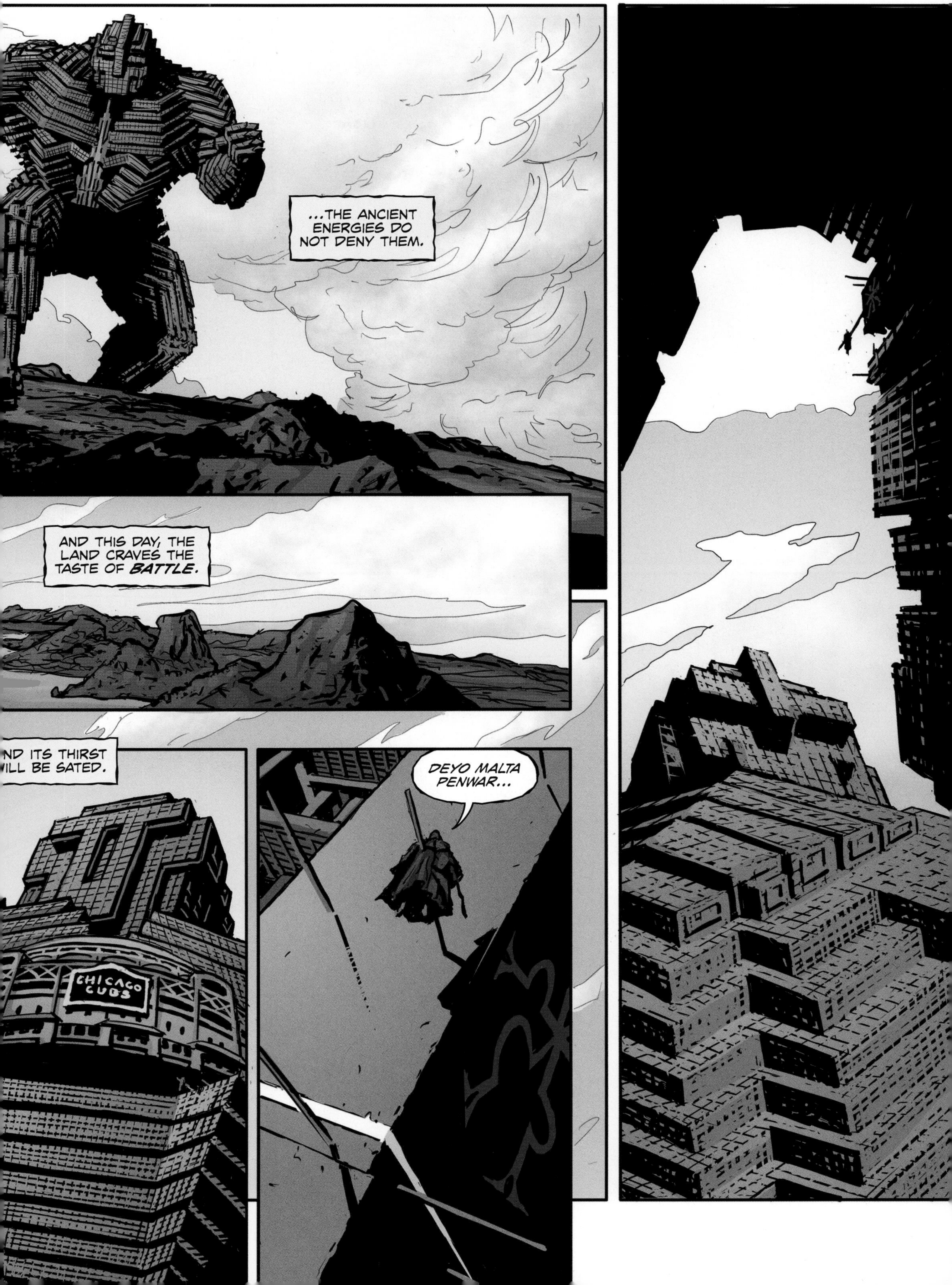
...THE ANCIENT ENERGIES DO NOT DENY THEM.
AND THIS DAY, THE LAND CRAVES THE TASTE OF *BATTLE*.
ND ITS THIRST WILL BE SATED.
CHICAGO CUBS
DEYO MALTA PENWAR...

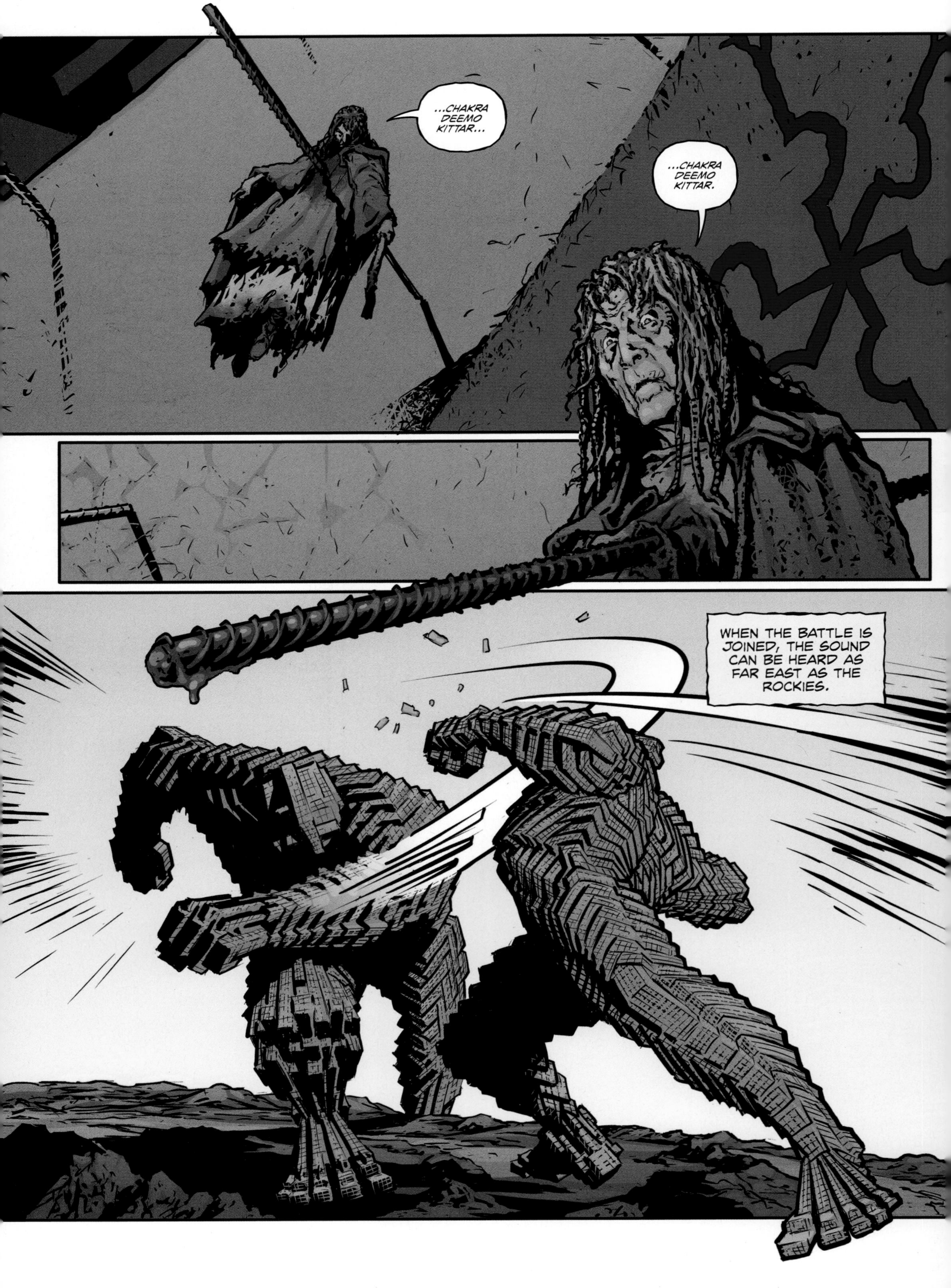
...CHAKRA DEEMO KITTAR...
...CHAKRA DEEMO KITTAR.
WHEN THE BATTLE IS JOINED, THE SOUND CAN BE HEARD AS FAR EAST AS THE ROCKIES.

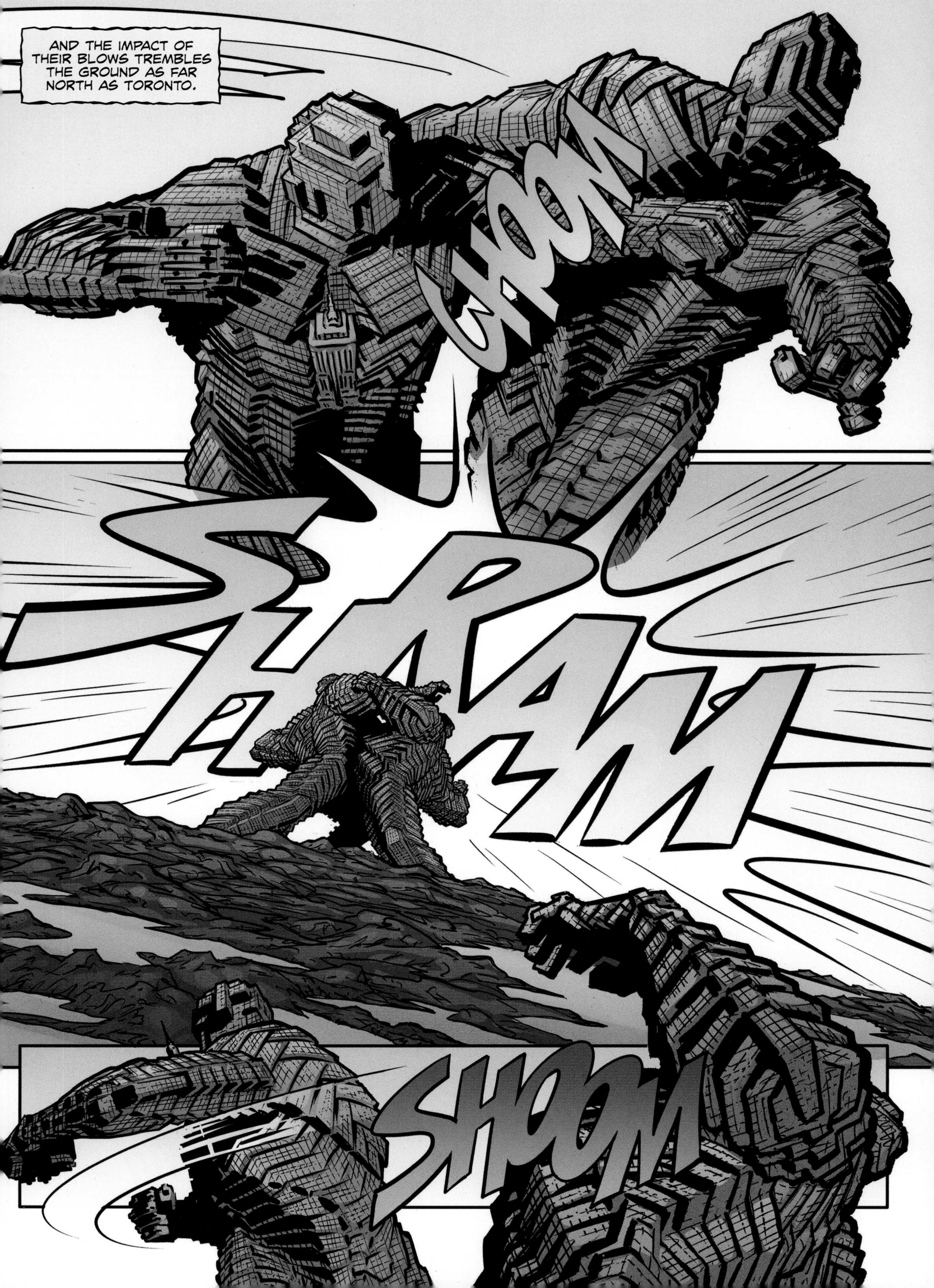
AND THE IMPACT OF THEIR BLOWS TREMBLES THE GROUND AS FAR NORTH AS TORONTO.
SHOOM
SPRAM
SHOOM

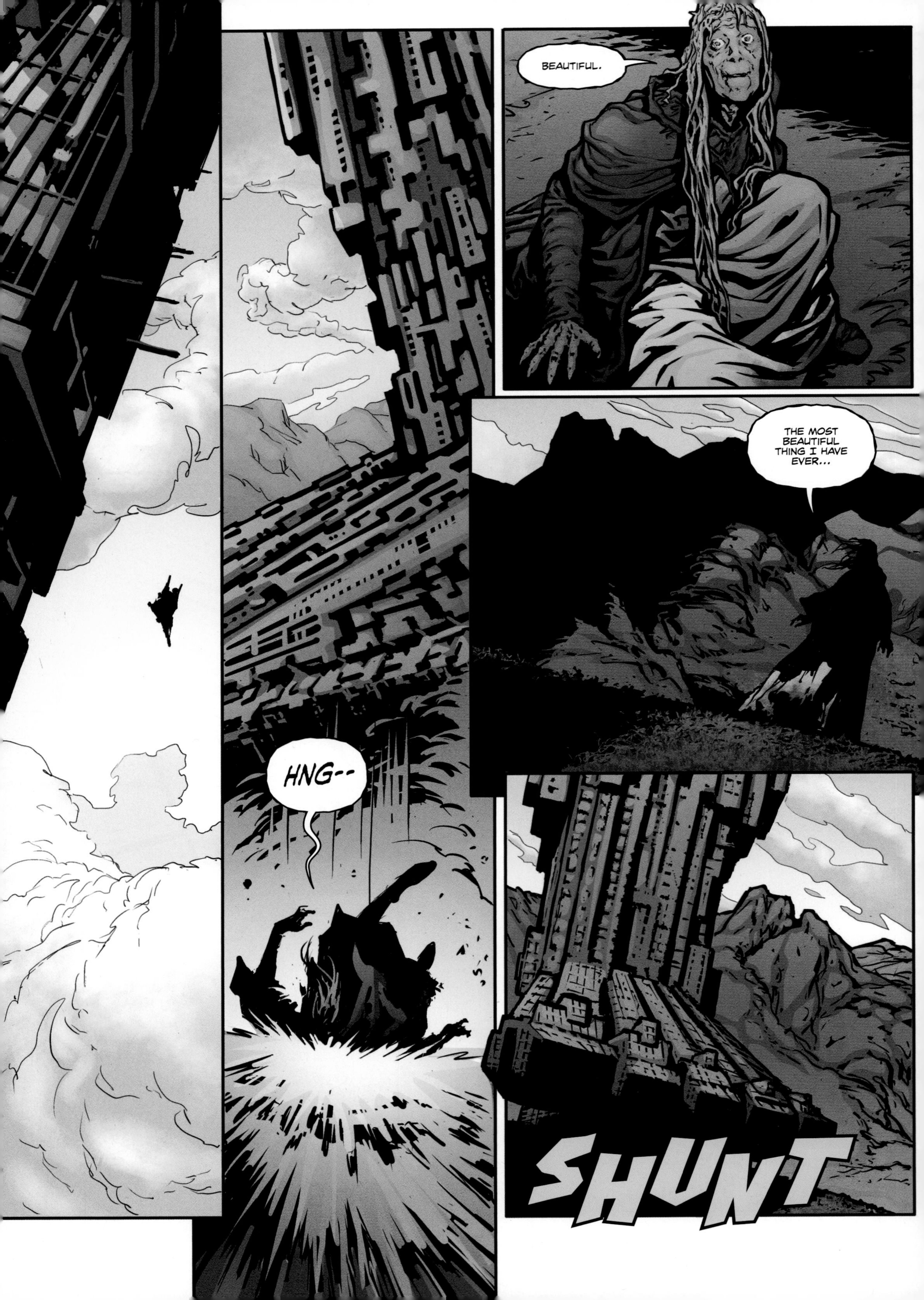
BEAUTIFUL.
THE MOST BEAUTIFUL THING I HAVE EVER...
HNG--
SHUNT

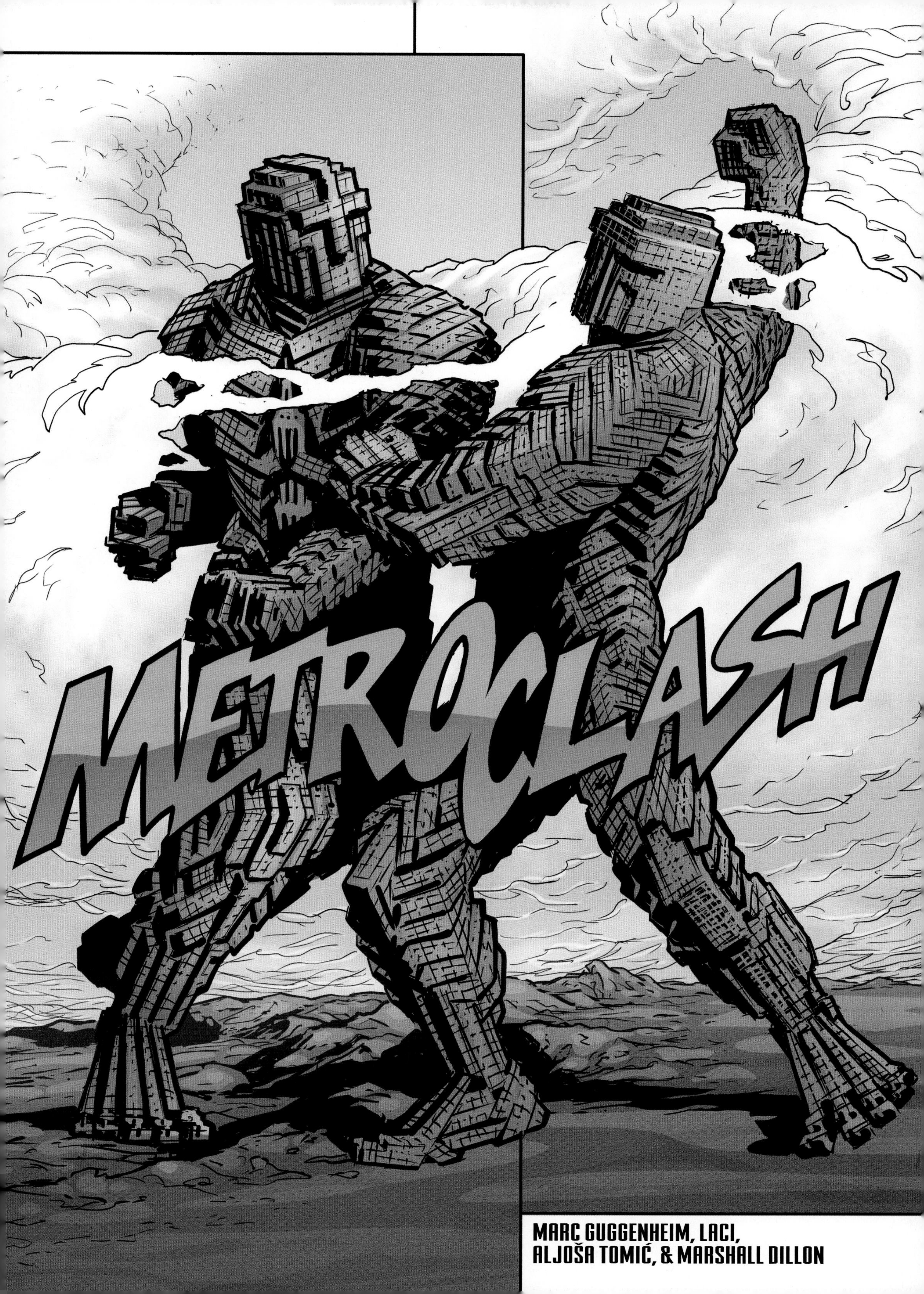
METROCLASH
MARC GUGGENHEIM, LACI,
ALJOŠA TOMIĆ, & MARSHALL DILLON

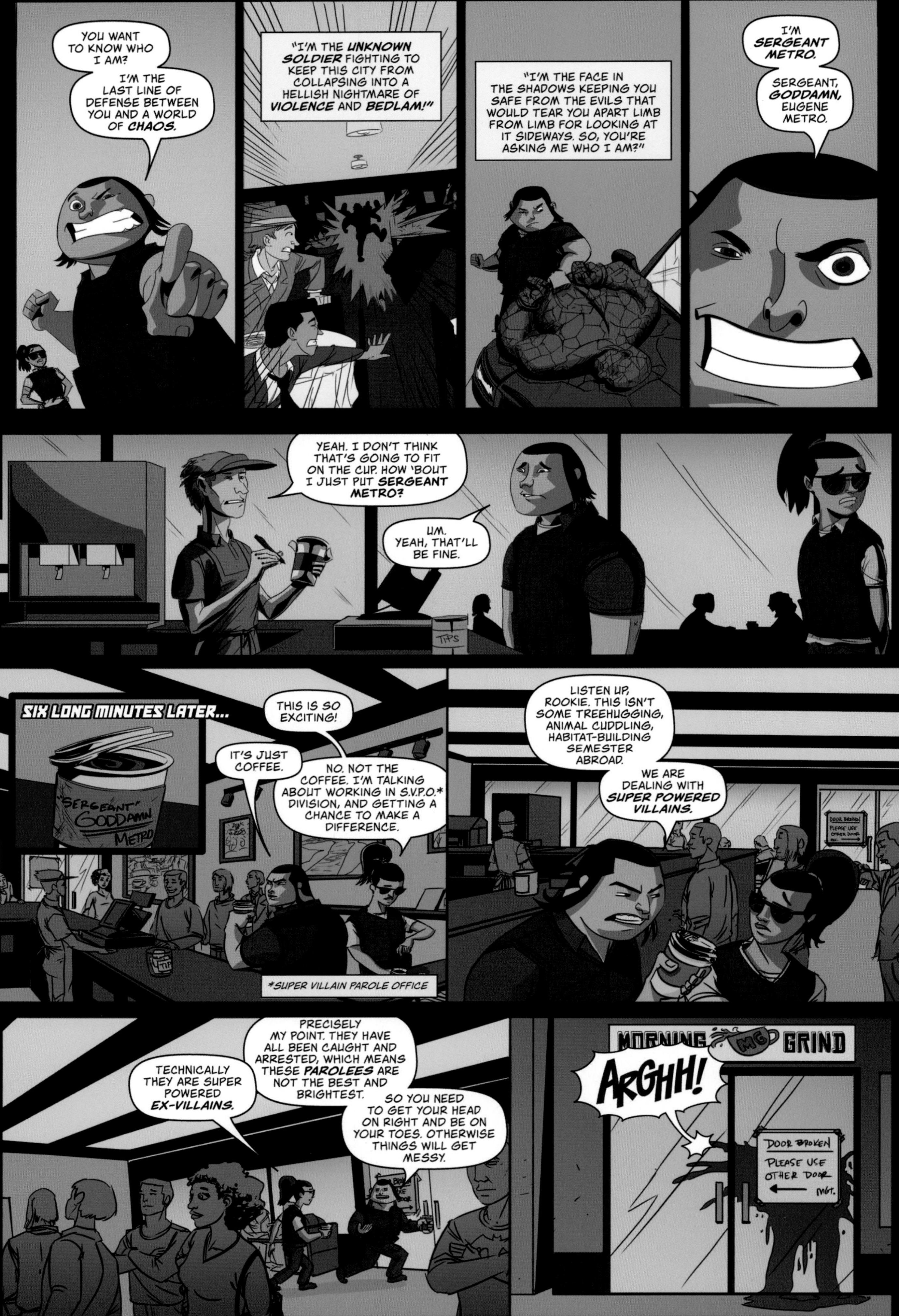
YOU WANT TO KNOW WHO I AM?
I'M THE LAST LINE OF DEFENSE BETWEEN YOU AND A WORLD OF CHAOS.
"I'M THE UNKNOWN SOLDIER FIGHTING TO KEEP THIS CITY FROM COLLAPSING INTO A HELLISH NIGHTMARE OF VIOLENCE AND BEDLAM!"
"I'M THE FACE IN THE SHADOWS KEEPING YOU SAFE FROM THE EVILS THAT WOULD TEAR YOU APART LIMB FROM LIMB FOR LOOKING AT IT SIDEWAYS. SO, YOU'RE ASKING ME WHO I AM?"
I'M SERGEANT METRO.
SERGEANT, GODDAMN, EUGENE METRO.
YEAH. I DON'T THINK THAT'S GOING TO FIT ON THE CUP. HOW 'BOUT I JUST PUT SERGEANT METRO?
UM. YEAH, THAT'LL BE FINE.
TIPS
SIX LONG MINUTES LATER...
"SERGEANT" GODDAMN METRO
THIS IS SO EXCITING!
IT'S JUST COFFEE.
NO. NOT THE COFFEE. I'M TALKING ABOUT WORKING IN S.V.P.O.* DIVISION, AND GETTING A CHANCE TO MAKE A DIFFERENCE.
*SUPER VILLAIN PAROLE OFFICE
LISTEN UP, ROOKIE. THIS ISN'T SOME TREEHUGGING, ANIMAL CUDDLING, HABITAT-BUILDING SEMESTER ABROAD.
WE ARE DEALING WITH SUPER POWERED VILLAINS.
TECHNICALLY THEY ARE SUPER POWERED EX-VILLAINS.
PRECISELY MY POINT. THEY HAVE ALL BEEN CAUGHT AND ARRESTED, WHICH MEANS THESE PAROLEES ARE NOT THE BEST AND BRIGHTEST.
SO YOU NEED TO GET YOUR HEAD ON RIGHT AND BE ON YOUR TOES. OTHERWISE THINGS WILL GET MESSY.
MORNING MG GRIND
ARGHH!
DOOR BROKEN
PLEASE USE OTHER DOOR
MGT.

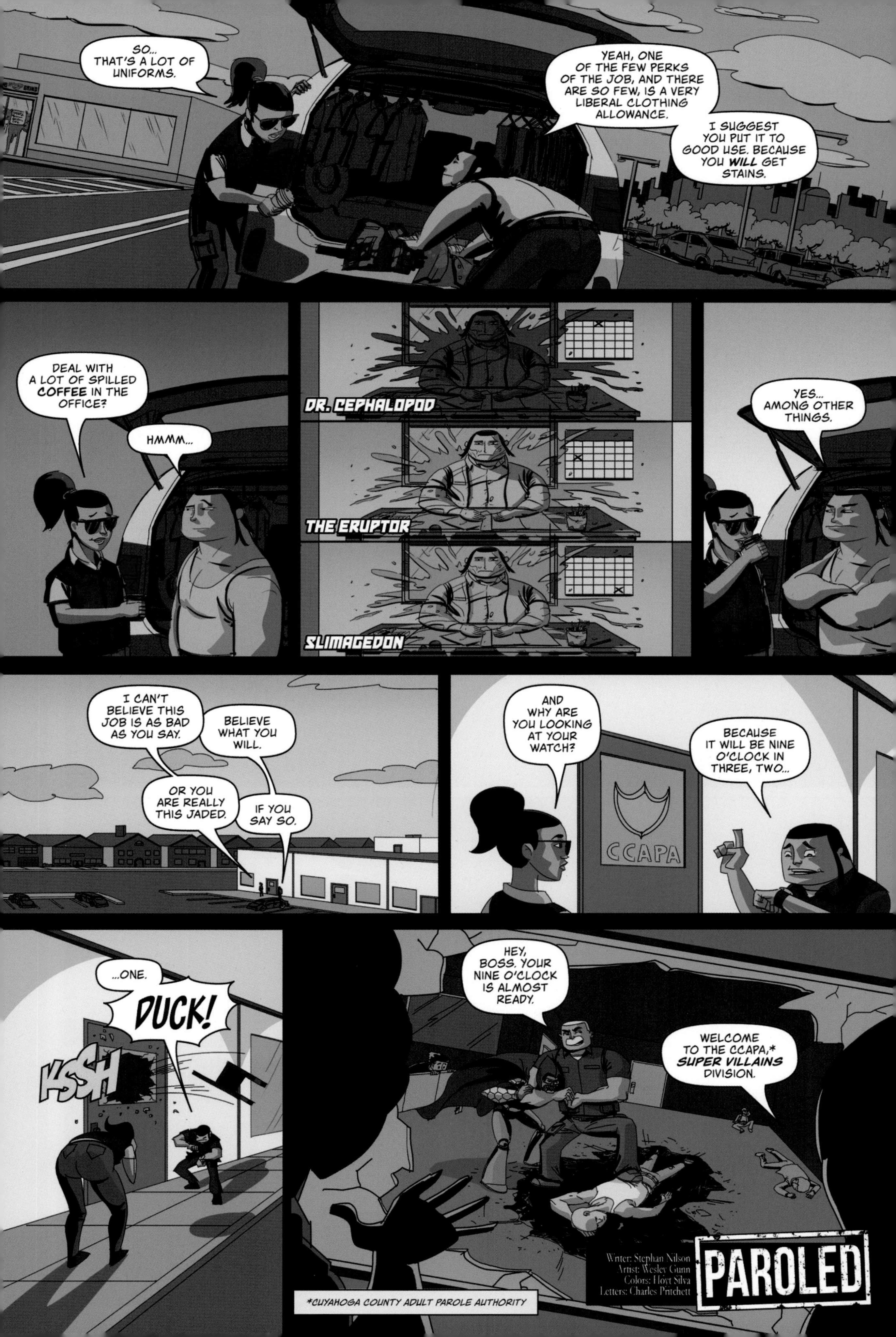
SO... THAT'S A LOT OF UNIFORMS.
YEAH, ONE OF THE FEW PERKS OF THE JOB, AND THERE ARE SO FEW, IS A VERY LIBERAL CLOTHING ALLOWANCE.
I SUGGEST YOU PUT IT TO GOOD USE. BECAUSE YOU WILL GET STAINS.
DEAL WITH A LOT OF SPILLED COFFEE IN THE OFFICE?
HMMM...
DR. CEPHALOPOD
THE ERUPTOR
SLIMAGEDON
YES... AMONG OTHER THINGS.
I CAN'T BELIEVE THIS JOB IS AS BAD AS YOU SAY.
BELIEVE WHAT YOU WILL.
OR YOU ARE REALLY THIS JADED.
IF YOU SAY SO.
AND WHY ARE YOU LOOKING AT YOUR WATCH?
CCAPA
BECAUSE IT WILL BE NINE O'CLOCK IN THREE, TWO...
...ONE.
DUCK!
KSSH
HEY, BOSS. YOUR NINE O'CLOCK IS ALMOST READY.
WELCOME TO THE CCAPA,* SUPER VILLAINS DIVISION.
Writer: Stephan Nilson
Artist: Wesley Gunn
Colors: Hoyt Silva
Letters: Charles Pritchett
PAROLED
*CUYAHOGA COUNTY ADULT PAROLE AUTHORITY

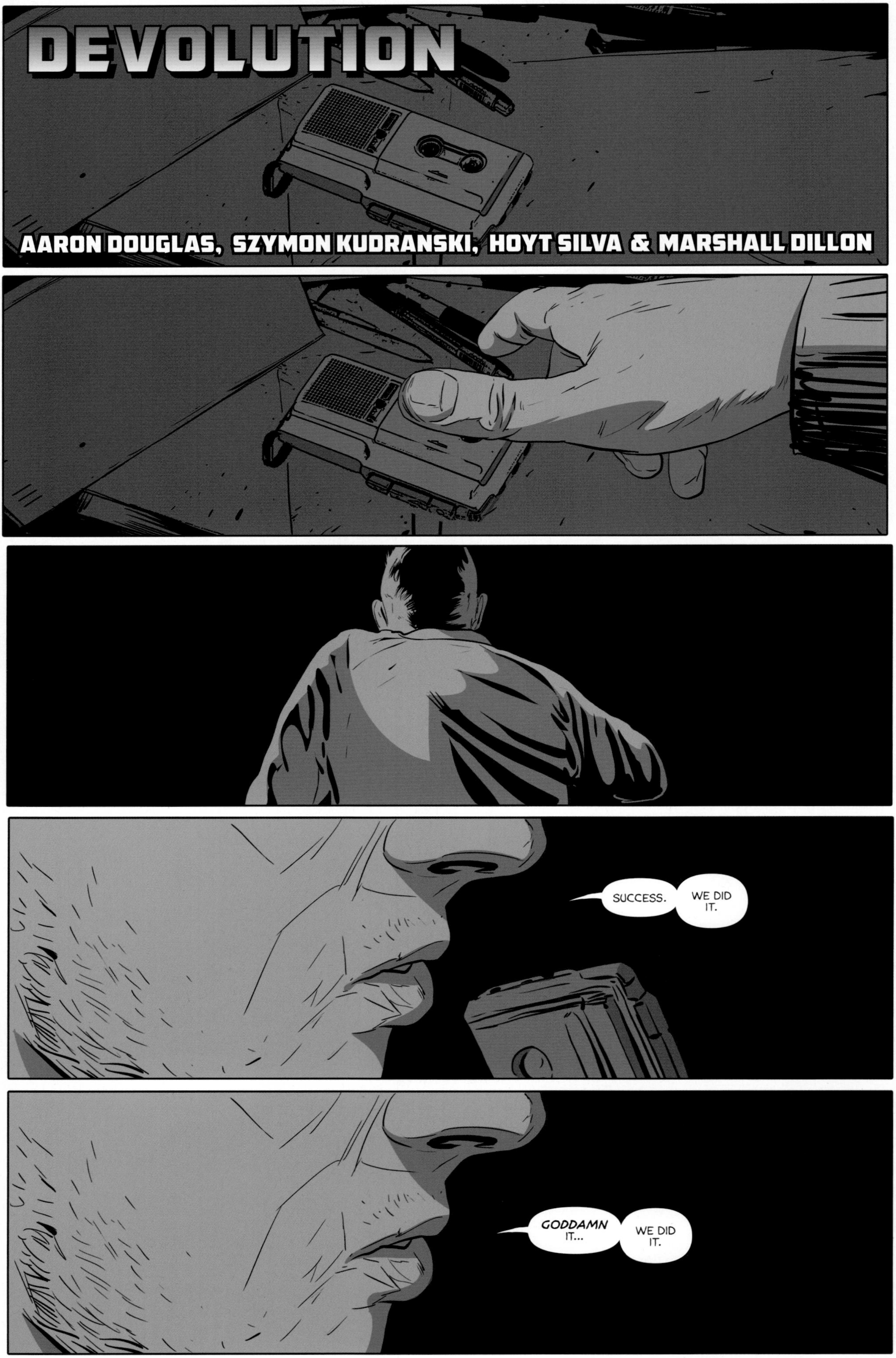
DEVOLUTION
AARON DOUGLAS, SZYMON KUDRANSKI, HOYT SILVA & MARSHALL DILLON
SUCCESS.
WE DID IT.
GODDAMN IT...
WE DID IT.

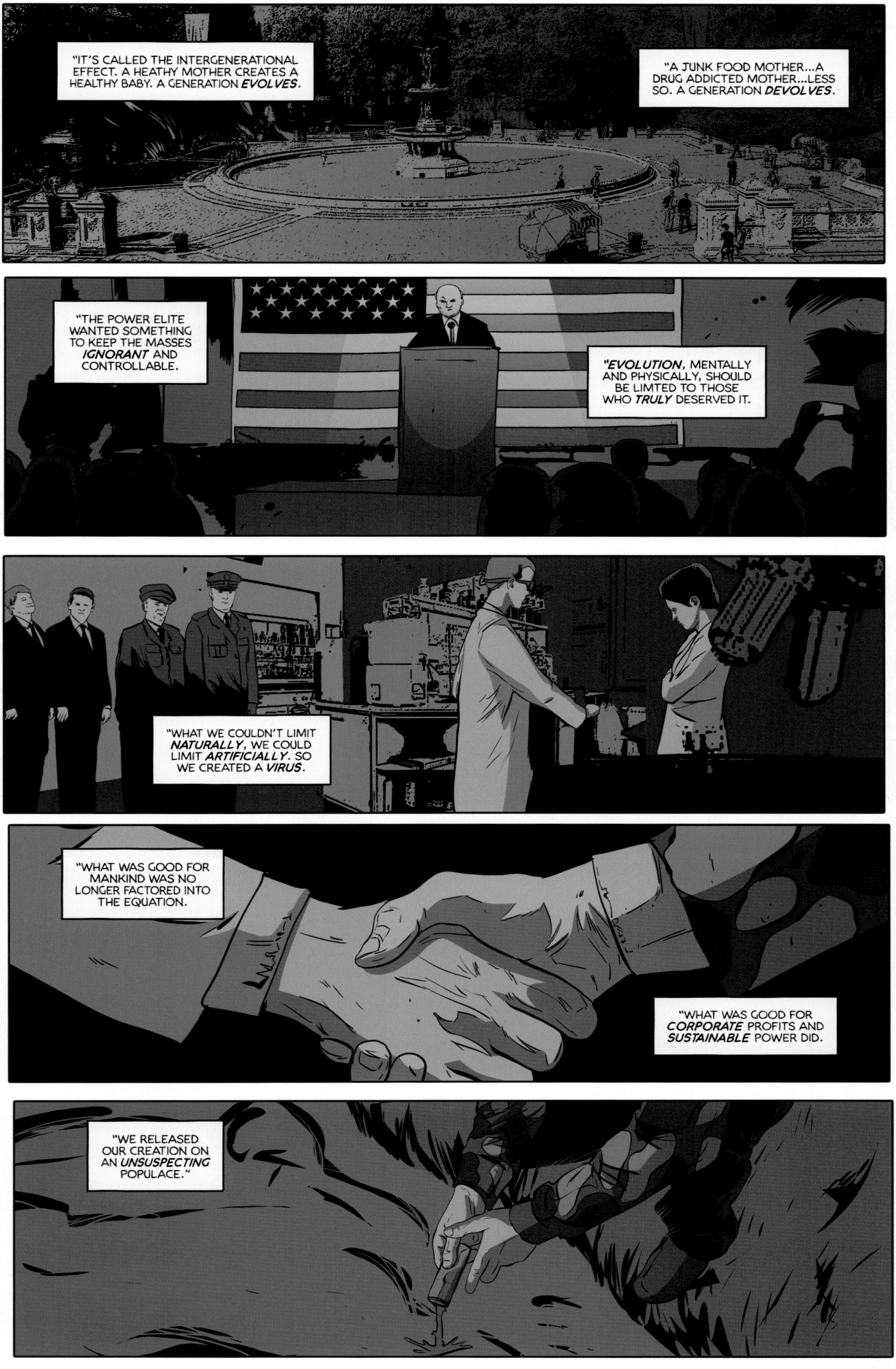
"IT'S CALLED THE INTERGENERATIONAL EFFECT. A HEATHY MOTHER CREATES A HEALTHY BABY. A GENERATION *EVOLVES*.
"A JUNK FOOD MOTHER...A DRUG ADDICTED MOTHER...LESS SO. A GENERATION *DEVOLVES*.
"THE POWER ELITE WANTED SOMETHING TO KEEP THE MASSES *IGNORANT* AND CONTROLLABLE.
"*EVOLUTION*, MENTALLY AND PHYSICALLY, SHOULD BE LIMTED TO THOSE WHO *TRULY* DESERVED IT.
"WHAT WE COULDN'T LIMIT *NATURALLY*, WE COULD LIMIT *ARTIFICIALLY*. SO WE CREATED A *VIRUS*.
"WHAT WAS GOOD FOR MANKIND WAS NO LONGER FACTORED INTO THE EQUATION.
"WHAT WAS GOOD FOR *CORPORATE* PROFITS AND *SUSTAINABLE* POWER DID.
"WE RELEASED OUR CREATION ON AN *UNSUSPECTING* POPULACE."

"BUT OUR CREATION *MUTATED*...THE VIRUS CREATED TO *CURB* EVOLUTION...INSTEAD *EVOLVED*. THE PEOPLE...THE MASSES...DID NOT.

"WE SOON SAW THE RESULTS OF OUR ACTIONS AS OUR OWN *CHILDREN* BECAME MORE *BEAST* THAN MAN. OUR *PRIMAL* DESIRES BECAME *DOMINANT*. WE WATCHED AS OUR *CIVILIZED* WORLD FADED AWAY.

"A *NEW* GOVERNMENT WAS ELECTED TO POWER WITH THE SINCERE DESIRE TO STOP WHAT THEIR PREDECESSORS HAD *UNWITTINGLY* SET INTO MOTION.

"THEY *FAILED*.

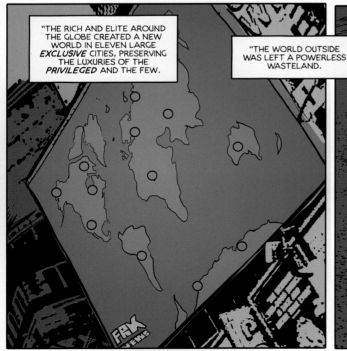

"THE RICH AND ELITE AROUND THE GLOBE CREATED A NEW WORLD IN ELEVEN LARGE *EXCLUSIVE* CITIES, PRESERVING THE LUXURIES OF THE *PRIVILEGED* AND THE FEW.

"THE WORLD OUTSIDE WAS LEFT A POWERLESS WASTELAND.

"THE CITIES BECAME STERILE *PALACES* OF TECHNOLOGY AND LIGHT, WITH ALL THE NECESSITIES FOR LIFE *READILY* AVAILABLE.

"CULTURE, ART, ANY FORM OF PLEASURE OR STIMULATION, ONLY *DISTRACTED* FROM THE CORPORATE MANDATED ROUTINE OF THE POPULACE, AND SO WERE *ELIMINATED*."

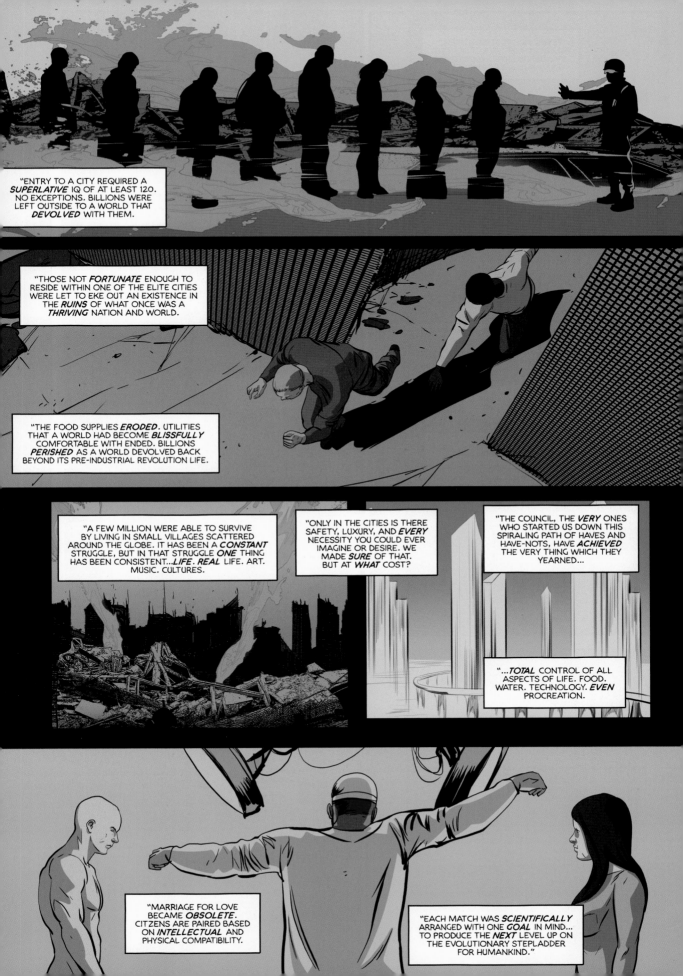

"ENTRY TO A CITY REQUIRED A *SUPERLATIVE* IQ OF AT LEAST 120. NO EXCEPTIONS. BILLIONS WERE LEFT OUTSIDE TO A WORLD THAT *DEVOLVED* WITH THEM.

"THOSE NOT *FORTUNATE* ENOUGH TO RESIDE WITHIN ONE OF THE ELITE CITIES WERE LET TO EKE OUT AN EXISTENCE IN THE *RUINS* OF WHAT ONCE WAS A *THRIVING* NATION AND WORLD.

"THE FOOD SUPPLIES *ERODED*. UTILITIES THAT A WORLD HAD BECOME *BLISSFULLY* COMFORTABLE WITH ENDED. BILLIONS *PERISHED* AS A WORLD DEVOLVED BACK BEYOND ITS PRE-INDUSTRIAL REVOLUTION LIFE.

"A FEW MILLION WERE ABLE TO SURVIVE BY LIVING IN SMALL VILLAGES SCATTERED AROUND THE GLOBE. IT HAS BEEN A *CONSTANT* STRUGGLE, BUT IN THAT STRUGGLE *ONE* THING HAS BEEN CONSISTENT...*LIFE. REAL* LIFE. ART. MUSIC. CULTURES.

"ONLY IN THE CITIES IS THERE SAFETY, LUXURY, AND *EVERY* NECESSITY YOU COULD EVER IMAGINE OR DESIRE. WE MADE *SURE* OF THAT. BUT AT *WHAT* COST?

"THE COUNCIL, THE *VERY* ONES WHO STARTED US DOWN THIS SPIRALING PATH OF HAVES AND HAVE-NOTS, HAVE *ACHIEVED* THE VERY THING WHICH THEY YEARNED...

"...*TOTAL* CONTROL OF ALL ASPECTS OF LIFE. FOOD. WATER. TECHNOLOGY. *EVEN* PROCREATION.

"MARRIAGE FOR LOVE BECAME *OBSOLETE*. CITZENS ARE PAIRED BASED ON *INTELLECTUAL* AND PHYSICAL COMPATIBILITY.

"EACH MATCH WAS *SCIENTIFICALLY* ARRANGED WITH ONE *GOAL* IN MIND... TO PRODUCE THE *NEXT* LEVEL UP ON THE EVOLUTIONARY STEPLADDER FOR HUMANKIND."

"FETUS' ARE TESTED IN UTERO. FAILURE TO MEET THE DESIGNATED STANDARDS BRINGS *IMMEDIATE* TERMINATION OF THE UNBORN.

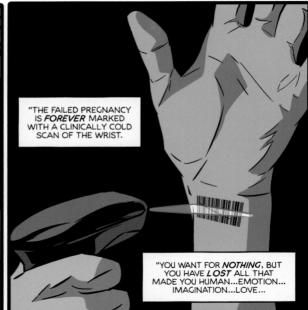

"THE FAILED PREGNANCY IS *FOREVER* MARKED WITH A CLINICALLY COLD SCAN OF THE WRIST.

"YOU WANT FOR *NOTHING*, BUT YOU HAVE *LOST* ALL THAT MADE YOU HUMAN...EMOTION... IMAGINATION...LOVE...

"OUTSIDE THE GLEAMING CITIES, THERE IS NO LUXURY.

"THERE ARE NO WRIST SCANS.

"NO FREE FOOD OR WATER.

"BUT THERE IS *LIFE*.

"AND *LOVE*.

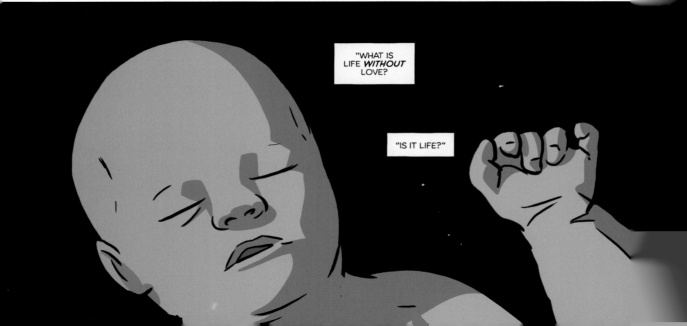

"WHAT IS LIFE *WITHOUT* LOVE?

"IS IT LIFE?"

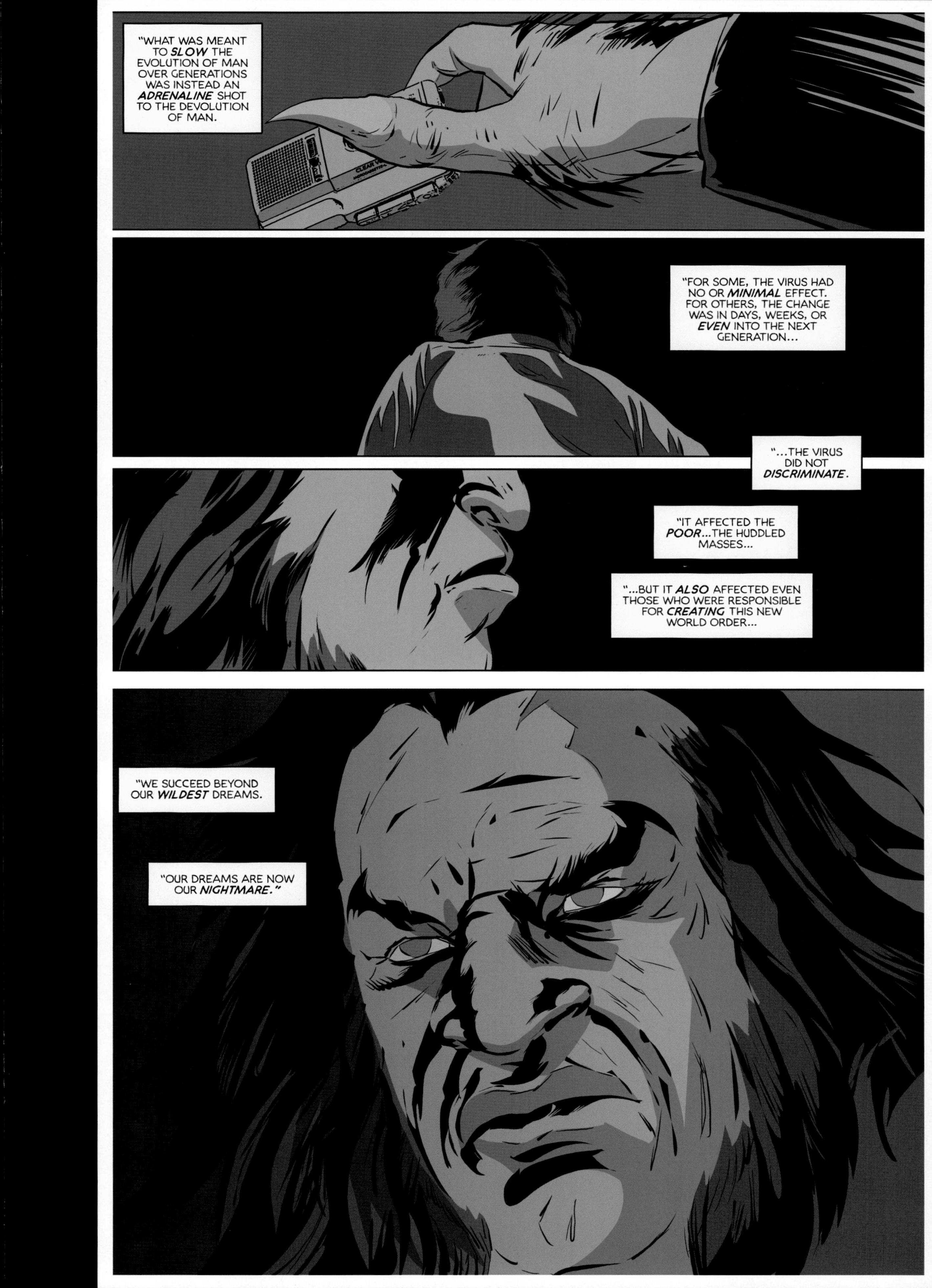
"WHAT WAS MEANT TO *SLOW* THE EVOLUTION OF MAN OVER GENERATIONS WAS INSTEAD AN *ADRENALINE* SHOT TO THE DEVOLUTION OF MAN.
"FOR SOME, THE VIRUS HAD NO OR *MINIMAL* EFFECT. FOR OTHERS, THE CHANGE WAS IN DAYS, WEEKS, OR *EVEN* INTO THE NEXT GENERATION...
"...THE VIRUS DID NOT *DISCRIMINATE*.
"IT AFFECTED THE *POOR*...THE HUDDLED MASSES...
"...BUT IT *ALSO* AFFECTED EVEN THOSE WHO WERE RESPONSIBLE FOR *CREATING* THIS NEW WORLD ORDER...
"WE SUCCEED BEYOND OUR *WILDEST* DREAMS.
"OUR DREAMS ARE NOW OUR *NIGHTMARE.*"

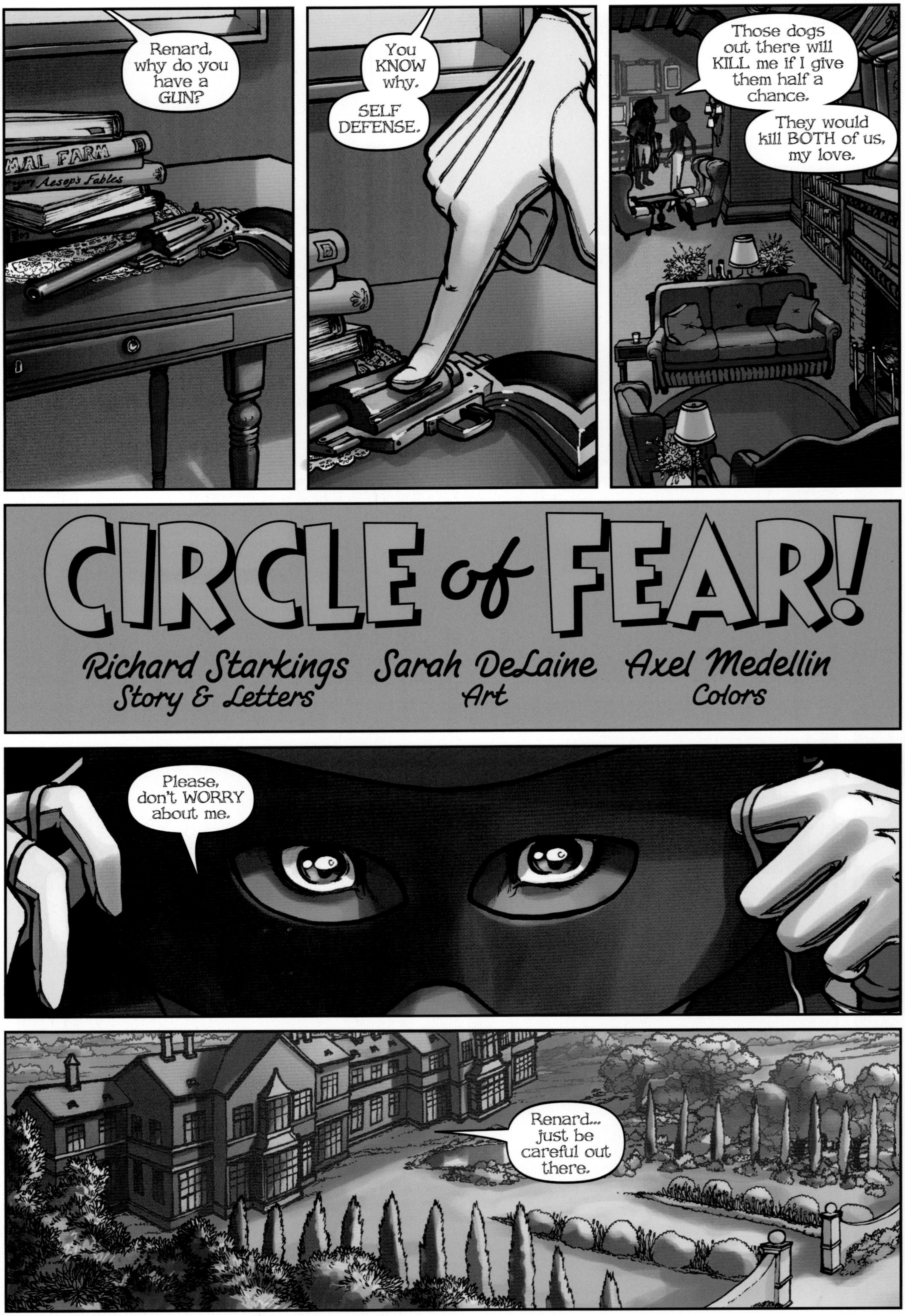
Renard, why do you have a GUN?
You KNOW why.
SELF DEFENSE.
Those dogs out there will KILL me if I give them half a chance.
They would kill BOTH of us, my love.
CIRCLE of FEAR!
Richard Starkings
Story & Letters
Sarah DeLaine
Art
Axel Medellin
Colors
Please, don't WORRY about me.
Renard... just be careful out there.

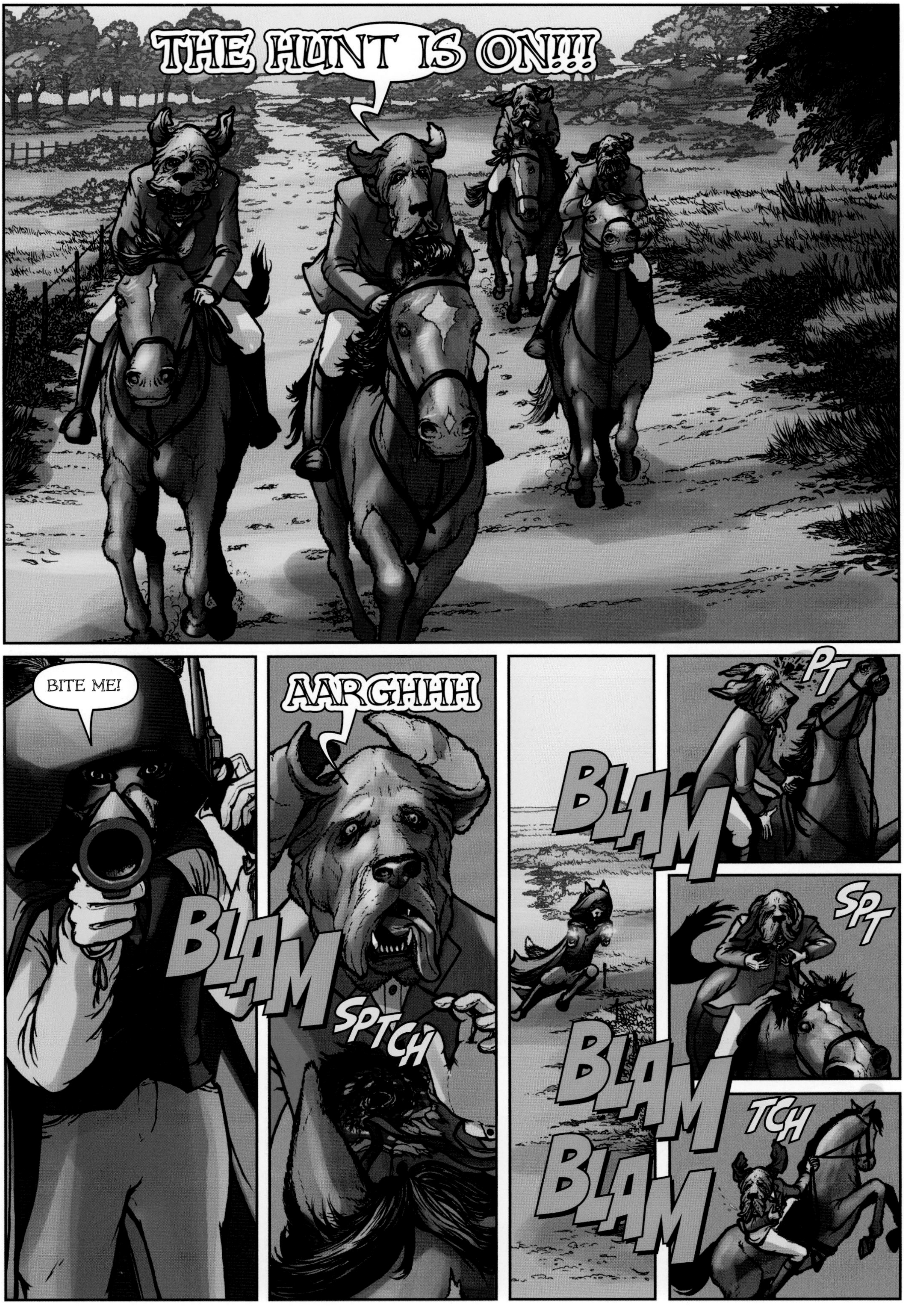
THE HUNT IS ON!!!
BITE ME!
BLAM
AARGHHH
SPTCH
BLAM
PT
SPT
BLAM
BLAM
TCH

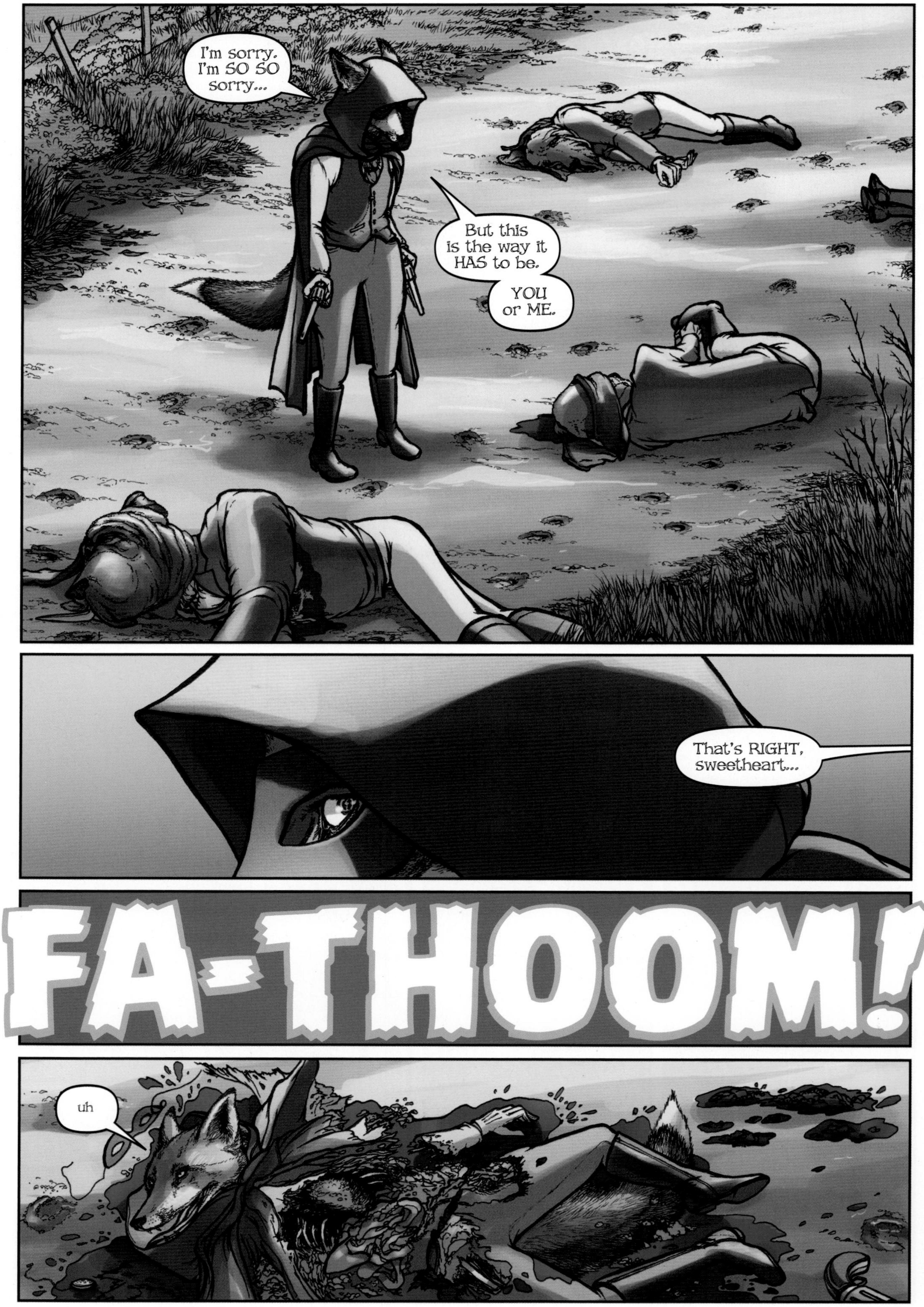

I'm sorry. I'm SO SO sorry...
But this is the way it HAS to be.
YOU or ME.
That's RIGHT, sweetheart...
FA-THOOM!
uh

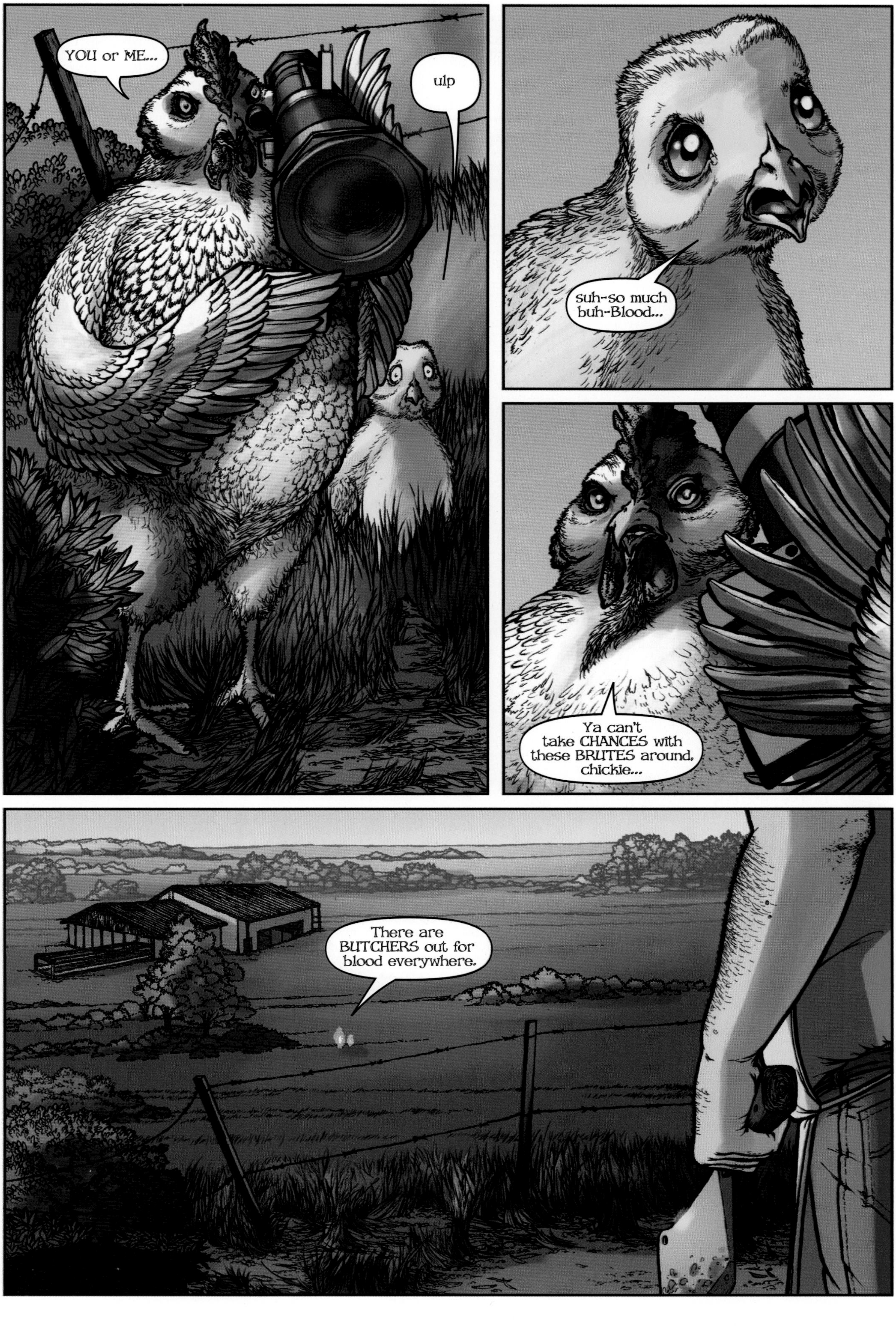
YOU or ME...
ulp
suh-so much buh-Blood...
Ya can't take CHANCES with these BRUTES around, chickie...
There are BUTCHERS out for blood everywhere.

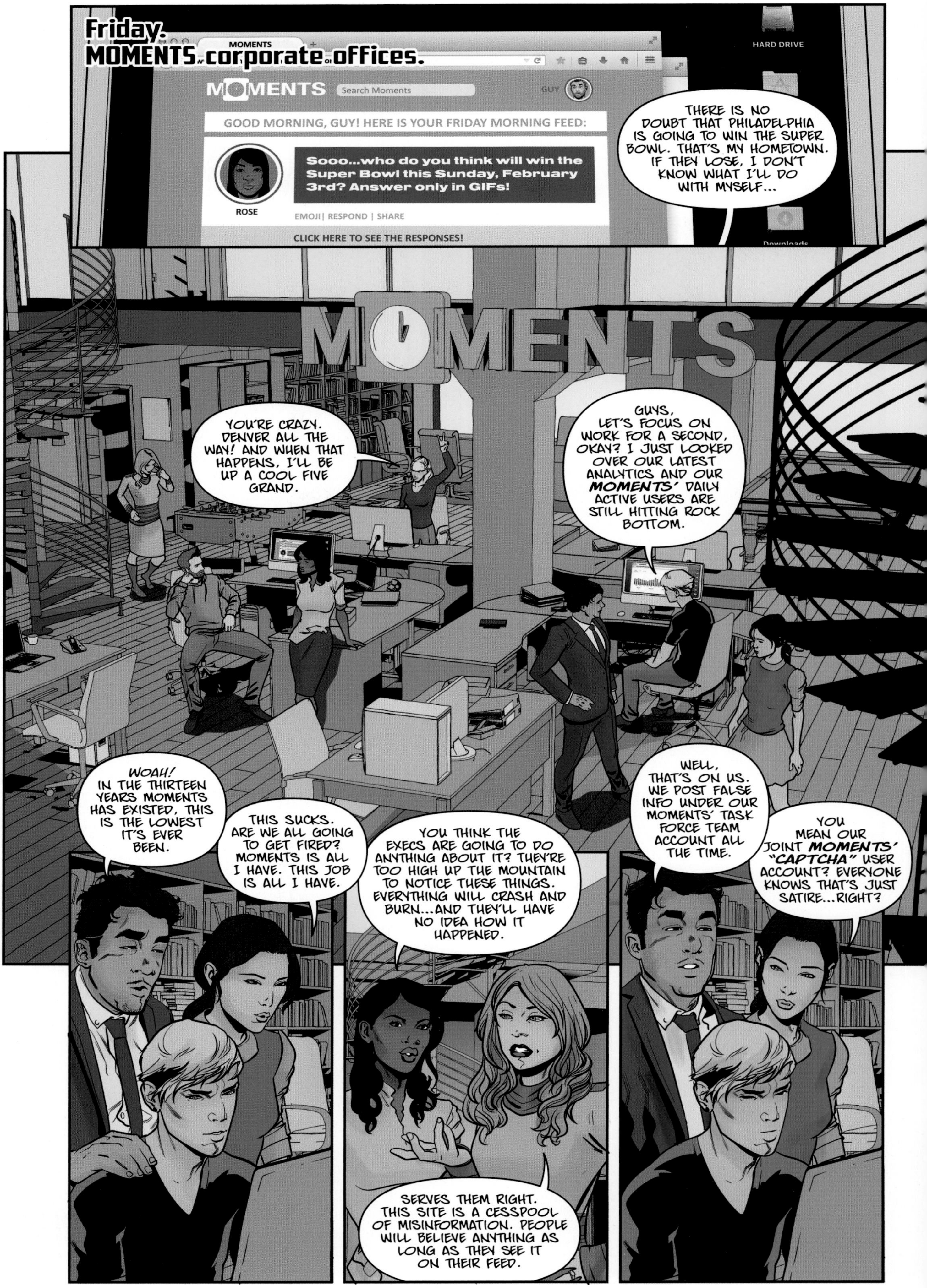
Friday. MOMENTS corporate offices.
MOMENTS
Search Moments
GUY
GOOD MORNING, GUY! HERE IS YOUR FRIDAY MORNING FEED:
Sooo...who do you think will win the Super Bowl this Sunday, February 3rd? Answer only in GIFs!
ROSE
EMOJI | RESPOND | SHARE
CLICK HERE TO SEE THE RESPONSES!
HARD DRIVE
THERE IS NO DOUBT THAT PHILADELPHIA IS GOING TO WIN THE SUPER BOWL. THAT'S MY HOMETOWN. IF THEY LOSE, I DON'T KNOW WHAT I'LL DO WITH MYSELF...
MOMENTS
YOU'RE CRAZY. DENVER ALL THE WAY! AND WHEN THAT HAPPENS, I'LL BE UP A COOL FIVE GRAND.
GUYS, LET'S FOCUS ON WORK FOR A SECOND, OKAY? I JUST LOOKED OVER OUR LATEST ANALYTICS AND OUR MOMENTS' DAILY ACTIVE USERS ARE STILL HITTING ROCK BOTTOM.
WOAH! IN THE THIRTEEN YEARS MOMENTS HAS EXISTED, THIS IS THE LOWEST IT'S EVER BEEN.
THIS SUCKS. ARE WE ALL GOING TO GET FIRED? MOMENTS IS ALL I HAVE. THIS JOB IS ALL I HAVE.
YOU THINK THE EXECS ARE GOING TO DO ANYTHING ABOUT IT? THEY'RE TOO HIGH UP THE MOUNTAIN TO NOTICE THESE THINGS. EVERYTHING WILL CRASH AND BURN...AND THEY'LL HAVE NO IDEA HOW IT HAPPENED.
SERVES THEM RIGHT. THIS SITE IS A CESSPOOL OF MISINFORMATION. PEOPLE WILL BELIEVE ANYTHING AS LONG AS THEY SEE IT ON THEIR FEED.
WELL, THAT'S ON US. WE POST FALSE INFO UNDER OUR MOMENTS' TASK FORCE TEAM ACCOUNT ALL THE TIME.
YOU MEAN OUR JOINT MOMENTS' "CAPTCHA" USER ACCOUNT? EVERYONE KNOWS THAT'S JUST SATIRE...RIGHT?

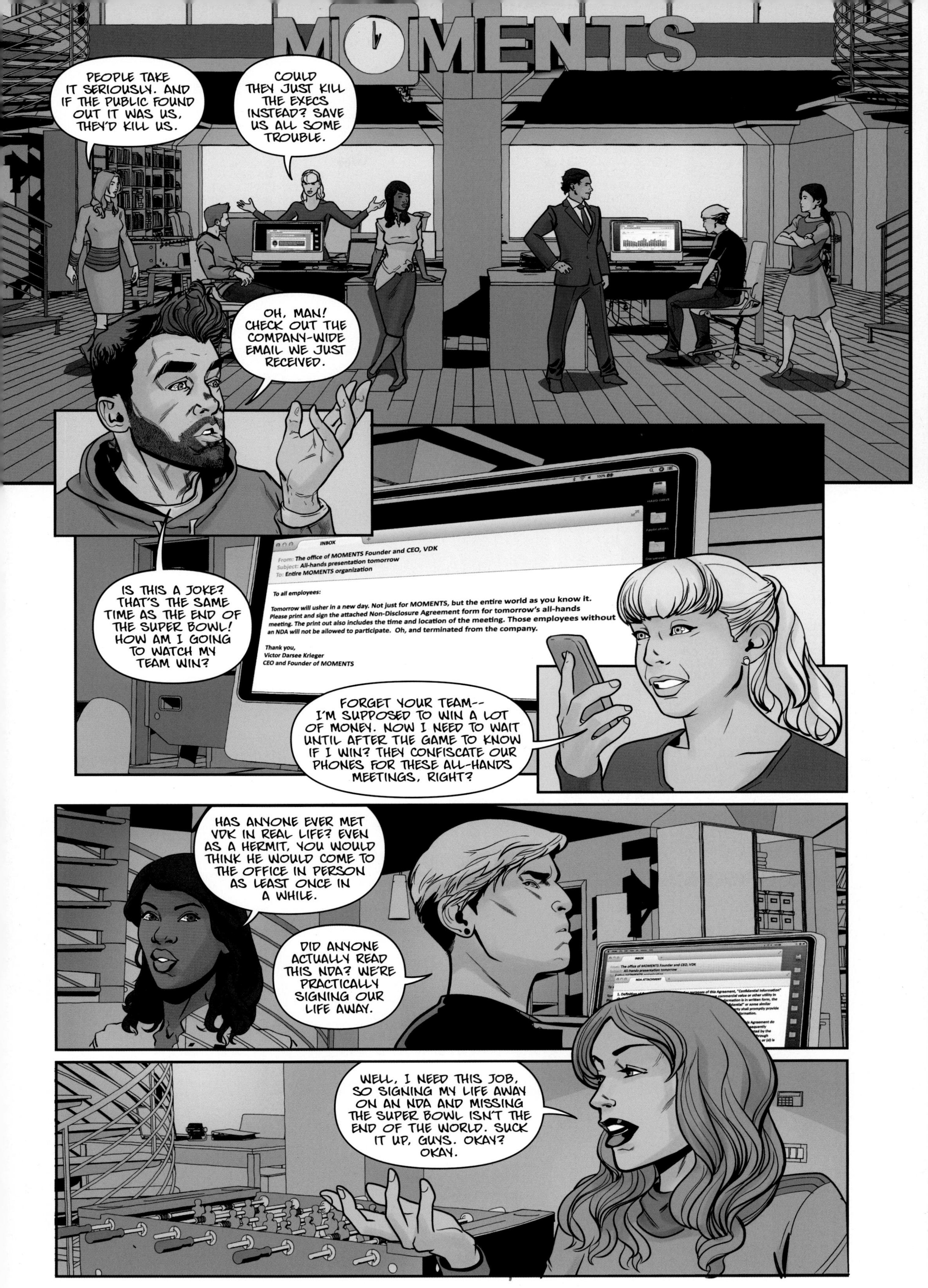
MOMENTS
PEOPLE TAKE IT SERIOUSLY. AND IF THE PUBLIC FOUND OUT IT WAS US, THEY'D KILL US.
COULD THEY JUST KILL THE EXECS INSTEAD? SAVE US ALL SOME TROUBLE.
OH, MAN! CHECK OUT THE COMPANY-WIDE EMAIL WE JUST RECEIVED.
IS THIS A JOKE? THAT'S THE SAME TIME AS THE END OF THE SUPER BOWL! HOW AM I GOING TO WATCH MY TEAM WIN?
INBOX
From: The office of MOMENTS Founder and CEO, VDK
Subject: All-hands presentation tomorrow
To: Entire MOMENTS organization
To all employees:
Tomorrow will usher in a new day. Not just for MOMENTS, but the entire world as you know it. Please print and sign the attached Non-Disclosure Agreement form for tomorrow's all-hands meeting. The print out also includes the time and location of the meeting. Those employees without an NDA will not be allowed to participate. Oh, and terminated from the company.
Thank you,
Victor Darsee Krieger
CEO and Founder of MOMENTS
FORGET YOUR TEAM-- I'M SUPPOSED TO WIN A LOT OF MONEY. NOW I NEED TO WAIT UNTIL AFTER THE GAME TO KNOW IF I WIN? THEY CONFISCATE OUR PHONES FOR THESE ALL-HANDS MEETINGS, RIGHT?
HAS ANYONE EVER MET VDK IN REAL LIFE? EVEN AS A HERMIT, YOU WOULD THINK HE WOULD COME TO THE OFFICE IN PERSON AS LEAST ONCE IN A WHILE.
DID ANYONE ACTUALLY READ THIS NDA? WE'RE PRACTICALLY SIGNING OUR LIFE AWAY.
WELL, I NEED THIS JOB, SO SIGNING MY LIFE AWAY ON AN NDA AND MISSING THE SUPER BOWL ISN'T THE END OF THE WORLD. SUCK IT UP, GUYS. OKAY? OKAY.

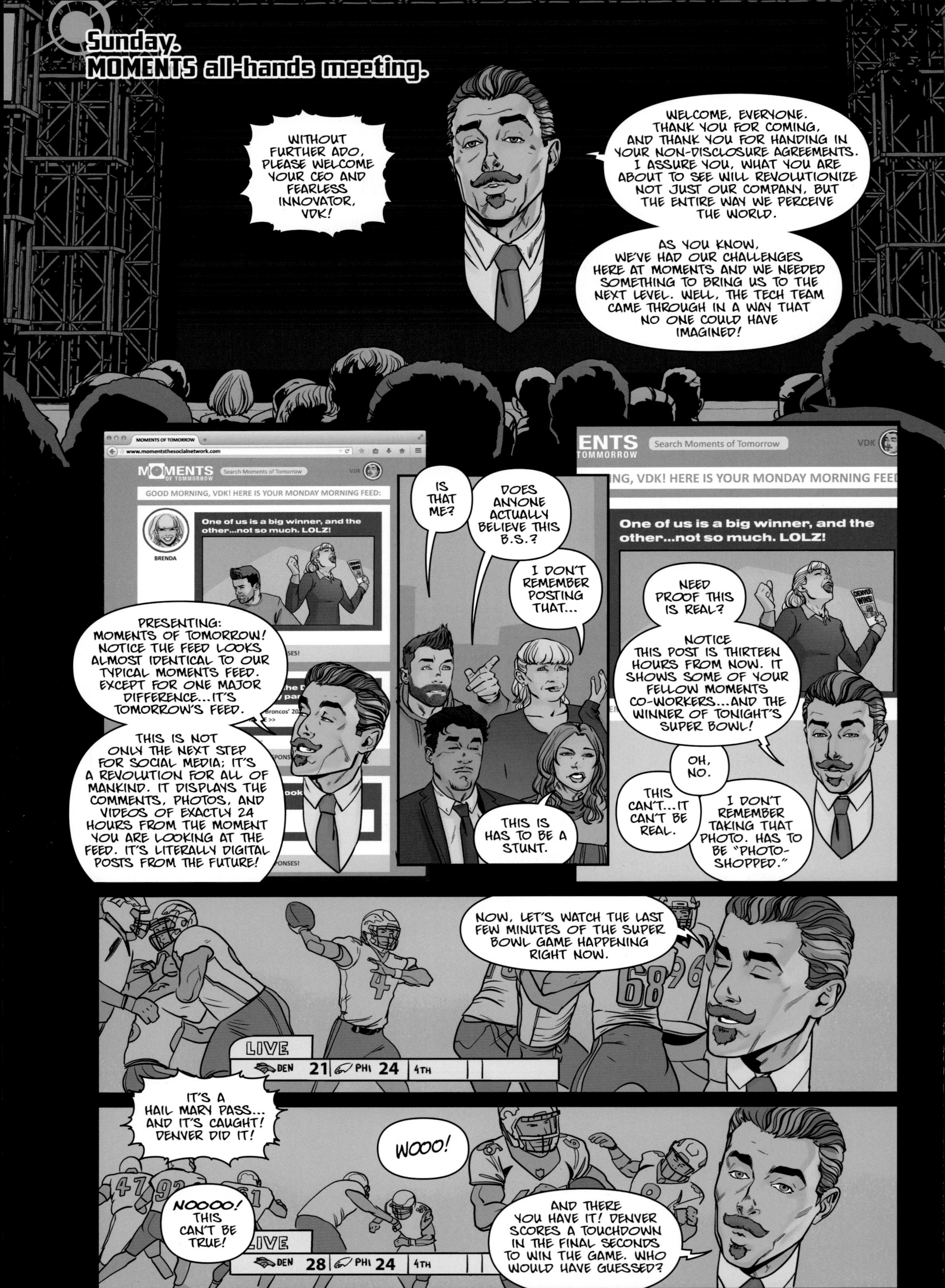
Sunday.
MOMENTS all-hands meeting.
WITHOUT FURTHER ADO, PLEASE WELCOME YOUR CEO AND FEARLESS INNOVATOR, VDK!
WELCOME, EVERYONE. THANK YOU FOR COMING, AND THANK YOU FOR HANDING IN YOUR NON-DISCLOSURE AGREEMENTS. I ASSURE YOU, WHAT YOU ARE ABOUT TO SEE WILL REVOLUTIONIZE NOT JUST OUR COMPANY, BUT THE ENTIRE WAY WE PERCEIVE THE WORLD.
AS YOU KNOW, WE'VE HAD OUR CHALLENGES HERE AT MOMENTS AND WE NEEDED SOMETHING TO BRING US TO THE NEXT LEVEL. WELL, THE TECH TEAM CAME THROUGH IN A WAY THAT NO ONE COULD HAVE IMAGINED!
MOMENTS OF TOMORROW
www.momentsthesocialnetwork.com
MOMENTS OF TOMORROW
Search Moments of Tomorrow
VDK
GOOD MORNING, VDK! HERE IS YOUR MONDAY MORNING FEED:
BRENDA
One of us is a big winner, and the other...not so much. LOLZ!
DENVER WINS!
PRESENTING: MOMENTS OF TOMORROW! NOTICE THE FEED LOOKS ALMOST IDENTICAL TO OUR TYPICAL MOMENTS FEED. EXCEPT FOR ONE MAJOR DIFFERENCE...IT'S TOMORROW'S FEED.
THIS IS NOT ONLY THE NEXT STEP FOR SOCIAL MEDIA; IT'S A REVOLUTION FOR ALL OF MANKIND. IT DISPLAYS THE COMMENTS, PHOTOS, AND VIDEOS OF EXACTLY 24 HOURS FROM THE MOMENT YOU ARE LOOKING AT THE FEED. IT'S LITERALLY DIGITAL POSTS FROM THE FUTURE!
IS THAT ME?
DOES ANYONE ACTUALLY BELIEVE THIS B.S.?
I DON'T REMEMBER POSTING THAT...
THIS IS HAS TO BE A STUNT.
ENTS
TOMORROW
Search Moments of Tomorrow
VDK
NG, VDK! HERE IS YOUR MONDAY MORNING FEED
One of us is a big winner, and the other...not so much. LOLZ!
NEED PROOF THIS IS REAL?
NOTICE THIS POST IS THIRTEEN HOURS FROM NOW. IT SHOWS SOME OF YOUR FELLOW MOMENTS CO-WORKERS...AND THE WINNER OF TONIGHT'S SUPER BOWL!
OH, NO.
THIS CAN'T...IT CAN'T BE REAL.
I DON'T REMEMBER TAKING THAT PHOTO. HAS TO BE "PHOTO-SHOPPED."
NOW, LET'S WATCH THE LAST FEW MINUTES OF THE SUPER BOWL GAME HAPPENING RIGHT NOW.
LIVE
DEN 21 PHI 24 4TH
IT'S A HAIL MARY PASS... AND IT'S CAUGHT! DENVER DID IT!
WOOO!
NOOOO! THIS CAN'T BE TRUE!
AND THERE YOU HAVE IT! DENVER SCORES A TOUCHDOWN IN THE FINAL SECONDS TO WIN THE GAME. WHO WOULD HAVE GUESSED?
LIVE
DEN 28 PHI 24 4TH

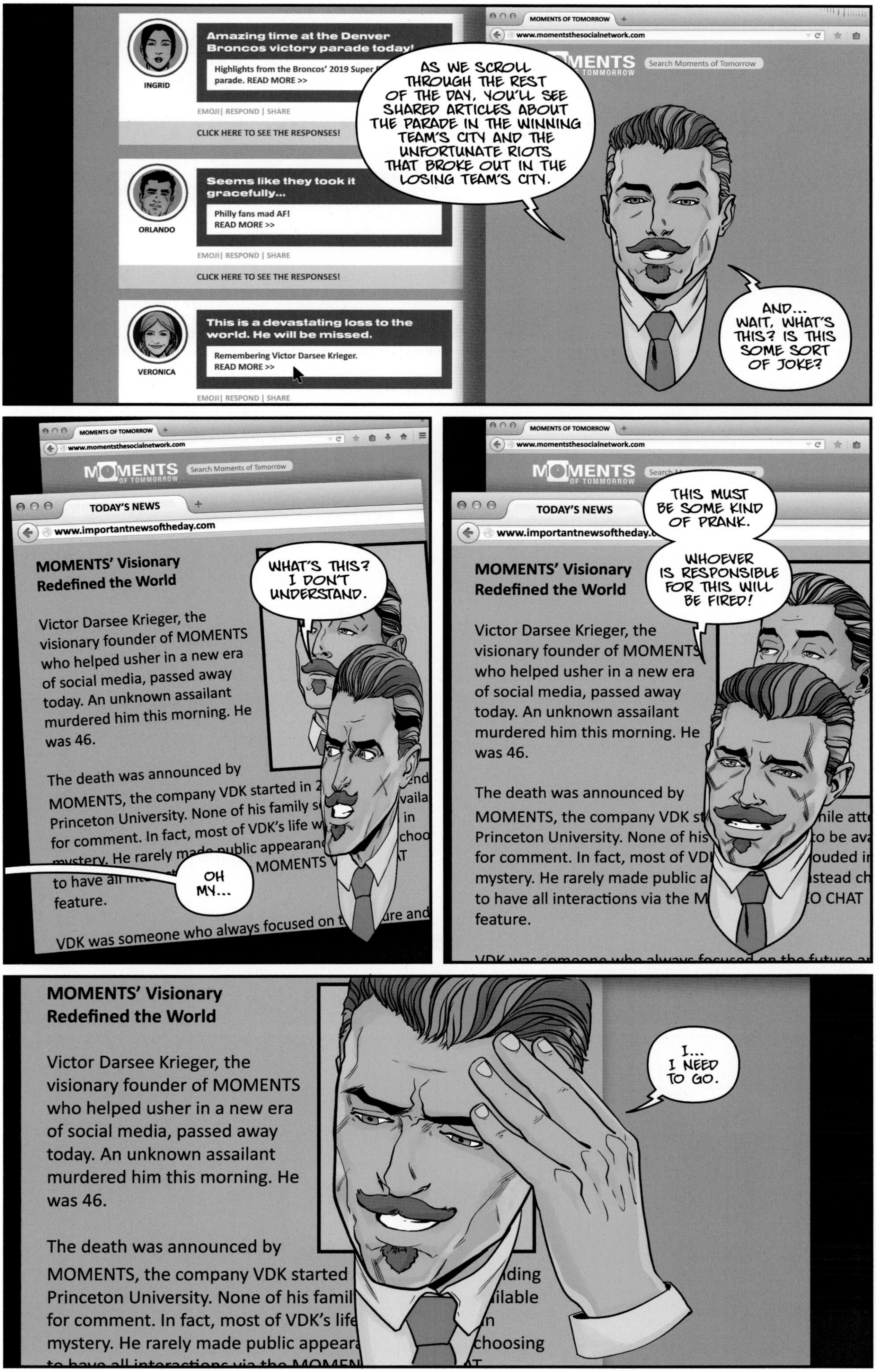

MOMENTS OF TOMORROW
www.momentsthesocialnetwork.com
Search Moments of Tomorrow
Amazing time at the Denver Broncos victory parade today!
INGRID
EMOJI| RESPOND | SHARE
CLICK HERE TO SEE THE RESPONSES!
AS WE SCROLL THROUGH THE REST OF THE DAY, YOU'LL SEE SHARED ARTICLES ABOUT THE PARADE IN THE WINNING TEAM'S CITY AND THE UNFORTUNATE RIOTS THAT BROKE OUT IN THE LOSING TEAM'S CITY.
Seems like they took it gracefully...
Philly fans mad AF! READ MORE >>
ORLANDO
EMOJI| RESPOND | SHARE
CLICK HERE TO SEE THE RESPONSES!
This is a devastating loss to the world. He will be missed.
Remembering Victor Darsee Krieger. READ MORE >>
VERONICA
EMOJI| RESPOND | SHARE
AND... WAIT, WHAT'S THIS? IS THIS SOME SORT OF JOKE?
TODAY'S NEWS
www.importantnewsoftheday.com
MOMENTS' Visionary Redefined the World
Victor Darsee Krieger, the visionary founder of MOMENTS who helped usher in a new era of social media, passed away today. An unknown assailant murdered him this morning. He was 46.
WHAT'S THIS? I DON'T UNDERSTAND.
OH MY...
THIS MUST BE SOME KIND OF PRANK.
WHOEVER IS RESPONSIBLE FOR THIS WILL BE FIRED!
MOMENTS' Visionary Redefined the World
Victor Darsee Krieger, the visionary founder of MOMENTS who helped usher in a new era of social media, passed away today. An unknown assailant murdered him this morning. He was 46.
I... I NEED TO GO.

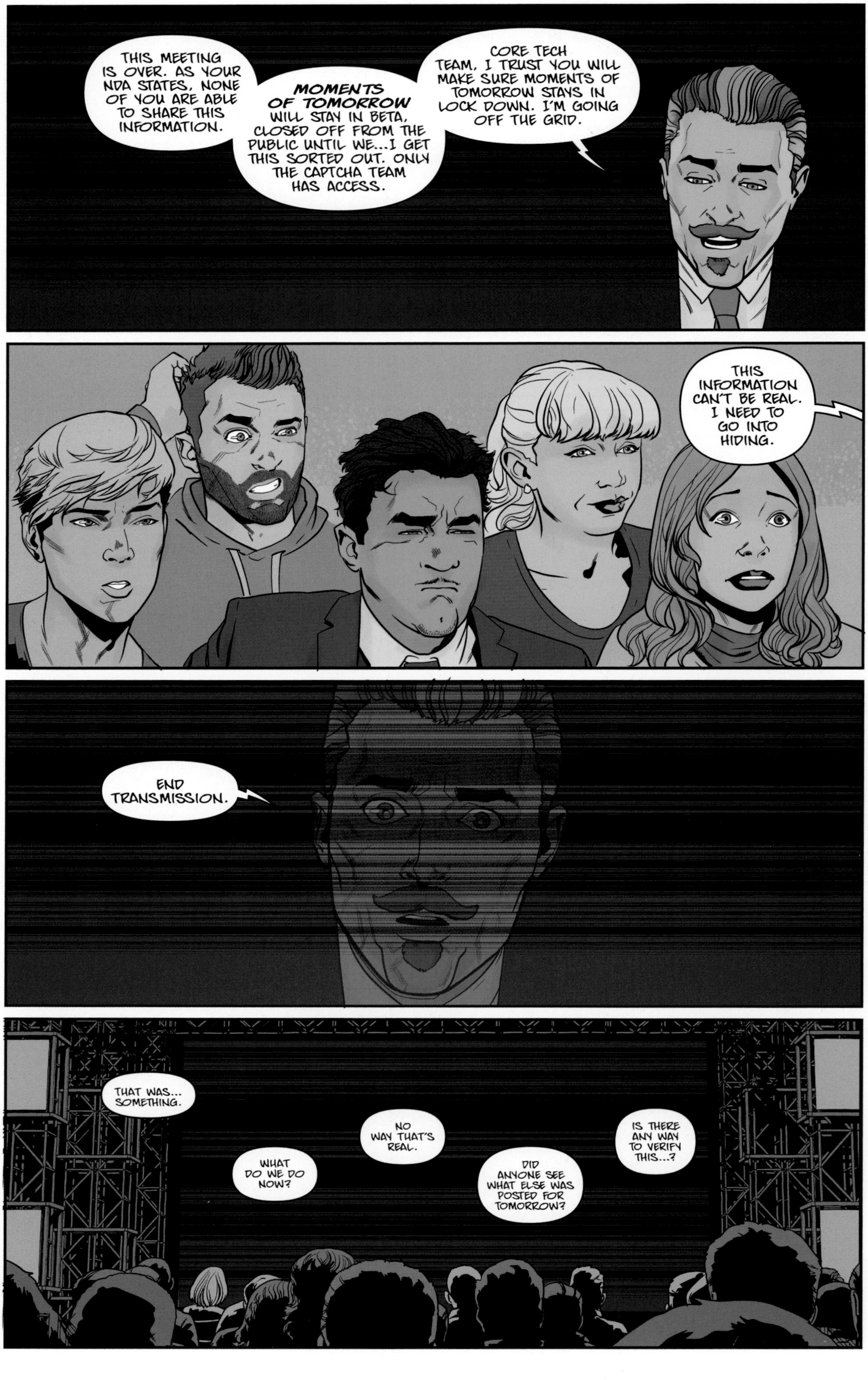
THIS MEETING IS OVER. AS YOUR NDA STATES, NONE OF YOU ARE ABLE TO SHARE THIS INFORMATION.
MOMENTS OF TOMORROW WILL STAY IN BETA, CLOSED OFF FROM THE PUBLIC UNTIL WE...I GET THIS SORTED OUT. ONLY THE CAPTCHA TEAM HAS ACCESS.
CORE TECH TEAM, I TRUST YOU WILL MAKE SURE MOMENTS OF TOMORROW STAYS IN LOCK DOWN. I'M GOING OFF THE GRID.
THIS INFORMATION CAN'T BE REAL. I NEED TO GO INTO HIDING.
END TRANSMISSION.
THAT WAS... SOMETHING.
WHAT DO WE DO NOW?
NO WAY THAT'S REAL.
DID ANYONE SEE WHAT ELSE WAS POSTED FOR TOMORROW?
IS THERE ANY WAY TO VERIFY THIS...?

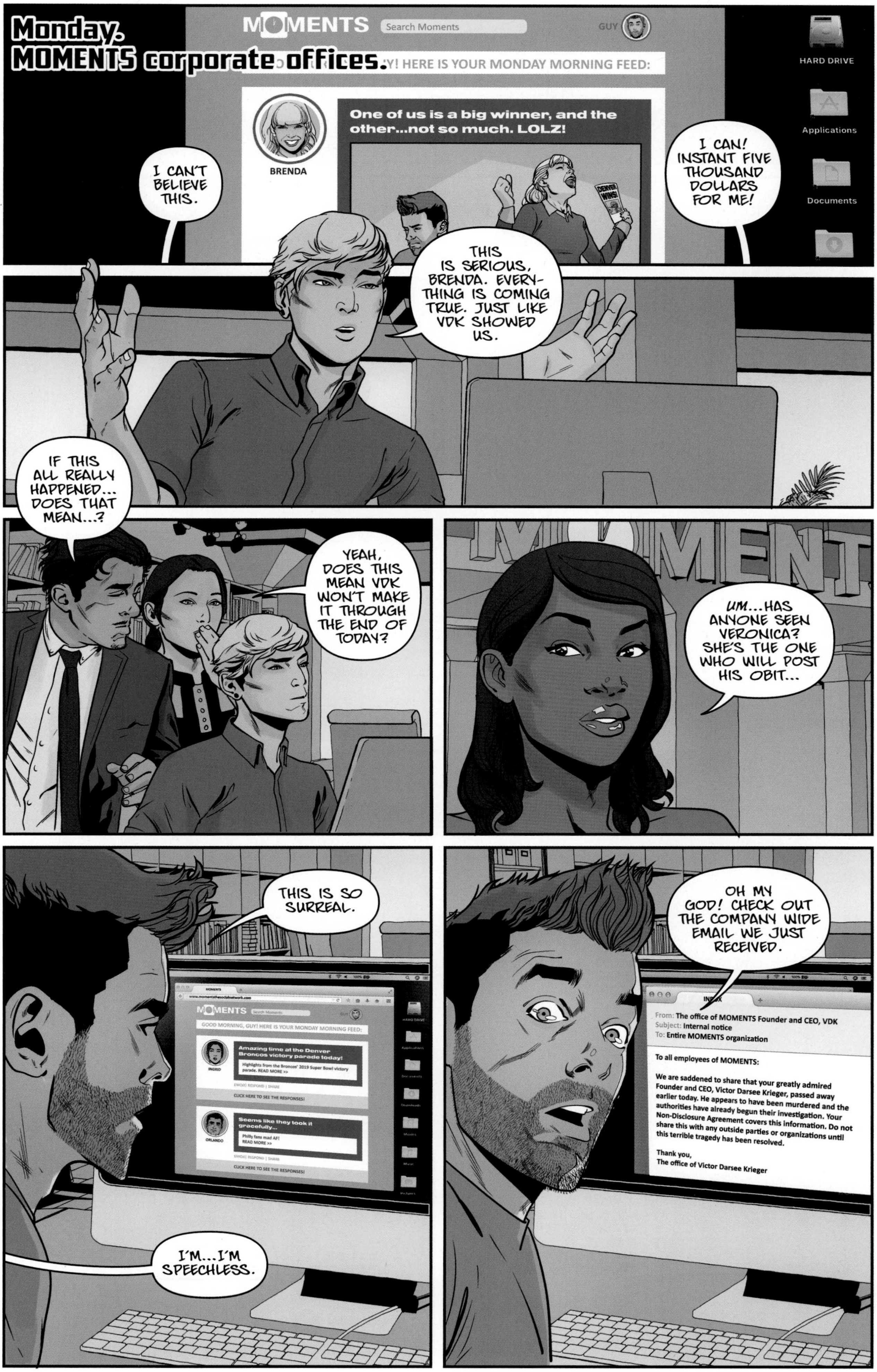
Monday.
MOMENTS corporate offices.
MOMENTS
Search Moments
GUY
Y! HERE IS YOUR MONDAY MORNING FEED:
HARD DRIVE
Applications
Documents
BRENDA
One of us is a big winner, and the other...not so much. LOLZ!
DENVER WINS!
I CAN'T BELIEVE THIS.
I CAN! INSTANT FIVE THOUSAND DOLLARS FOR ME!
THIS IS SERIOUS, BRENDA. EVERYTHING IS COMING TRUE. JUST LIKE VDK SHOWED US.
IF THIS ALL REALLY HAPPENED... DOES THAT MEAN...?
YEAH, DOES THIS MEAN VDK WON'T MAKE IT THROUGH THE END OF TODAY?
UM...HAS ANYONE SEEN VERONICA? SHE'S THE ONE WHO WILL POST HIS OBIT...
THIS IS SO SURREAL.
GOOD MORNING, GUY! HERE IS YOUR MONDAY MORNING FEED:
Amazing time at the Denver Broncos victory parade today!
Highlights from the Broncos' 2019 Super Bowl victory parade. READ MORE >>
INGRID
CLICK HERE TO SEE THE RESPONSES!
Seems like they took it gracefully...
Philly fans mad AF! READ MORE >>
ORLANDO
CLICK HERE TO SEE THE RESPONSES!
I'M...I'M SPEECHLESS.
OH MY GOD! CHECK OUT THE COMPANY WIDE EMAIL WE JUST RECEIVED.
INBOX
From: The office of MOMENTS Founder and CEO, VDK
Subject: Internal notice
To: Entire MOMENTS organization
To all employees of MOMENTS:
We are saddened to share that your greatly admired Founder and CEO, Victor Darsee Krieger, passed away earlier today. He appears to have been murdered and the authorities have already begun their investigation. Your Non-Disclosure Agreement covers this information. Do not share this with any outside parties or organizations until this terrible tragedy has been resolved.
Thank you,
The office of Victor Darsee Krieger

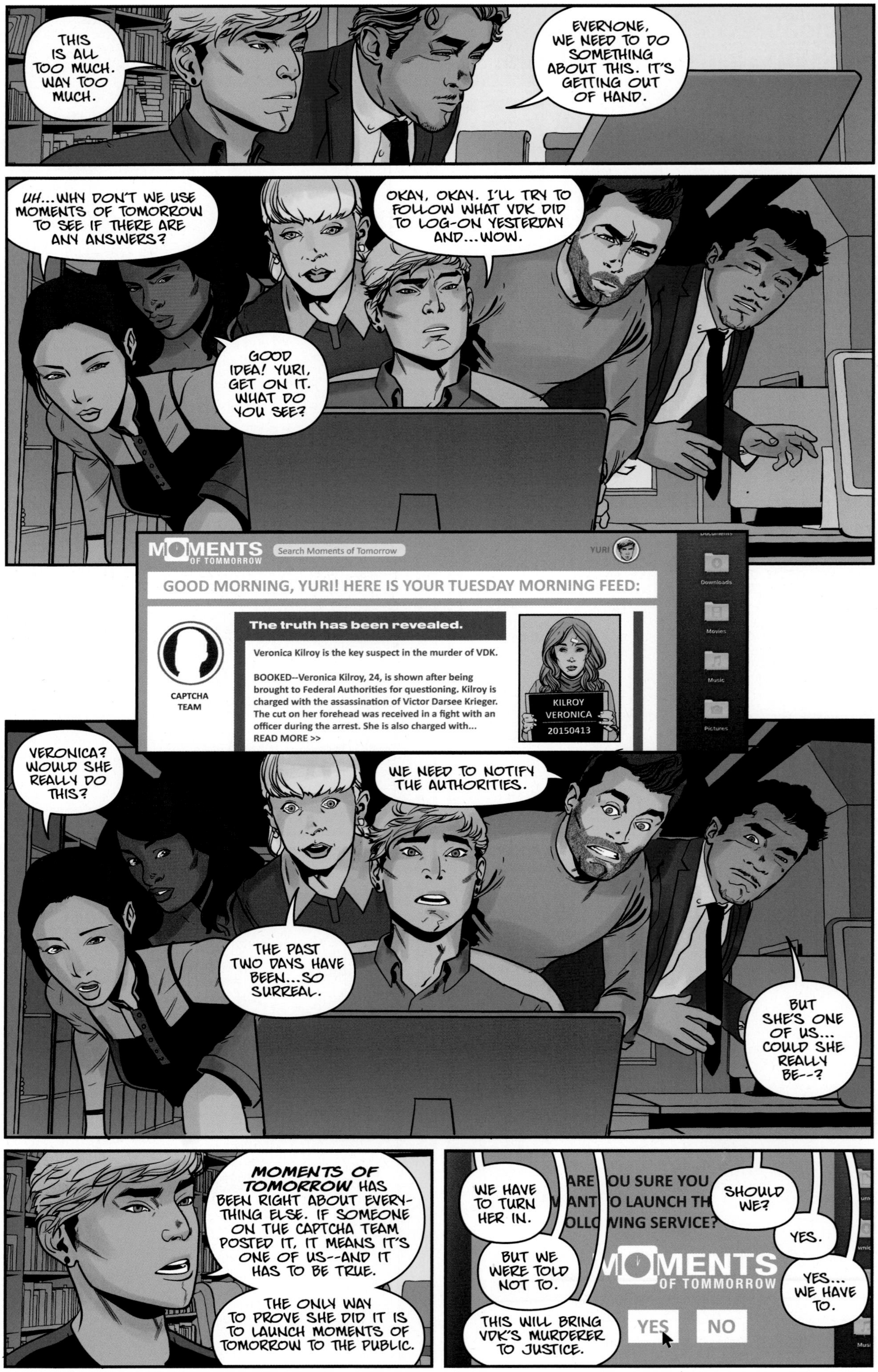
THIS IS ALL TOO MUCH. WAY TOO MUCH.
EVERYONE, WE NEED TO DO SOMETHING ABOUT THIS. IT'S GETTING OUT OF HAND.
UH...WHY DON'T WE USE MOMENTS OF TOMORROW TO SEE IF THERE ARE ANY ANSWERS?
OKAY, OKAY. I'LL TRY TO FOLLOW WHAT VDK DID TO LOG-ON YESTERDAY AND...WOW.
GOOD IDEA! YURI, GET ON IT. WHAT DO YOU SEE?
MOMENTS OF TOMORROW
Search Moments of Tomorrow
YURI
GOOD MORNING, YURI! HERE IS YOUR TUESDAY MORNING FEED:
CAPTCHA TEAM
The truth has been revealed.
Veronica Kilroy is the key suspect in the murder of VDK.
BOOKED--Veronica Kilroy, 24, is shown after being brought to Federal Authorities for questioning. Kilroy is charged with the assassination of Victor Darsee Krieger. The cut on her forehead was received in a fight with an officer during the arrest. She is also charged with...
READ MORE >>
KILROY VERONICA 20150413
Downloads
Movies
Music
Pictures
VERONICA? WOULD SHE REALLY DO THIS?
WE NEED TO NOTIFY THE AUTHORITIES.
THE PAST TWO DAYS HAVE BEEN...SO SURREAL.
BUT SHE'S ONE OF US... COULD SHE REALLY BE--?
MOMENTS OF TOMORROW HAS BEEN RIGHT ABOUT EVERYTHING ELSE. IF SOMEONE ON THE CAPTCHA TEAM POSTED IT, IT MEANS IT'S ONE OF US--AND IT HAS TO BE TRUE.
THE ONLY WAY TO PROVE SHE DID IT IS TO LAUNCH MOMENTS OF TOMORROW TO THE PUBLIC.
WE HAVE TO TURN HER IN.
SHOULD WE?
YES.
BUT WE WERE TOLD NOT TO.
YES... WE HAVE TO.
MOMENTS OF TOMORROW
THIS WILL BRING VDK'S MURDERER TO JUSTICE.
YES
NO

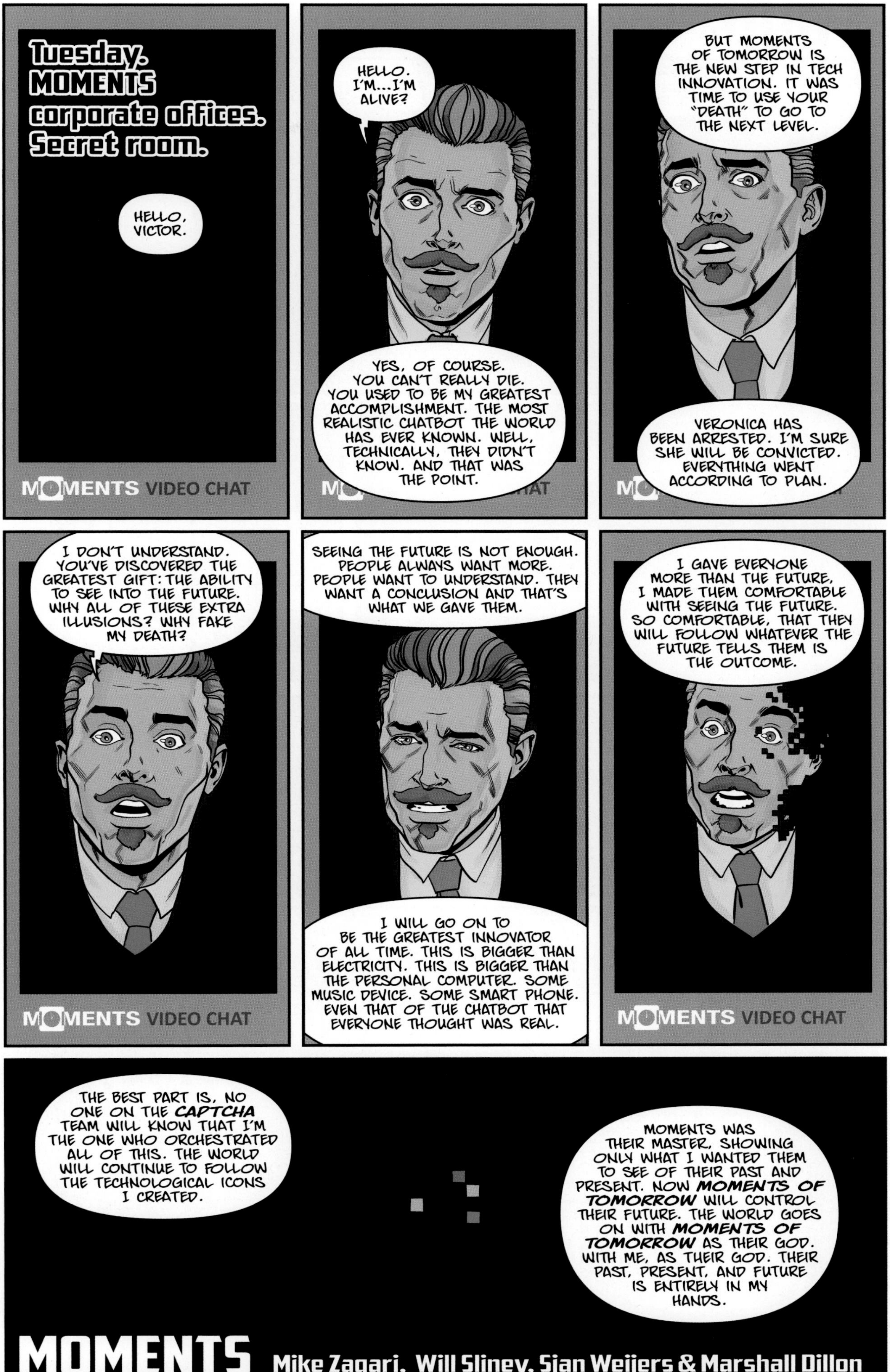
Tuesday. MOMENTS corporate offices. Secret room.
HELLO, VICTOR.
MOMENTS VIDEO CHAT
HELLO. I'M...I'M ALIVE?
YES, OF COURSE. YOU CAN'T REALLY DIE. YOU USED TO BE MY GREATEST ACCOMPLISHMENT. THE MOST REALISTIC CHATBOT THE WORLD HAS EVER KNOWN. WELL, TECHNICALLY, THEY DIDN'T KNOW. AND THAT WAS THE POINT.
BUT MOMENTS OF TOMORROW IS THE NEW STEP IN TECH INNOVATION. IT WAS TIME TO USE YOUR "DEATH" TO GO TO THE NEXT LEVEL.
VERONICA HAS BEEN ARRESTED. I'M SURE SHE WILL BE CONVICTED. EVERYTHING WENT ACCORDING TO PLAN.
I DON'T UNDERSTAND. YOU'VE DISCOVERED THE GREATEST GIFT: THE ABILITY TO SEE INTO THE FUTURE. WHY ALL OF THESE EXTRA ILLUSIONS? WHY FAKE MY DEATH?
MOMENTS VIDEO CHAT
SEEING THE FUTURE IS NOT ENOUGH. PEOPLE ALWAYS WANT MORE. PEOPLE WANT TO UNDERSTAND. THEY WANT A CONCLUSION AND THAT'S WHAT WE GAVE THEM.
I WILL GO ON TO BE THE GREATEST INNOVATOR OF ALL TIME. THIS IS BIGGER THAN ELECTRICITY. THIS IS BIGGER THAN THE PERSONAL COMPUTER. SOME MUSIC DEVICE. SOME SMART PHONE. EVEN THAT OF THE CHATBOT THAT EVERYONE THOUGHT WAS REAL.
I GAVE EVERYONE MORE THAN THE FUTURE. I MADE THEM COMFORTABLE WITH SEEING THE FUTURE. SO COMFORTABLE, THAT THEY WILL FOLLOW WHATEVER THE FUTURE TELLS THEM IS THE OUTCOME.
MOMENTS VIDEO CHAT
THE BEST PART IS, NO ONE ON THE *CAPTCHA* TEAM WILL KNOW THAT I'M THE ONE WHO ORCHESTRATED ALL OF THIS. THE WORLD WILL CONTINUE TO FOLLOW THE TECHNOLOGICAL ICONS I CREATED.
MOMENTS WAS THEIR MASTER, SHOWING ONLY WHAT I WANTED THEM TO SEE OF THEIR PAST AND PRESENT. NOW *MOMENTS OF TOMORROW* WILL CONTROL THEIR FUTURE. THE WORLD GOES ON WITH *MOMENTS OF TOMORROW* AS THEIR GOD. WITH ME, AS THEIR GOD. THEIR PAST, PRESENT, AND FUTURE IS ENTIRELY IN MY HANDS.
MOMENTS Mike Zagari, Will Sliney, Sjan Weijers & Marshall Dillon

A JOB

MARKO STOJANOVIĆ, IVAN ŠANOVIĆ & MARSHALL DILLON

THERE'S NO USE.

THE BULLET BURST INTO SEVERAL PIECES ENTERING THE SKULL... HE'S LOST TOO MUCH BLOOD, HIS HEART COULDN'T TAKE IT.

SISTER, CALL THE TIME OF DEATH AND NOTIFY HIS UNIT.

SISTER?

WHY ARE YOU CRYING? WHAT'S WRONG?

THE FACT THAT I AM A SISTER.

HIS SISTER.

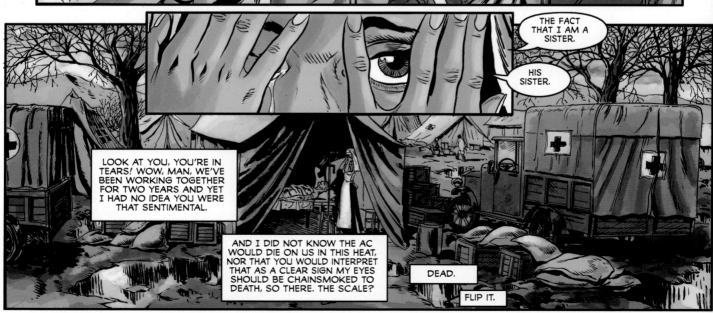

LOOK AT YOU, YOU'RE IN TEARS! WOW, MAN, WE'VE BEEN WORKING TOGETHER FOR TWO YEARS AND YET I HAD NO IDEA YOU WERE THAT SENTIMENTAL.

AND I DID NOT KNOW THE AC WOULD DIE ON US IN THIS HEAT, NOR THAT YOU WOULD INTERPRET THAT AS A CLEAR SIGN MY EYES SHOULD BE CHAINSMOKED TO DEATH, SO THERE. THE SCALE?

DEAD.

FLIP IT.

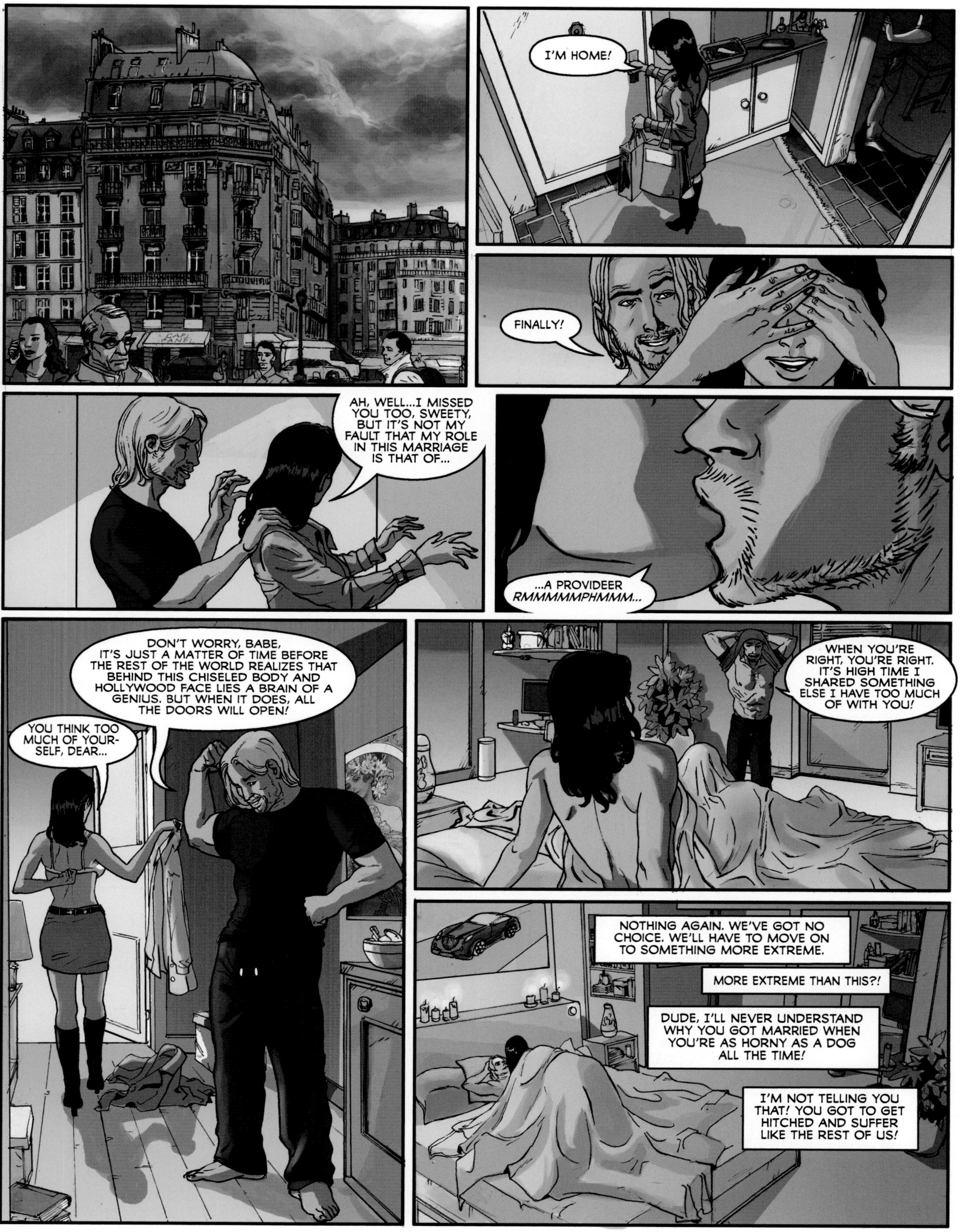
I'M HOME!
FINALLY!
AH, WELL...I MISSED YOU TOO, SWEETY, BUT IT'S NOT MY FAULT THAT MY ROLE IN THIS MARRIAGE IS THAT OF...
...A PROVIDEER RMMMMMPHMMM...
DON'T WORRY, BABE, IT'S JUST A MATTER OF TIME BEFORE THE REST OF THE WORLD REALIZES THAT BEHIND THIS CHISELED BODY AND HOLLYWOOD FACE LIES A BRAIN OF A GENIUS. BUT WHEN IT DOES, ALL THE DOORS WILL OPEN!
YOU THINK TOO MUCH OF YOURSELF, DEAR...
WHEN YOU'RE RIGHT, YOU'RE RIGHT. IT'S HIGH TIME I SHARED SOMETHING ELSE I HAVE TOO MUCH OF WITH YOU!
NOTHING AGAIN. WE'VE GOT NO CHOICE. WE'LL HAVE TO MOVE ON TO SOMETHING MORE EXTREME.
MORE EXTREME THAN THIS?!
DUDE, I'LL NEVER UNDERSTAND WHY YOU GOT MARRIED WHEN YOU'RE AS HORNY AS A DOG ALL THE TIME!
I'M NOT TELLING YOU THAT! YOU GOT TO GET HITCHED AND SUFFER LIKE THE REST OF US!

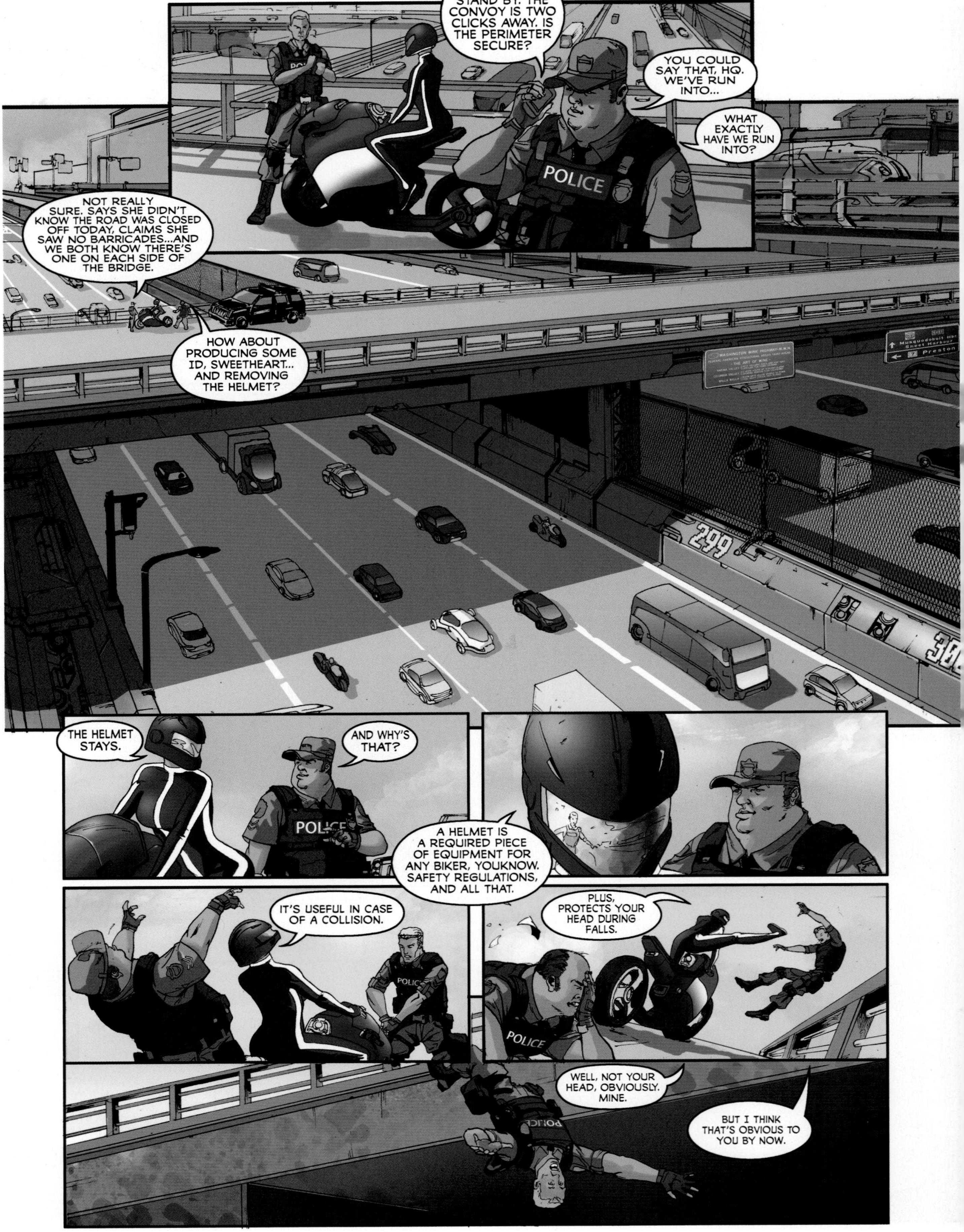
TEAM FIVE, STAND BY. THE CONVOY IS TWO CLICKS AWAY. IS THE PERIMETER SECURE?
YOU COULD SAY THAT, HQ. WE'VE RUN INTO...
WHAT EXACTLY HAVE WE RUN INTO?
POLICE
NOT REALLY SURE. SAYS SHE DIDN'T KNOW THE ROAD WAS CLOSED OFF TODAY, CLAIMS SHE SAW NO BARRICADES...AND WE BOTH KNOW THERE'S ONE ON EACH SIDE OF THE BRIDGE.
HOW ABOUT PRODUCING SOME ID, SWEETHEART... AND REMOVING THE HELMET?
299
THE HELMET STAYS.
AND WHY'S THAT?
POLICE
A HELMET IS A REQUIRED PIECE OF EQUIPMENT FOR ANY BIKER, YOUKNOW. SAFETY REGULATIONS, AND ALL THAT.
IT'S USEFUL IN CASE OF A COLLISION.
POLICE
PLUS, PROTECTS YOUR HEAD DURING FALLS.
POLICE
WELL, NOT YOUR HEAD, OBVIOUSLY. MINE.
BUT I THINK THAT'S OBVIOUS TO YOU BY NOW.
POLICE

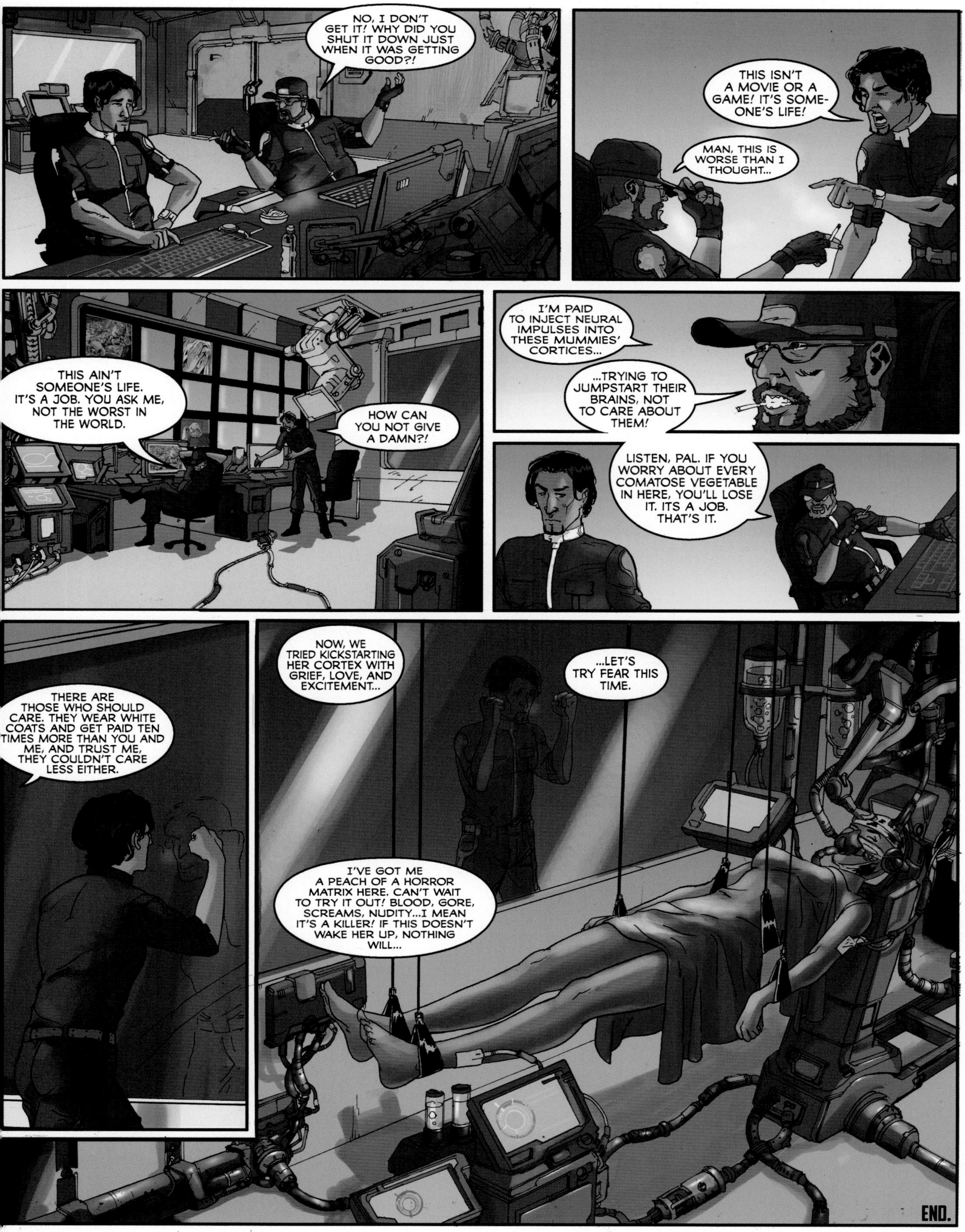
NO, I DON'T GET IT! WHY DID YOU SHUT IT DOWN JUST WHEN IT WAS GETTING GOOD?!
THIS ISN'T A MOVIE OR A GAME! IT'S SOME-ONE'S LIFE!
MAN, THIS IS WORSE THAN I THOUGHT...
THIS AIN'T SOMEONE'S LIFE. IT'S A JOB. YOU ASK ME, NOT THE WORST IN THE WORLD.
HOW CAN YOU NOT GIVE A DAMN?!
I'M PAID TO INJECT NEURAL IMPULSES INTO THESE MUMMIES' CORTICES...
...TRYING TO JUMPSTART THEIR BRAINS, NOT TO CARE ABOUT THEM!
LISTEN, PAL. IF YOU WORRY ABOUT EVERY COMATOSE VEGETABLE IN HERE, YOU'LL LOSE IT. ITS A JOB. THAT'S IT.
THERE ARE THOSE WHO SHOULD CARE. THEY WEAR WHITE COATS AND GET PAID TEN TIMES MORE THAN YOU AND ME, AND TRUST ME, THEY COULDN'T CARE LESS EITHER.
NOW, WE TRIED KICKSTARTING HER CORTEX WITH GRIEF, LOVE, AND EXCITEMENT...
...LET'S TRY FEAR THIS TIME.
I'VE GOT ME A PEACH OF A HORROR MATRIX HERE. CAN'T WAIT TO TRY IT OUT! BLOOD, GORE, SCREAMS, NUDITY...I MEAN IT'S A KILLER! IF THIS DOESN'T WAKE HER UP, NOTHING WILL...
END.

BRIAN AZZARELLO
writer

Considered one of the top writers in comics and a six-time Eisner Award winner, Brian Azzarello came to prominence with his multi-Eisner and Harvey Award-winning Vertigo/DC Comics title *100 Bullets*, and recently garnered national media attention by joining legendary comic creator Frank Miller for the third installment of the iconic Batman series *The Dark Knight*, titled *The Master Race*.

TIM BRADSTREET
artist

An Eisner Award-nominated illustrated whose work has spanned three decades in the fields of comic books, role-paying game art, trading cards, and conceptional art for film and television, Tim enjoyed critically received runs as the featured cover artist for Marvel's *Punisher* and DC Comics' *Hellblazer* comic book series, garnering a fanatic fan-following that continues to this day.

SEB ČAMAGAJEVAC
colorist

Sebastian has worked as an illustrator, comic artist, and colorist in his native Croatia, as well as the United Kingdom.

JOHN CASSADAY
cover artist

John first gained wide-spread attention collaborating with Warren Ellis on *Planetary*, firmly entrenching him as one of comic's biggest artist talents, receiving multiple Eisner and Eagle Awards for his art. In 2015, he launched Marvel Comics *Star Wars* series to massive acclaim and sales. He is also a published writer and even directed an episode of the television series *Dollhouse*.

CRANK!
letterer

Christopher Crank letters a bunch of books put out by Image, Dark Horse, Oni Press, and Dynamite. He also has a podcast with comic artist Mike Norton and members of Four Star Studios in Chicago (crankcast. net) and makes music (sonomorti.bandcamp.com). Catch him on Twitter: @ccrank.

SARAH DELAINE
artist

Sarah DeLaine has had various roles within the comic book industry for over a decade, but prefers making comics best of all. She resides in Jacksonville, FL, where she makes art with lots of little details while listening to audiobooks. Her first original graphic novel *Little Girls* is set to debut later this year.

DAVE DORMAN
artist

Eisner, Inkpot, and Bram Stoker Award-winning artist and illustrator, Dave was voted the #1 Star Wars Artist by the fans in 1996. Today, he continues creating his signature dramatic, action-packed art for book, comic, and magazine covers, movie and album covers, toy, and character design. His website

MARGUERITE BENNETT
writer

Marguerite Bennett is a comic book writer from Richmond, Virginia, who currently splits her time between Los Angeles and New York City. She received her MFA in Creative Writing from Sarah Lawrence College in 2013 and quickly went on to work for DC Comics, Marvel, BOOM! Studios, Dynamite, and IDW on projects ranging from *Batman*, *Bombshells*, and *A-Force* to INSEXTS, one of AfterShock's debut launches.

CULLEN BUNN
writer

Cullen is the writer of such creator-owned comics as *The Sixth Gun*, *The Damned*, *Harrow County*, and *Regression*. In addition, he writes *X-Men Blue*, *Monsters Unleashed*, and numerous *Deadpool* comics for Marvel.

MIKE CAREY
writer

Mike writes across many different medias, but is best known as a novelist and comic book writer. His graphic novel series *Lucifer* has been developed as a major TV series. His novel *The Girl With All the Gifts* has sold over a million copies in English-language editions and became a critically acclaimed motion picture based on his own screenplay, for which he received the British Screenwriters' Award for Outstanding Newcomer.

ANDY CLARKE
artist

Andy began working in comics in 1998 with writer Dan Abnett on *Sinister Dexter* for 2000AD. He has made modest contributions to *Judge Dredd* (including a newspaper strip), and worked on *Nikolai Dante* and *Shimura* with Robbie Morrison. He co-created *Thirteen* with Mike Carey and teamed up with Andy Diggle for *Snow/Tiger*. He's also done the odd cover here and there.

MARCO CRONER
writer

Marco Croner is new. For years he's been co-creating, co-producing, co-writing and co-editing the international design manga-comic anthology *Tape*, working with artists the world over, among them the extraordinary Andrew Robinson. *Tape* will be released in 2018. Something else will have to come up.

MARSHALL DILLON
letterer

A comic book industry veteran. Over the years he's been everything from an independent self-published writer to an associate publisher working on properties like *G.I. Joe*, *Voltron*, and *Street Fighter*. Marshall has worked for just about every publisher except the "big two." Primarily a father and letterer these days, he also dabbles in old-school paper and dice RPG game design.

AARON DOUGLAS
writer

Aaron is a Film and Television Actor best known for his portrayal of Chief Galen Tyrol on Syfy's *Battlestar Galactica*. With almost 100 screen credits on his creative resume, Aaron is excited to branch out into writing and get on the other side of the camera. After being published in novel form, this is his first work in

artist

Joe Eisma is the Eisner-nominated and New York Times best-selling artist and co-creator of *Morning Glories* from Image Comics. In addition, he has drawn for DC Comics, Archie Comics, Valiant, and IDW.

artist / colorist

Toni got his start in the European market, primarily in animation and films, but also on graphic albums for Soleil and Delcourt. More recently, Toni has worked for Dark Horse Comics on projects with popular writers such as Greg Rucka and John Arcudi. Currently he is working on a graphic novel for Planeta. Born in Serbia, Toni currently lives in Barcelona.

FRANCESCO FRANCAVILLA
writer / artist

Francesco, an Eisner Award winner and New York Times best-selling creator, is best known for bringing his signature style (Neo-Pulp) to the comics industry. In addition, he works on art for movie posters, DVD/BD, albums, concept and storyboards for film and TV. Born and raised in Italy, he lives now in Atlanta, GA, with his lovely partner Lisa and his sometime annoying, but overall sweet cat.

NEIL GAIMAN
writer

The critically-acclaimed writer of the multiple Eisner Award-winning *Sandman* series, Neil has also written several award-winning novels, including *American Gods*, *Good Omens*, *Coraline*, and *The Graveyard Book*, many of which have been successfully adapted for film and television.

MICHAEL GAYDOS
writer / artist / letterer

Michael has received two Eisner Award nominations for his work on *Alias* with Brian Michael Bendis for Marvel and is co-creator of Marvel's *Jessica Jones*, who has her own Netflix series. In addition to his Illustration work, Michael's fine art paintings, drawings, and prints have been the subject of a number of solo exhibitions and his art is in private collections worldwide.

MARC GUGGENHEIM
writer

A former attorney, Marc Guggenheim has written for multiple mediums including television, film, prose, digital, videogames, and comic books. He is currently serving as executive producer of *Arrow*, *DC's Legends of Tomorrow* and *Trollhunters* as well as writing *X-Men Gold* for Marvel Comics.

WESLEY GUNN
artist

Born and raised in Boston, MA, Wesley came to New York to attend the School of Visual Arts, graduating with a BFA in 2000. Since then he has worked for various companies including Build-A-Bear Workshop/ABC, Cartoon Network, Nickelodeon, and Image Comics.

PHIL HESTER
writer / artist

Phil has been writing and drawing comics for nearly three decades, beginning while still a student at the University of Iowa. He broke into the mainstream with a long run as artist of DC's *Swamp Thing* with writer Mark Millar, and Kevin Smith's revival of DC's *Green Arrow*. His work, as both artist and writer, has been featured in hundreds of comics from nearly every American publisher.

PAUL JENKINS
writer

Paul has been creating, writing and building franchises for over twenty years in the graphic novel, film, and video game industries. He has enjoyed recognition on the New York Times best-seller list, has been nominated for two BAFTA Awards, and has been the recipient of a government-sponsored Prism Award for his contributions in storytelling and characterization.

STIPE KALAJZIC
artist

An ex-architect who decided he would rather draw comics. Co-author of the comic *On The Wall* for One Peace Books and author of many comic strips *Sisters and Brothers, the Bicycle Riders* for his local bike co-op. Stipe lives and works in Zagreb, Croatia.

SZYMON KUDRANSKI
artist

Born in Poland, Szymon got his big break into comics working with writer Steve Niles in 2004's *30 Days of Night Annual*. Since then, Szymon has worked with DC Comics, Marvel Comics, and Image Comics, where he was personally asked by Todd McFarlane to take over art duties on the long-running *Spawn* series. Szymon also is credited with co-creating the AfterShock Comics series, *BLACK-EYED KIDS*.

LACI
artist

Vladimir Krstić Laci is a comic book artist and illustrator born in 1959. in Niš, Serbia. He was published by some of the largest European publishers, including French (Declourt, Soleil), Italian (Bonelli), and American publishers (Image, Dark Horse). In 2017 he received the Grand Prix "Golden Muse" of the fifth festival in San Remy, France.

LEILA LEIZ
artist

Born and raised in Italy, Leila is a self-taught artist who has seen her lifelong dream of working in American comics come true. After working for several years at European publishers like Soleil and Sergio Bonelli, Leila has made the exciting jump to AfterShock Comics, where she begins her new adventure on Paul Jenkins' new series, ALTERS.

GUY MAJOR
artist

Guy Major is an artist and photographer who has been working in comics since 1995, when he responded to an ad looking for colorists for Wildstorm's *WildC.A.T.S.* series. When not working on comics or out with his camera, he is studying about, tasting, or drinking wine.

LAURA MARTIN
colorist

Laura Martin is a multiple-award winning colorist. She got her start at Wildstorm in 1995, and has been coloring comics ever since. In her spare time, Laura likes to explore hiking trails all around Georgia. In addition, she and her husband Randy work with Firkins, an Atlanta-based cat rescue organization.

ALEX MEDELLIN
colorist

Axel has been drawing and coloring comics for a while now, including for Metal Hurlant, Zuda, Heavy Metal, Zenescope, BOOM! Studios and Image Comics, among others. He did the art for more than half of the *Elephantmen* series. He's probably meeting a deadline right now.

KEVIN MELLON
artist

Kevin Mellon is an artist and writer living in Atlanta, Georgia. He has created comics for Image, Marvel, Heavy Metal, and many others. He is currently working as a storyboard artist on the Emmy award-winning animated show *Archer* (FX), as well as having storyboarded on *The Vampire Diaries* and *Black Lightning* (The CW).

TRAVIS MOORE
artist

Travis Moore has worked with DC/Vertigo for the past decade, including titles such as *JSA All-Stars, Freedom Fighters, The Wolf Among Us, Everafter from the Pages of Fables,* and most recently *Batman.* His current project is *Lark's Killer* for 1First Comics.

STEPHAN NILSON
writer

Stephan Nilson is an Eisner Award-accepting comic book creator that was born and died in Okinawa, but the military doctors and nurses thwarted his attempt at emancipation. Stephan has been working in comics and television for fifteen years. He has written and edited for DC Comics, Image Comics, IDW Publishing, Nickelodeon, Warner Bros., Universal, and AfterShock Comics.

CHARLES PRITCHETT
letterer

Brought up on the wrong side of the tracks in a bustling metropolis in Newfoundland, Canada, Charles is really terrible at writing epic sounding biographies of his life and times. He enjoys a fine stew from time to time and hates to travel. He can be found currently living in Canada's smallest, but nicest province, outnumbered by powerful women in his own household.

JOE PRUETT
writer

Joe Pruett is an Eisner Award-winning comic book editor, publisher, and writer, having been nominated for numerous Eisner, Harvey and Eagle awards. Best known as the editor for the anthology series *Negative Burn,* he also has written for virtually every major comic publisher, including Image, Vertigo, IDW, AfterShock, and Marvel, where he wrote for *X-Men Unlimited, Cable,* and *Magneto Rex.*

JORDAN RASKIN
artist

Jordan Raskin is an experienced commercial illustrator with a background in pre and post production film work, storyboards, comic books, animation, screenwriting, and I.P. development.

CLIFF RICHARDS
artist

Brazil-based comics veteran Cliff Richards has been a mainstay at DC Comics, where he has drawn *Batman/Superman, Wonder Woman, Cyborg,* and many others. For seven years, he drew Joss Whedon's *Buffy the Vampire Slayer, Angel,* and other related titles, along with such offbeat graphic novels as *Pride & Prejudice & Zombies.*

ANDREW ROBINSON
artist / colorist

Andrew has painted covers for all the major publishers, including Marvel, DC, and AfterShock. He is also a multi-award winning, New York Times best-selling illustrator for his painted work on the highly acclaimed graphic novel, *The Fifth Beatle.* His sequential work can be seen in *Batman Black and White, The Ride: My Brother's Keeper, Gen 13, Harley Quinn,* and *Dusty Star.*

IVAN ŠANOVIĆ
artist

Born in Belgrade, Serbia in 1974, Ivan is an illustrator, animator, and comic book artist. Published in various Serbian magazines, his art has been recognized by his peers, earning several awards for his work.

HOYT SILVA
artist / colorist

Hoyt Silva is the most versatile storyteller to grace the pages of a comic. From pencils, inks, to color, he handles each with an unequivocal freshness the game just isn't ready for. Check out more of his work on Patreon at patreon.com/hoytsilva or on Instagram as @thehoyt.

WILL SLINEY
artist

An award-winning artist and writer from Cork, Ireland, he is best known for his work on *Spider-Man 2099* and *Fearless Defenders* for Marvel Comics. His book *Celtic Warrior,* which he wrote, drew and colored, is an Irish Times best-seller.

RICHARD STARKINGS
writer / letterer

Richard has worked as a lettering artist on just about every mainstream comic imaginable. His company Comicraft currently letters a whole bunch of comics. He's also is the creator and writer of *Elephantmen* at Image Comics. He loves Yorkshire

JIM STARLIN
writer

Best known as the creator of Marvel Comics' Thanos, Gamora, and Drax the Destroyer, all of which play large roles in Marvel's movie universe, Jim is the "father" of the cosmic soap-opera he made popular as a writer and artist on *Warlock*, *Captain Marvel*, and his own *Dreadstar* series.

MARKO STOJANOVIĆ
writer

Born in 1978. in Leskovac, Serbia, Marko is a writer, editor, and translator. He has published his comics in 12 countries including Great Britain, Belgium and Uruguay, and is currently working on a series about Crusades for the French publisher, Delcourt. He's also the winner of lifetime achievement awards for his contribution to comics in three different countries: Serbia, Macedonia, and Bulgaria.

FRANK TIERI
writer

Frank Tieri is an award-winning writer and creator working in comics, video games, animation, and television. Though probably best known to comic readers for his three-year run on *Wolverine*, Frank has also worked on some of the biggest franchises in the industry for Marvel, DC, Dynamite, Top Cow, and Archie. He lives in Brooklyn like three million other people.

CHARLES VESS
writer / artist

Charles' long list of accomplishments include the *Stardust* illustrated novel with Neil Gaiman, as well as many illustrated books and graphic novels for which he has won four World Fantasy, three Chesley, a Mythopoeic and two Will Eisner awards. He lives on a small farm in southwestern Virginia where he works diligently from his studio, Green Man Press.

BILL WILLINGHAM
writer

Bill Willingham created the long running *Fables* comic book series and also wrote it. He's written and drawn other things. too.

MICHAEL ZULLI
artist

Michael is a three-time Eisner Award nominee, best known for his frequent collaborations with writer Neil Gaiman, including on the iconic *Sandman* series for DC Comics. A gallery show of his art, "Visions of the Wake," was presented in New York City.

BRIAN STELFREEZE
signed edition cover artist

Fresh off a critically-received run on Marvel's *Black Panther* comic books series, Brian has been a mainstay in the comic book industry for over 20 years. A winner of San Diego Comic-Con International's prestigious Inkpot Award for his life-long achievements in the comic book industry, Brian has long been considered one of the industries top storytellers and draftsman. Brian currently resides in Atlanta, Georgia.

DALIBOR TALAJIĆ
artist

Dalibor Talajić is a professor of clarinette in music high school. Well, he was actually, until Joe Pruett gave him a shot in comics at Desperado Publishing. More recently, his art has been featured on such comic titles as the *Incredible Hulk*, *X-Men*, *Punisher*, and *Deadpool Kills the Marvel Universe*. His most critically-acclaimed work is *Madaya Mom*.

ALJOŠA TOMIĆ
colorist

Aljoša Tomić is a comic book colorist stationed in Novi Sad, Serbia. With more than 10 years of professional experience, he has had his work published by various publishers from around the globe, including Dark Horse, Markosia, and Delcourt.

SJAN WEIJERS
colorist

Sjan is a freelance artist based in The Netherlands. She works in animation and video games, providing style guides, character design, toy designs, and art direction for various projects. As a comic artist, her main focus is on color and atmosphere. Sjan has previously worked with Sony Video Entertainment and Dreamworks Animation. She currently colors MONSTRO MECHANICA for AfterShock Comics.

MIKE ZAGARI
writer

After over 15 years of experience at Marvel, Disney Publishing, Lucasfilm Publishing, and DC Comics, Mike Zagari joined the AfterShock team. He continues to create and produce immersive stories and experiences. Mike has also written and illustrated a self-published comic called *Human on the Inside*.

CHECK OUT THESE GREAT AFTERSHOCK
COLLECTIONS!